CONTENTS

THE GENTLEMEN'S ✝ ALLIANCE CROSS™

Shojo Beat

Story & Art by
Arina Tanemura

Vol. 1

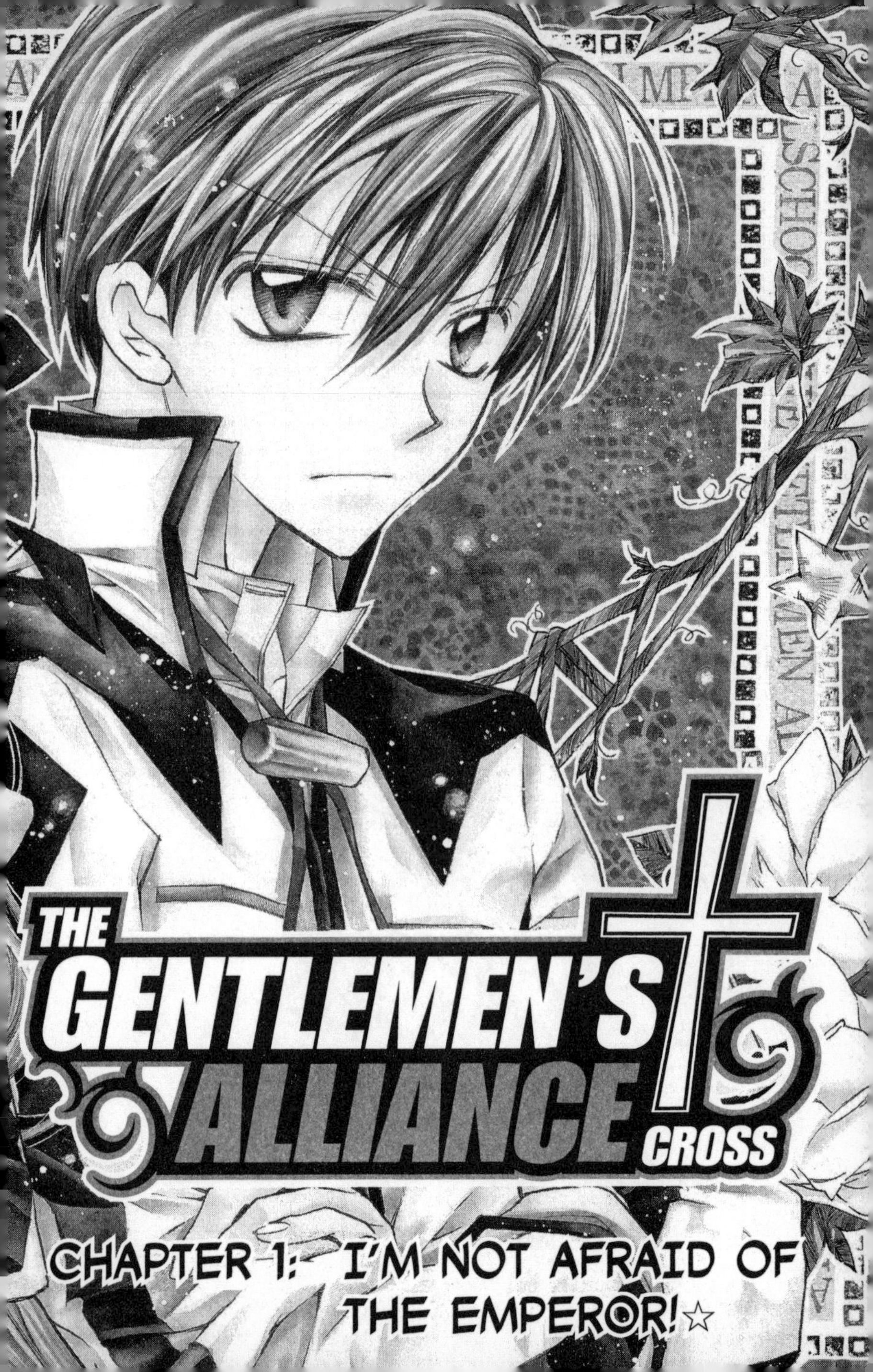
THE GENTLEMEN'S ALLIANCE CROSS
CHAPTER 1: I'M NOT AFRAID OF THE EMPEROR!☆

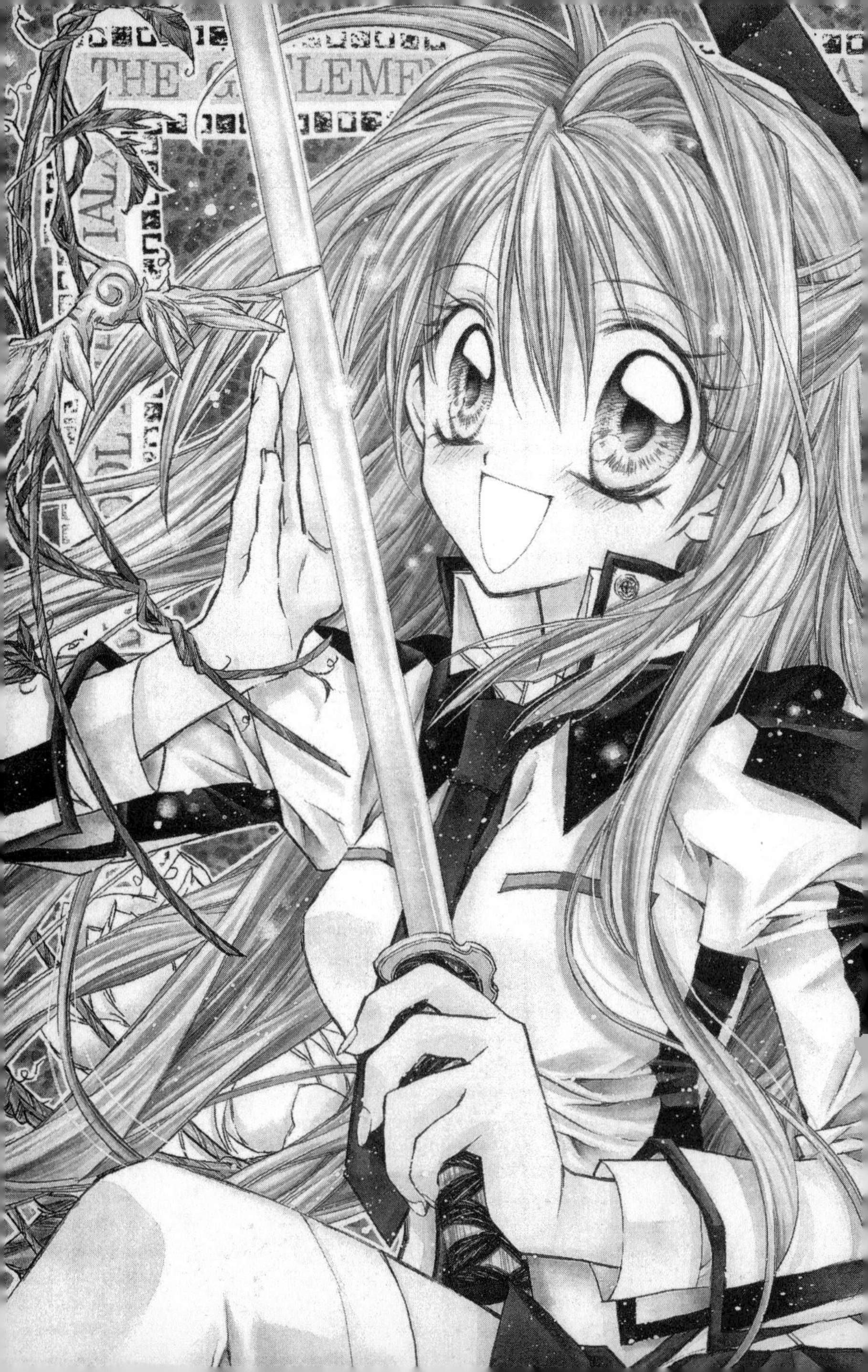
THE

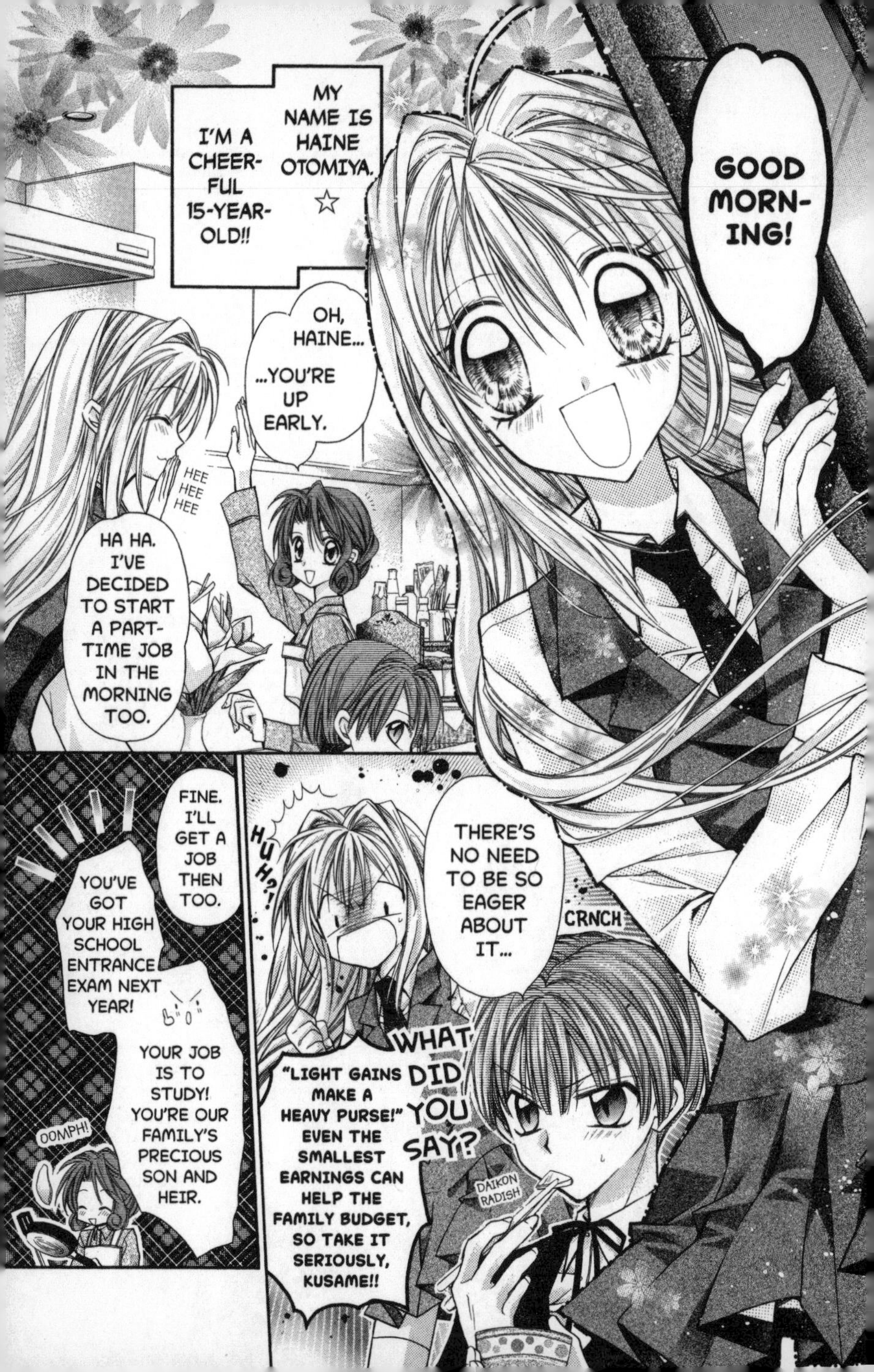
GOOD MORNING!
MY NAME IS HAINE OTOMIYA. ☆
I'M A CHEERFUL 15-YEAR-OLD!!
OH, HAINE...
...YOU'RE UP EARLY.
HEE HEE HEE
HA HA. I'VE DECIDED TO START A PART-TIME JOB IN THE MORNING TOO.
THERE'S NO NEED TO BE SO EAGER ABOUT IT...
CRNCH
HUH?!
WHAT DID YOU SAY?
"LIGHT GAINS MAKE A HEAVY PURSE!" EVEN THE SMALLEST EARNINGS CAN HELP THE FAMILY BUDGET, SO TAKE IT SERIOUSLY, KUSAME!!
DAIKON RADISH
FINE. I'LL GET A JOB THEN TOO.
YOU'VE GOT YOUR HIGH SCHOOL ENTRANCE EXAM NEXT YEAR!
YOUR JOB IS TO STUDY! YOU'RE OUR FAMILY'S PRECIOUS SON AND HEIR.
OOMPH!

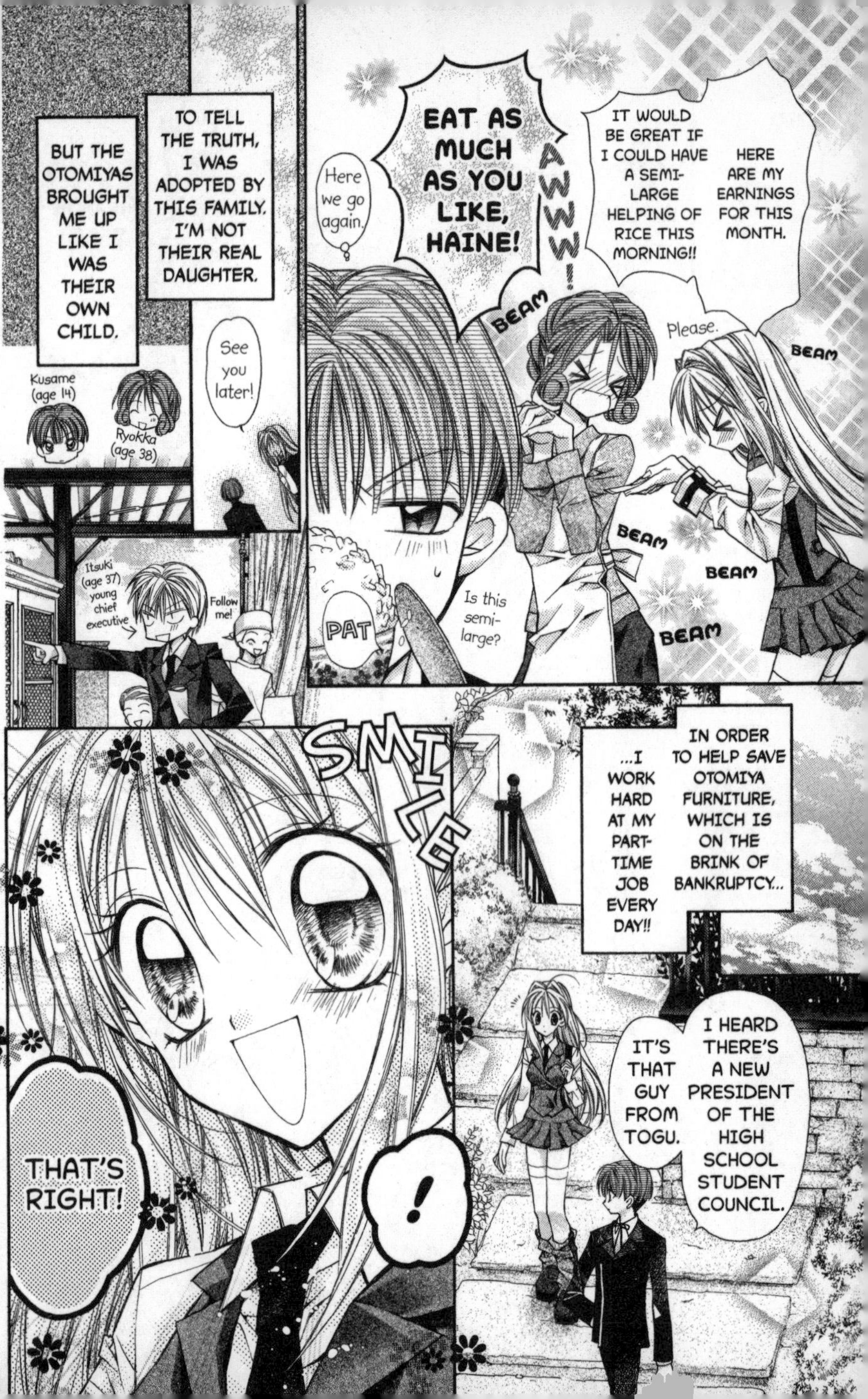
HERE ARE MY EARNINGS FOR THIS MONTH.
IT WOULD BE GREAT IF I COULD HAVE A SEMI-LARGE HELPING OF RICE THIS MORNING!!
Please.
BEAM
AWWW!
EAT AS MUCH AS YOU LIKE, HAINE!
BEAM
Here we go again.
BEAM
BEAM
BEAM
Is this semi-large?
PAT
TO TELL THE TRUTH, I WAS ADOPTED BY THIS FAMILY. I'M NOT THEIR REAL DAUGHTER.
See you later!
BUT THE OTOMIYAS BROUGHT ME UP LIKE I WAS THEIR OWN CHILD.
Ryokka (age 38)
Kusame (age 14)
Follow me!
Itsuki (age 37) young chief executive
IN ORDER TO HELP SAVE OTOMIYA FURNITURE, WHICH IS ON THE BRINK OF BANKRUPTCY...
...I WORK HARD AT MY PART-TIME JOB EVERY DAY!!
I HEARD THERE'S A NEW PRESIDENT OF THE HIGH SCHOOL STUDENT COUNCIL.
IT'S THAT GUY FROM TOGU.
SMILE
!
THAT'S RIGHT!

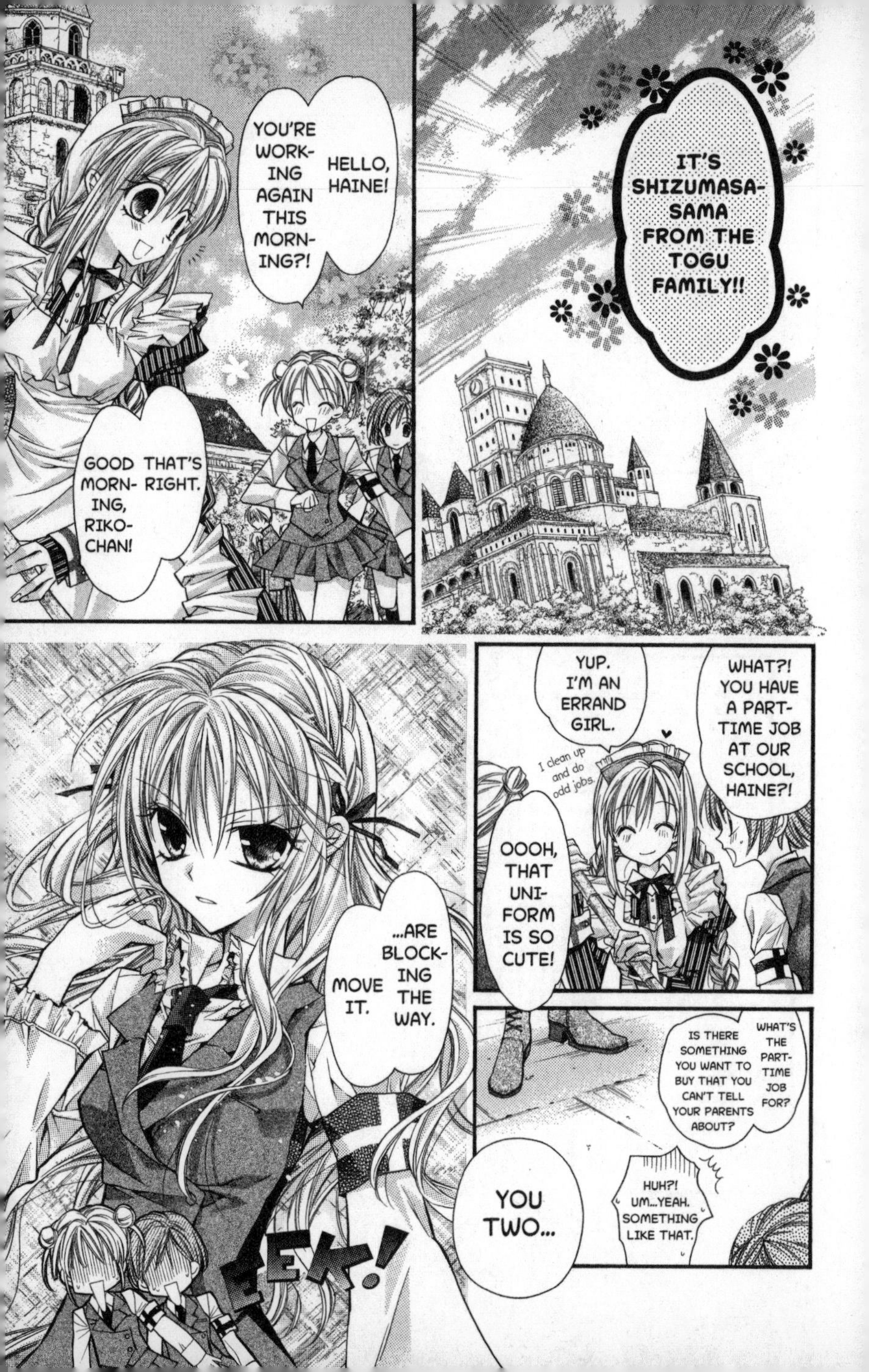
IT'S SHIZUMASA-SAMA FROM THE TOGU FAMILY!!
HELLO, HAINE!
YOU'RE WORKING AGAIN THIS MORNING?!
GOOD MORNING, RIKO-CHAN! THAT'S RIGHT.
WHAT?! YOU HAVE A PART-TIME JOB AT OUR SCHOOL, HAINE?!
YUP. I'M AN ERRAND GIRL.
I clean up and do odd jobs.
OOOH, THAT UNIFORM IS SO CUTE!
WHAT'S THE PART-TIME JOB FOR?
IS THERE SOMETHING YOU WANT TO BUY THAT YOU CAN'T TELL YOUR PARENTS ABOUT?
HUH?! UM...YEAH. SOMETHING LIKE THAT.
YOU TWO...
...ARE BLOCKING THE WAY.
MOVE IT.
EEK!

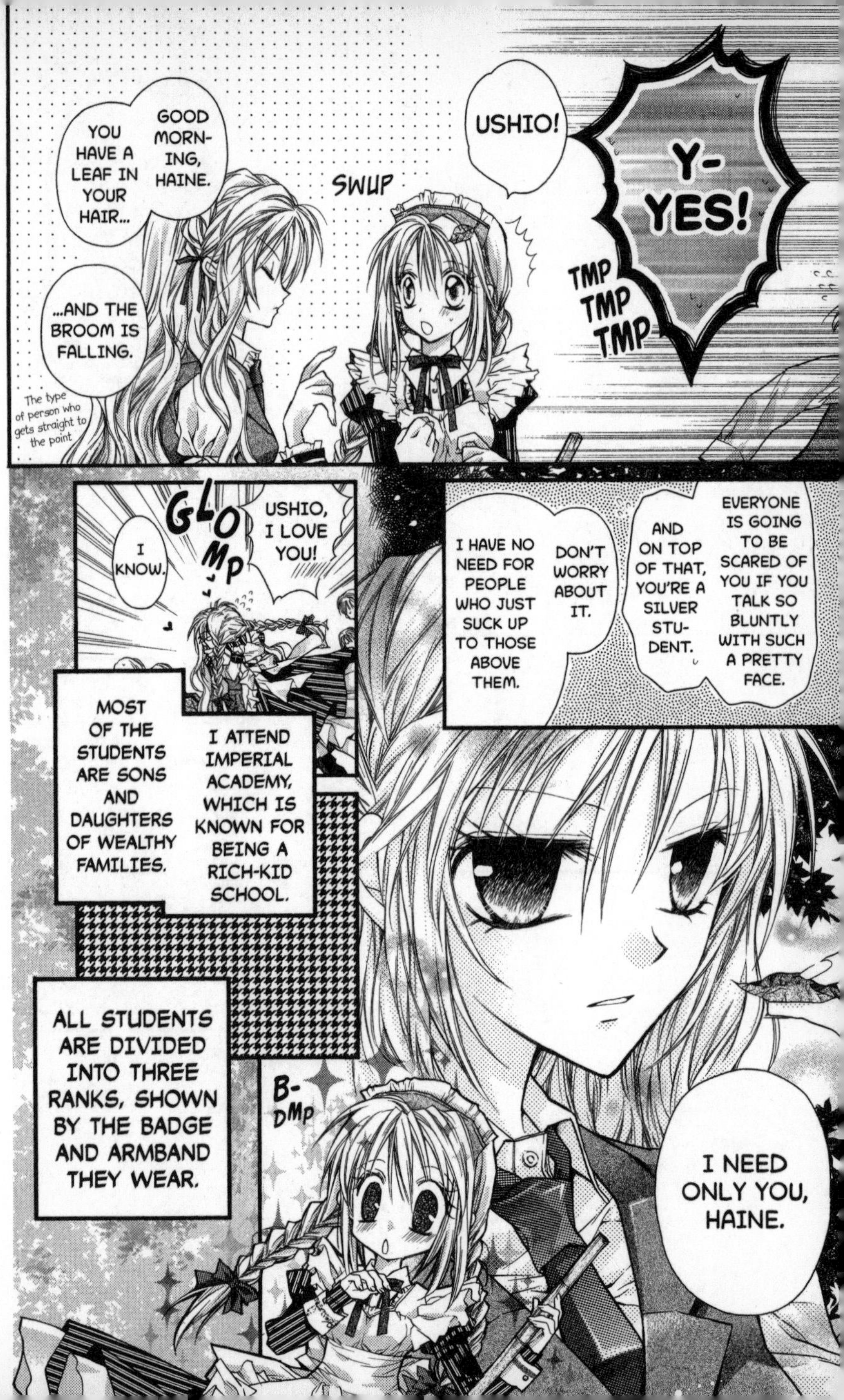
Y-YES!
TMP TMP TMP
USHIO!
SWUP
GOOD MORNING, HAINE.
YOU HAVE A LEAF IN YOUR HAIR...
...AND THE BROOM IS FALLING.
The type of person who gets straight to the point
EVERYONE IS GOING TO BE SCARED OF YOU IF YOU TALK SO BLUNTLY WITH SUCH A PRETTY FACE.
AND ON TOP OF THAT, YOU'RE A SILVER STU-DENT.
DON'T WORRY ABOUT IT.
I HAVE NO NEED FOR PEOPLE WHO JUST SUCK UP TO THOSE ABOVE THEM.
I NEED ONLY YOU, HAINE.
B-DMP
USHIO, I LOVE YOU!
GLOMP
I KNOW.
I ATTEND IMPERIAL ACADEMY, WHICH IS KNOWN FOR BEING A RICH-KID SCHOOL.
MOST OF THE STUDENTS ARE SONS AND DAUGHTERS OF WEALTHY FAMILIES.
ALL STUDENTS ARE DIVIDED INTO THREE RANKS, SHOWN BY THE BADGE AND ARMBAND THEY WEAR.

Hello!

I'm Arina Tanemura.
People who read my manga for the first time may not know this, but this actually happens to be my twentieth manga!!

The Gentlemen's Alliance ✝ started in the September 2004 edition of *Ribon*, and I have been enjoying myself in the creation of this story ever since.

I intend to write the profiles of the characters in these spaces. (They're going to give away some of the secrets so please read them after you finish the volume.)

*

I now have two cats, and I am so happy about it! Their names are Riku and Kai. Riku is a girl, and Kai is a boy. They are American Shorthair siblings.

I hope you enjoy *The Gentlemen's Alliance* ✝. Thank you!

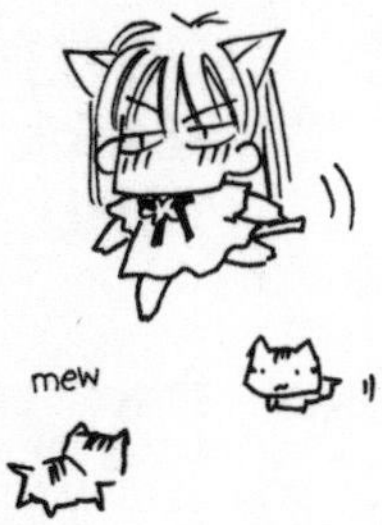
mew

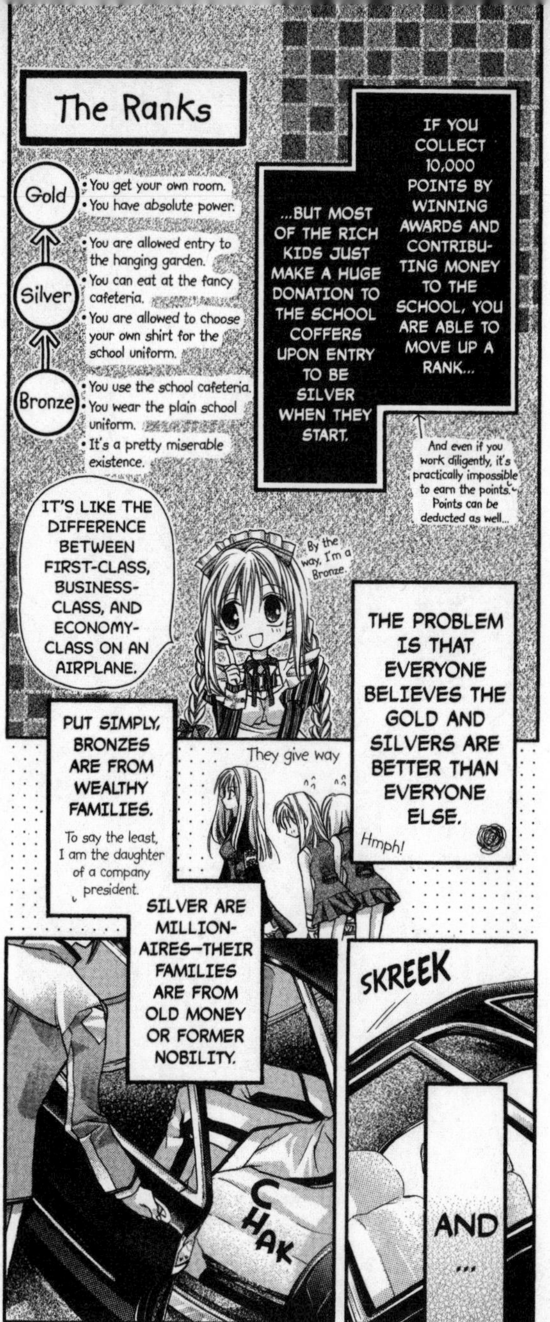
The Ranks
Gold
• You get your own room.
• You have absolute power.
Silver
• You are allowed entry to the hanging garden.
• You can eat at the fancy cafeteria.
• You are allowed to choose your own shirt for the school uniform.
Bronze
• You use the school cafeteria.
• You wear the plain school uniform.
• It's a pretty miserable existence.
IF YOU COLLECT 10,000 POINTS BY WINNING AWARDS AND CONTRIBUTING MONEY TO THE SCHOOL, YOU ARE ABLE TO MOVE UP A RANK...
...BUT MOST OF THE RICH KIDS JUST MAKE A HUGE DONATION TO THE SCHOOL COFFERS UPON ENTRY TO BE SILVER WHEN THEY START.
And even if you work diligently, it's practically impossible to earn the points. Points can be deducted as well...
By the way, I'm a Bronze.
IT'S LIKE THE DIFFERENCE BETWEEN FIRST-CLASS, BUSINESS-CLASS, AND ECONOMY-CLASS ON AN AIRPLANE.
THE PROBLEM IS THAT EVERYONE BELIEVES THE GOLD AND SILVERS ARE BETTER THAN EVERYONE ELSE.
Hmph!
They give way
PUT SIMPLY, BRONZES ARE FROM WEALTHY FAMILIES.
To say the least, I am the daughter of a company president.
SILVER ARE MILLIONAIRES—THEIR FAMILIES ARE FROM OLD MONEY OR FORMER NOBILITY.
SKREEK
AND...
CHAK

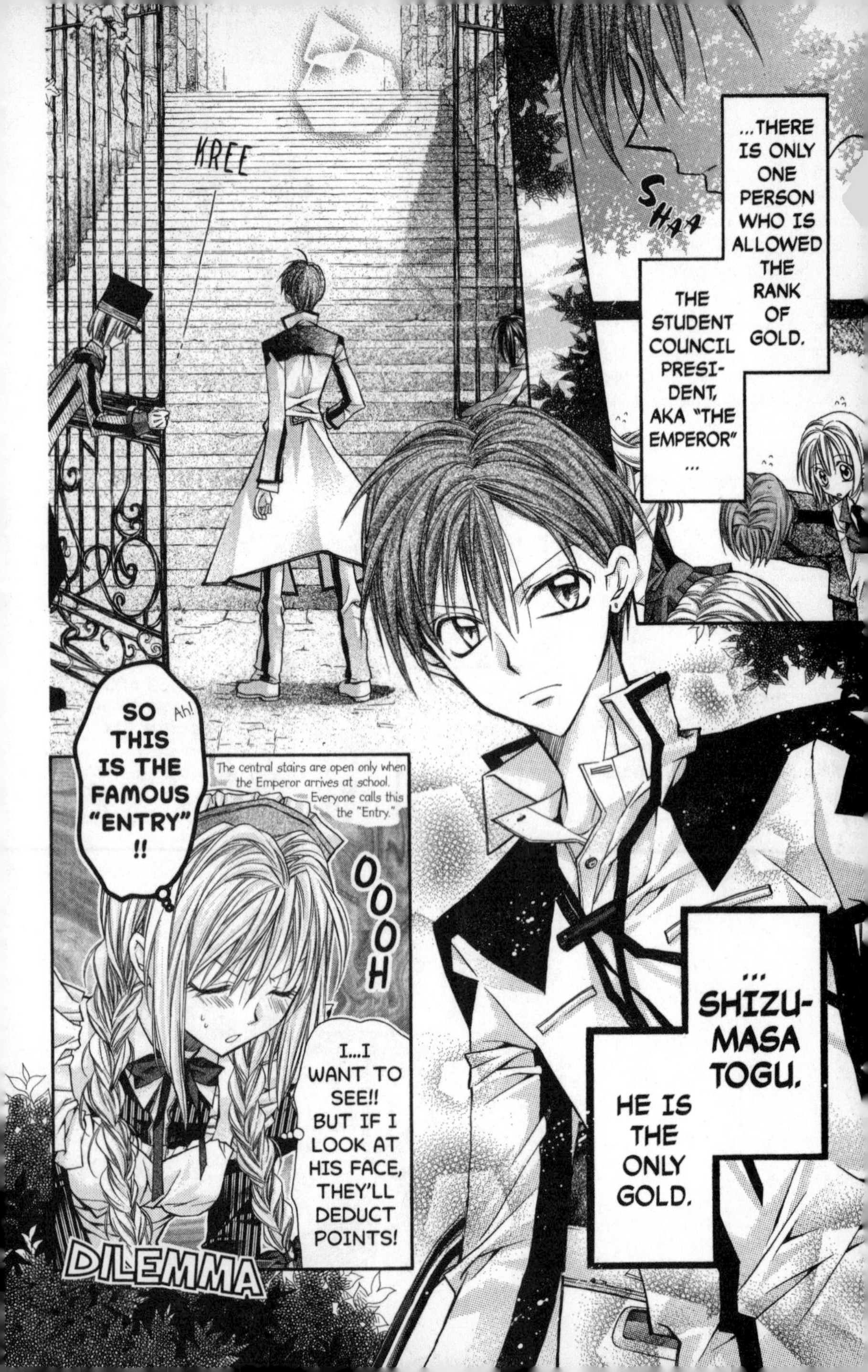

SHAA
...THERE IS ONLY ONE PERSON WHO IS ALLOWED THE RANK OF GOLD.
THE STUDENT COUNCIL PRESIDENT, AKA "THE EMPEROR" ...
... SHIZUMASA TOGU.
HE IS THE ONLY GOLD.
KREE
SO THIS IS THE FAMOUS "ENTRY" !!
Ah!
The central stairs are open only when the Emperor arrives at school. Everyone calls this the "Entry."
OOOH
I...I WANT TO SEE!! BUT IF I LOOK AT HIS FACE, THEY'LL DEDUCT POINTS!
DILEMMA

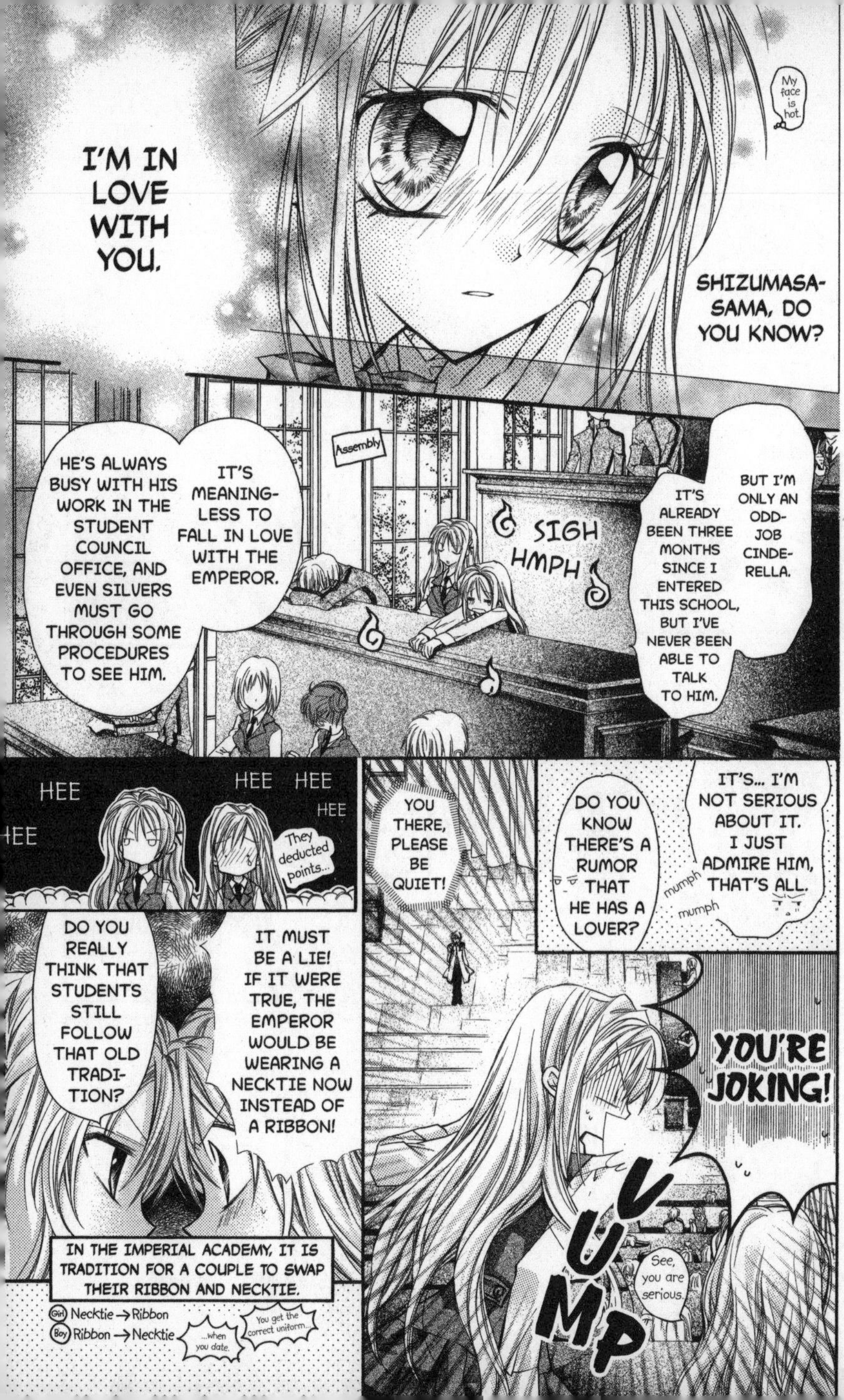
My face is hot.
SHIZUMASA-SAMA, DO YOU KNOW?
I'M IN LOVE WITH YOU.
BUT I'M ONLY AN ODD-JOB CINDERELLA.
IT'S ALREADY BEEN THREE MONTHS SINCE I ENTERED THIS SCHOOL, BUT I'VE NEVER BEEN ABLE TO TALK TO HIM.
SIGH
HMPH
Assembly
IT'S MEANINGLESS TO FALL IN LOVE WITH THE EMPEROR.
HE'S ALWAYS BUSY WITH HIS WORK IN THE STUDENT COUNCIL OFFICE, AND EVEN SILVERS MUST GO THROUGH SOME PROCEDURES TO SEE HIM.
IT'S... I'M NOT SERIOUS ABOUT IT. I JUST ADMIRE HIM, THAT'S ALL.
mumph
mumph
DO YOU KNOW THERE'S A RUMOR THAT HE HAS A LOVER?
YOU'RE JOKING!
VUMP
See, you are serious.
YOU THERE, PLEASE BE QUIET!
HEE HEE
HEE
HEE
HEE
They deducted points...
IT MUST BE A LIE! IF IT WERE TRUE, THE EMPEROR WOULD BE WEARING A NECKTIE NOW INSTEAD OF A RIBBON!
DO YOU REALLY THINK THAT STUDENTS STILL FOLLOW THAT OLD TRADITION?
IN THE IMPERIAL ACADEMY, IT IS TRADITION FOR A COUPLE TO SWAP THEIR RIBBON AND NECKTIE.
Girl Necktie → Ribbon
Boy Ribbon → Necktie
...when you date.
You get the correct uniform...

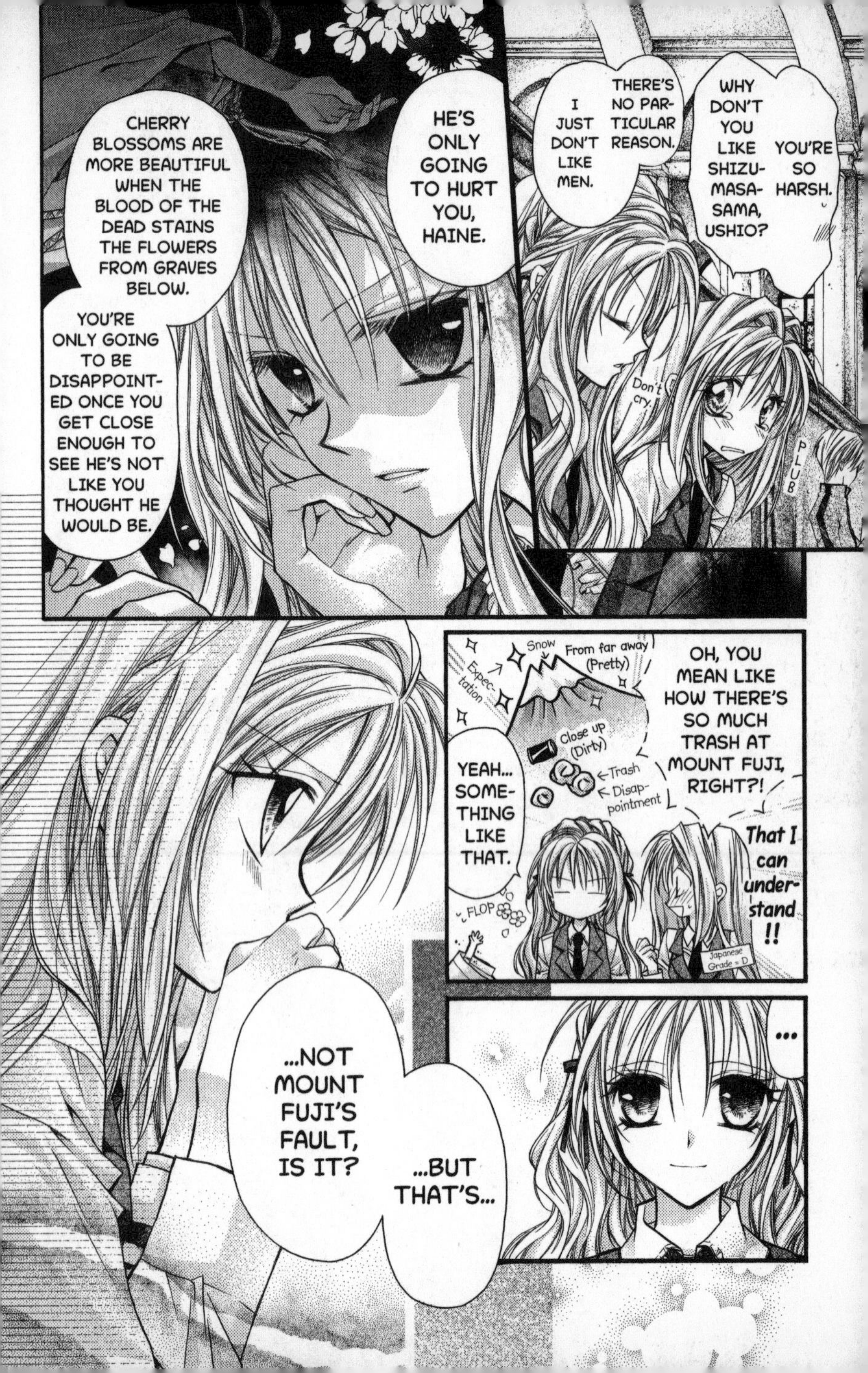
YOU'RE SO HARSH.
WHY DON'T YOU LIKE SHIZUMASA-SAMA, USHIO?
THERE'S NO PARTICULAR REASON.
I JUST DON'T LIKE MEN.
Don't cry.
PLUB
HE'S ONLY GOING TO HURT YOU, HAINE.
CHERRY BLOSSOMS ARE MORE BEAUTIFUL WHEN THE BLOOD OF THE DEAD STAINS THE FLOWERS FROM GRAVES BELOW.
YOU'RE ONLY GOING TO BE DISAPPOINTED ONCE YOU GET CLOSE ENOUGH TO SEE HE'S NOT LIKE YOU THOUGHT HE WOULD BE.
OH, YOU MEAN LIKE HOW THERE'S SO MUCH TRASH AT MOUNT FUJI, RIGHT?!
Snow
From far away (Pretty)
Expectation
Close up (Dirty)
Trash
Disappointment
YEAH... SOMETHING LIKE THAT.
That I can understand!!
FLOP
Japanese Grade = D
...
...BUT THAT'S...
...NOT MOUNT FUJI'S FAULT, IS IT?

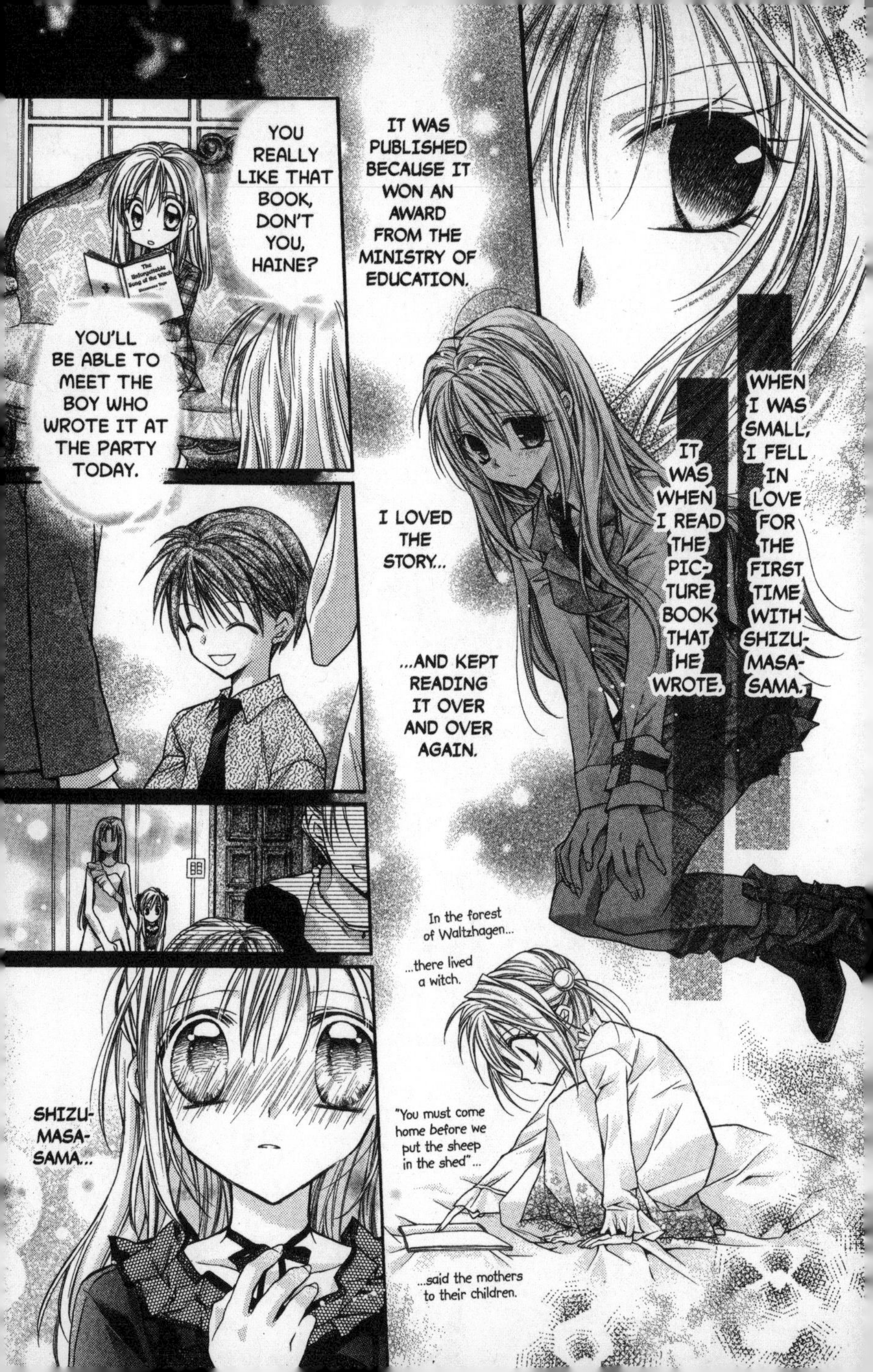
WHEN I WAS SMALL, I FELL IN LOVE FOR THE FIRST TIME WITH SHIZU-MASA-SAMA.
IT WAS WHEN I READ THE PIC-TURE BOOK THAT HE WROTE.
I LOVED THE STORY...
...AND KEPT READING IT OVER AND OVER AGAIN.
In the forest of Waltzhagen...
...there lived a witch.
"You must come home before we put the sheep in the shed"...
...said the mothers to their children.
YOU REALLY LIKE THAT BOOK, DON'T YOU, HAINE?
IT WAS PUBLISHED BECAUSE IT WON AN AWARD FROM THE MINISTRY OF EDUCATION.
YOU'LL BE ABLE TO MEET THE BOY WHO WROTE IT AT THE PARTY TODAY.
SHIZU-MASA-SAMA...

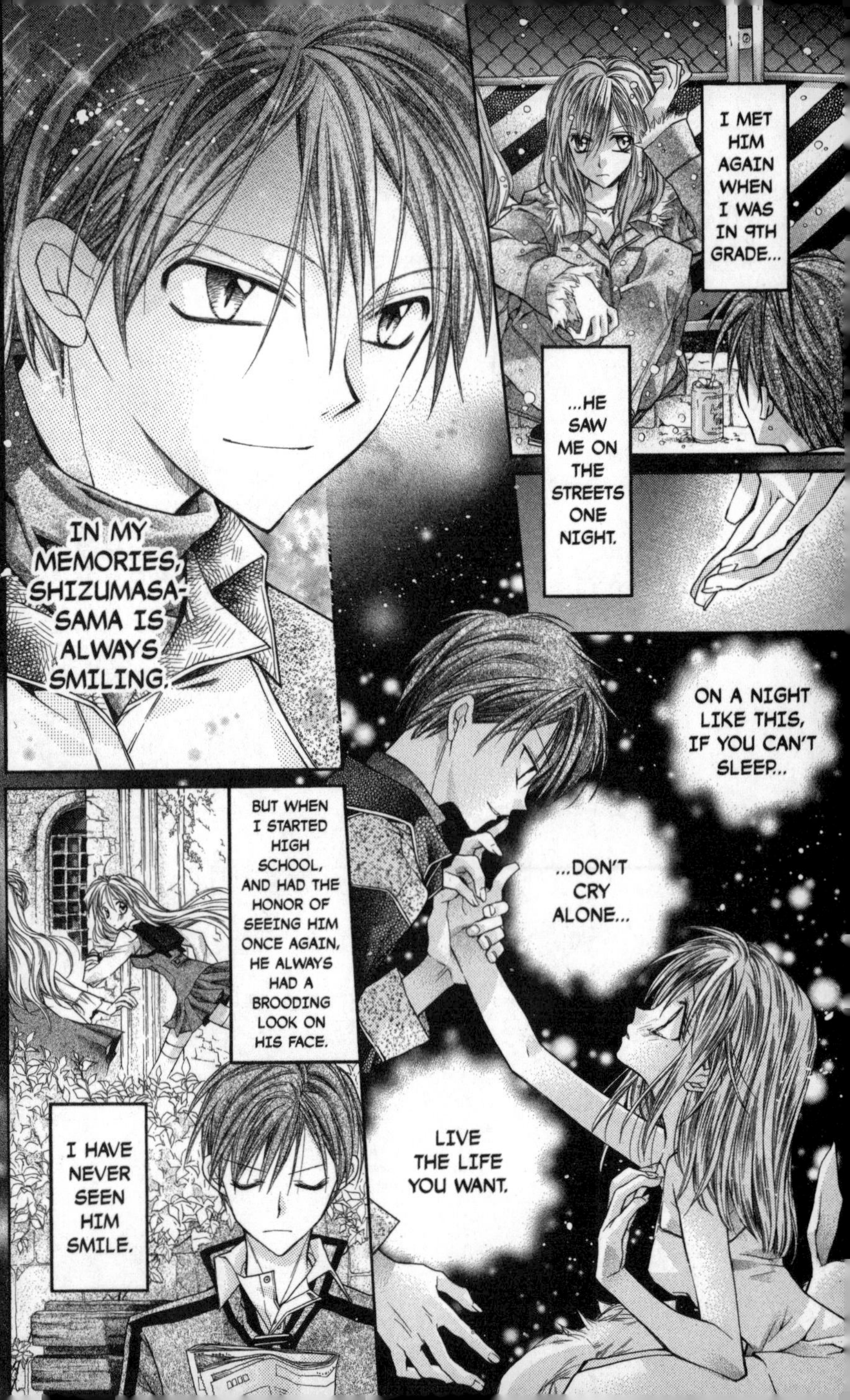
I MET HIM AGAIN WHEN I WAS IN 9TH GRADE...
...HE SAW ME ON THE STREETS ONE NIGHT.
IN MY MEMORIES, SHIZUMASA-SAMA IS ALWAYS SMILING.
ON A NIGHT LIKE THIS, IF YOU CAN'T SLEEP...
...DON'T CRY ALONE...
LIVE THE LIFE YOU WANT.
BUT WHEN I STARTED HIGH SCHOOL, AND HAD THE HONOR OF SEEING HIM ONCE AGAIN, HE ALWAYS HAD A BROODING LOOK ON HIS FACE.
I HAVE NEVER SEEN HIM SMILE.

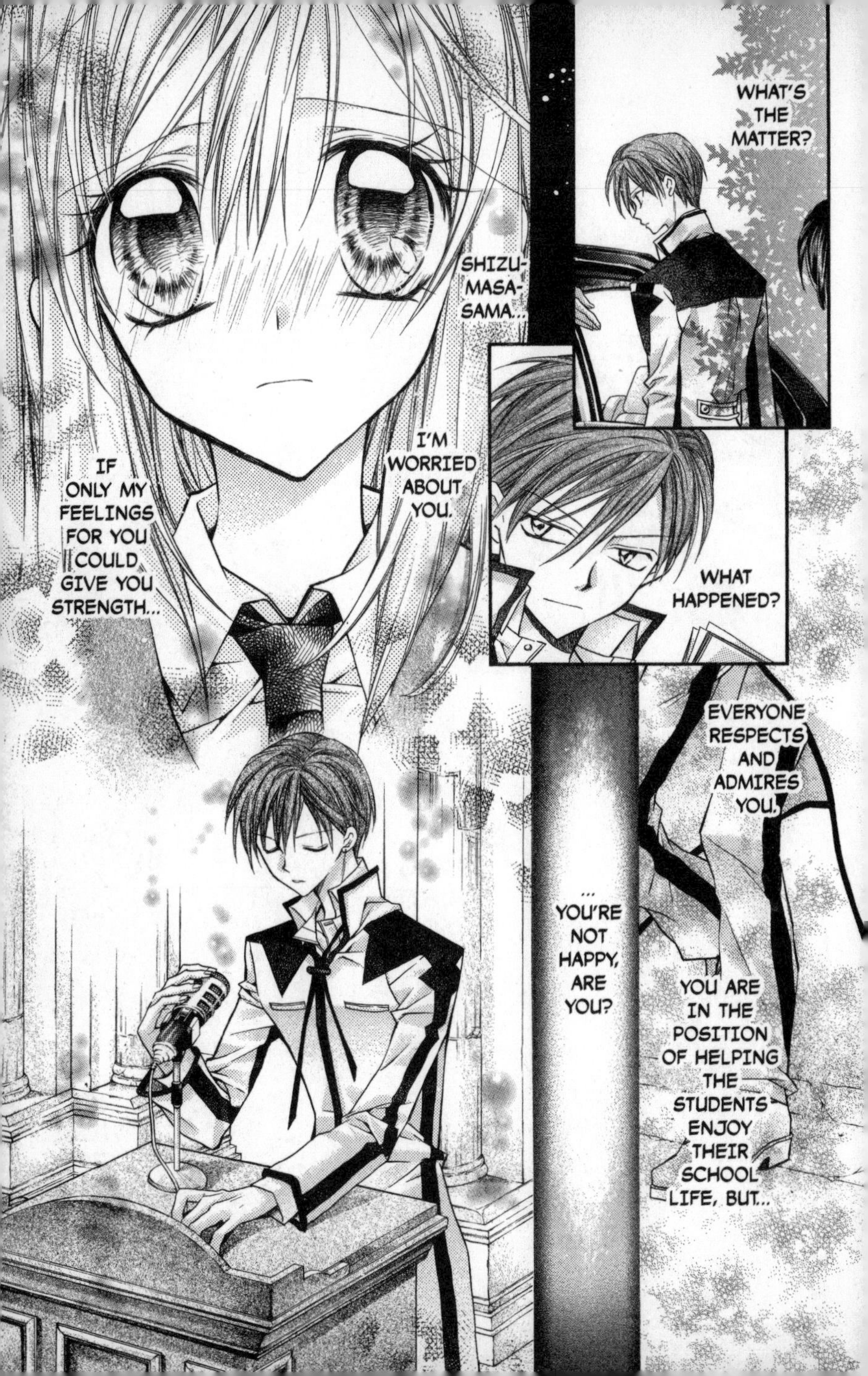
WHAT'S THE MATTER?
WHAT HAPPENED?
EVERYONE RESPECTS AND ADMIRES YOU.
YOU ARE IN THE POSITION OF HELPING THE STUDENTS ENJOY THEIR SCHOOL LIFE, BUT...
... YOU'RE NOT HAPPY, ARE YOU?
SHIZU-MASA-SAMA...
I'M WORRIED ABOUT YOU.
IF ONLY MY FEELINGS FOR YOU COULD GIVE YOU STRENGTH...

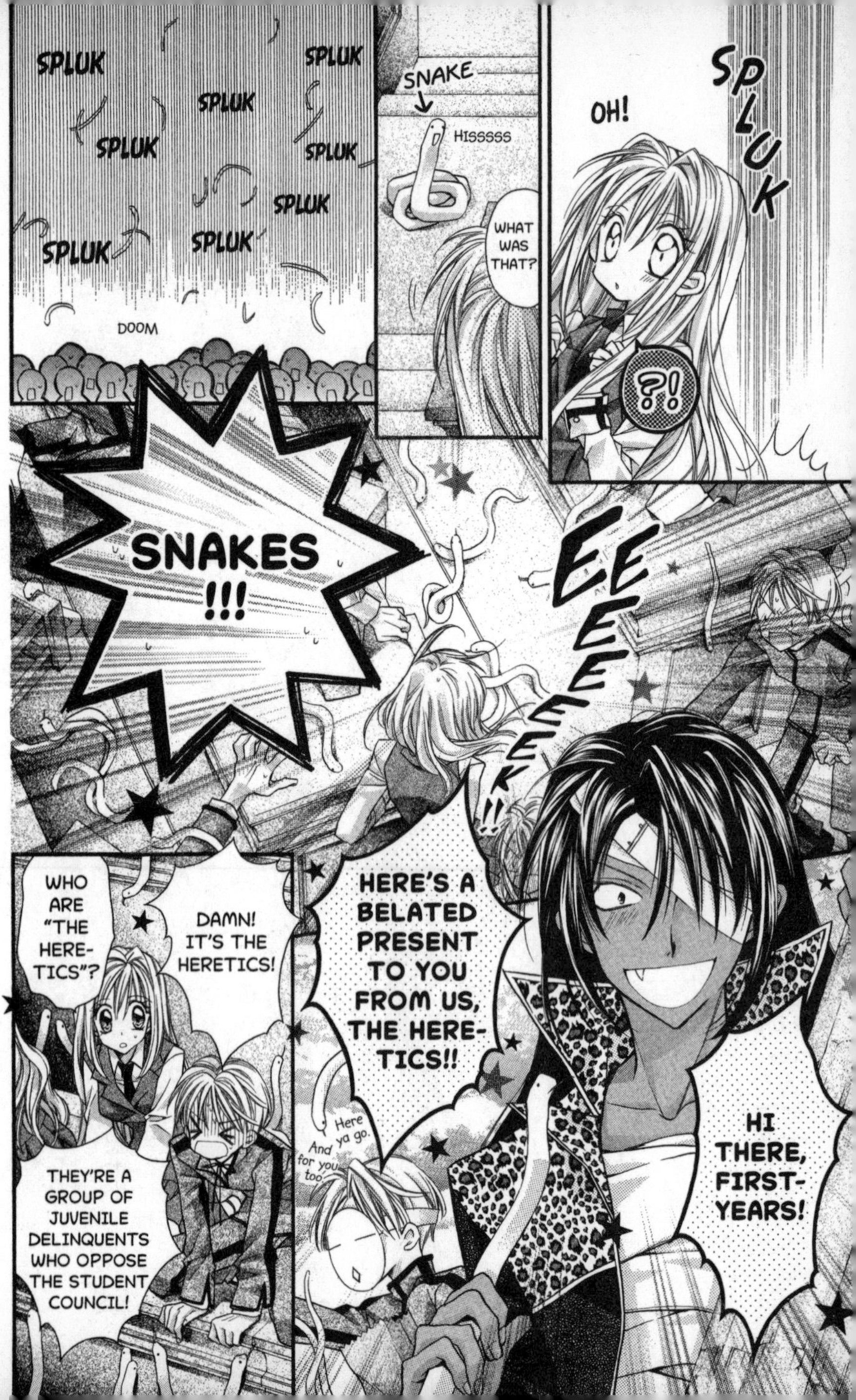
SPLUK
OH!
?!
SNAKE
HISSSSS
WHAT WAS THAT?
SPLUK
SPLUK
SPLUK
SPLUK
SPLUK
SPLUK
SPLUK
SPLUK
DOOM
EEEEEEEK!!
SNAKES!!!
HI THERE, FIRST-YEARS!
HERE'S A BELATED PRESENT TO YOU FROM US, THE HERE-TICS!!
Here ya go.
And for you too.
DAMN! IT'S THE HERETICS!
WHO ARE "THE HERE-TICS"?
THEY'RE A GROUP OF JUVENILE DELINQUENTS WHO OPPOSE THE STUDENT COUNCIL!

Haine Otomiya

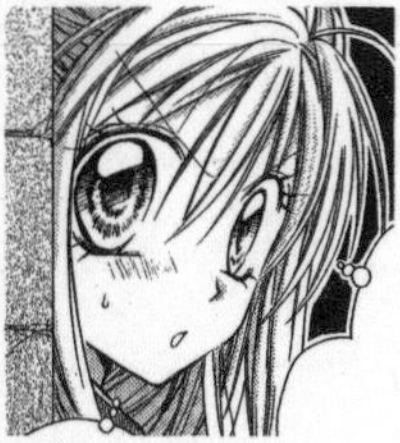

Birthday: January 21
Blood Type: O

A 15-year-old who used to be a yanki.

The picture book she read when she was young triggered her love for Shizumasa-sama.

At the age of 10, the Otomiya family adopted her from the Kamiya family.

She dislikes her real father. She seems to have been close to her mother, but...?

Comments

Haine is a very unlikely heroine for my manga. She messes up her one-liners, she makes mistakes when using kanji—basically she's rather stupid. (But my fans kindly tell me that is what's good about her...)

But Haine is a character who I can draw in a very relaxed mood. She's cheerful and is never discouraged.

I just hope that one day she and the Emperor will become a true couple...

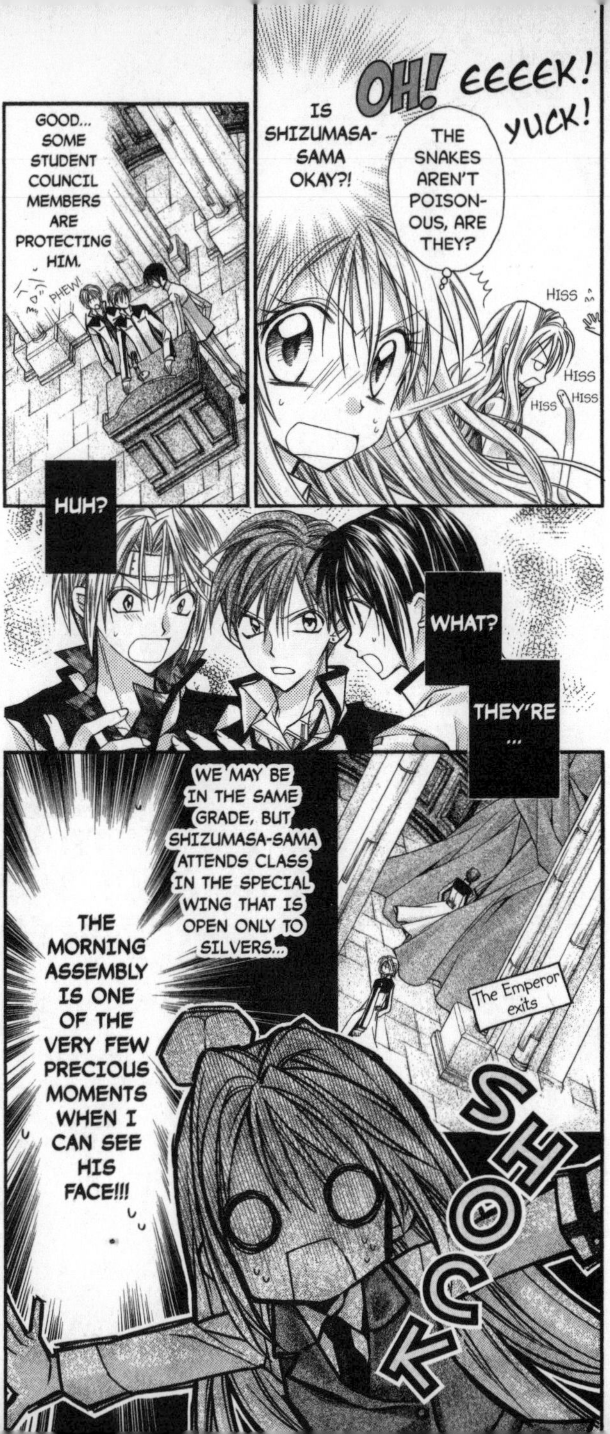
EEEEK! YUCK!
OH!
THE SNAKES AREN'T POISONOUS, ARE THEY?
IS SHIZUMASA-SAMA OKAY?!
HISS
HISS
HISS
HISS
GOOD... SOME STUDENT COUNCIL MEMBERS ARE PROTECTING HIM.
PHEW!
WHAT?
THEY'RE ...
HUH?
WE MAY BE IN THE SAME GRADE, BUT SHIZUMASA-SAMA ATTENDS CLASS IN THE SPECIAL WING THAT IS OPEN ONLY TO SILVERS...
The Emperor exits
THE MORNING ASSEMBLY IS ONE OF THE VERY FEW PRECIOUS MOMENTS WHEN I CAN SEE HIS FACE!!!
SHOCK

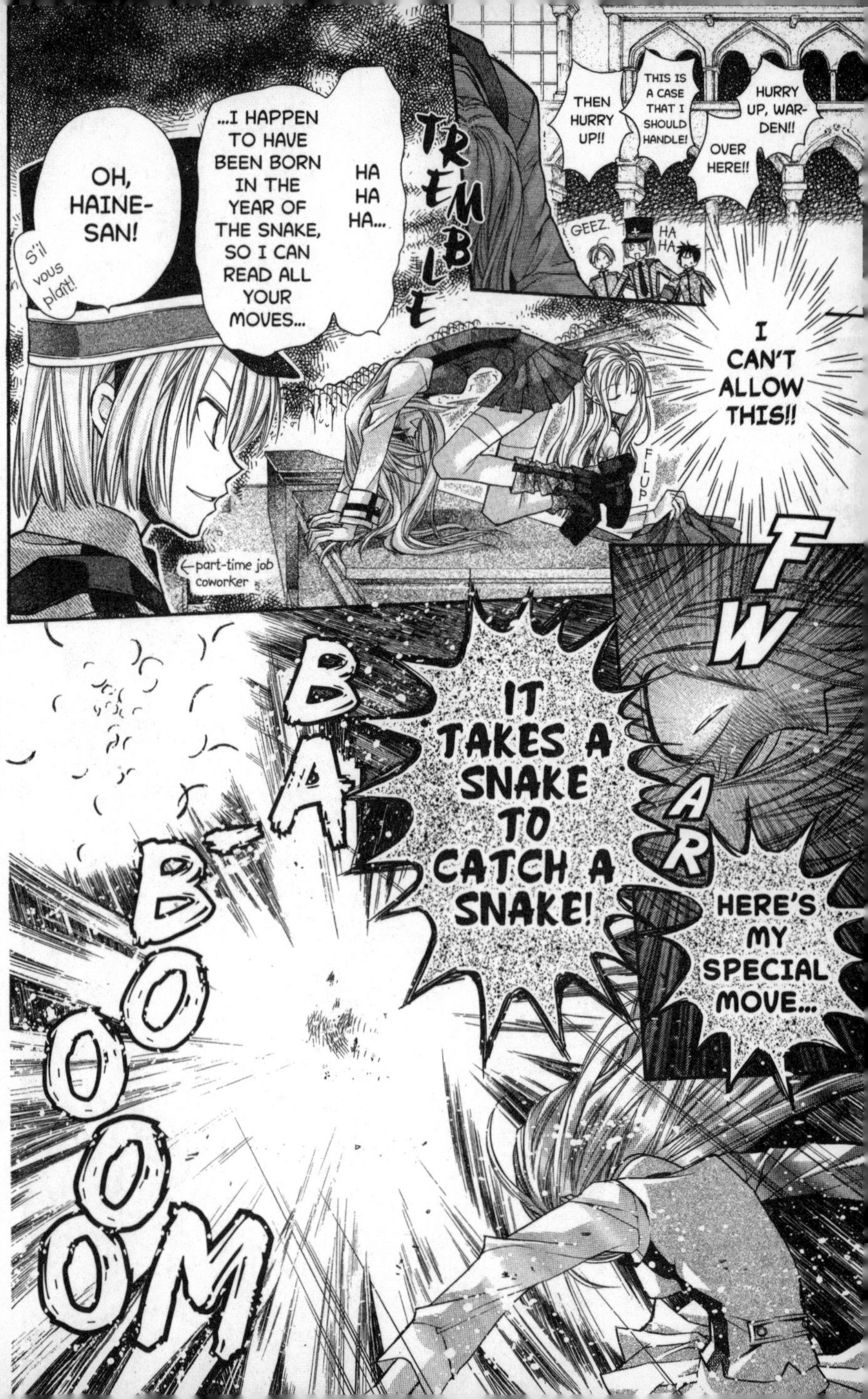
HURRY UP, WARDEN!!
OVER HERE!!
THIS IS A CASE THAT I SHOULD HANDLE!
THEN HURRY UP!!
HA HA
GEEZ.
I CAN'T ALLOW THIS!!
TREMBLE
HA HA HA...
...I HAPPEN TO HAVE BEEN BORN IN THE YEAR OF THE SNAKE, SO I CAN READ ALL YOUR MOVES...
OH, HAINE-SAN!
S'il vous plaît!
FLUP
←part-time job coworker
FWAR
HERE'S MY SPECIAL MOVE...
IT TAKES A SNAKE TO CATCH A SNAKE!
BA
BOOOOOOM

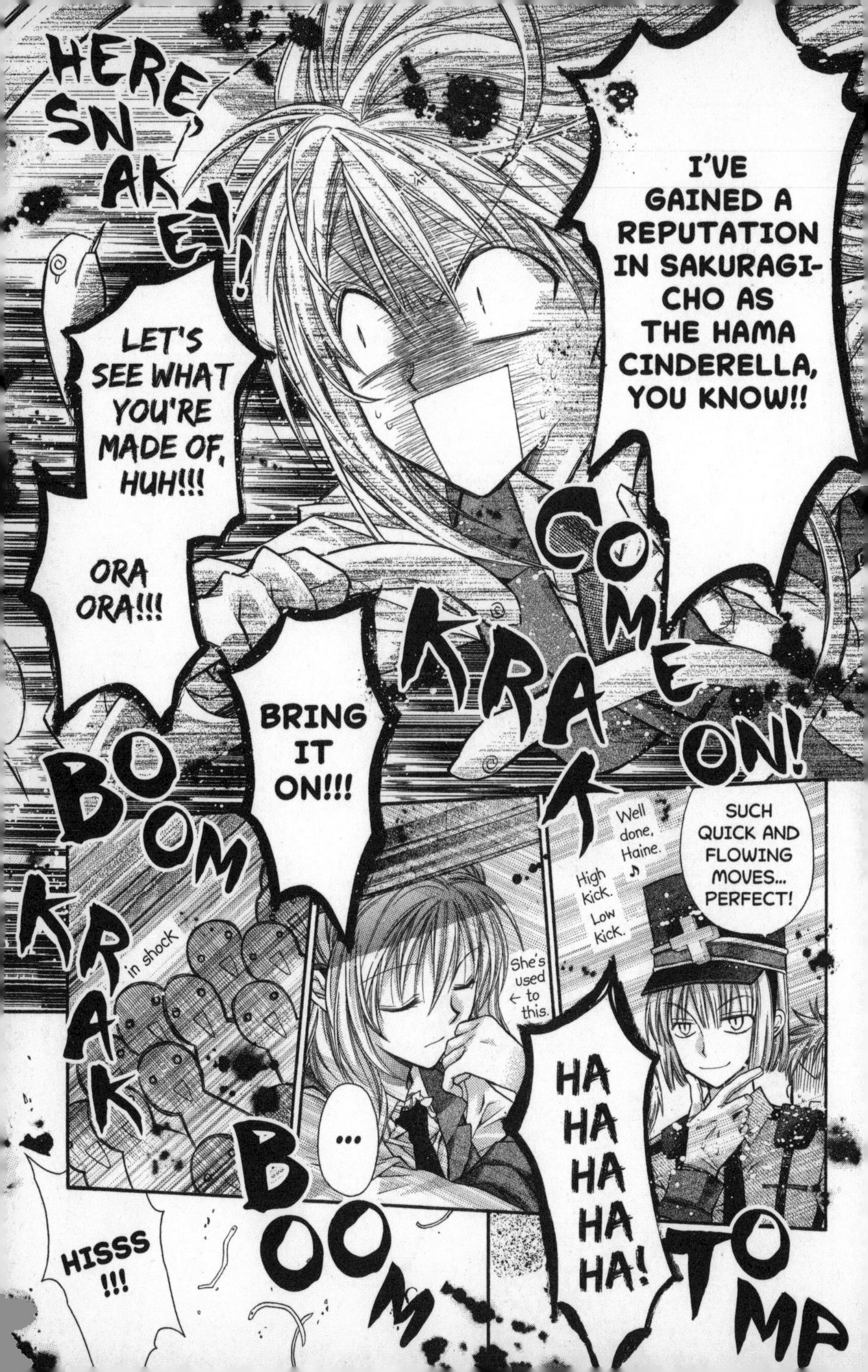
I'VE GAINED A REPUTATION IN SAKURAGI-CHO AS THE HAMA CINDERELLA, YOU KNOW!!
COME ON!
HERE'S SNAKEY!
LET'S SEE WHAT YOU'RE MADE OF, HUH!!!
ORA ORA!!!
KRAAK
BRING IT ON!!!
BOOM
KRAK
SUCH QUICK AND FLOWING MOVES... PERFECT!
Well done, Haine. ♪
High Kick. Low Kick.
HA HA HA HA HA!
STOMP
She's used ← to this.
in shock
...
BOOM
HISSS !!!

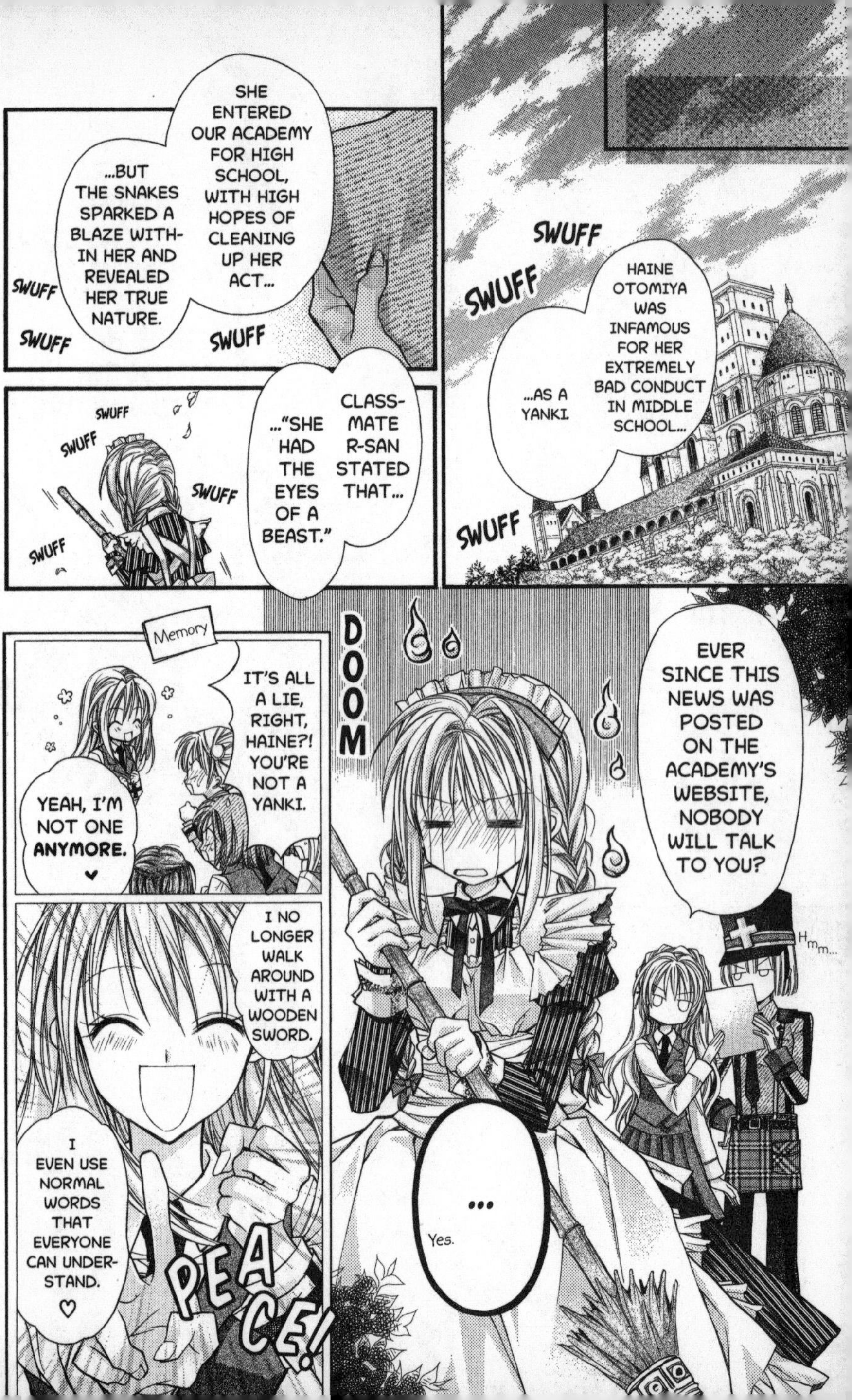
SWUFF
SWUFF
HAINE OTOMIYA WAS INFAMOUS FOR HER EXTREMELY BAD CONDUCT IN MIDDLE SCHOOL...
...AS A YANKI
SWUFF
SHE ENTERED OUR ACADEMY FOR HIGH SCHOOL, WITH HIGH HOPES OF CLEANING UP HER ACT...
...BUT THE SNAKES SPARKED A BLAZE WITH-IN HER AND REVEALED HER TRUE NATURE.
SWUFF
SWUFF
SWUFF
CLASS-MATE R-SAN STATED THAT...
..."SHE HAD THE EYES OF A BEAST."
SWUFF
SWUFF
SWUFF
SWUFF
EVER SINCE THIS NEWS WAS POSTED ON THE ACADEMY'S WEBSITE, NOBODY WILL TALK TO YOU?
Hmm...
DOOM
...
Yes.
Memory
IT'S ALL A LIE, RIGHT, HAINE?! YOU'RE NOT A YANKI.
YEAH, I'M NOT ONE **ANYMORE.** ❤
I NO LONGER WALK AROUND WITH A WOODEN SWORD.
I EVEN USE NORMAL WORDS THAT EVERYONE CAN UNDER-STAND. ♡
PEACE!

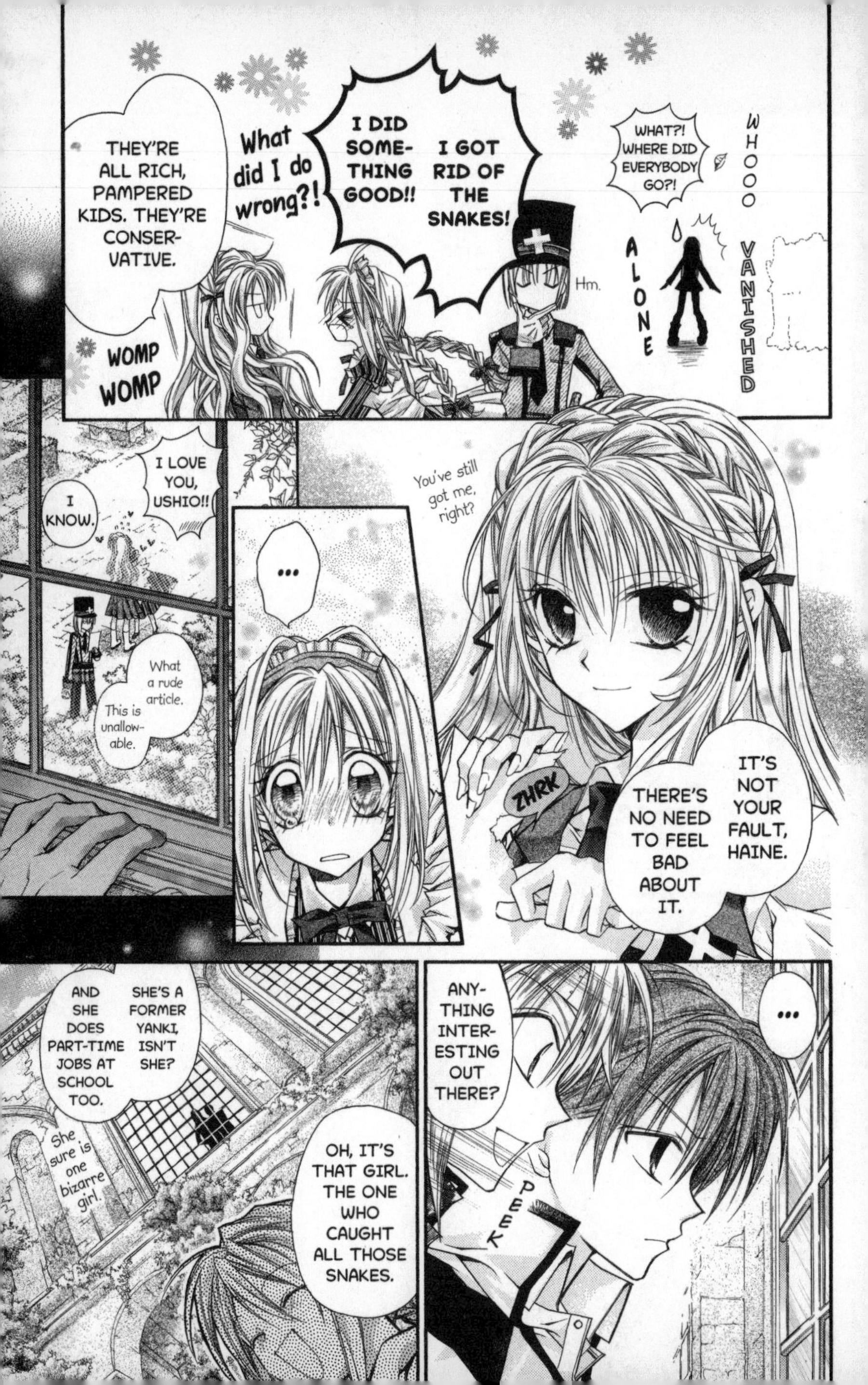
WHOOO
VANISHED
WHAT?! WHERE DID EVERYBODY GO?!
ALONE
Hm.
I GOT RID OF THE SNAKES!
I DID SOME-THING GOOD!!
What did I do wrong?!
THEY'RE ALL RICH, PAMPERED KIDS. THEY'RE CONSER-VATIVE.
WOMP WOMP
You've still got me, right?
IT'S NOT YOUR FAULT, HAINE.
THERE'S NO NEED TO FEEL BAD ABOUT IT.
ZHRK
...
I LOVE YOU, USHIO!!
I KNOW.
What a rude article.
This is unallowable.
...
ANY-THING INTER-ESTING OUT THERE?
PEEK
OH, IT'S THAT GIRL. THE ONE WHO CAUGHT ALL THOSE SNAKES.
SHE'S A FORMER YANKI, ISN'T SHE?
AND SHE DOES PART-TIME JOBS AT SCHOOL TOO.
She sure is one bizarre girl.

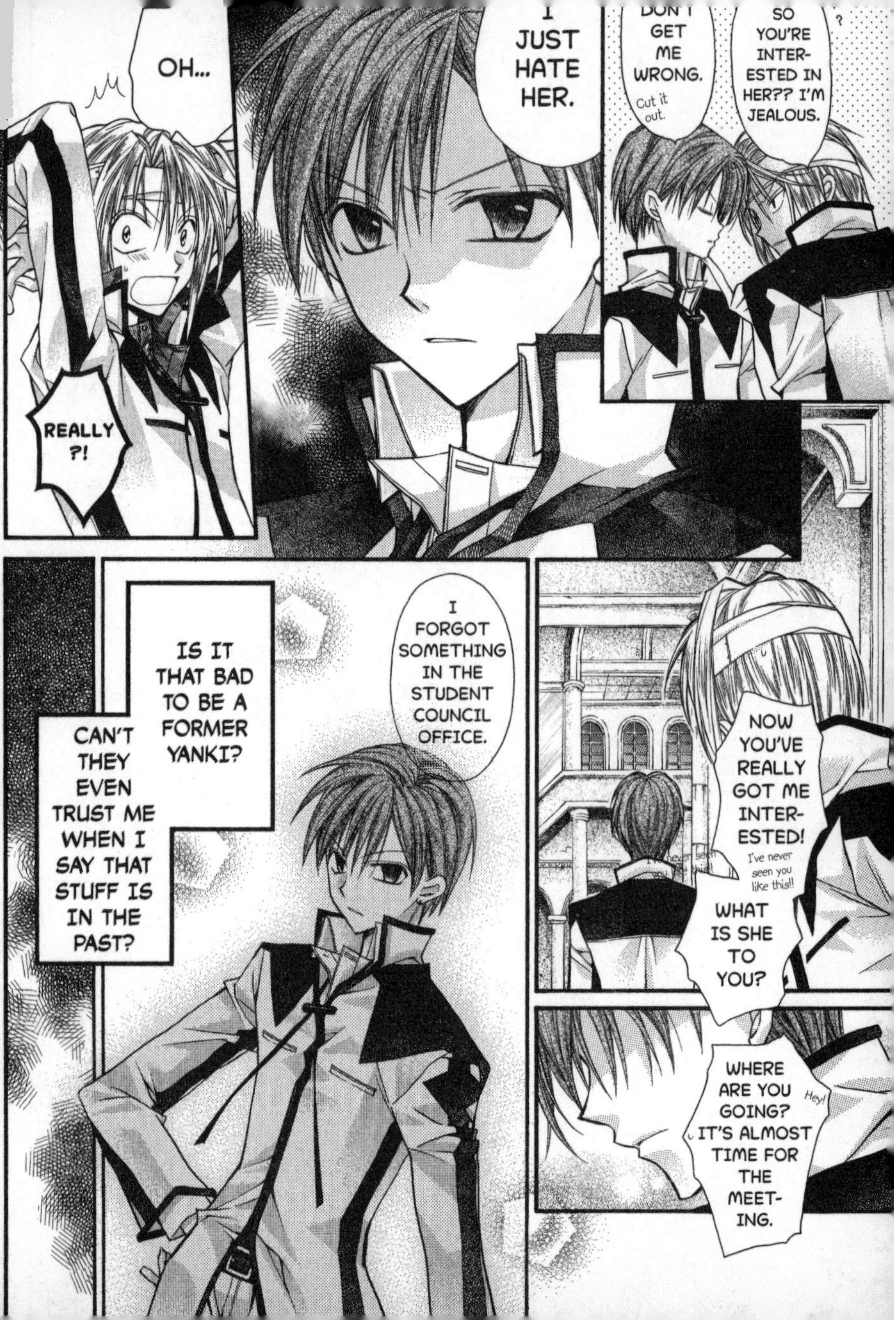
SO YOU'RE INTER-ESTED IN HER?? I'M JEALOUS.
?
DON'T GET ME WRONG.
Cut it out.
I JUST HATE HER.
OH...
REALLY ?!
NOW YOU'VE REALLY GOT ME INTER-ESTED!
I've never seen you like this!!
WHAT IS SHE TO YOU?
WHERE ARE YOU GOING? IT'S ALMOST TIME FOR THE MEET-ING.
Hey!
I FORGOT SOMETHING IN THE STUDENT COUNCIL OFFICE.
IS IT THAT BAD TO BE A FORMER YANKI?
CAN'T THEY EVEN TRUST ME WHEN I SAY THAT STUFF IS IN THE PAST?

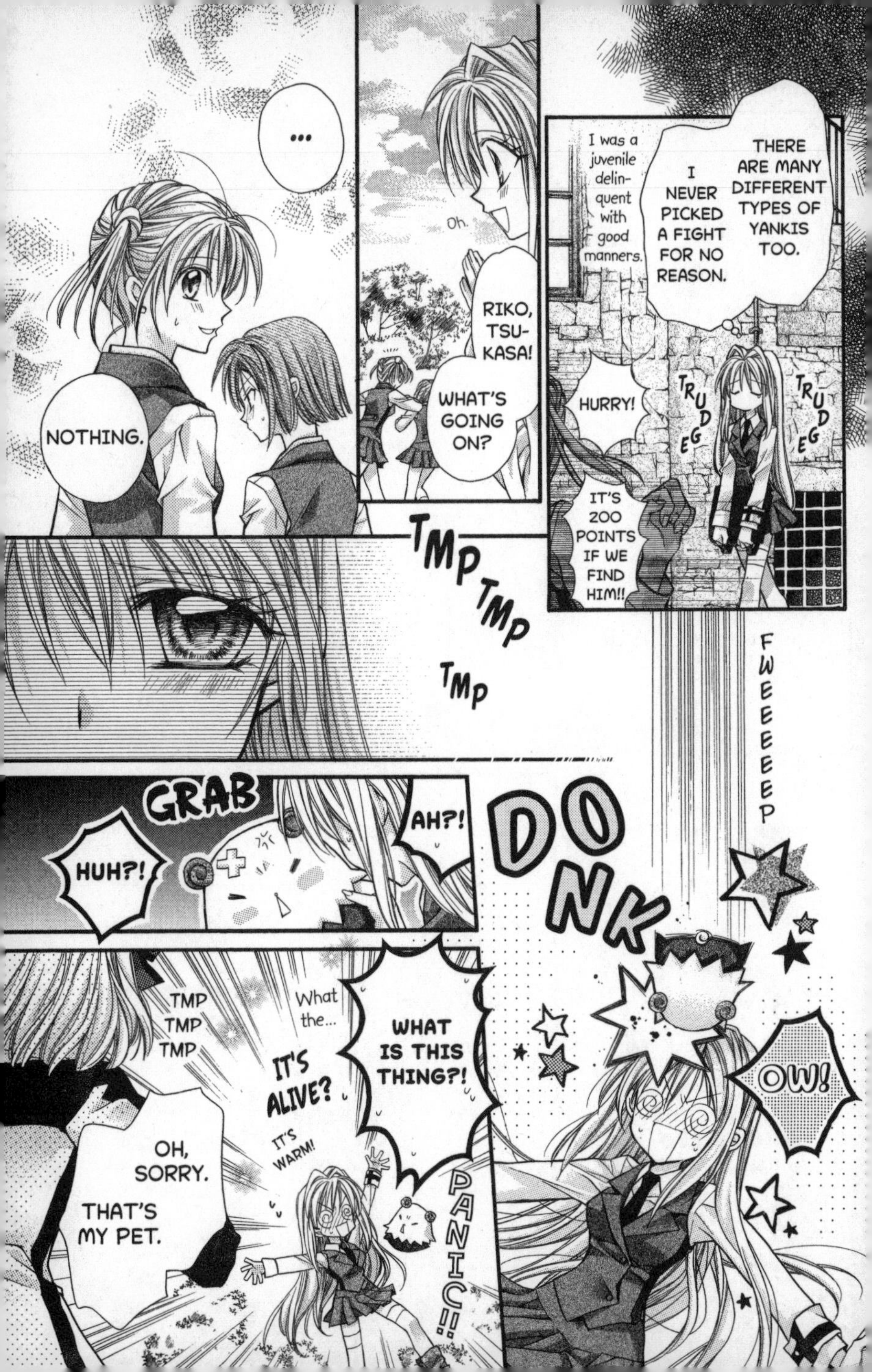

TRUDGE
TRUDGE
THERE ARE MANY DIFFERENT TYPES OF YANKIS TOO.
I NEVER PICKED A FIGHT FOR NO REASON.
I was a juvenile delinquent with good manners.
HURRY!
IT'S 200 POINTS IF WE FIND HIM!!
Oh.
RIKO, TSUKASA!
WHAT'S GOING ON?
...
NOTHING.
TMP TMP TMP
TMP
FWEEEEEEEP
DONK
OW!
GRAB
AH?!
HUH?!
WHAT IS THIS THING?!
What the...
IT'S ALIVE?
IT'S WARM!
PANIC!!
TMP TMP TMP
OH, SORRY.
THAT'S MY PET.

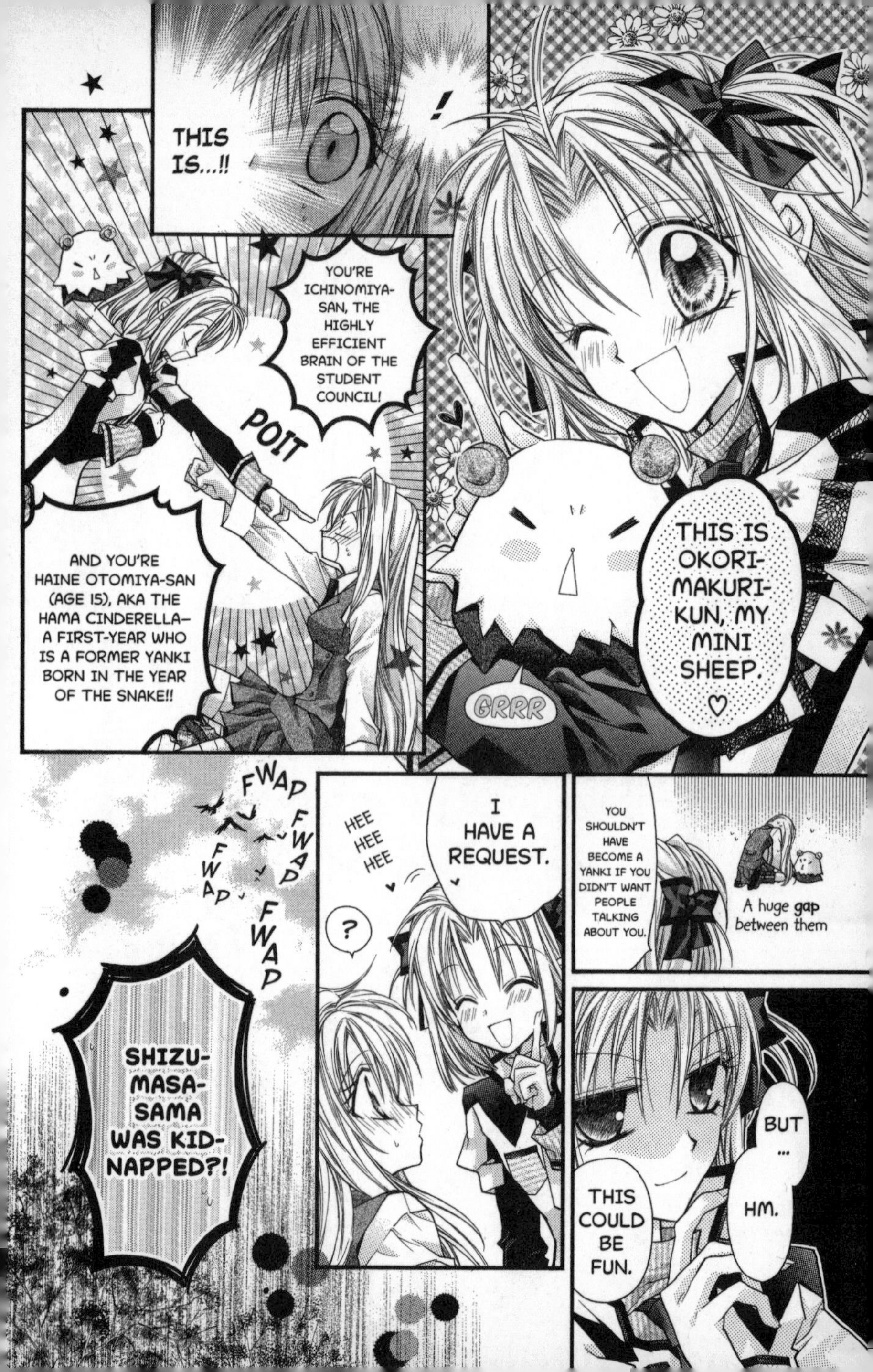
THIS IS OKORI-MAKURI-KUN, MY MINI SHEEP. ♡
GRRR
!
THIS IS...!!
YOU'RE ICHINOMIYA-SAN, THE HIGHLY EFFICIENT BRAIN OF THE STUDENT COUNCIL!
POIT
AND YOU'RE HAINE OTOMIYA-SAN (AGE 15), AKA THE HAMA CINDERELLA—A FIRST-YEAR WHO IS A FORMER YANKI BORN IN THE YEAR OF THE SNAKE!!
YOU SHOULDN'T HAVE BECOME A YANKI IF YOU DIDN'T WANT PEOPLE TALKING ABOUT YOU.
A huge gap between them
BUT ...
HM.
THIS COULD BE FUN.
I HAVE A REQUEST.
HEE HEE HEE
?
FWAP
FWAP
FWAP
FWAP
FWAP
SHIZU-MASA-SAMA WAS KID-NAPPED?!

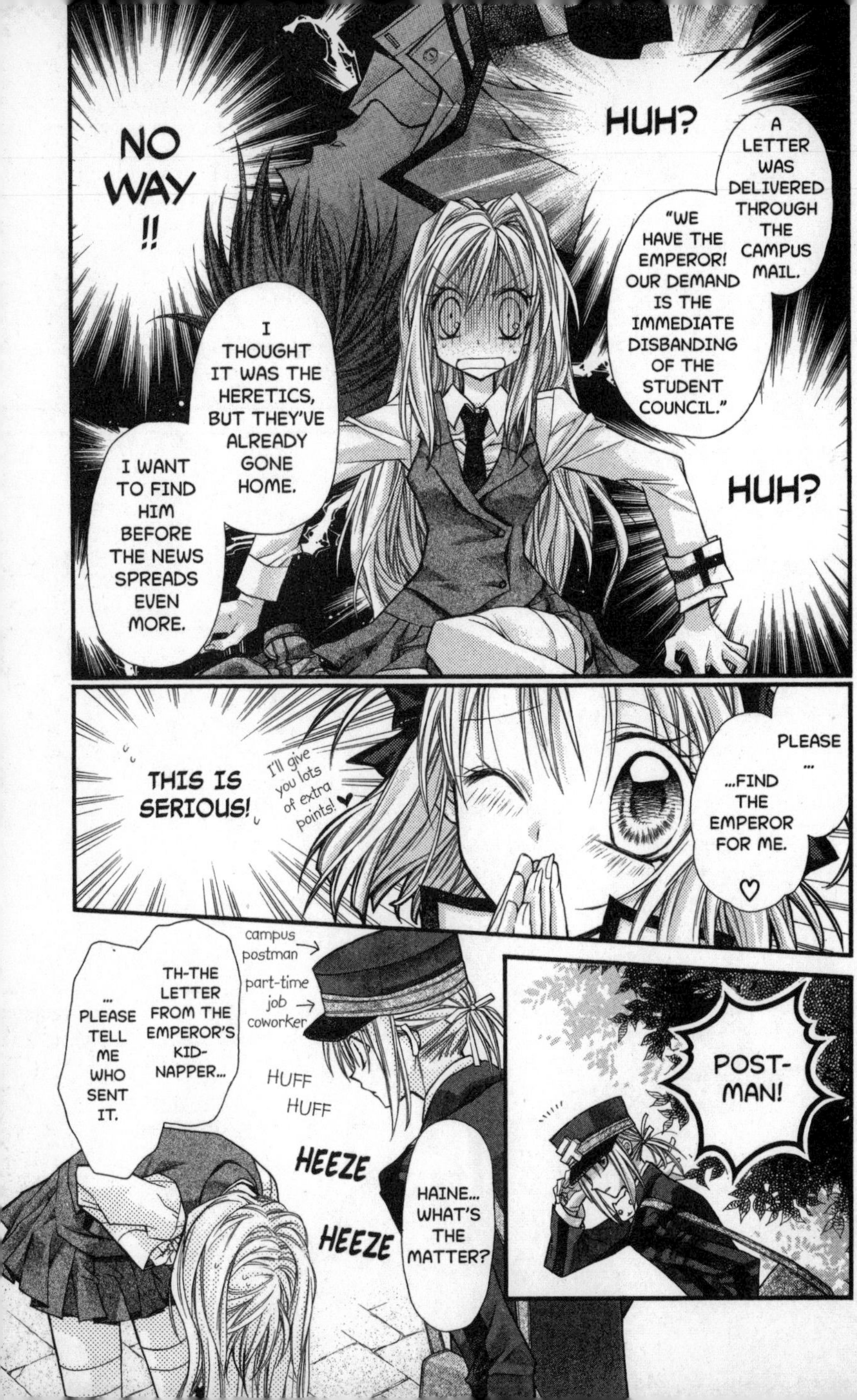
A LETTER WAS DELIVERED THROUGH THE CAMPUS MAIL.
HUH?
“WE HAVE THE EMPEROR! OUR DEMAND IS THE IMMEDIATE DISBANDING OF THE STUDENT COUNCIL.”
HUH?
NO WAY !!
I THOUGHT IT WAS THE HERETICS, BUT THEY'VE ALREADY GONE HOME.
I WANT TO FIND HIM BEFORE THE NEWS SPREADS EVEN MORE.
PLEASE ... ...FIND THE EMPEROR FOR ME. ♡
THIS IS SERIOUS!
I'll give you lots of extra points! ♥
POST-MAN!
HAINE... WHAT'S THE MATTER?
HEEZE
HEEZE
HUFF HUFF
campus postman
part-time job coworker
TH-THE LETTER FROM THE EMPEROR'S KID-NAPPER...
... PLEASE TELL ME WHO SENT IT.

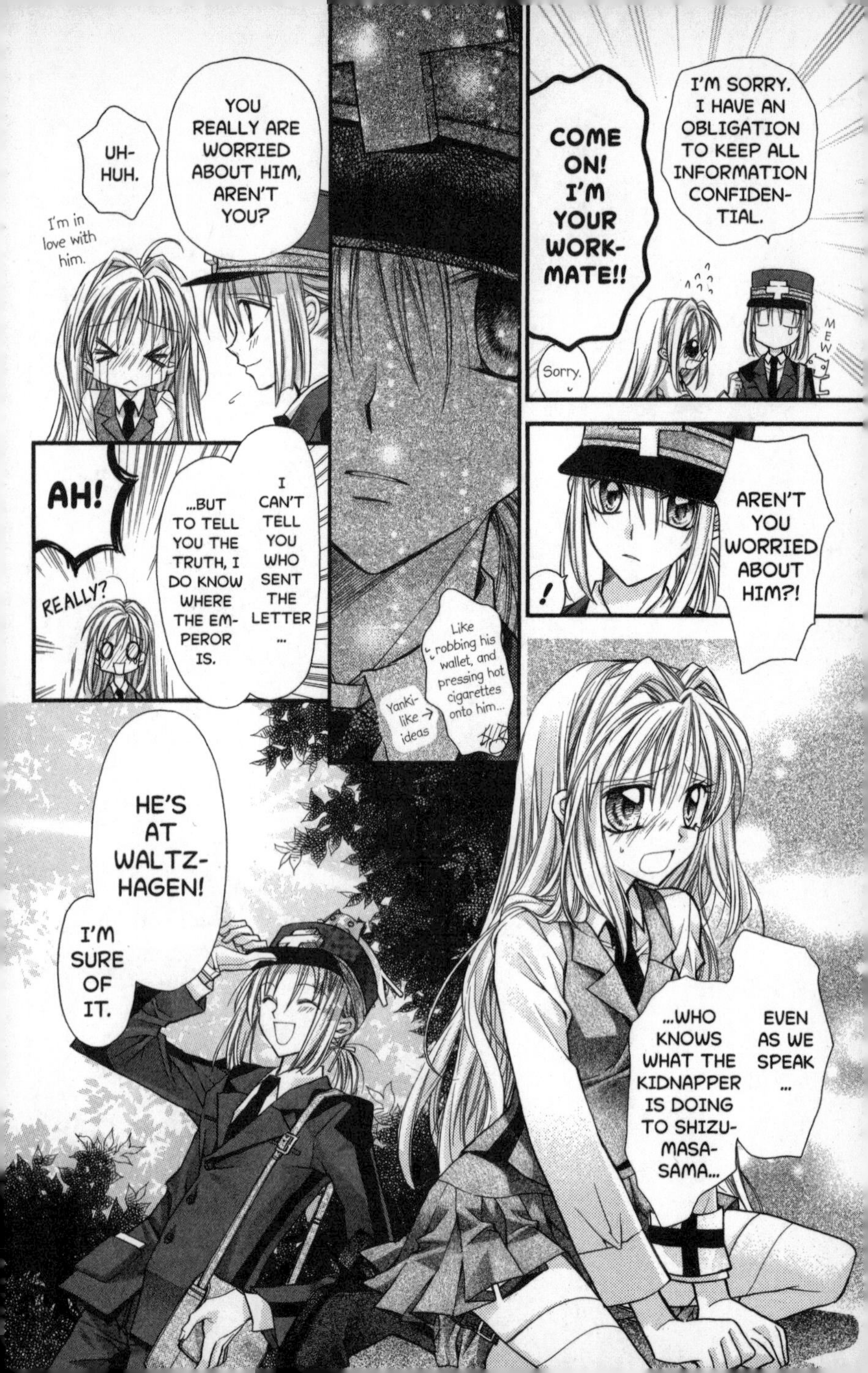
I'M SORRY. I HAVE AN OBLIGATION TO KEEP ALL INFORMATION CONFIDEN-TIAL.
COME ON! I'M YOUR WORK-MATE!!
MEW
Sorry.
AREN'T YOU WORRIED ABOUT HIM?!
!
Like robbing his wallet, and pressing hot cigarettes onto him...
Yanki-like → ideas
YOU REALLY ARE WORRIED ABOUT HIM, AREN'T YOU?
UH-HUH.
I'm in love with him.
I CAN'T TELL YOU WHO SENT THE LETTER...
...BUT TO TELL YOU THE TRUTH, I DO KNOW WHERE THE EM-PEROR IS.
AH!
REALLY?
EVEN AS WE SPEAK...
...WHO KNOWS WHAT THE KIDNAPPER IS DOING TO SHIZU-MASA-SAMA...
HE'S AT WALTZ-HAGEN!
I'M SURE OF IT.

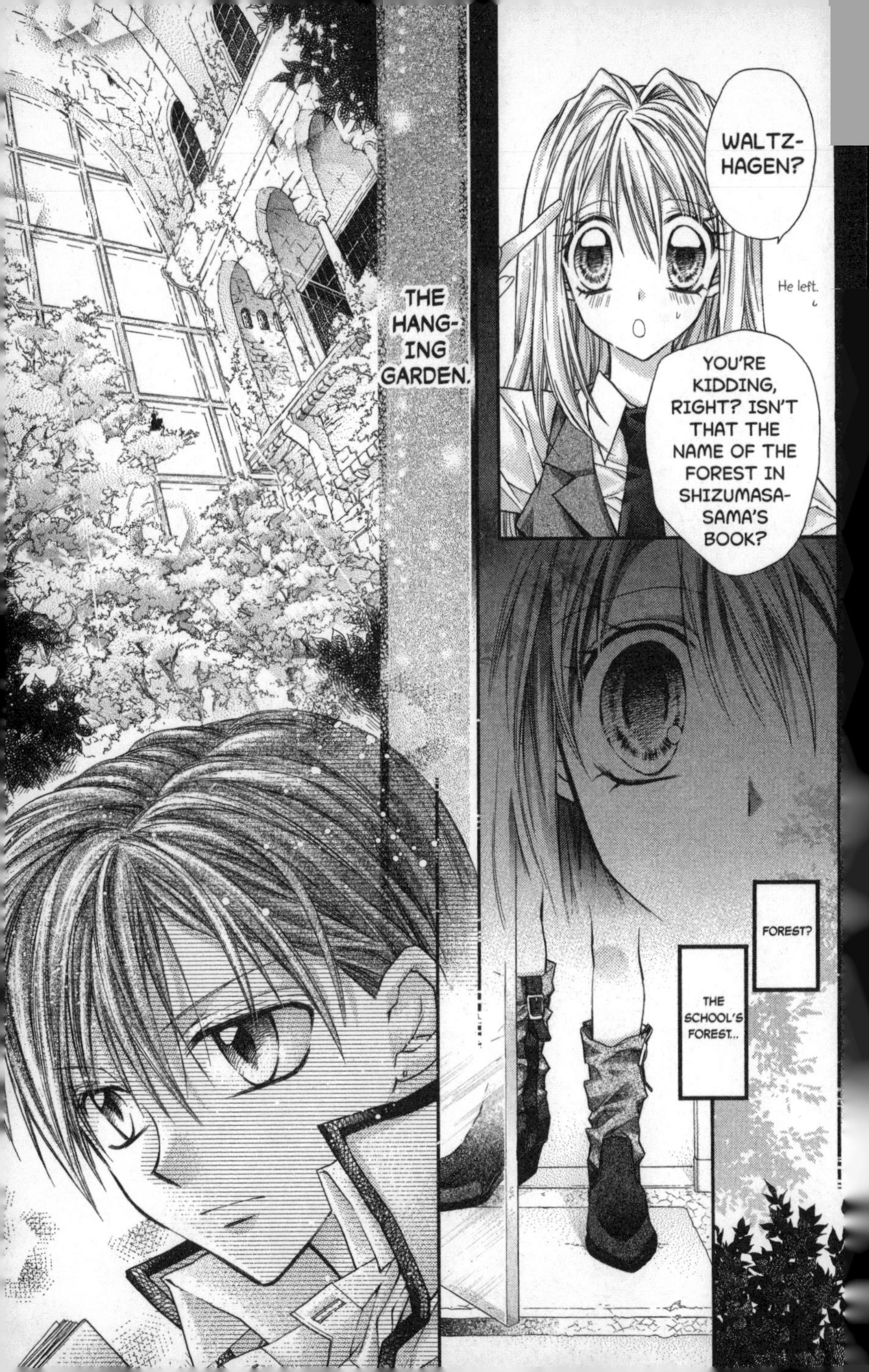
WALTZ-HAGEN?
He left.
YOU'RE KIDDING, RIGHT? ISN'T THAT THE NAME OF THE FOREST IN SHIZUMASA-SAMA'S BOOK?
FOREST?
THE SCHOOL'S FOREST...
THE HANG-ING GARDEN.

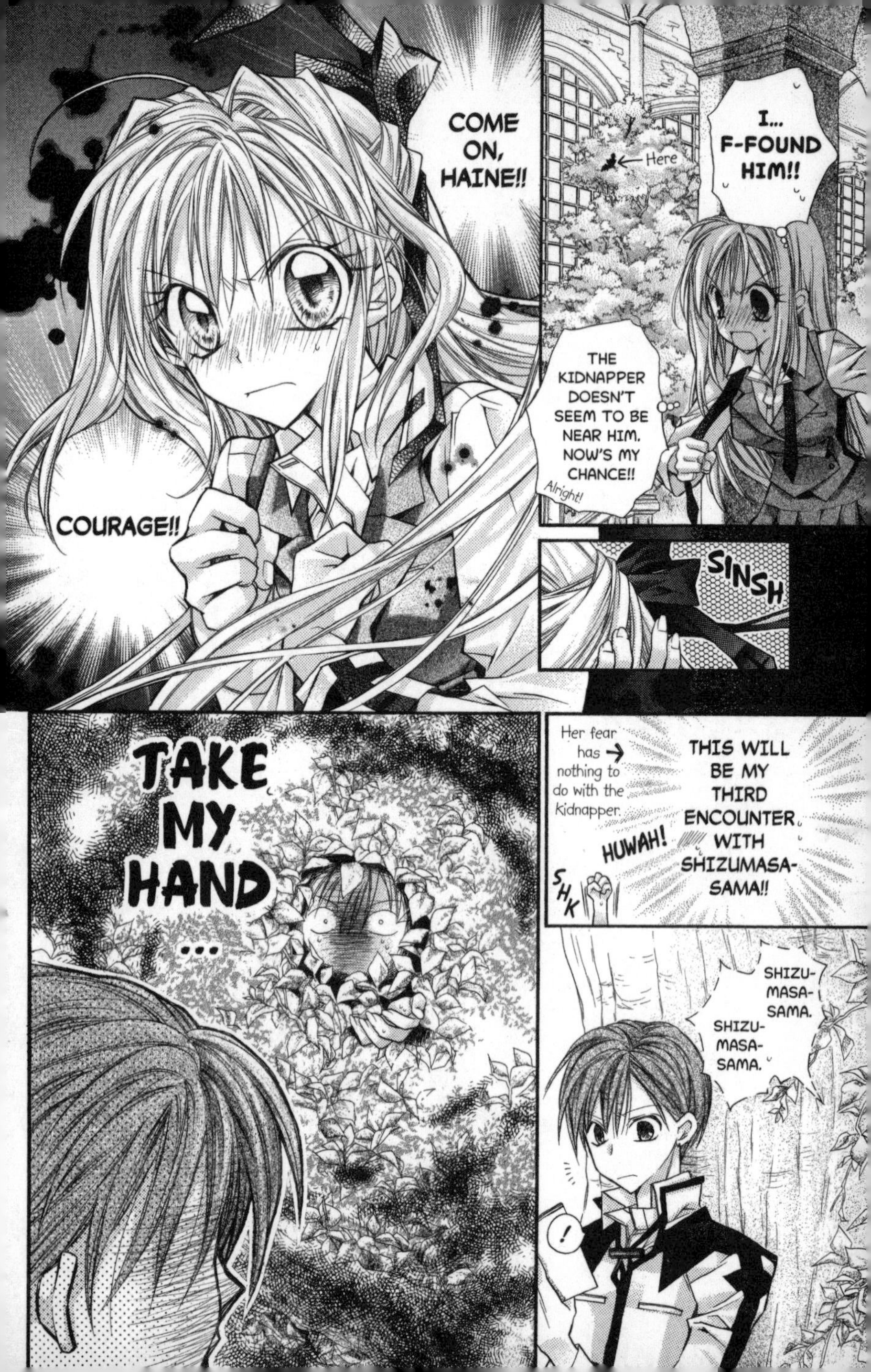

I... F-FOUND HIM!!
Here
THE KIDNAPPER DOESN'T SEEM TO BE NEAR HIM. NOW'S MY CHANCE!!
Alright!
SINSH
COME ON, HAINE!!
COURAGE!!
THIS WILL BE MY THIRD ENCOUNTER WITH SHIZUMASA-SAMA!!
Her fear has nothing to do with the kidnapper.
HUWAH!
SHK
SHIZU-MASA-SAMA.
SHIZU-MASA-SAMA.
!
TAKE MY HAND...

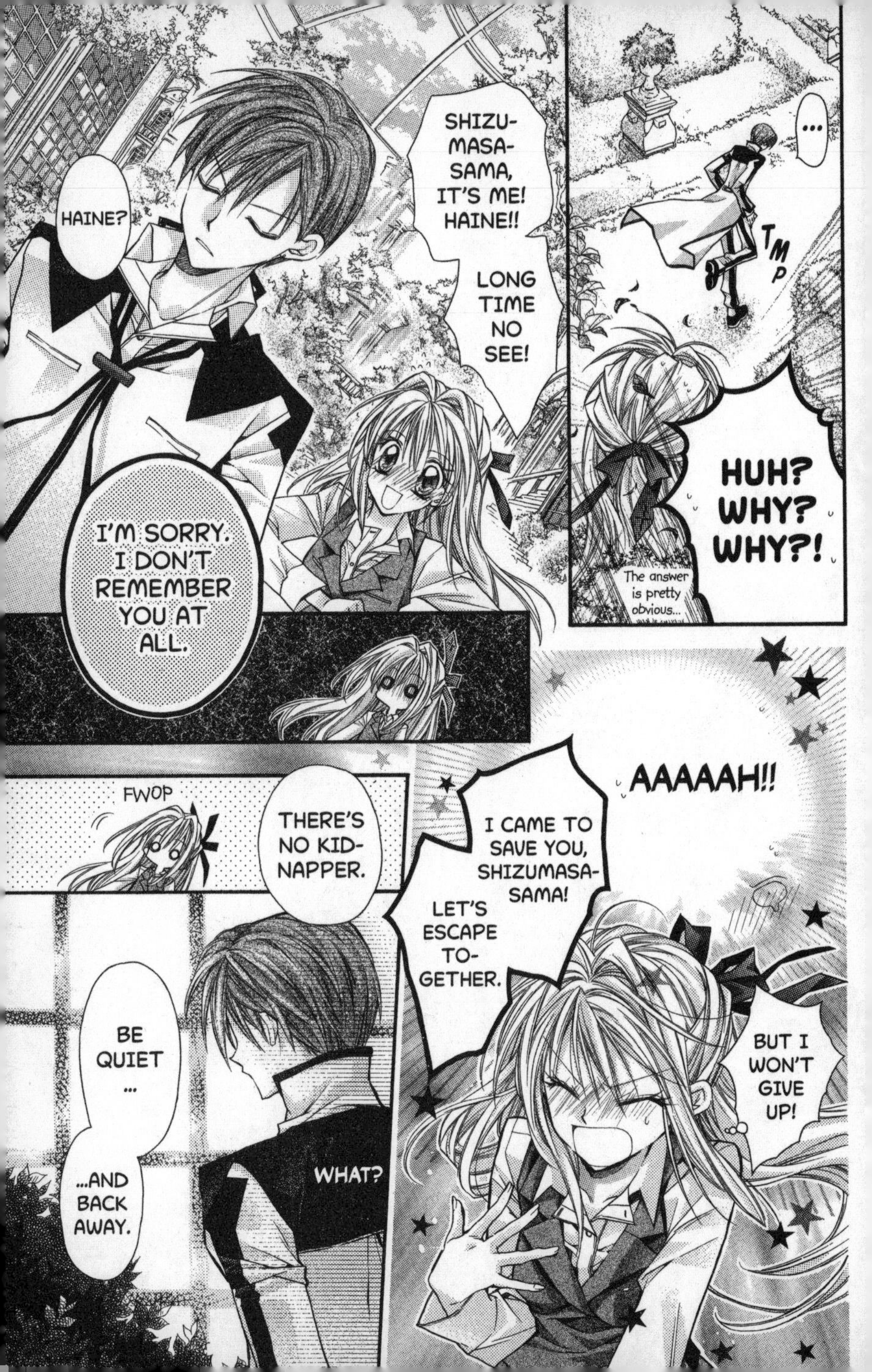
...
TMP
HUH? WHY? WHY?!
The answer is pretty obvious...
SHIZU-MASA-SAMA, IT'S ME! HAINE!!
LONG TIME NO SEE!
HAINE?
I'M SORRY. I DON'T REMEMBER YOU AT ALL.
AAAAAH!!
I CAME TO SAVE YOU, SHIZUMASA-SAMA!
LET'S ESCAPE TO-GETHER.
BUT I WON'T GIVE UP!
FWOP
THERE'S NO KID-NAPPER.
BE QUIET ...
...AND BACK AWAY.
WHAT?

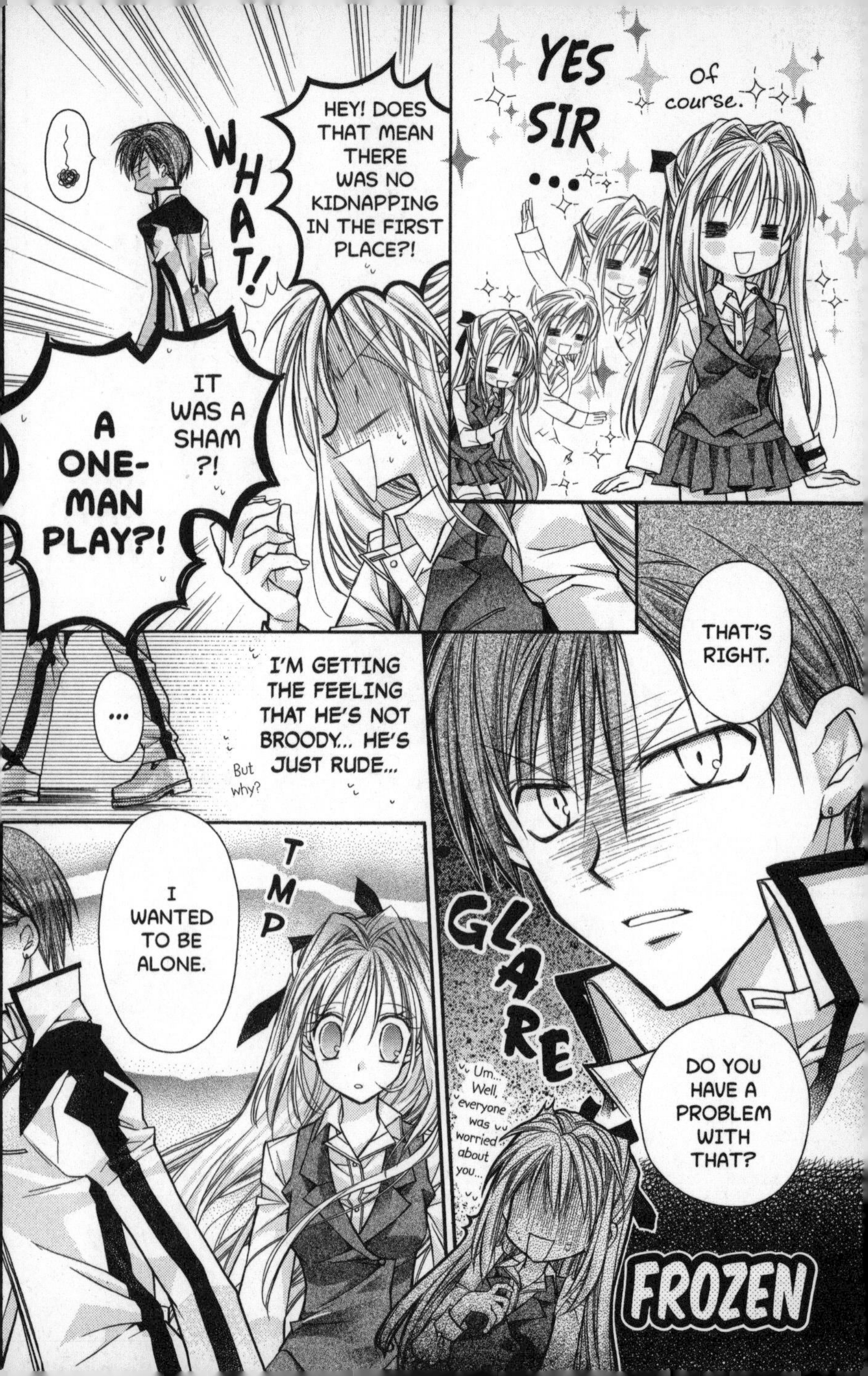
YES SIR...
Of course.
HEY! DOES THAT MEAN THERE WAS NO KIDNAPPING IN THE FIRST PLACE?!
WHAT!
!
IT WAS A SHAM?!
A ONE-MAN PLAY?!
THAT'S RIGHT.
GLARE
DO YOU HAVE A PROBLEM WITH THAT?
Um... Well, everyone was worried about you...
FROZEN
...
I'M GETTING THE FEELING THAT HE'S NOT BROODY... HE'S JUST RUDE...
But why?
I WANTED TO BE ALONE.
TMP

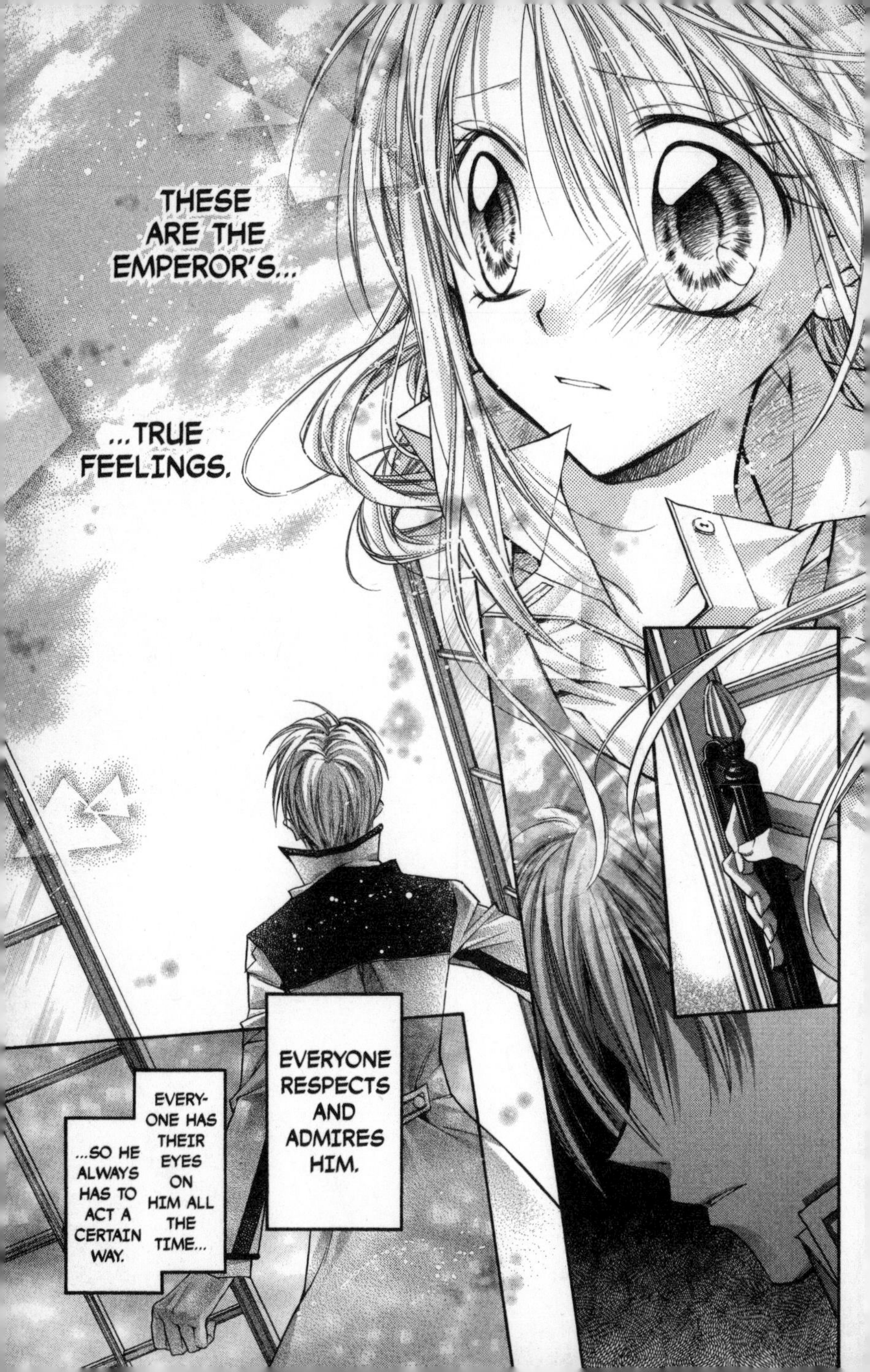
THESE ARE THE EMPEROR'S...
...TRUE FEELINGS.
EVERYONE RESPECTS AND ADMIRES HIM.
EVERY-ONE HAS THEIR EYES ON HIM ALL THE TIME...
...SO HE ALWAYS HAS TO ACT A CERTAIN WAY.

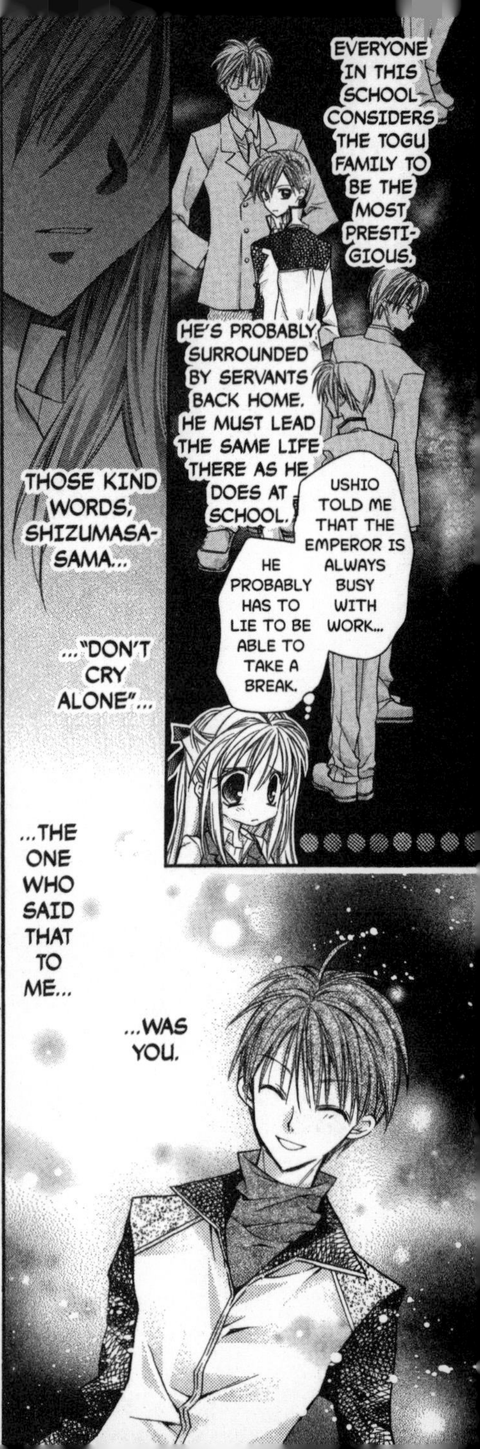
EVERYONE IN THIS SCHOOL CONSIDERS THE TOGU FAMILY TO BE THE MOST PRESTIGIOUS.
HE'S PROBABLY SURROUNDED BY SERVANTS BACK HOME. HE MUST LEAD THE SAME LIFE THERE AS HE DOES AT SCHOOL.
USHIO TOLD ME THAT THE EMPEROR IS ALWAYS BUSY WITH WORK...
HE PROBABLY HAS TO LIE TO BE ABLE TO TAKE A BREAK.
THOSE KIND WORDS, SHIZUMASA-SAMA...
..."DON'T CRY ALONE"...
...THE ONE WHO SAID THAT TO ME...
...WAS YOU.

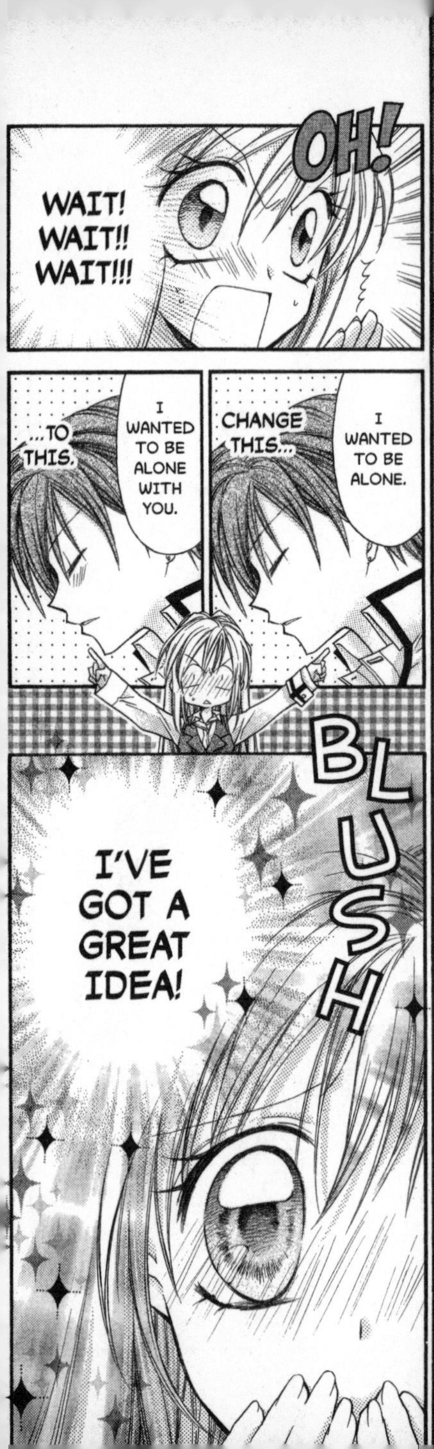
OH!
WAIT! WAIT!! WAIT!!!
I WANTED TO BE ALONE.
CHANGE THIS...
I WANTED TO BE ALONE WITH YOU.
...TO THIS.
BLUSH
I'VE GOT A GREAT IDEA!

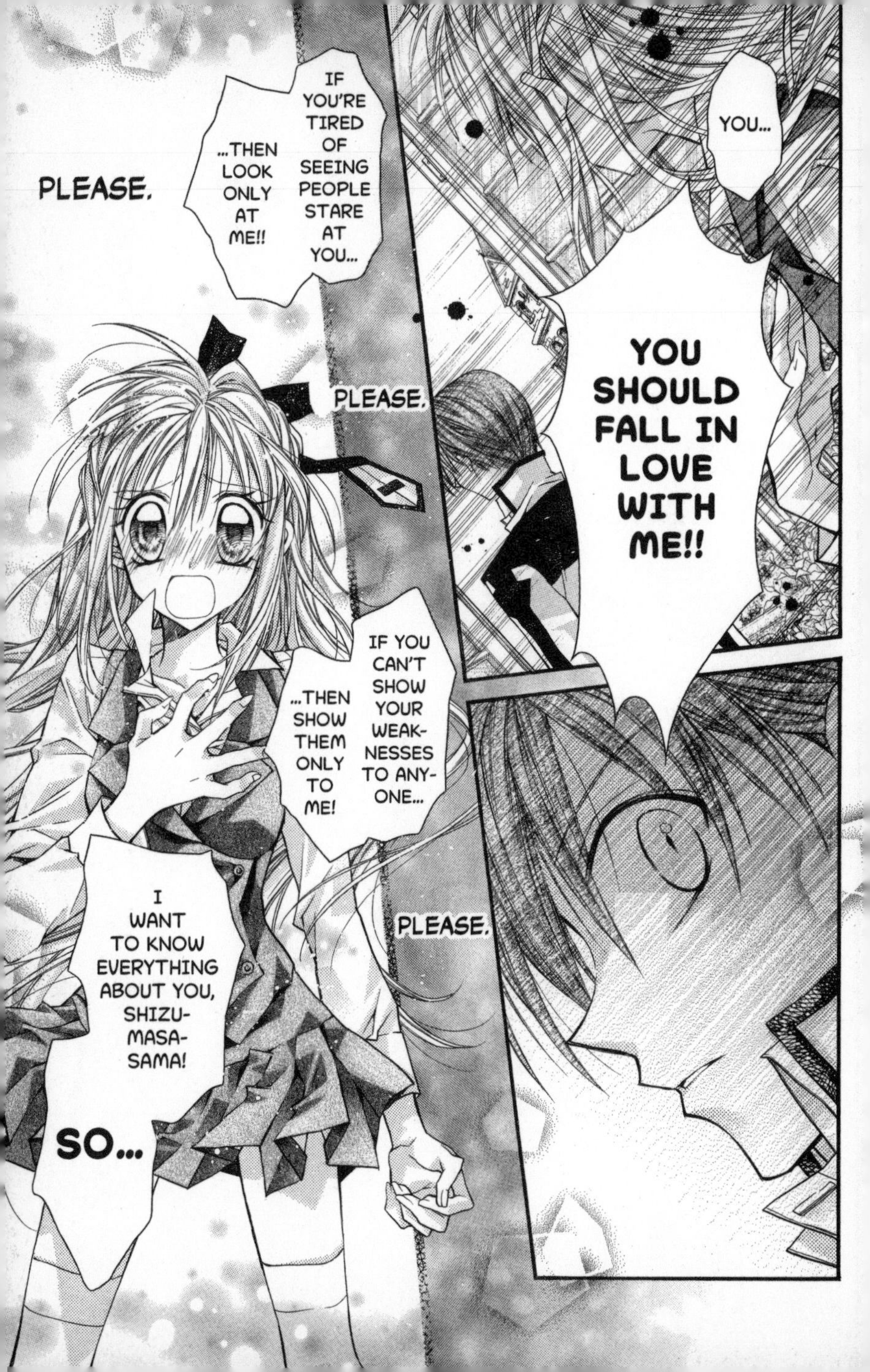
YOU...
YOU SHOULD FALL IN LOVE WITH ME!!
PLEASE.
IF YOU'RE TIRED OF SEEING PEOPLE STARE AT YOU...
...THEN LOOK ONLY AT ME!!
PLEASE.
IF YOU CAN'T SHOW YOUR WEAK-NESSES TO ANY-ONE...
...THEN SHOW THEM ONLY TO ME!
PLEASE.
I WANT TO KNOW EVERYTHING ABOUT YOU, SHIZU-MASA-SAMA!
SO...

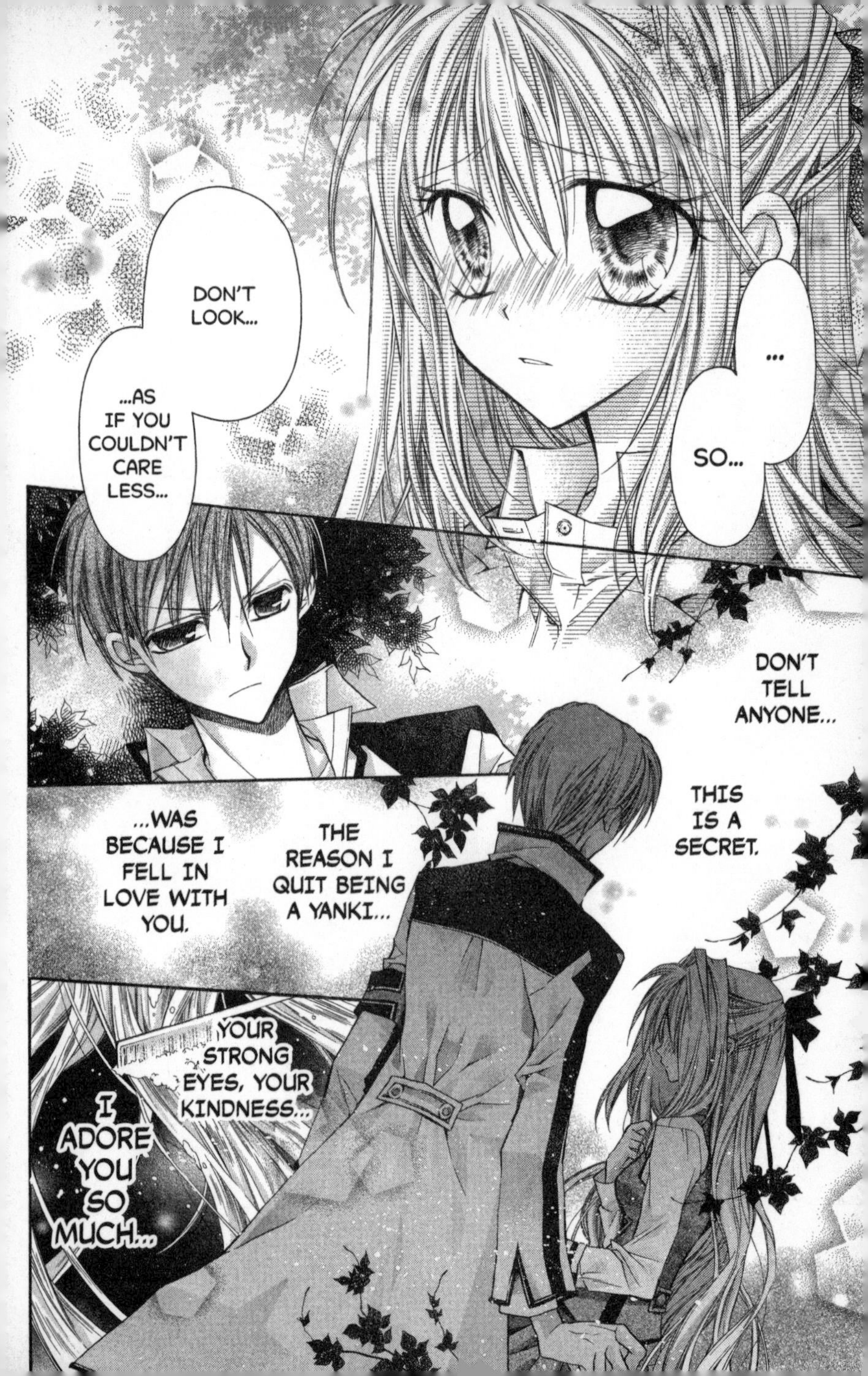
...
SO...
DON'T LOOK...
...AS IF YOU COULDN'T CARE LESS...
DON'T TELL ANYONE...
THIS IS A SECRET.
THE REASON I QUIT BEING A YANKI...
...WAS BECAUSE I FELL IN LOVE WITH YOU.
YOUR STRONG EYES, YOUR KINDNESS...
I ADORE YOU SO MUCH...

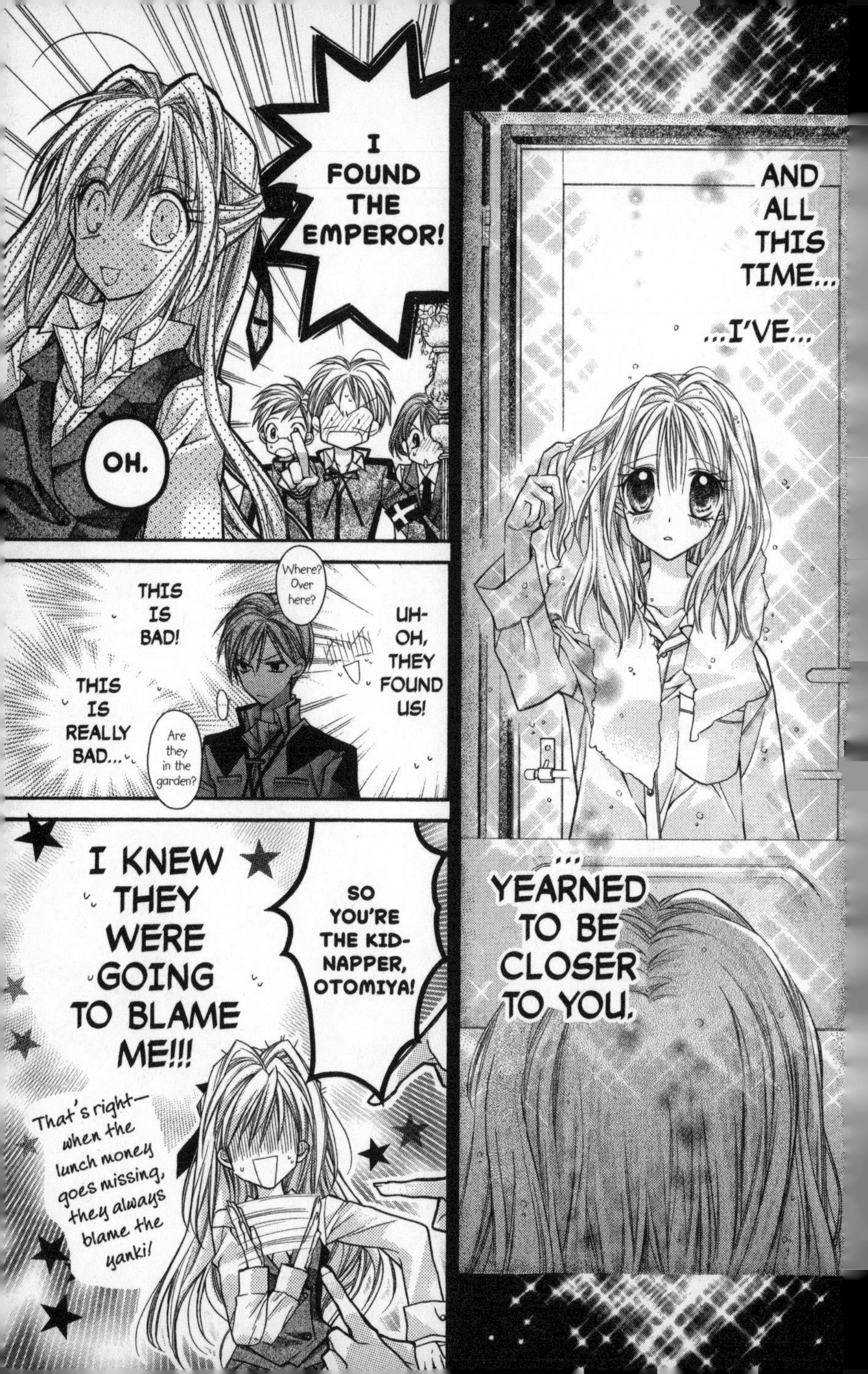
AND ALL THIS TIME...
...I'VE...
...YEARNED TO BE CLOSER TO YOU.
I FOUND THE EMPEROR!
OH.
UH-OH, THEY FOUND US!
Where? Over here?
THIS IS BAD!
THIS IS REALLY BAD...
Are they in the garden?
SO YOU'RE THE KID-NAPPER, OTOMIYA!
I KNEW THEY WERE GOING TO BLAME ME!!!
That's right—when the lunch money goes missing, they always blame the yanki!

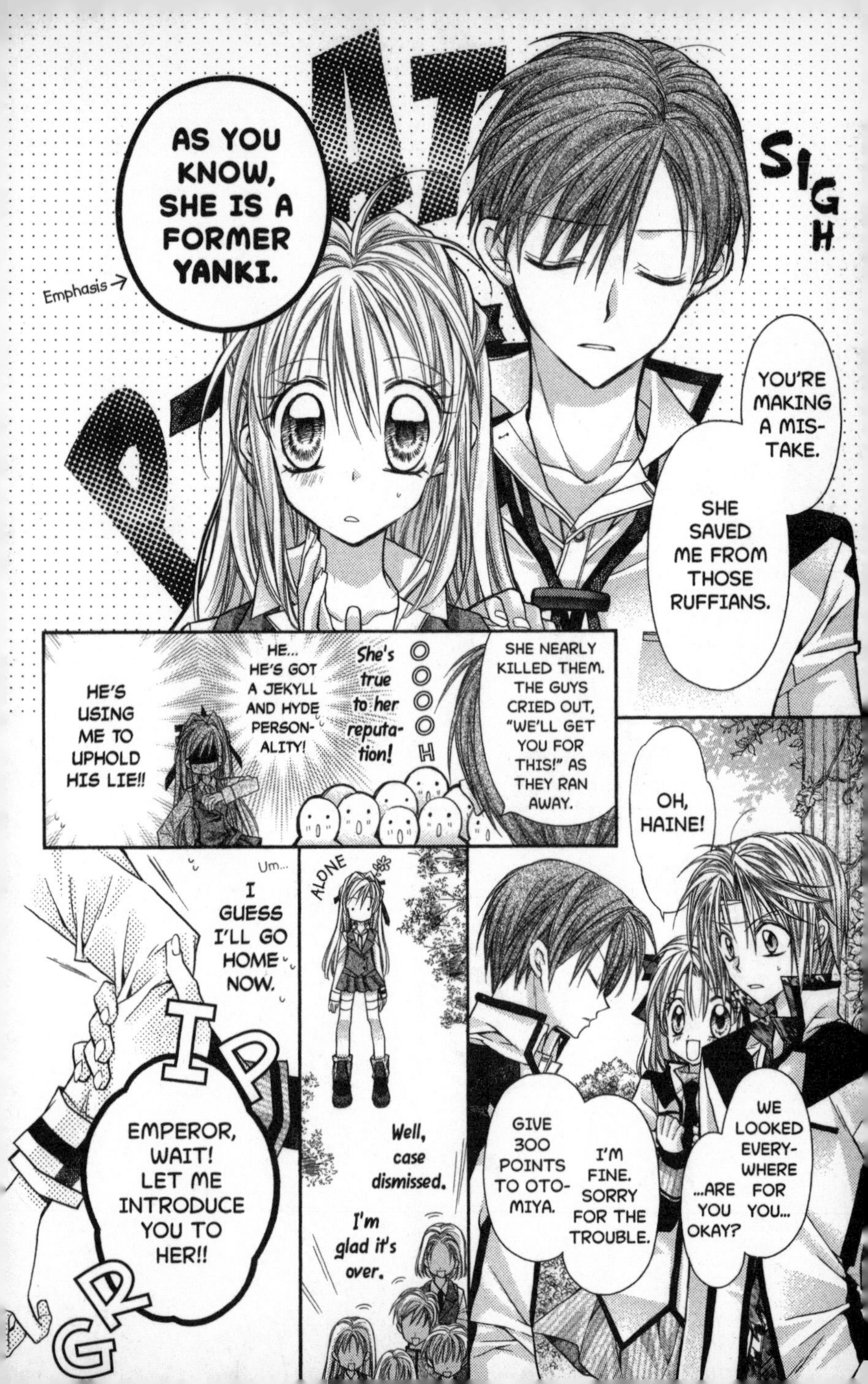
AS YOU KNOW, SHE IS A FORMER YANKI.
Emphasis
PAT
SIGH
YOU'RE MAKING A MIS-TAKE.
SHE SAVED ME FROM THOSE RUFFIANS.
SHE NEARLY KILLED THEM. THE GUYS CRIED OUT, "WE'LL GET YOU FOR THIS!" AS THEY RAN AWAY.
OOOOH
She's true to her reputa-tion!
HE... HE'S GOT A JEKYLL AND HYDE PERSON-ALITY!
HE'S USING ME TO UPHOLD HIS LIE!!
OH, HAINE!
WE LOOKED EVERY-WHERE FOR YOU...
...ARE YOU OKAY?
I'M FINE. SORRY FOR THE TROUBLE.
GIVE 300 POINTS TO OTO-MIYA.
ALONE
Well, case dismissed.
I'm glad it's over.
Um...
I GUESS I'LL GO HOME NOW.
RIP
EMPEROR, WAIT! LET ME INTRODUCE YOU TO HER!!
GR

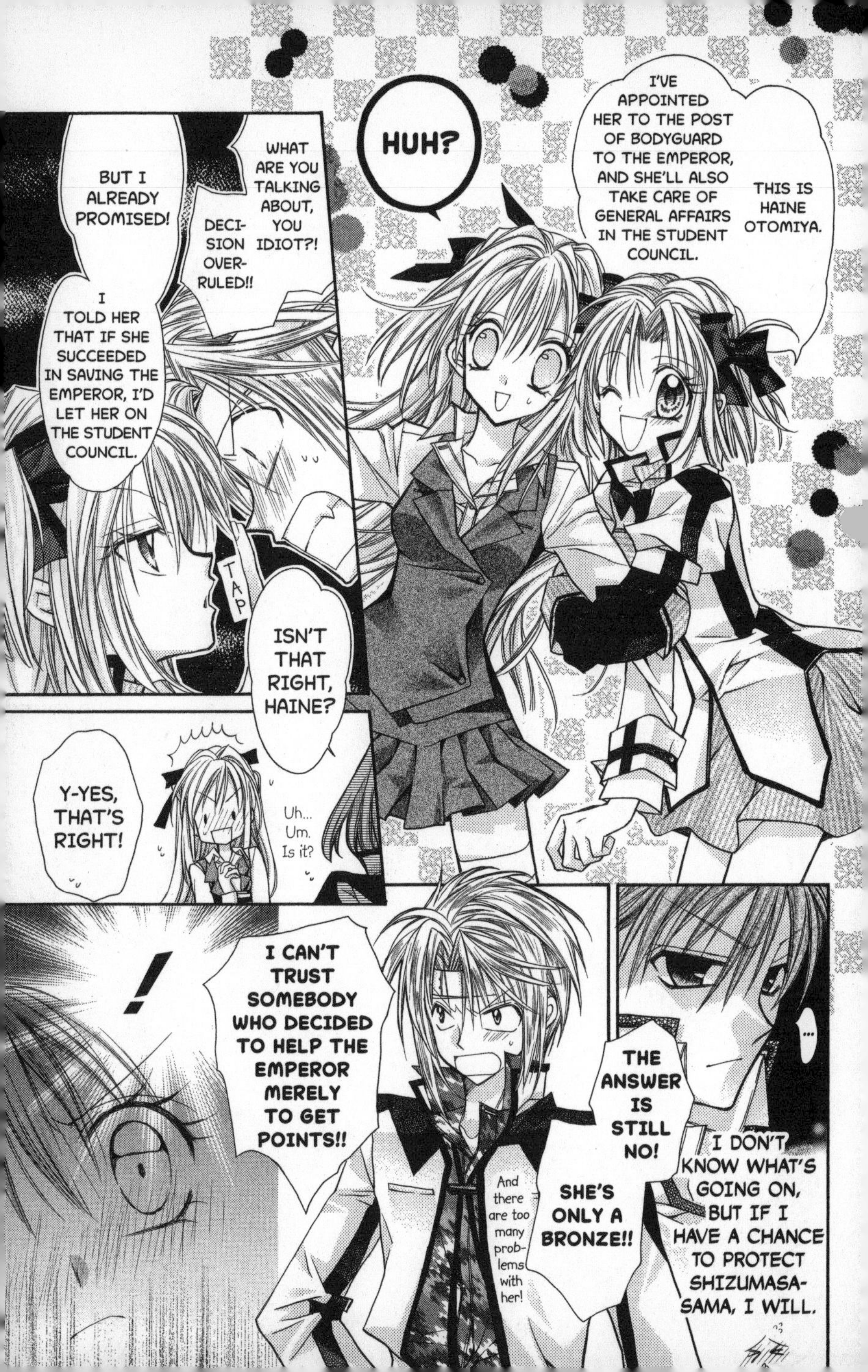
THIS IS HAINE OTOMIYA.
I'VE APPOINTED HER TO THE POST OF BODYGUARD TO THE EMPEROR, AND SHE'LL ALSO TAKE CARE OF GENERAL AFFAIRS IN THE STUDENT COUNCIL.
HUH?
WHAT ARE YOU TALKING ABOUT, YOU IDIOT?!
DECISION OVERRULED!!
BUT I ALREADY PROMISED!
I TOLD HER THAT IF SHE SUCCEEDED IN SAVING THE EMPEROR, I'D LET HER ON THE STUDENT COUNCIL.
TAP
ISN'T THAT RIGHT, HAINE?
Uh... Um. Is it?
Y-YES, THAT'S RIGHT!
...
I DON'T KNOW WHAT'S GOING ON, BUT IF I HAVE A CHANCE TO PROTECT SHIZUMASA-SAMA, I WILL.
THE ANSWER IS STILL NO!
SHE'S ONLY A BRONZE!!
And there are too many problems with her!
I CAN'T TRUST SOMEBODY WHO DECIDED TO HELP THE EMPEROR MERELY TO GET POINTS!!
!

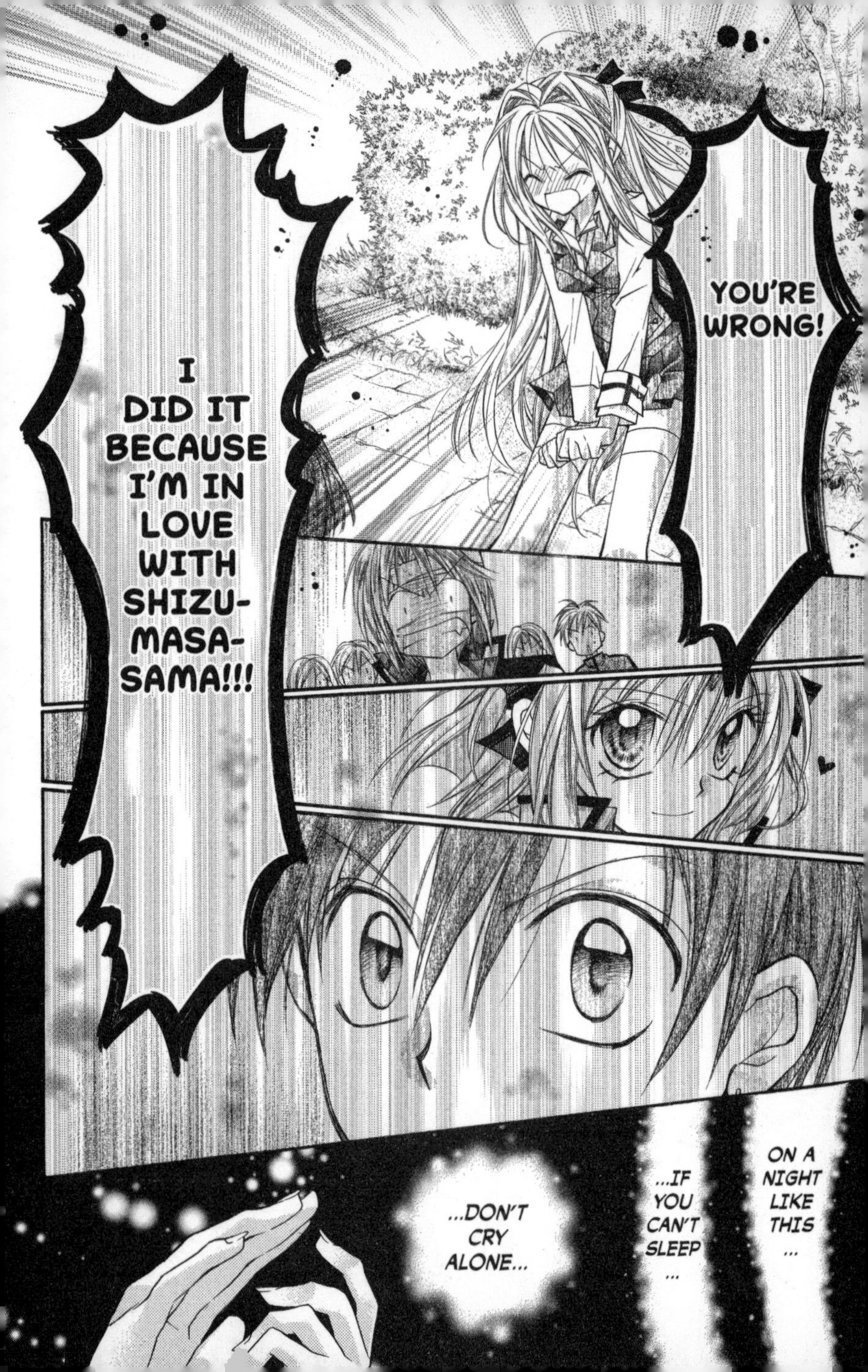
YOU'RE WRONG!
I DID IT BECAUSE I'M IN LOVE WITH SHIZU-MASA-SAMA!!!
ON A NIGHT LIKE THIS...
...IF YOU CAN'T SLEEP...
...DON'T CRY ALONE...

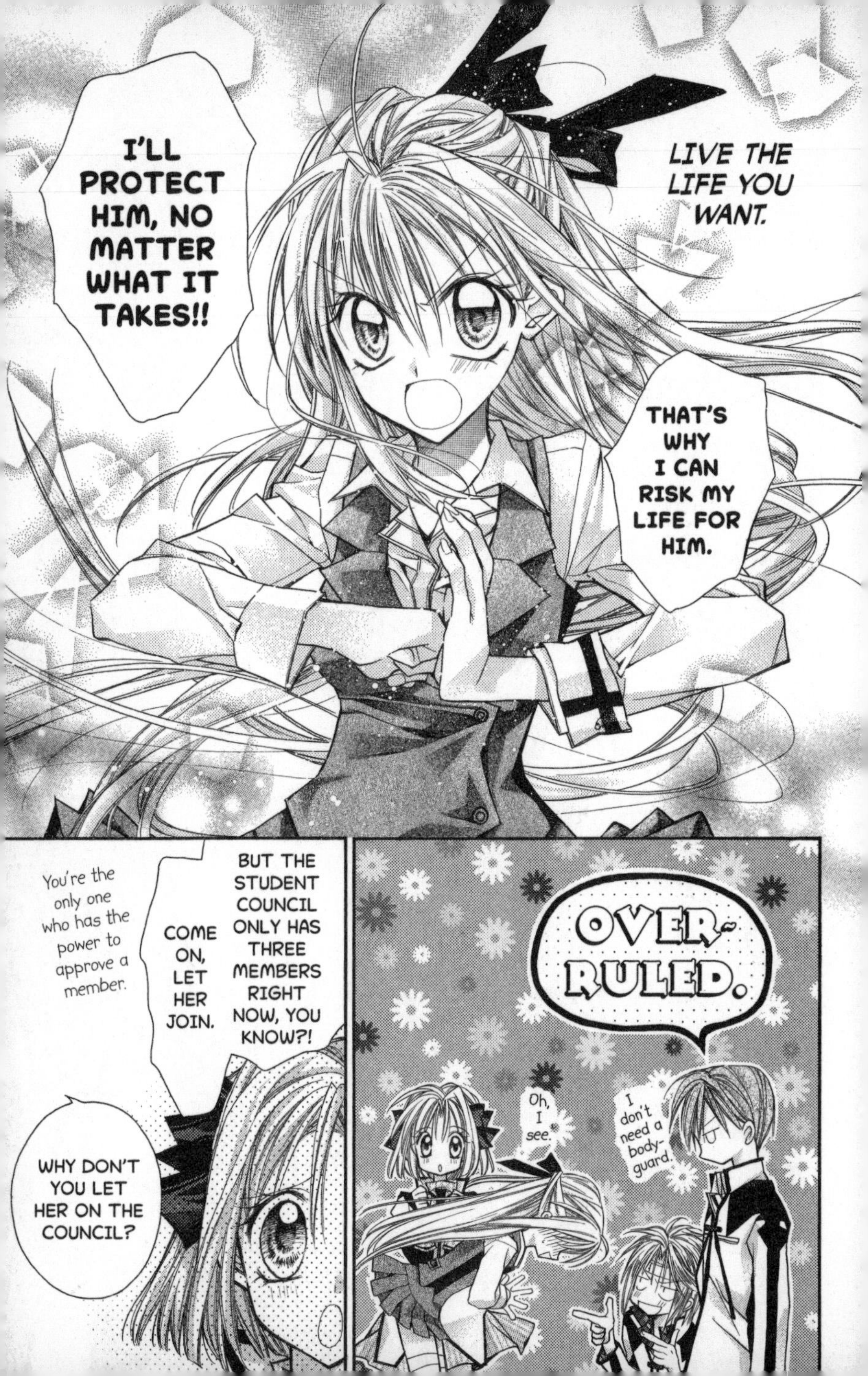
LIVE THE LIFE YOU WANT.
I'LL PROTECT HIM, NO MATTER WHAT IT TAKES!!
THAT'S WHY I CAN RISK MY LIFE FOR HIM.
OVER-RULED.
I don't need a body-guard.
Oh, I see.
BUT THE STUDENT COUNCIL ONLY HAS THREE MEMBERS RIGHT NOW, YOU KNOW?!
COME ON, LET HER JOIN.
You're the only one who has the power to approve a member.
WHY DON'T YOU LET HER ON THE COUNCIL?

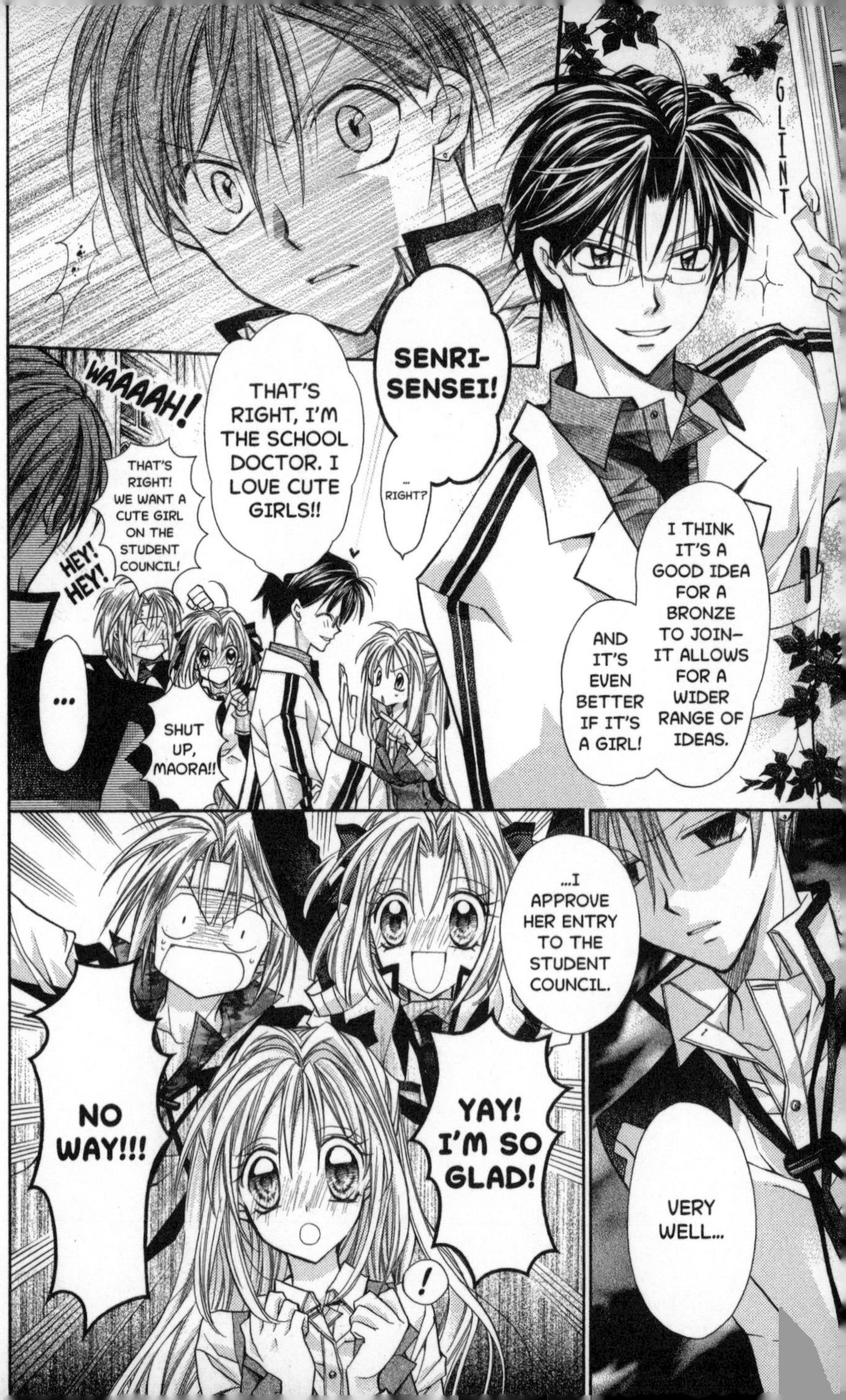
GLINT
SENRI-SENSEI!
I THINK IT'S A GOOD IDEA FOR A BRONZE TO JOIN— IT ALLOWS FOR A WIDER RANGE OF IDEAS.
AND IT'S EVEN BETTER IF IT'S A GIRL!
...RIGHT?
THAT'S RIGHT, I'M THE SCHOOL DOCTOR. I LOVE CUTE GIRLS!!
WAAAAAH!
THAT'S RIGHT! WE WANT A CUTE GIRL ON THE STUDENT COUNCIL!
HEY! HEY!
SHUT UP, MAORA!!
...
VERY WELL...
...I APPROVE HER ENTRY TO THE STUDENT COUNCIL.
YAY! I'M SO GLAD!
NO WAY!!!
!

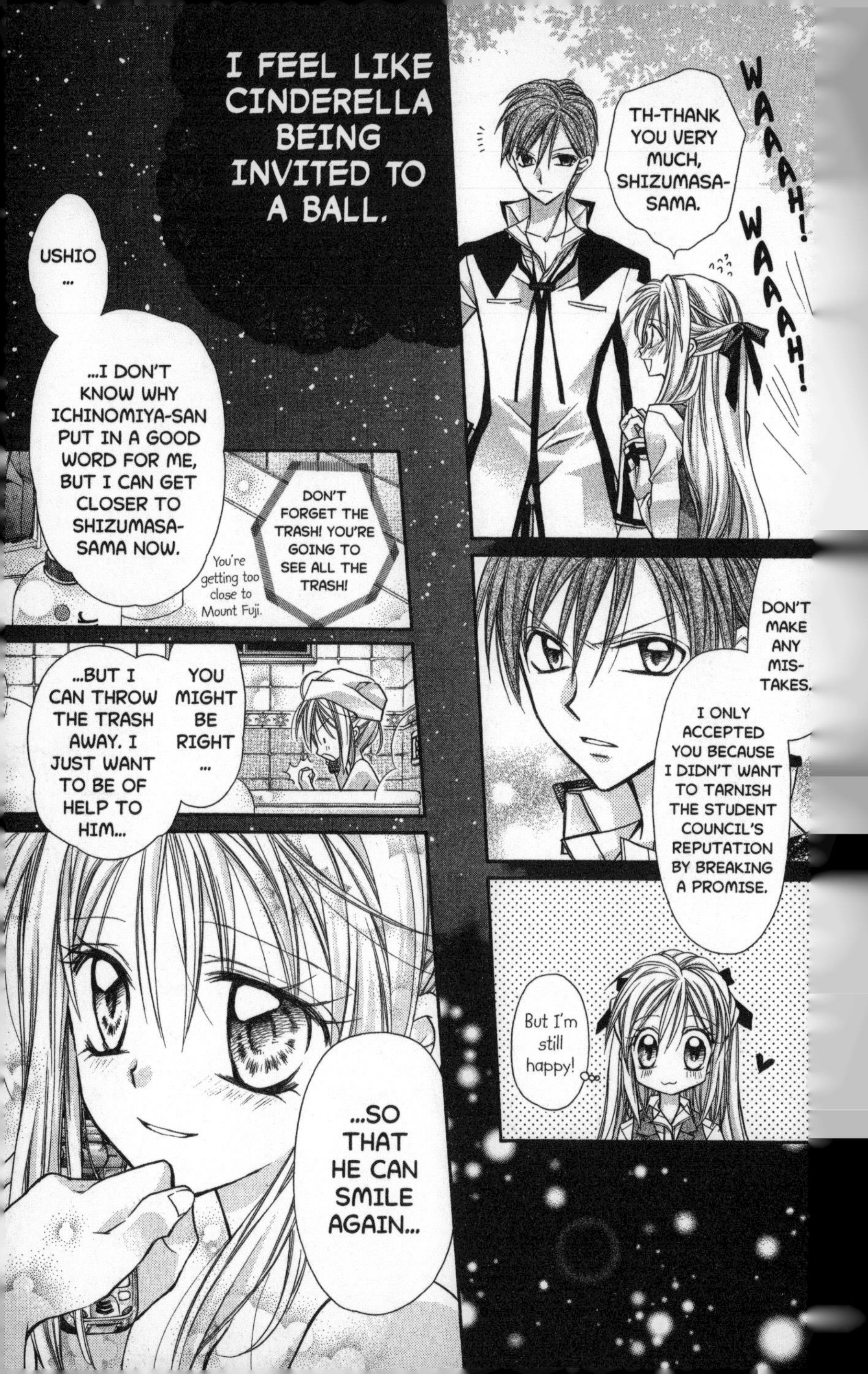
TH-THANK YOU VERY MUCH, SHIZUMASA-SAMA.
WAAAH! WAAAAH!
DON'T MAKE ANY MIS-TAKES.
I ONLY ACCEPTED YOU BECAUSE I DIDN'T WANT TO TARNISH THE STUDENT COUNCIL'S REPUTATION BY BREAKING A PROMISE.
But I'm still happy!
I FEEL LIKE CINDERELLA BEING INVITED TO A BALL.
USHIO ...
...I DON'T KNOW WHY ICHINOMIYA-SAN PUT IN A GOOD WORD FOR ME, BUT I CAN GET CLOSER TO SHIZUMASA-SAMA NOW.
DON'T FORGET THE TRASH! YOU'RE GOING TO SEE ALL THE TRASH!
You're getting too close to Mount Fuji.
YOU MIGHT BE RIGHT ...
...BUT I CAN THROW THE TRASH AWAY. I JUST WANT TO BE OF HELP TO HIM...
...SO THAT HE CAN SMILE AGAIN...

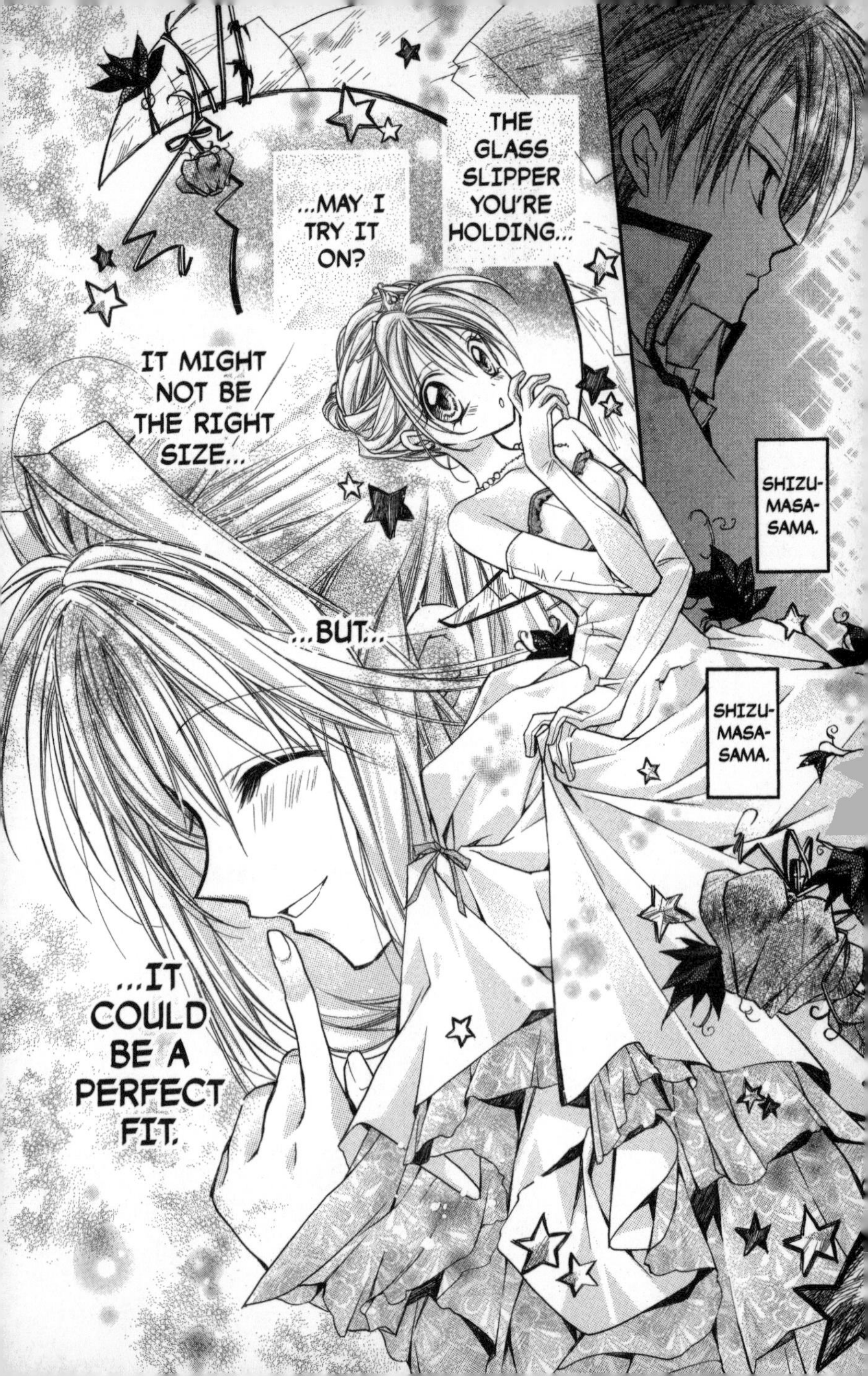
THE GLASS SLIPPER YOU'RE HOLDING...
...MAY I TRY IT ON?
SHIZU-MASA-SAMA.
SHIZU-MASA-SAMA.
IT MIGHT NOT BE THE RIGHT SIZE...
...BUT...
...IT COULD BE A PERFECT FIT.

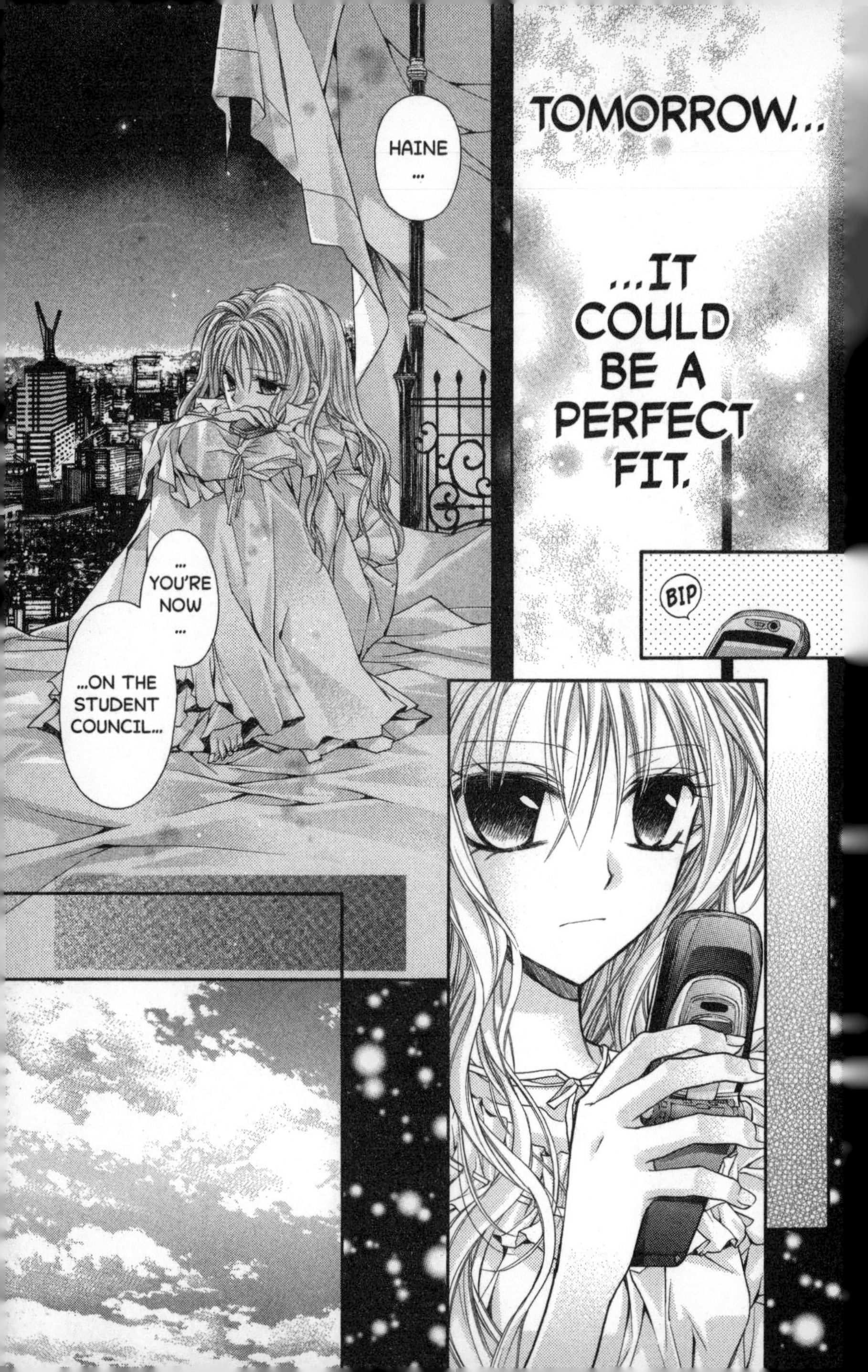
TOMORROW...
...IT COULD BE A PERFECT FIT.
BIP
HAINE...
...YOU'RE NOW...
...ON THE STUDENT COUNCIL...

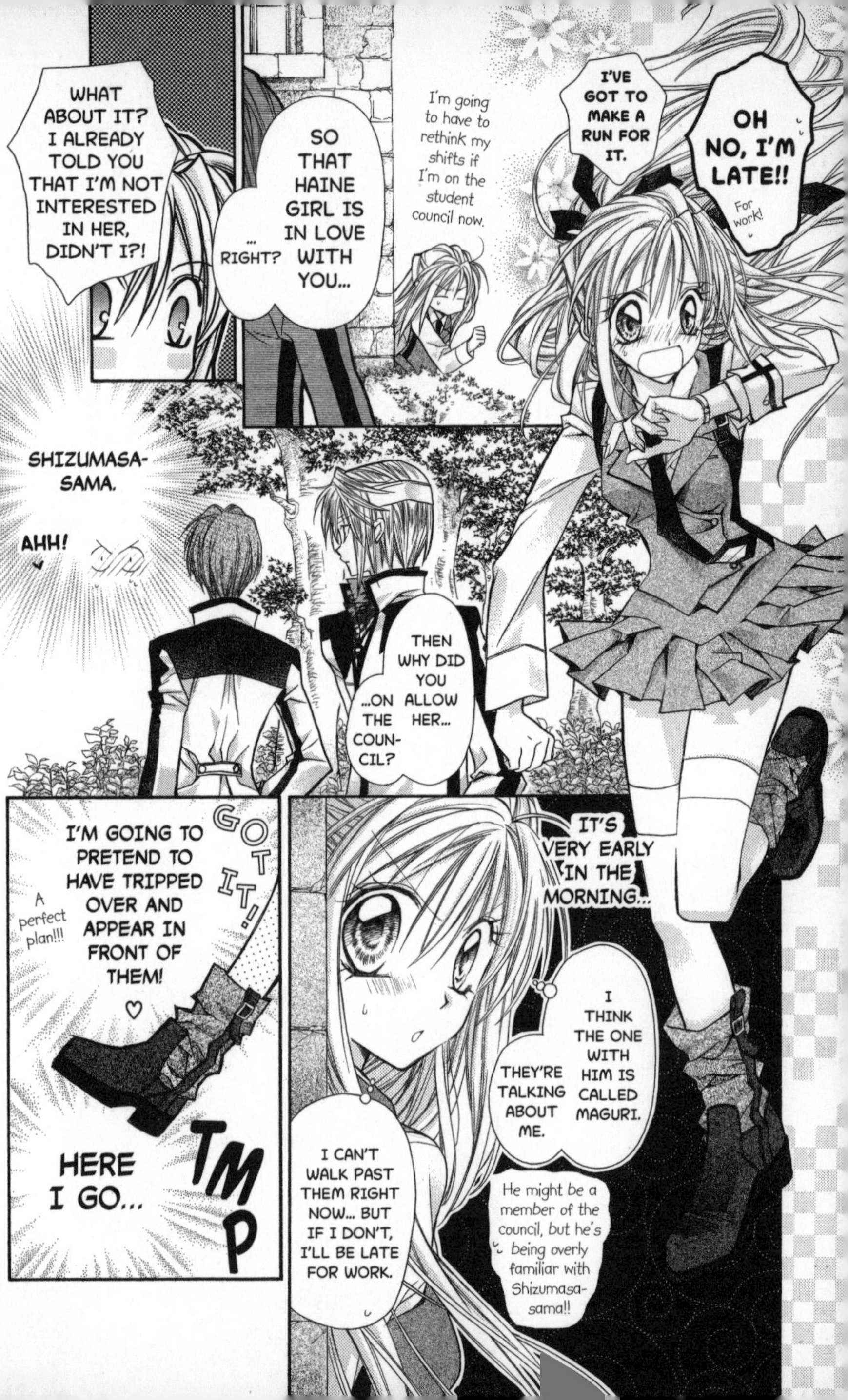
OH NO, I'M LATE!!
For work!
I'VE GOT TO MAKE A RUN FOR IT.
I'm going to have to rethink my shifts if I'm on the student council now.
SO THAT HAINE GIRL IS IN LOVE WITH YOU...
...RIGHT?
WHAT ABOUT IT? I ALREADY TOLD YOU THAT I'M NOT INTERESTED IN HER, DIDN'T I?!
THEN WHY DID YOU ALLOW HER...
...ON THE COUNCIL?
SHIZUMASA-SAMA.
AHH!
IT'S VERY EARLY IN THE MORNING...
I THINK THE ONE WITH HIM IS CALLED MAGURI.
THEY'RE TALKING ABOUT ME.
He might be a member of the council, but he's being overly familiar with Shizumasa-sama!!
I CAN'T WALK PAST THEM RIGHT NOW... BUT IF I DON'T, I'LL BE LATE FOR WORK.
GOT IT!
I'M GOING TO PRETEND TO HAVE TRIPPED OVER AND APPEAR IN FRONT OF THEM!
A perfect plan!!!
HERE I GO...
TMP

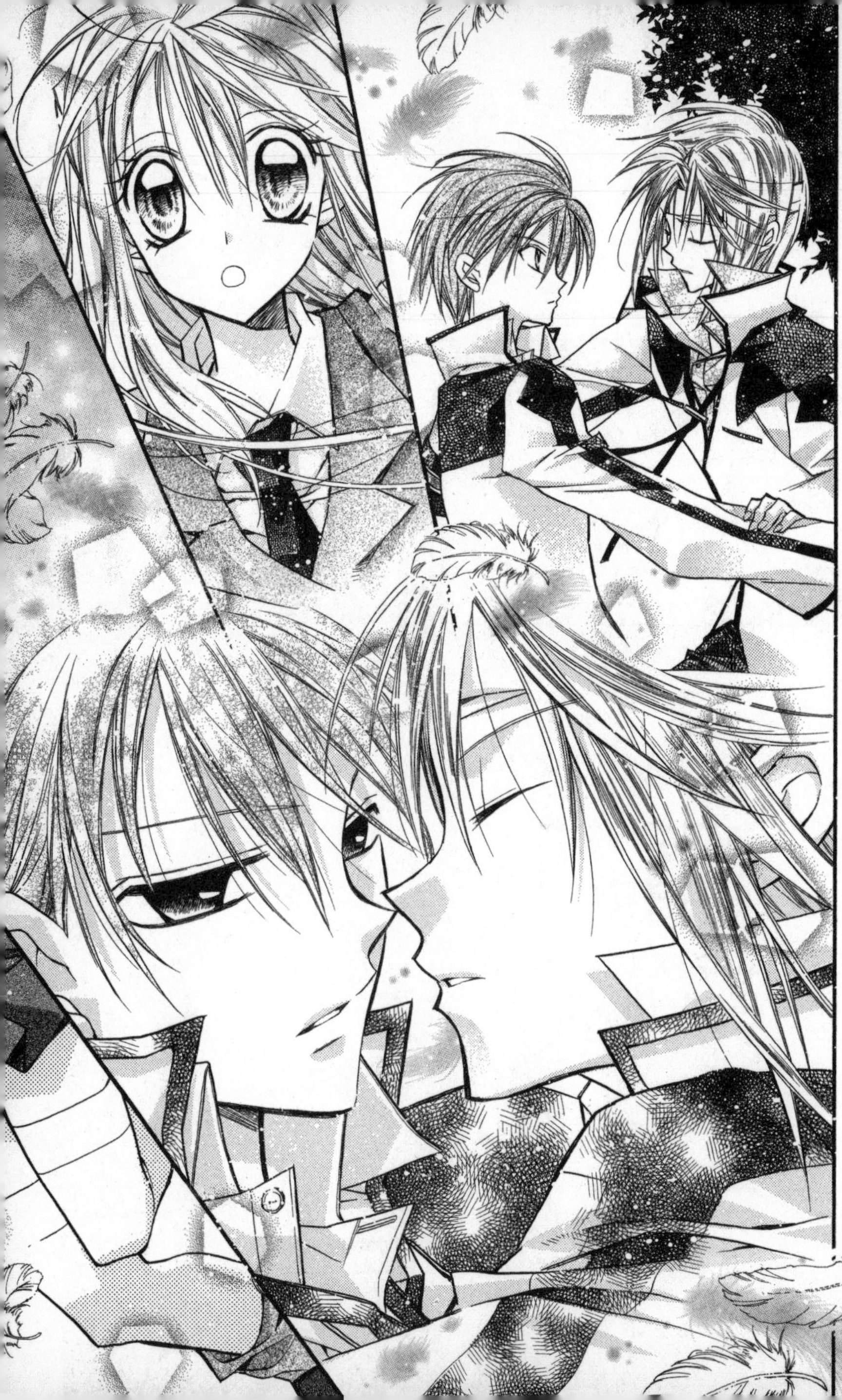

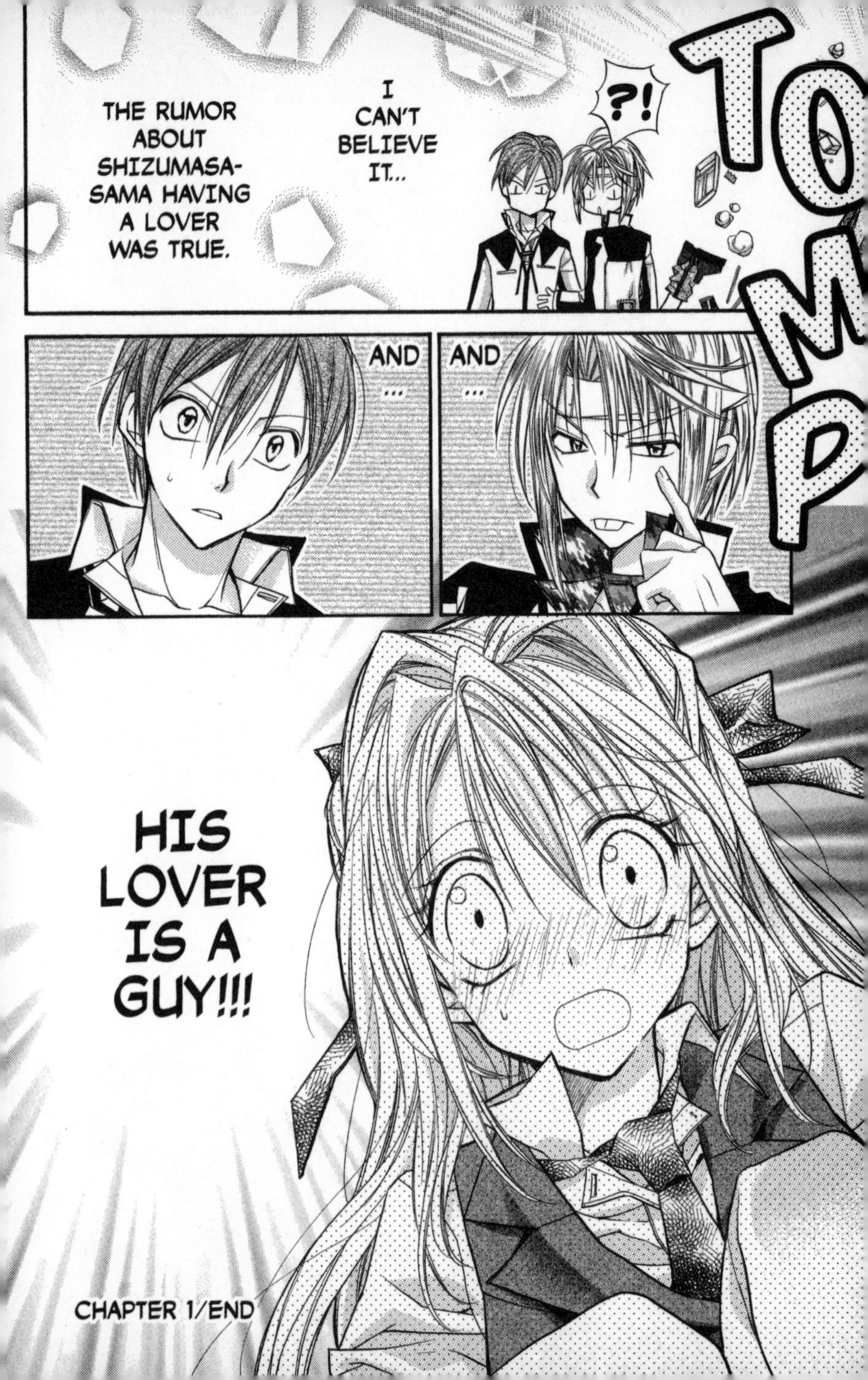
TOMP
?!
I CAN'T BELIEVE IT...
THE RUMOR ABOUT SHIZUMASA-SAMA HAVING A LOVER WAS TRUE.
AND ...
AND ...
HIS LOVER IS A GUY!!!
CHAPTER 1/END

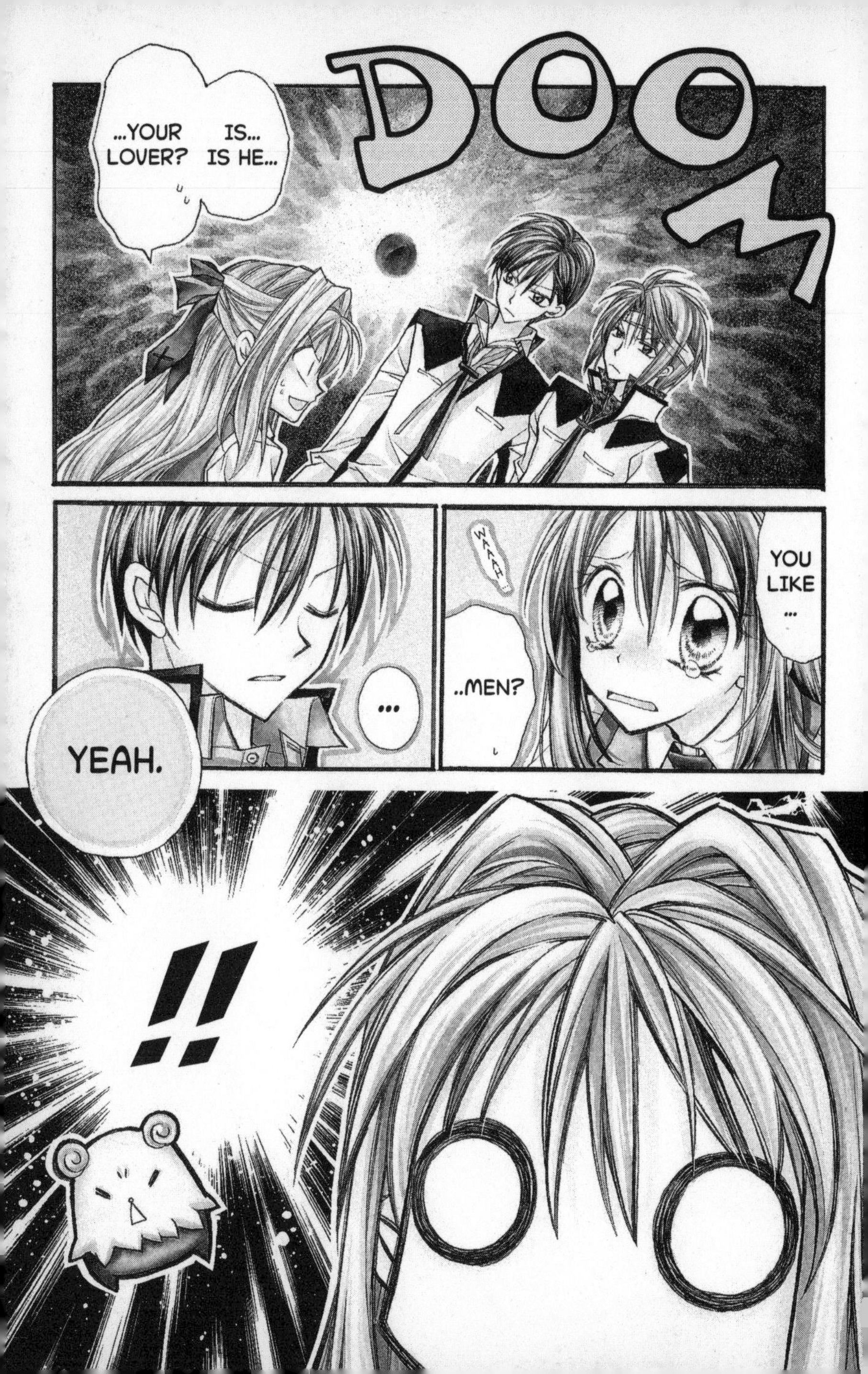
DOOM
IS... IS HE...
...YOUR LOVER?
YOU LIKE ...
WAAAH...
..MEN?
...
YEAH.
!!

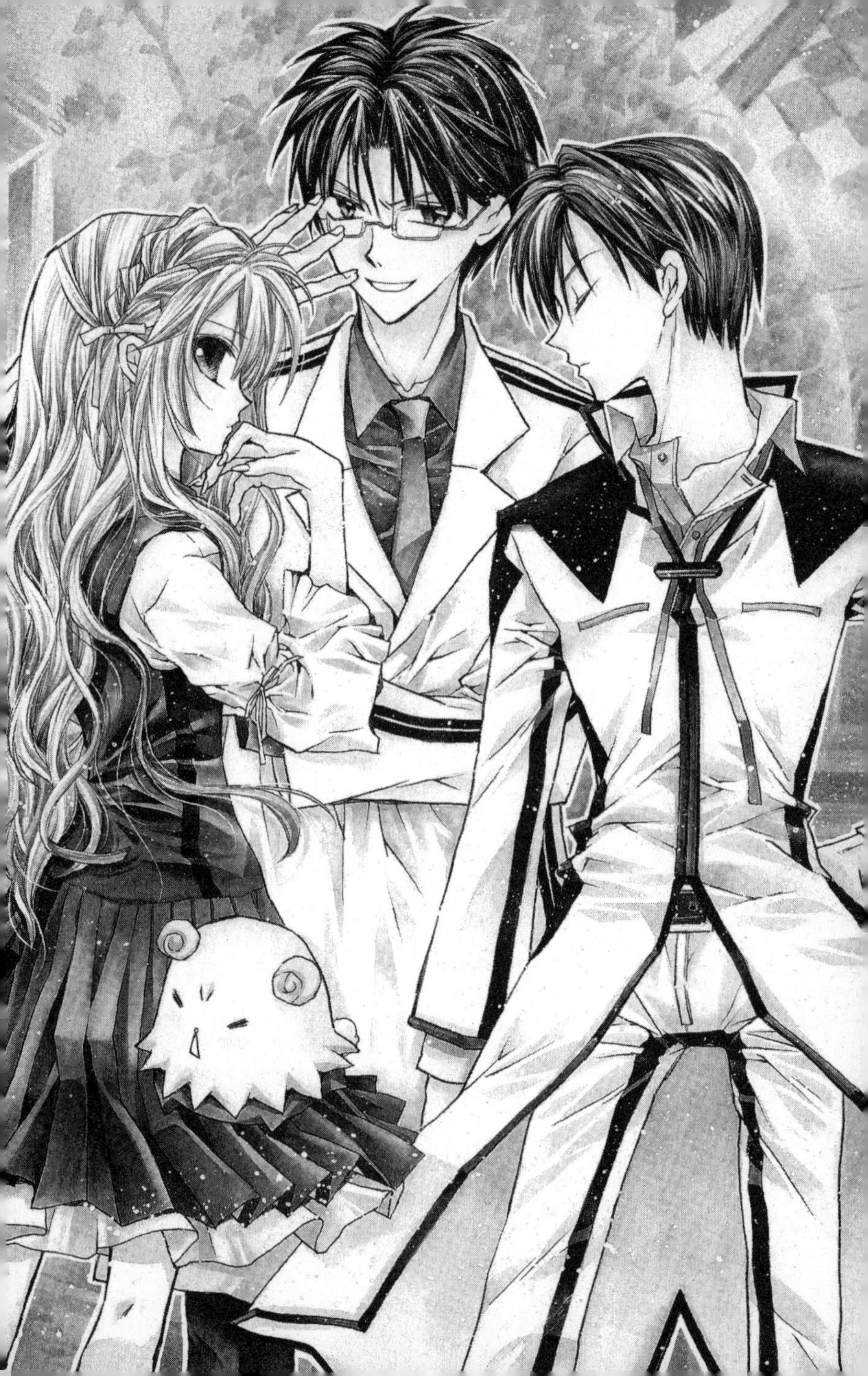

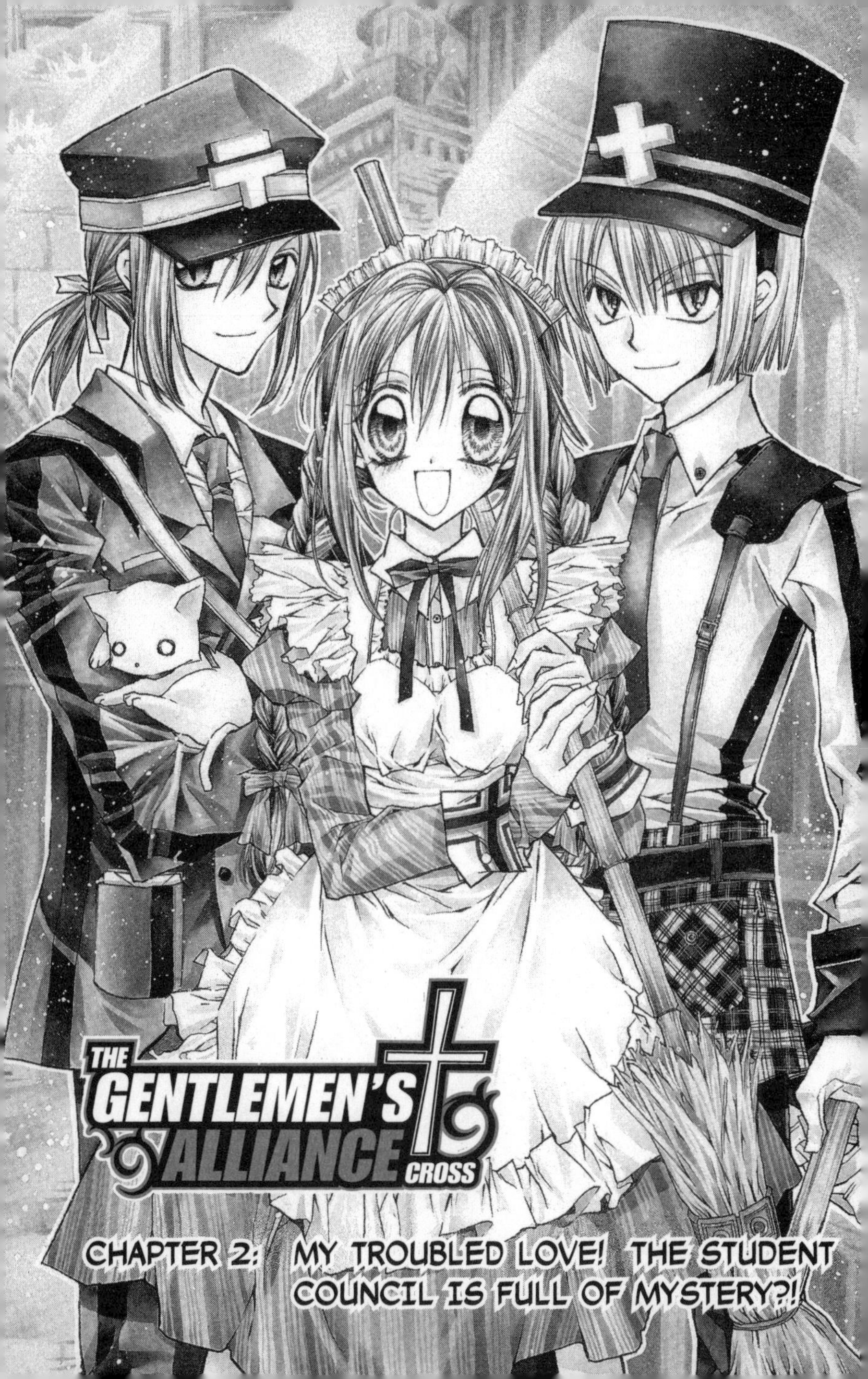
THE GENTLEMEN'S ALLIANCE CROSS
CHAPTER 2: MY TROUBLED LOVE! THE STUDENT COUNCIL IS FULL OF MYSTERY?!

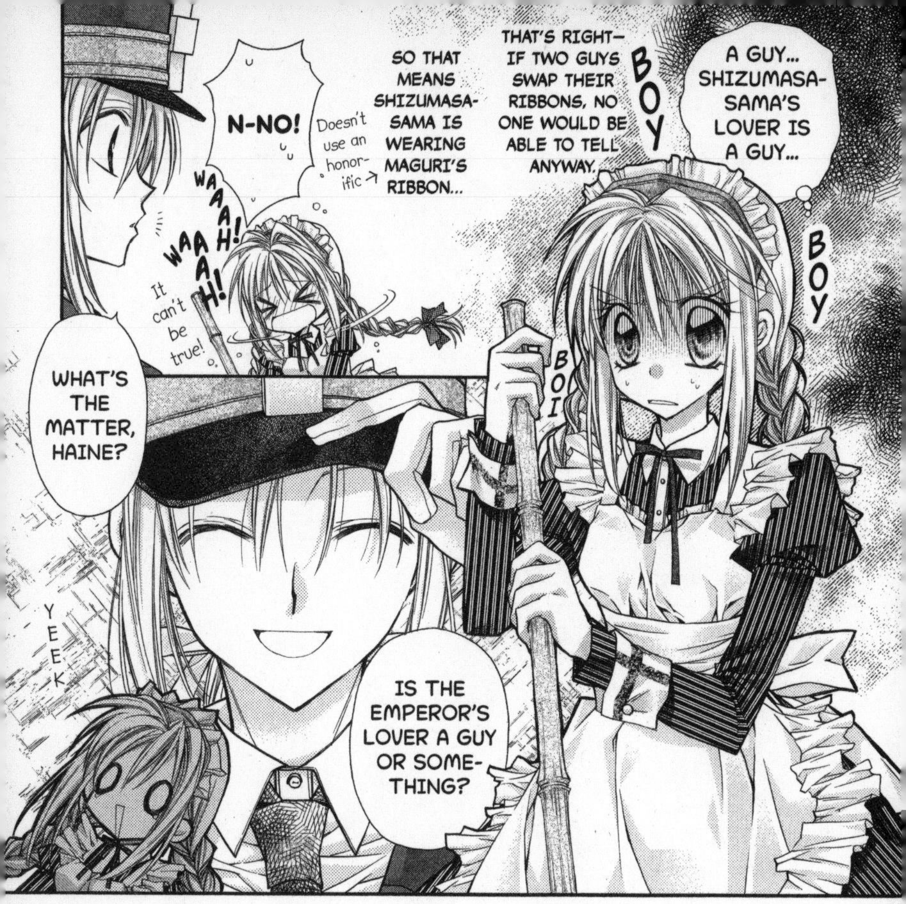
A GUY... SHIZUMASA-SAMA'S LOVER IS A GUY...
BOY
BOY
BOY
THAT'S RIGHT— IF TWO GUYS SWAP THEIR RIBBONS, NO ONE WOULD BE ABLE TO TELL ANYWAY.
SO THAT MEANS SHIZUMASA-SAMA IS WEARING MAGURI'S RIBBON...
Doesn't use an honor-ific
BOI
N-NO!
WAAAAH!
WAAAAH!
It can't be true!
WHAT'S THE MATTER, HAINE?
IS THE EMPEROR'S LOVER A GUY OR SOME-THING?
YEEK

Chapter 1: I'm Not Afraid of the Emperor! ☆ Lead-in I'm Haine! I'm 15 years old. ☆ And I'm in L-O-V-E with Shizumasa-sama!!

The drawing on the title page was used for a poster that was given as a present to 10,000 readers. Half of my assistants succeeded in getting hold of it, and the other half didn't, so I felt an uneasy atmosphere around me...(laugh)

There was a lot of information I had to incorporate in this episode, so I had a tough time putting it together... But there were a lot of characters I could play around with, so I could not help feeling I had "hit the jackpot" with my characters from the start.

Chapter 2: My Troubled Love! The Student Council Is Full of Mystery?! Lead-in Welcome to the Imperial Academy!

I like the drawing for this title page a lot. It was also popular with the readers, so I'm glad. The Emperor in this episode is very kind. He's actually a kind guy. Anyway, I think 50 million yen is pretty cheap price for a person. I thought about raising the price a little more, but Haine is even more aggravated about it since it is such a low price...so I decided not to change it.

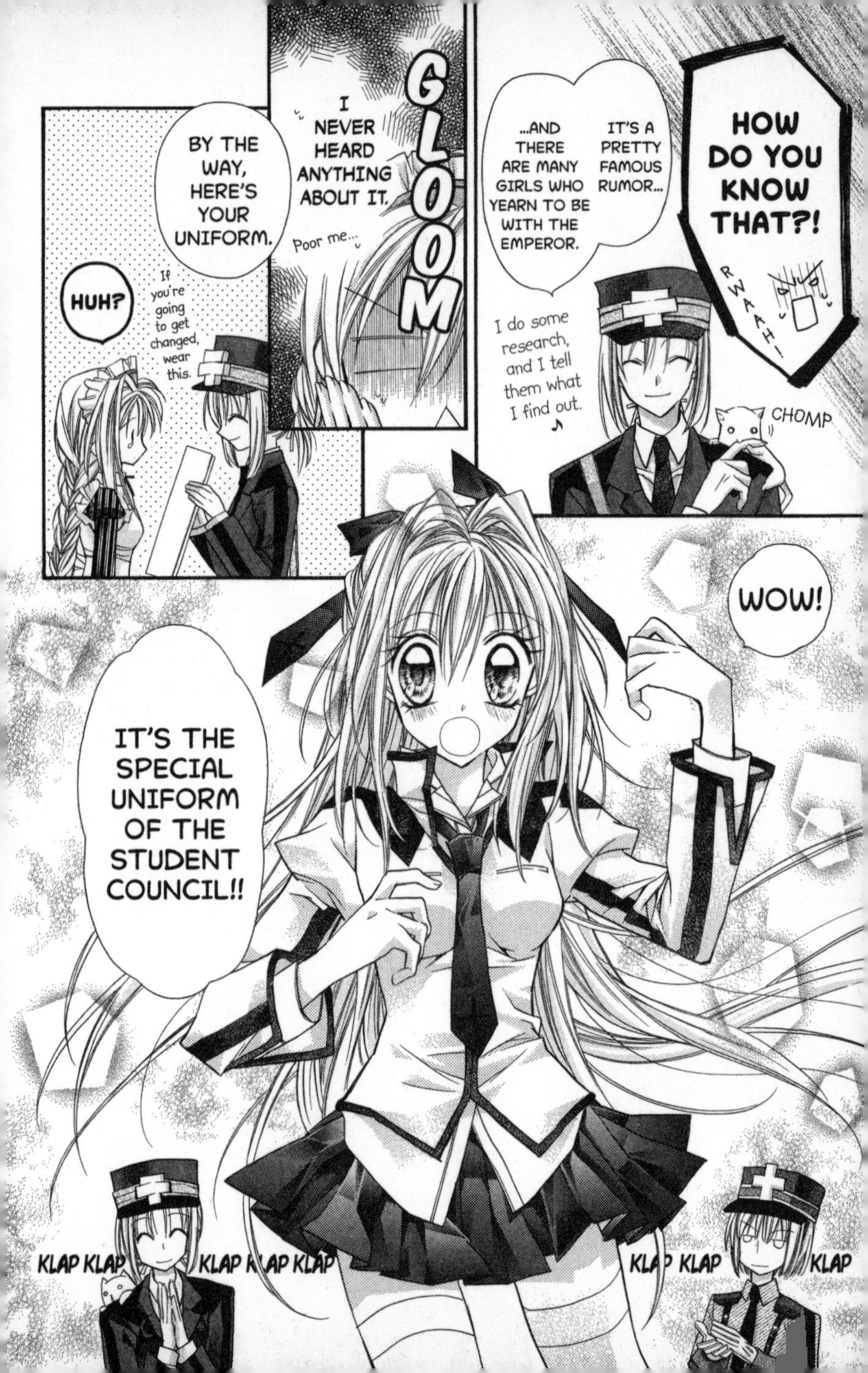
HOW DO YOU KNOW THAT?!
RWAAAH!
IT'S A PRETTY FAMOUS RUMOR...
...AND THERE ARE MANY GIRLS WHO YEARN TO BE WITH THE EMPEROR.
I do some research, and I tell them what I find out. ♪
CHOMP
GLOOM
I NEVER HEARD ANYTHING ABOUT IT.
Poor me...
BY THE WAY, HERE'S YOUR UNIFORM.
HUH?
If you're going to get changed, wear this.
WOW!
IT'S THE SPECIAL UNIFORM OF THE STUDENT COUNCIL!!
KLAP KLAP KLAP
KLAP KLAP
KLAP KLAP KLAP KLAP KLAP

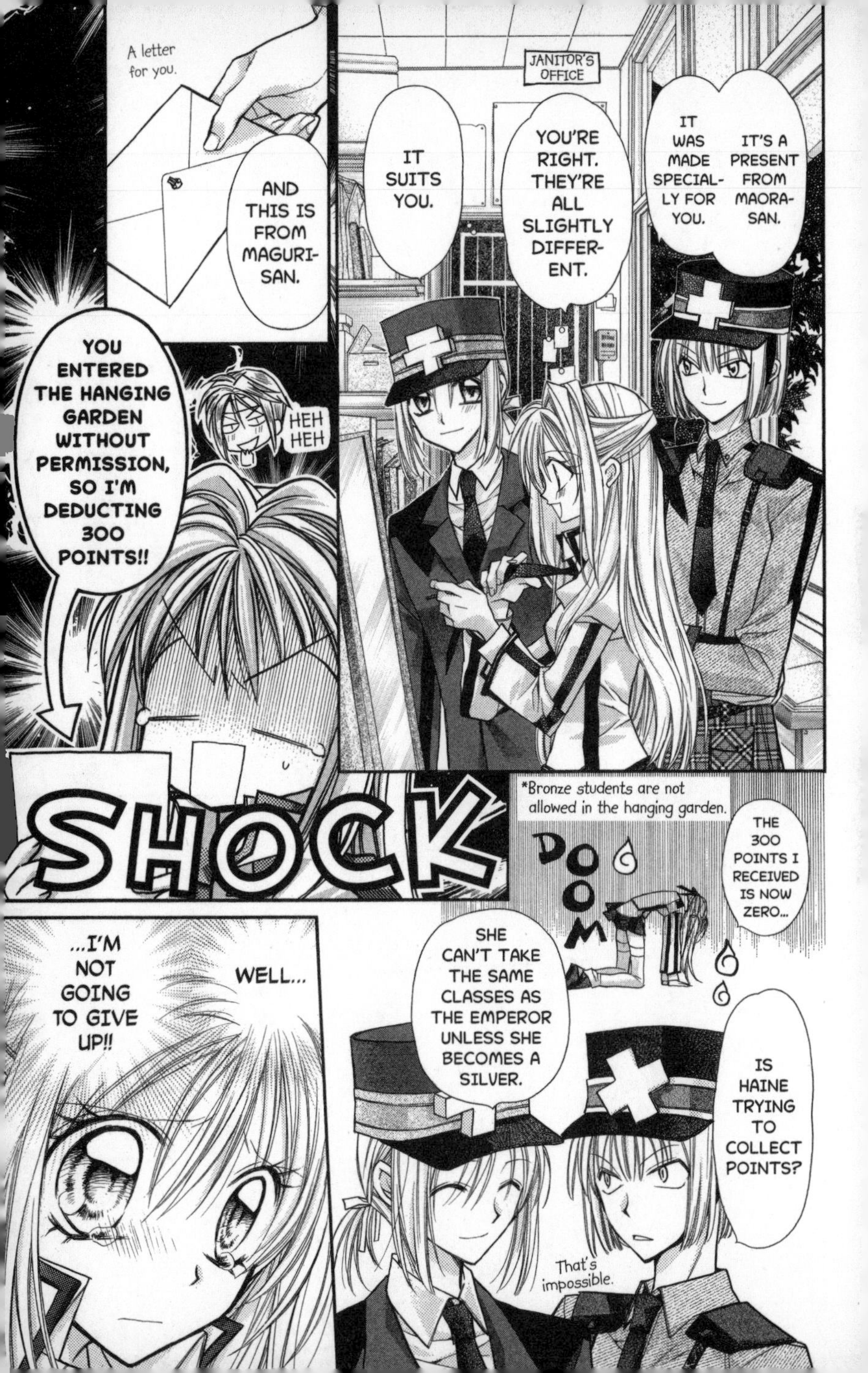
JANITOR'S OFFICE
IT'S A PRESENT FROM MAORA-SAN.
IT WAS MADE SPECIAL-LY FOR YOU.
YOU'RE RIGHT. THEY'RE ALL SLIGHTLY DIFFER-ENT.
IT SUITS YOU.
AND THIS IS FROM MAGURI-SAN.
A letter for you.
YOU ENTERED THE HANGING GARDEN WITHOUT PERMISSION, SO I'M DEDUCTING 300 POINTS!!
HEH HEH
*Bronze students are not allowed in the hanging garden.
THE 300 POINTS I RECEIVED IS NOW ZERO...
DOOOM
SHOCK
IS HAINE TRYING TO COLLECT POINTS?
SHE CAN'T TAKE THE SAME CLASSES AS THE EMPEROR UNLESS SHE BECOMES A SILVER.
That's impossible.
WELL...
...I'M NOT GOING TO GIVE UP!!

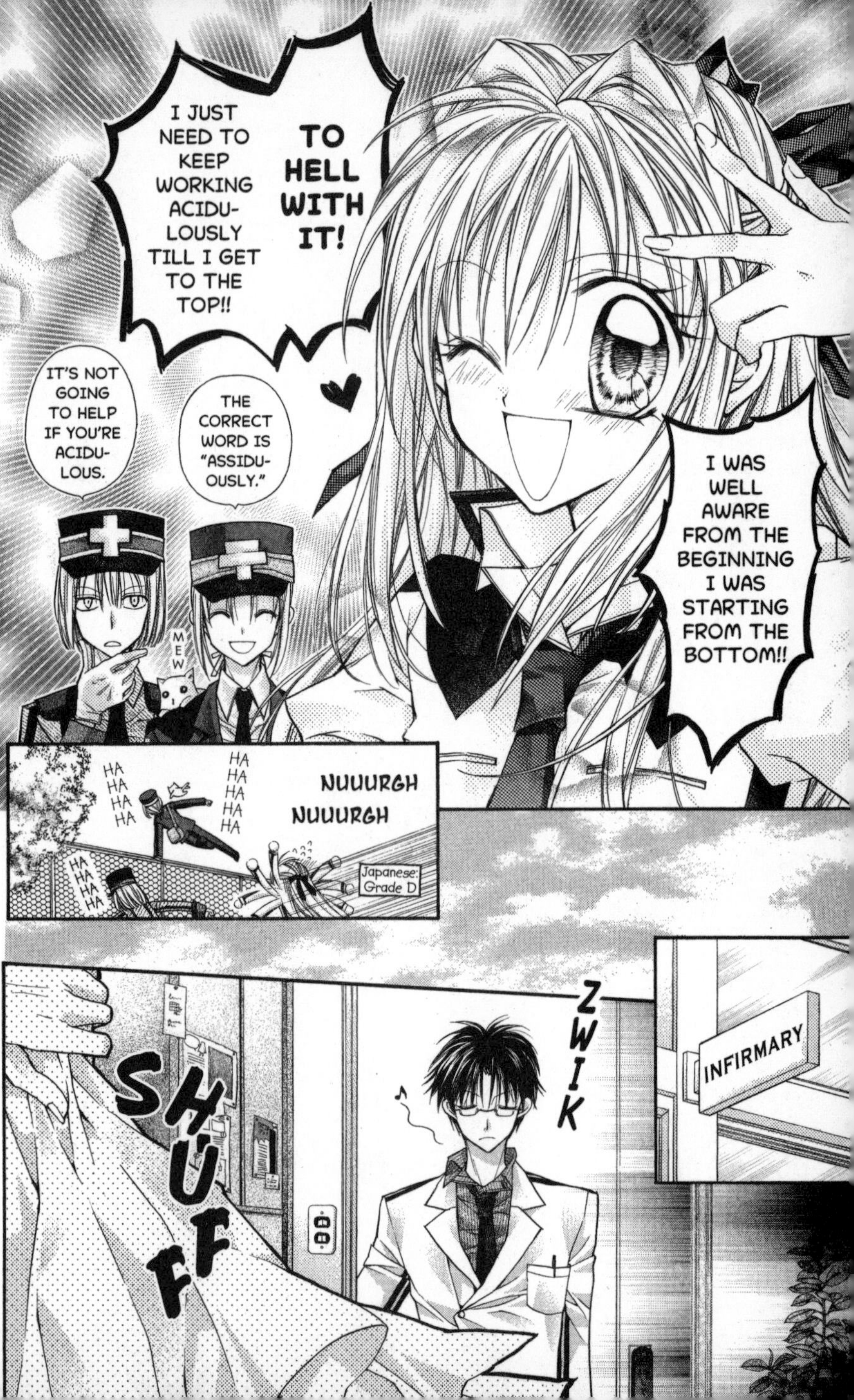
I WAS WELL AWARE FROM THE BEGINNING I WAS STARTING FROM THE BOTTOM!!
TO HELL WITH IT!
I JUST NEED TO KEEP WORKING ACIDU-LOUSLY TILL I GET TO THE TOP!!
THE CORRECT WORD IS "ASSIDU-OUSLY."
IT'S NOT GOING TO HELP IF YOU'RE ACIDU-LOUS.
MEW
NUUURGH NUUURGH
HA HA HA HA HA HA
HA HA HA HA
HA HA HA HA HA
Japanese: Grade D
INFIRMARY
ZWIK
SHUFF

Togu Shizumasa-sama

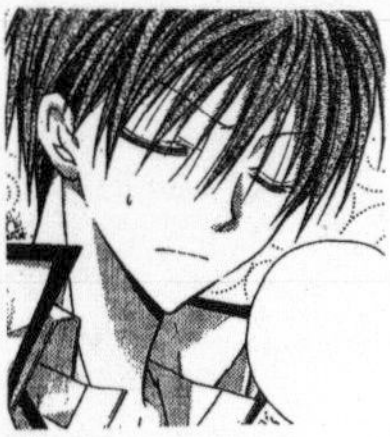

Birthday: October 17
Blood Type: A

He is the president of the student council, known to all as "the Emperor." He is the heir to the ultra-wealthy Togu Group.

He's a misanthrope who is difficult to work with. He seems to especially dislike Haine, but...

Comments

Here's one guy who is very hard to make comments about... (laugh) Even I'm not too sure about what kind of person he is, but I can tell you he is the coolest, most grown-up hero in all my manga.

Oooh, I just can't wait to get to all the details about him!!

By the way, all the characters in this series have the character Miya/Gu (宮) in their family names, and that's because...

- I knew there were going to be a lot of characters in this series, so I didn't want to be hassled with creating too many names.
- I wanted to give them a sense of unification.
- It sounds rich.

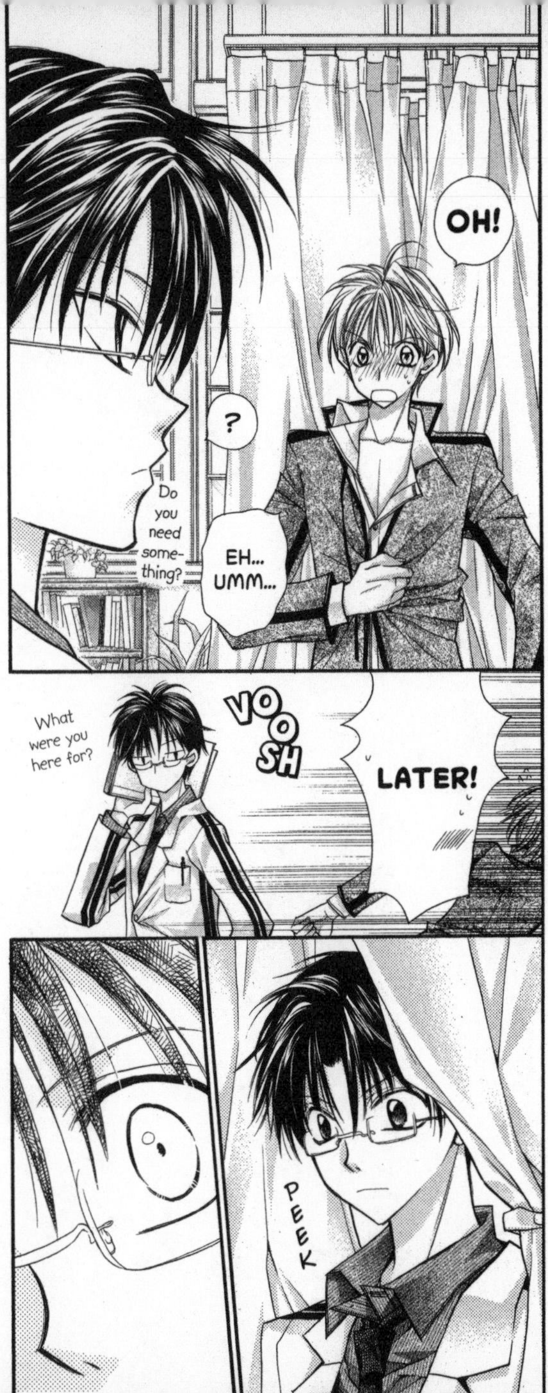
OH!
?
Do you need something?
EH... UMM...
LATER!
VOOSH
What were you here for?
PEEK

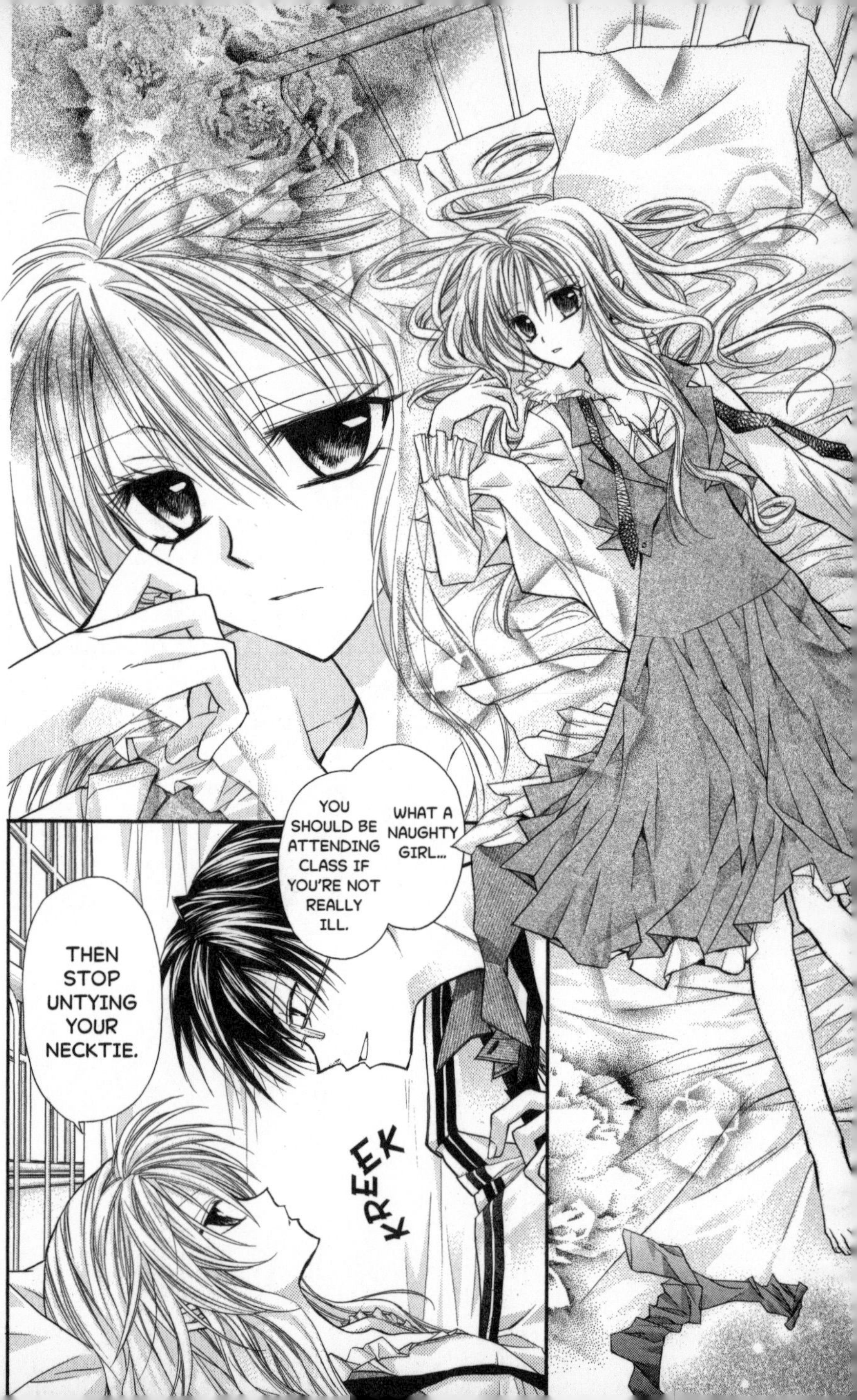
WHAT A NAUGHTY GIRL...
YOU SHOULD BE ATTENDING CLASS IF YOU'RE NOT REALLY ILL.
THEN STOP UNTYING YOUR NECKTIE.
KREEK

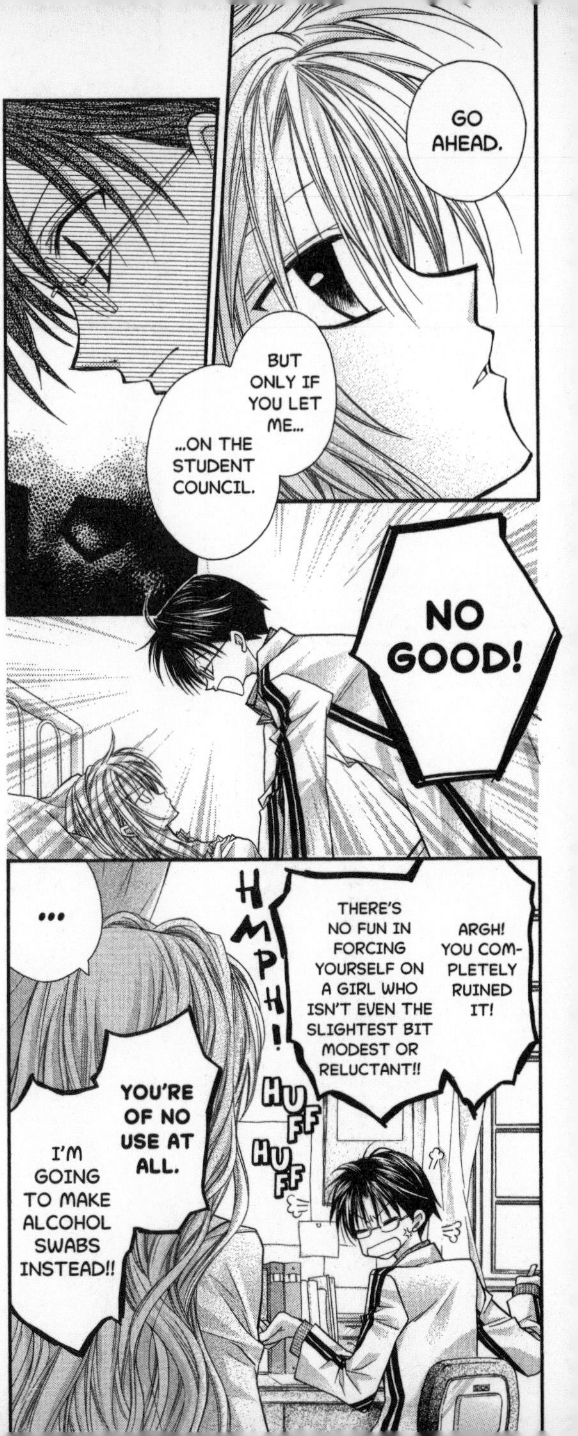
GO AHEAD.
BUT ONLY IF YOU LET ME...
...ON THE STUDENT COUNCIL.
NO GOOD!
ARGH! YOU COM-PLETELY RUINED IT!
THERE'S NO FUN IN FORCING YOURSELF ON A GIRL WHO ISN'T EVEN THE SLIGHTEST BIT MODEST OR RELUCTANT!!
HMPH!
HUFF HUFF
...
YOU'RE OF NO USE AT ALL.
I'M GOING TO MAKE ALCOHOL SWABS INSTEAD!!

Amamiya Ushio

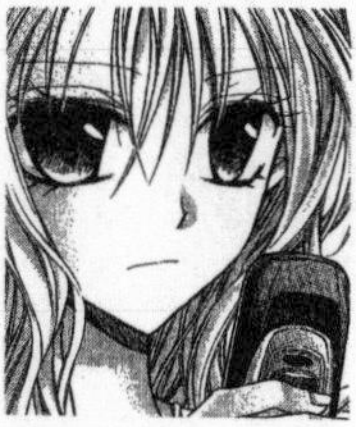

Birthday: February 27
Blood Type: A

This is Haine's friend who is extremely popular among the male students as "Lady Hydrangea." She's rather unsociable, and has never smiled at anybody except Haine.

She is extremely obsessed with Haine, who, by her very existence, helps Ushio keep a balanced mind.

Comments

"Will the *Ribon* readers accept her?" I worried about this, but she turned out to be much more popular than I expected. (She's basically as popular as Haine.)

She looks very girly on the outside, but maybe she's manly on the inside?

(Well, maybe not... She is girly in both good and bad ways.)

It was her encounter with Haine that changed her life forever.

I would very much like to write about it in the story. It's very important for me to include it.

She's my favorite. I find her very dear.

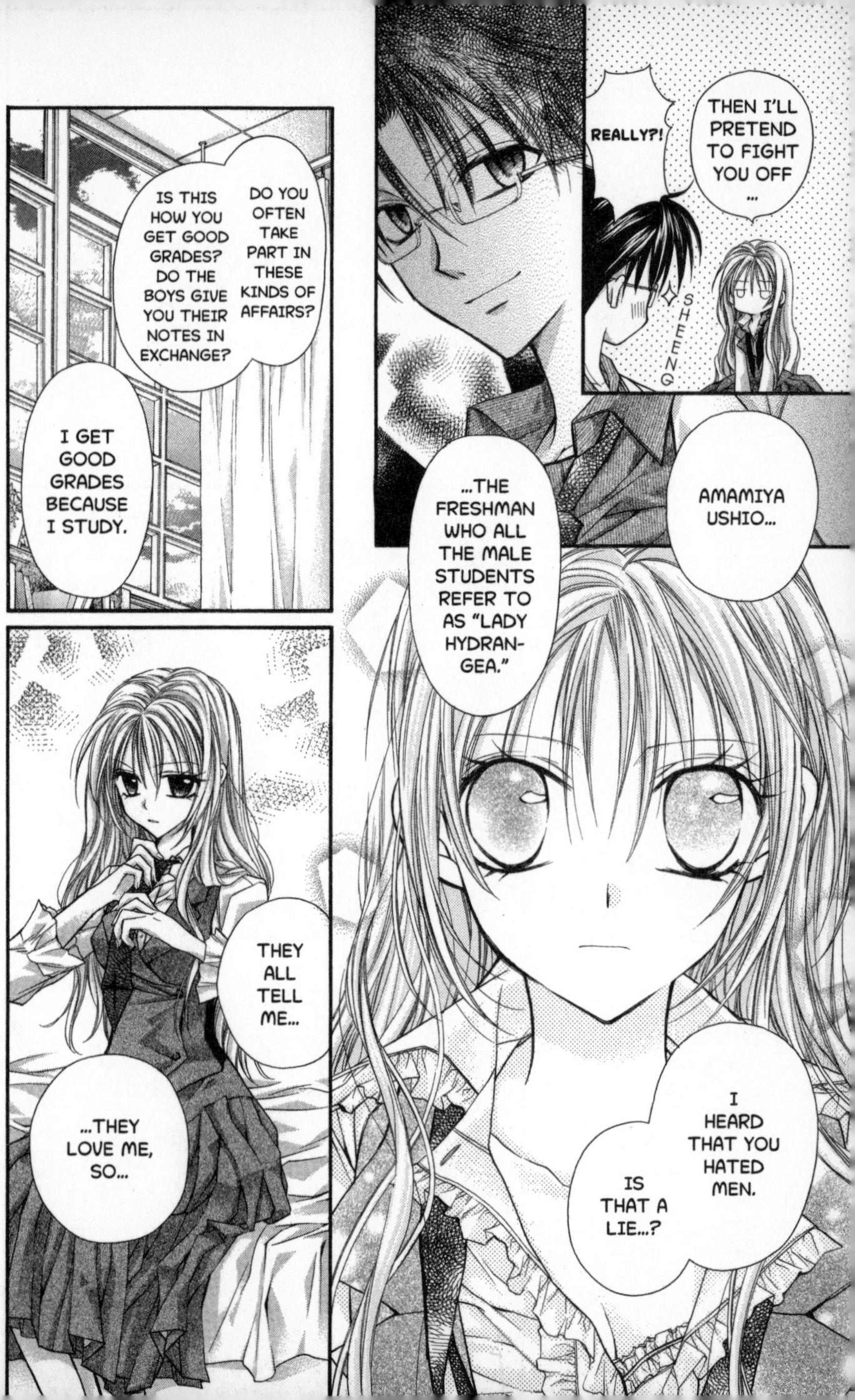
THEN I'LL PRETEND TO FIGHT YOU OFF ...
REALLY?!
SHEEENG
AMAMIYA USHIO...
...THE FRESHMAN WHO ALL THE MALE STUDENTS REFER TO AS "LADY HYDRANGEA."
I HEARD THAT YOU HATED MEN.
IS THAT A LIE...?
DO YOU OFTEN TAKE PART IN THESE KINDS OF AFFAIRS?
IS THIS HOW YOU GET GOOD GRADES? DO THE BOYS GIVE YOU THEIR NOTES IN EXCHANGE?
I GET GOOD GRADES BECAUSE I STUDY.
THEY ALL TELL ME...
...THEY LOVE ME, SO...

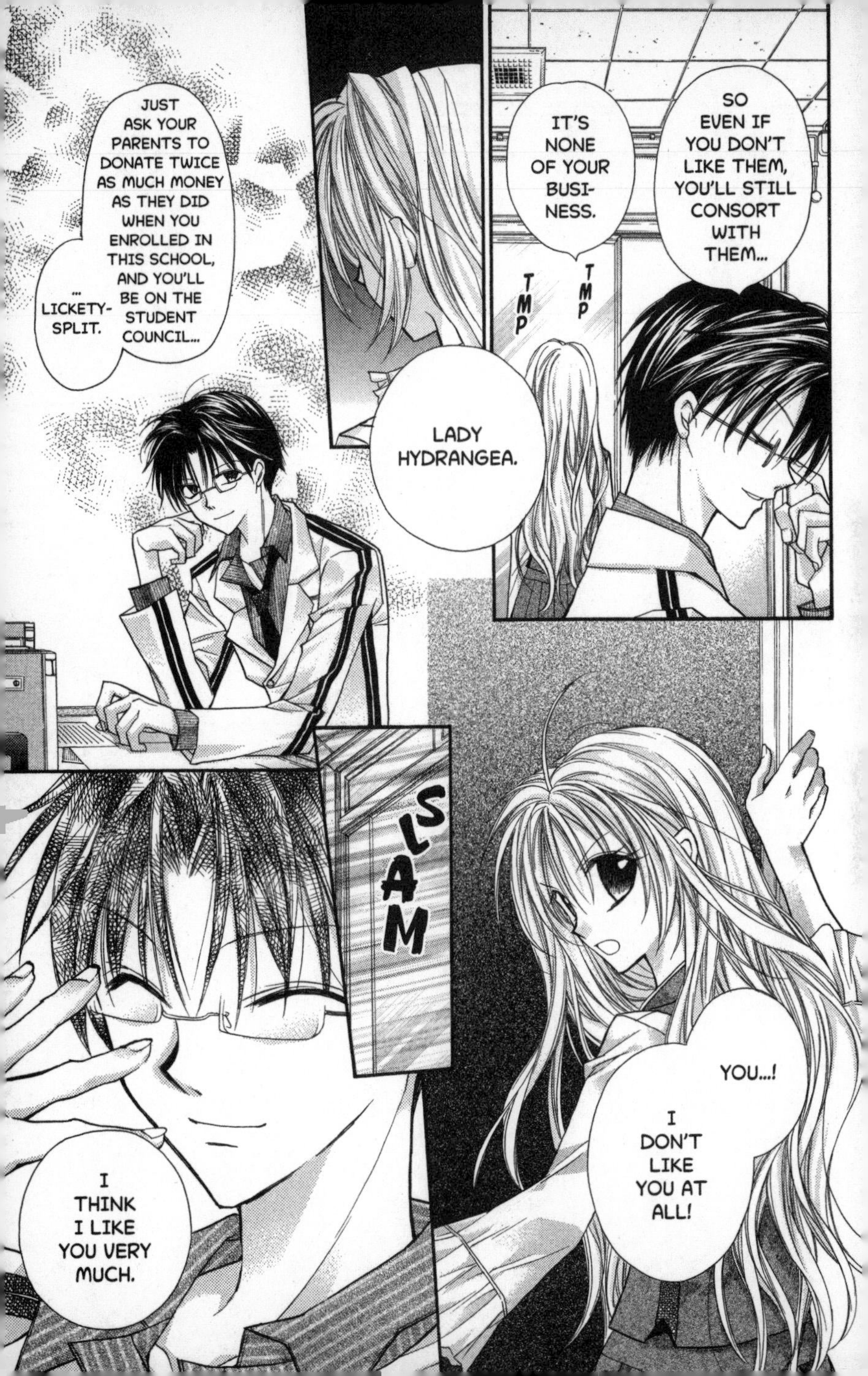
SO EVEN IF YOU DON'T LIKE THEM, YOU'LL STILL CONSORT WITH THEM...
IT'S NONE OF YOUR BUSI-NESS.
TMP
TMP
LADY HYDRANGEA.
JUST ASK YOUR PARENTS TO DONATE TWICE AS MUCH MONEY AS THEY DID WHEN YOU ENROLLED IN THIS SCHOOL, AND YOU'LL BE ON THE STUDENT COUNCIL...
... LICKETY-SPLIT.
SLAM
YOU...!
I DON'T LIKE YOU AT ALL!
I THINK I LIKE YOU VERY MUCH.

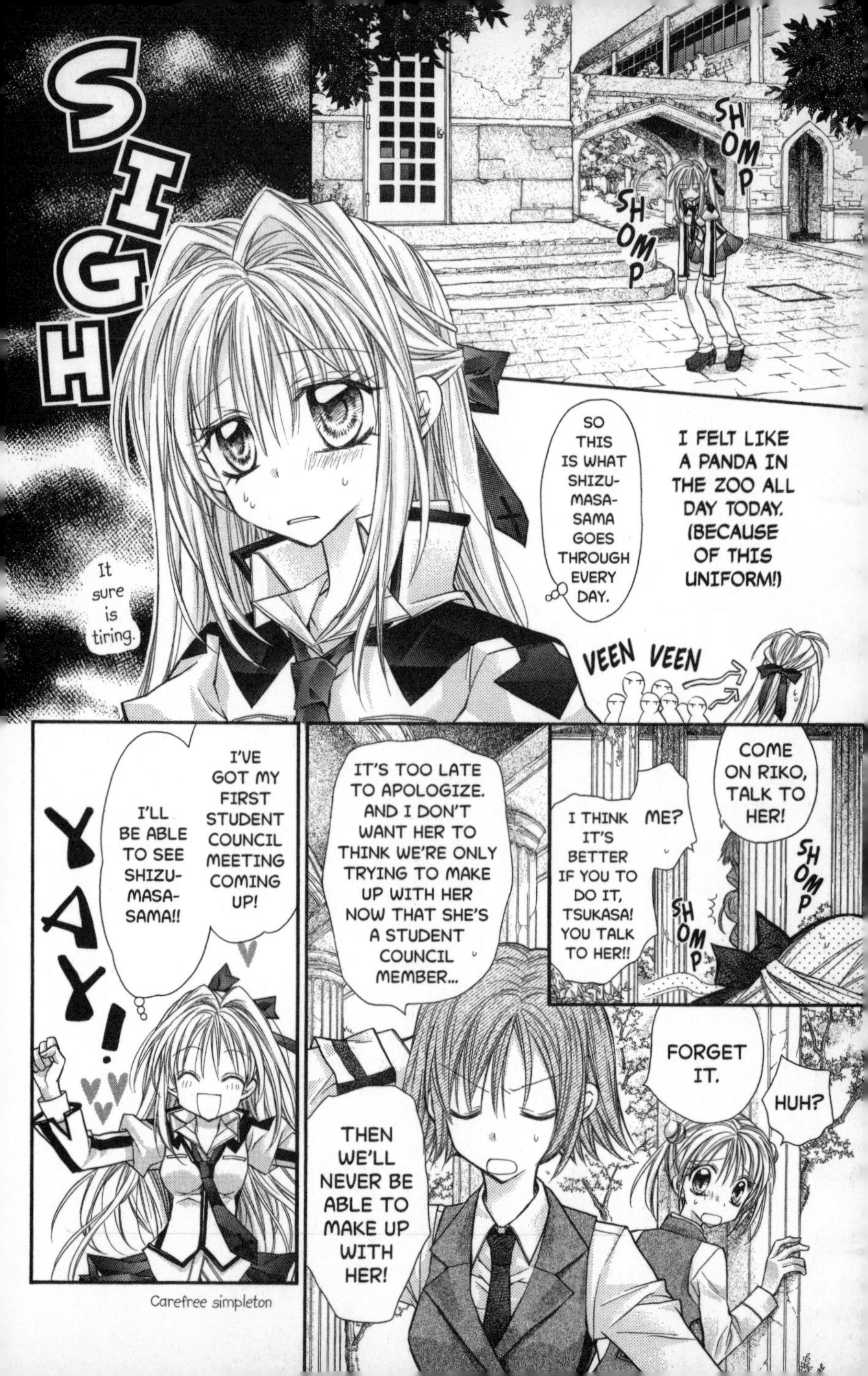
SHOMP
SHOMP
I FELT LIKE A PANDA IN THE ZOO ALL DAY TODAY. (BECAUSE OF THIS UNIFORM!)
SO THIS IS WHAT SHIZU-MASA-SAMA GOES THROUGH EVERY DAY.
SIGH
It sure is tiring.
VEEN VEEN
COME ON RIKO, TALK TO HER!
ME?
I THINK IT'S BETTER IF YOU TO DO IT, TSUKASA! YOU TALK TO HER!!
SHOMP
SHOMP
FORGET IT.
HUH?
IT'S TOO LATE TO APOLOGIZE. AND I DON'T WANT HER TO THINK WE'RE ONLY TRYING TO MAKE UP WITH HER NOW THAT SHE'S A STUDENT COUNCIL MEMBER...
THEN WE'LL NEVER BE ABLE TO MAKE UP WITH HER!
I'VE GOT MY FIRST STUDENT COUNCIL MEETING COMING UP!
I'LL BE ABLE TO SEE SHIZU-MASA-SAMA!!
YAY!
Carefree simpleton

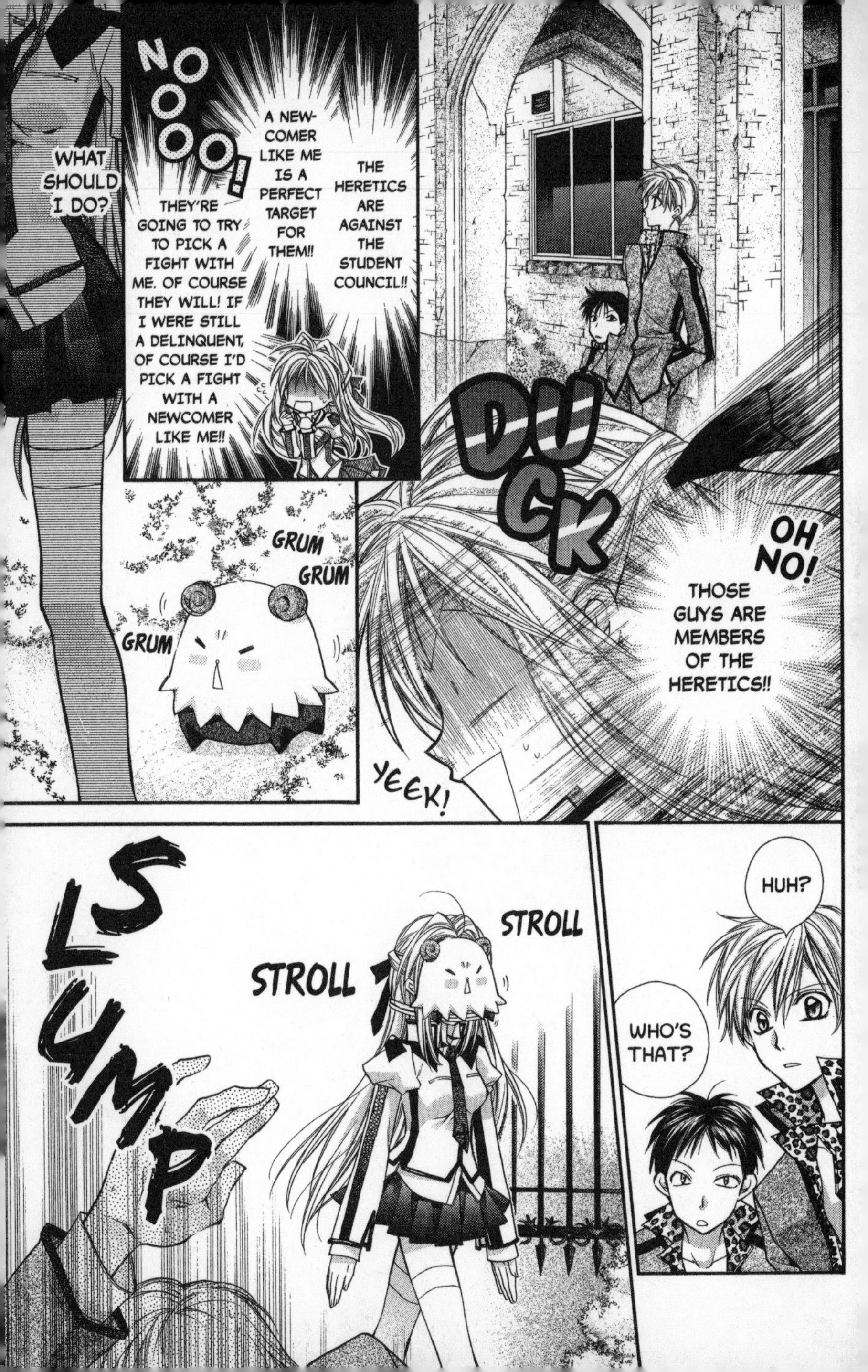

DUCK
OH NO!
THOSE GUYS ARE MEMBERS OF THE HERETICS!!
YEEK!
THE HERETICS ARE AGAINST THE STUDENT COUNCIL!!
A NEW-COMER LIKE ME IS A PERFECT TARGET FOR THEM!!
NOOOO!
THEY'RE GOING TO TRY TO PICK A FIGHT WITH ME. OF COURSE THEY WILL! IF I WERE STILL A DELINQUENT, OF COURSE I'D PICK A FIGHT WITH A NEWCOMER LIKE ME!!
WHAT SHOULD I DO?
GRUM
GRUM
GRUM
HUH?
WHO'S THAT?
STROLL
STROLL
SLUMP

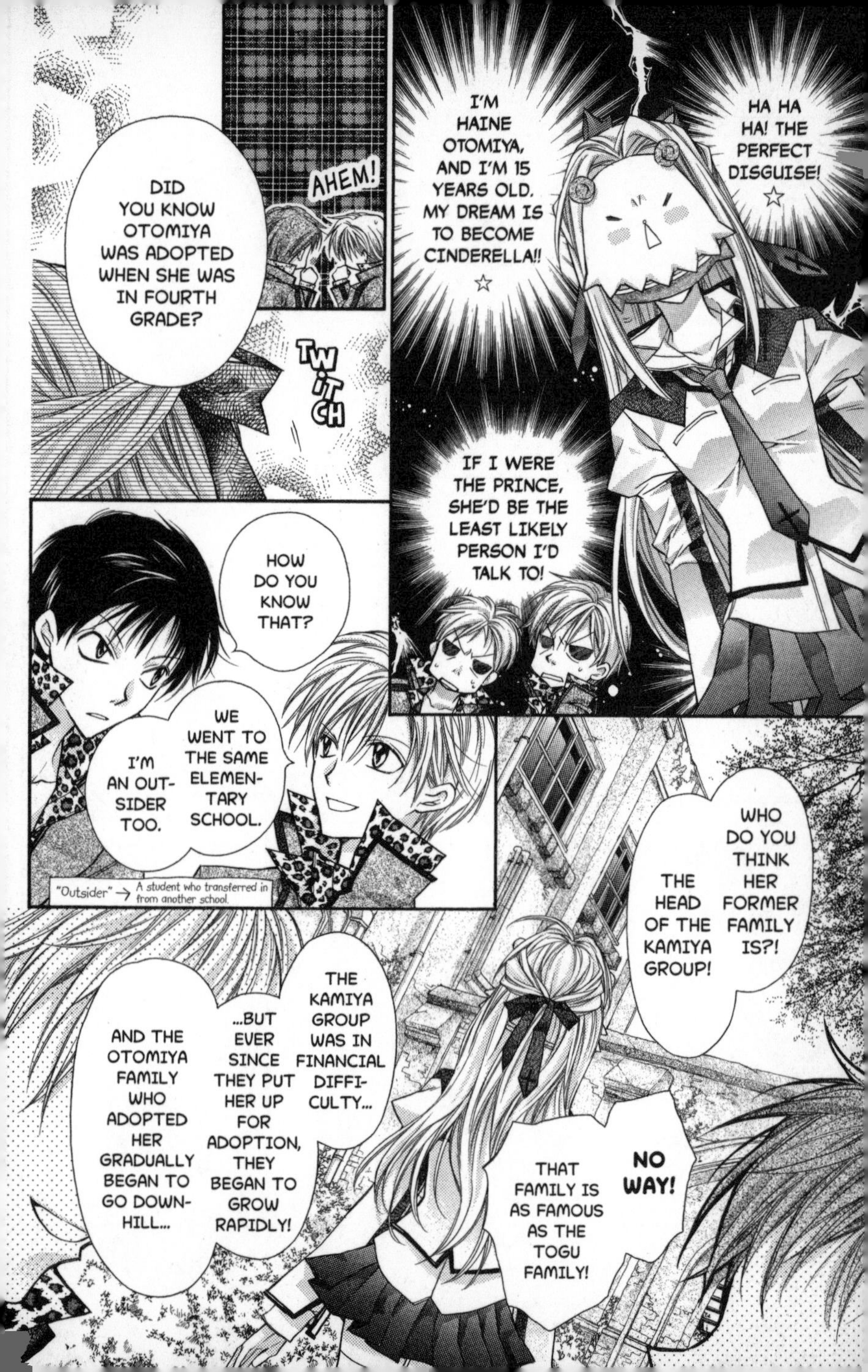
HA HA HA! THE PERFECT DISGUISE! ☆
I'M HAINE OTOMIYA, AND I'M 15 YEARS OLD. MY DREAM IS TO BECOME CINDERELLA!! ☆
IF I WERE THE PRINCE, SHE'D BE THE LEAST LIKELY PERSON I'D TALK TO!
AHEM!
DID YOU KNOW OTOMIYA WAS ADOPTED WHEN SHE WAS IN FOURTH GRADE?
TWITCH
HOW DO YOU KNOW THAT?
WE WENT TO THE SAME ELEMENTARY SCHOOL.
I'M AN OUTSIDER TOO.
"Outsider" → A student who transferred in from another school.
WHO DO YOU THINK HER FORMER FAMILY IS?!
THE HEAD OF THE KAMIYA GROUP!
NO WAY!
THAT FAMILY IS AS FAMOUS AS THE TOGU FAMILY!
THE KAMIYA GROUP WAS IN FINANCIAL DIFFICULTY...
...BUT EVER SINCE THEY PUT HER UP FOR ADOPTION, THEY BEGAN TO GROW RAPIDLY!
AND THE OTOMIYA FAMILY WHO ADOPTED HER GRADUALLY BEGAN TO GO DOWNHILL...

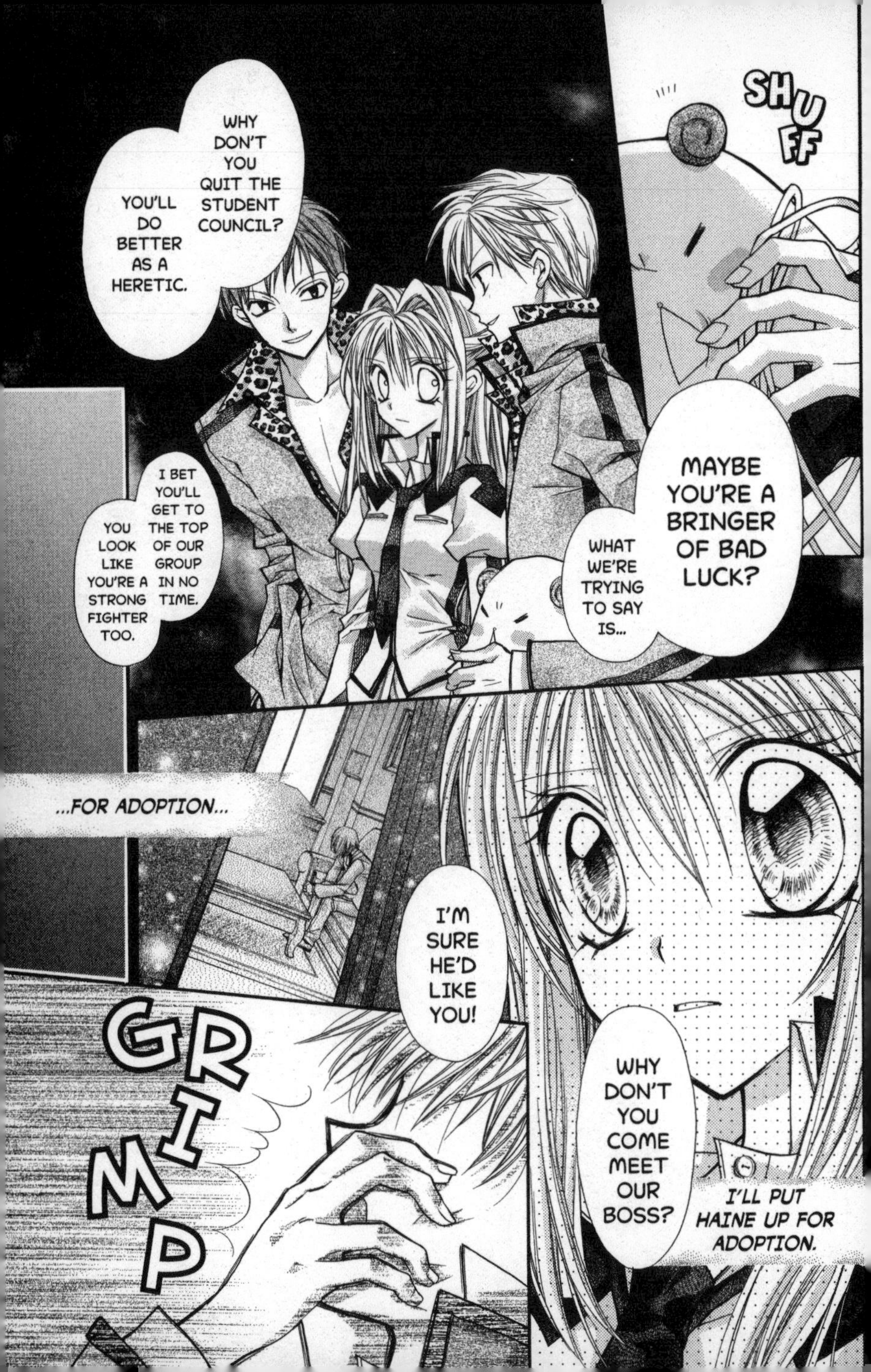
SHUFF
MAYBE YOU'RE A BRINGER OF BAD LUCK?
WHAT WE'RE TRYING TO SAY IS...
WHY DON'T YOU QUIT THE STUDENT COUNCIL?
YOU'LL DO BETTER AS A HERETIC.
I BET YOU'LL GET TO THE TOP OF OUR GROUP IN NO TIME.
YOU LOOK LIKE YOU'RE A STRONG FIGHTER TOO.
I'LL PUT HAINE UP FOR ADOPTION.
WHY DON'T YOU COME MEET OUR BOSS?
I'M SURE HE'D LIKE YOU!
...FOR ADOPTION...
GRIMP

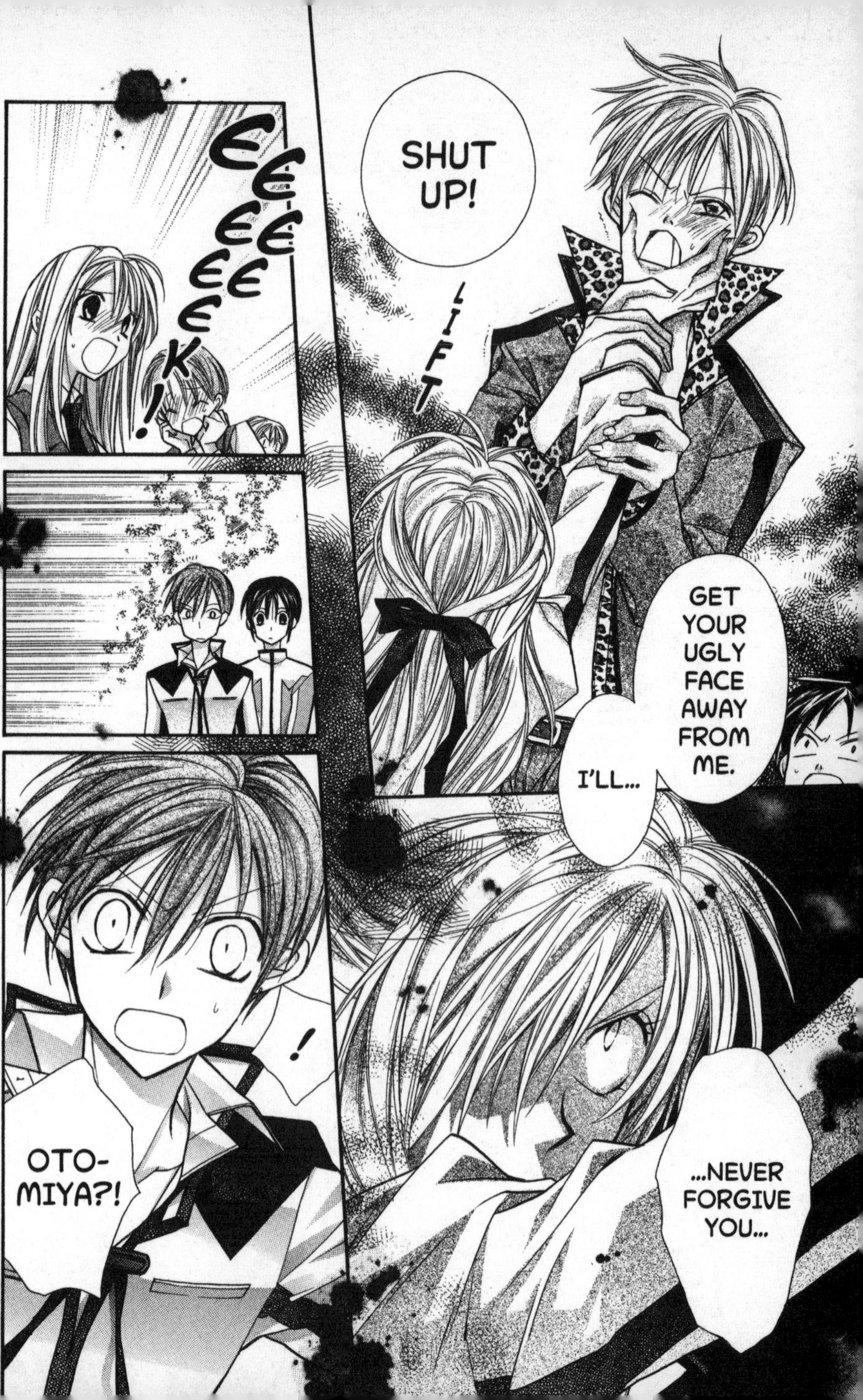
SHUT UP!
LIFT
GET YOUR UGLY FACE AWAY FROM ME.
EEEEEEEK!
I'LL...
...NEVER FORGIVE YOU...
!
OTO-MIYA?!

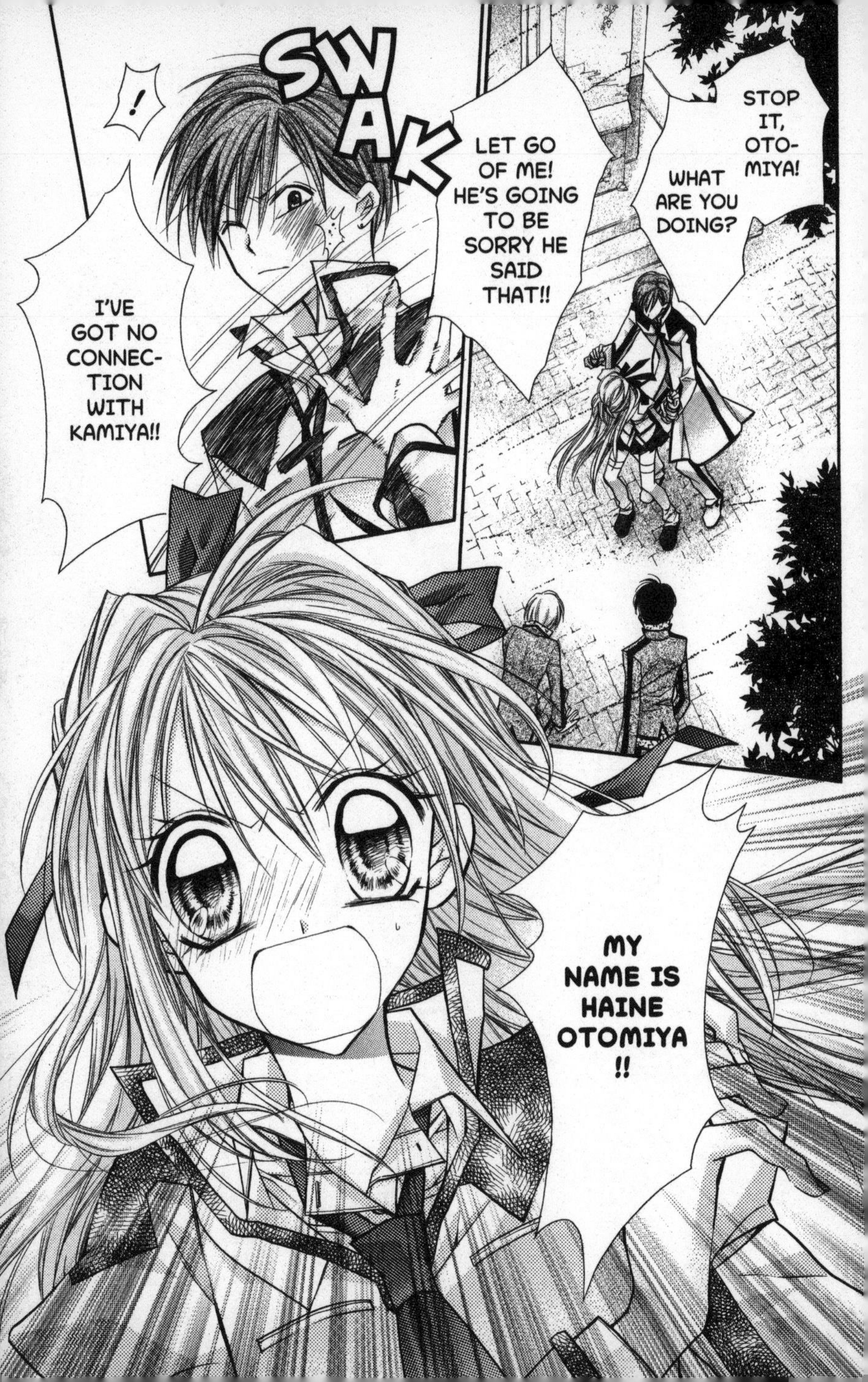
STOP IT, OTO-MIYA!
WHAT ARE YOU DOING?
LET GO OF ME! HE'S GOING TO BE SORRY HE SAID THAT!!
SWAK
!
I'VE GOT NO CONNECTION WITH KAMIYA!!
MY NAME IS HAINE OTOMIYA !!

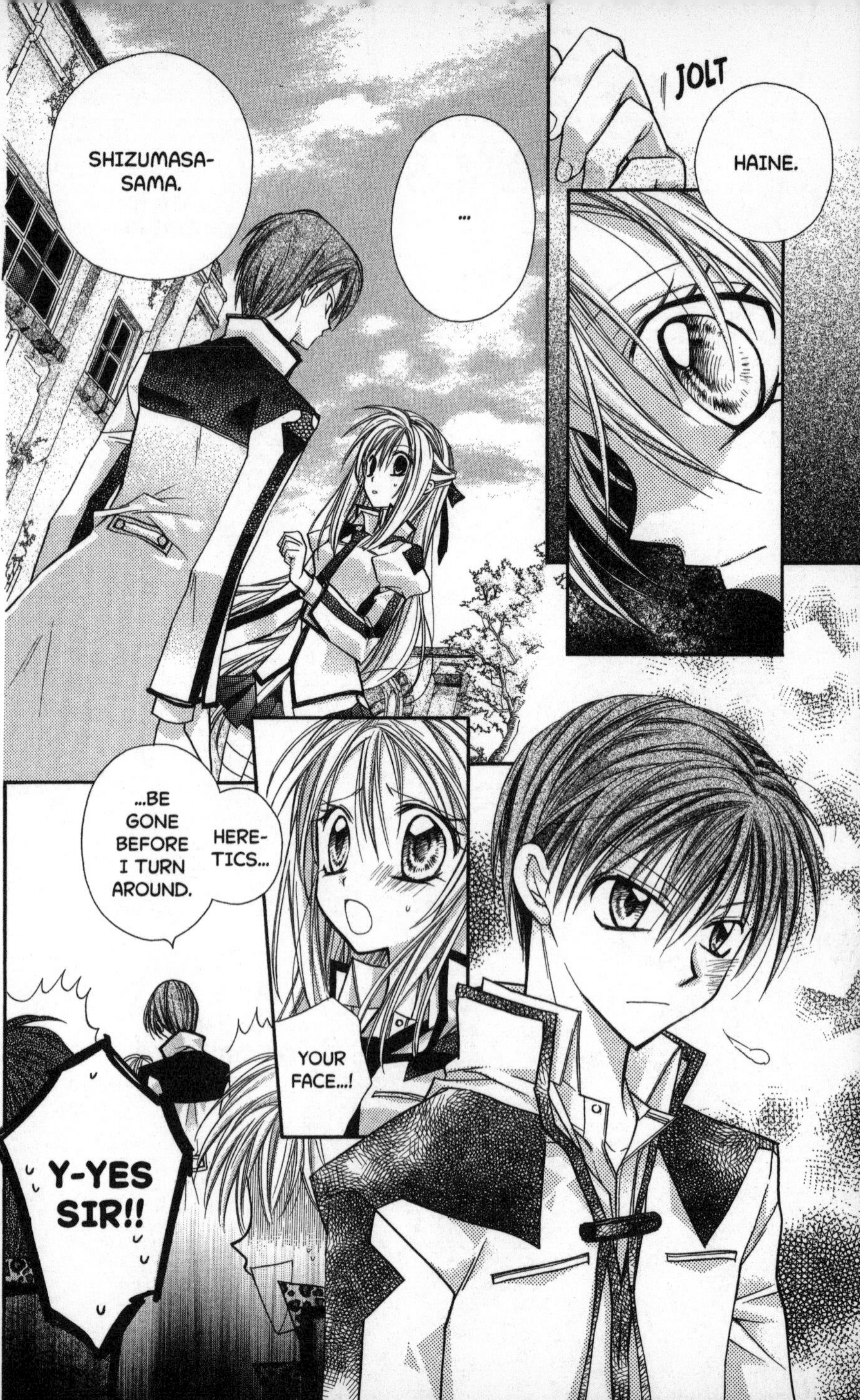
JOLT
HAINE.
...
SHIZUMASA-SAMA.
YOUR FACE...!
HERETICS...
...BE GONE BEFORE I TURN AROUND.
Y-YES SIR!!

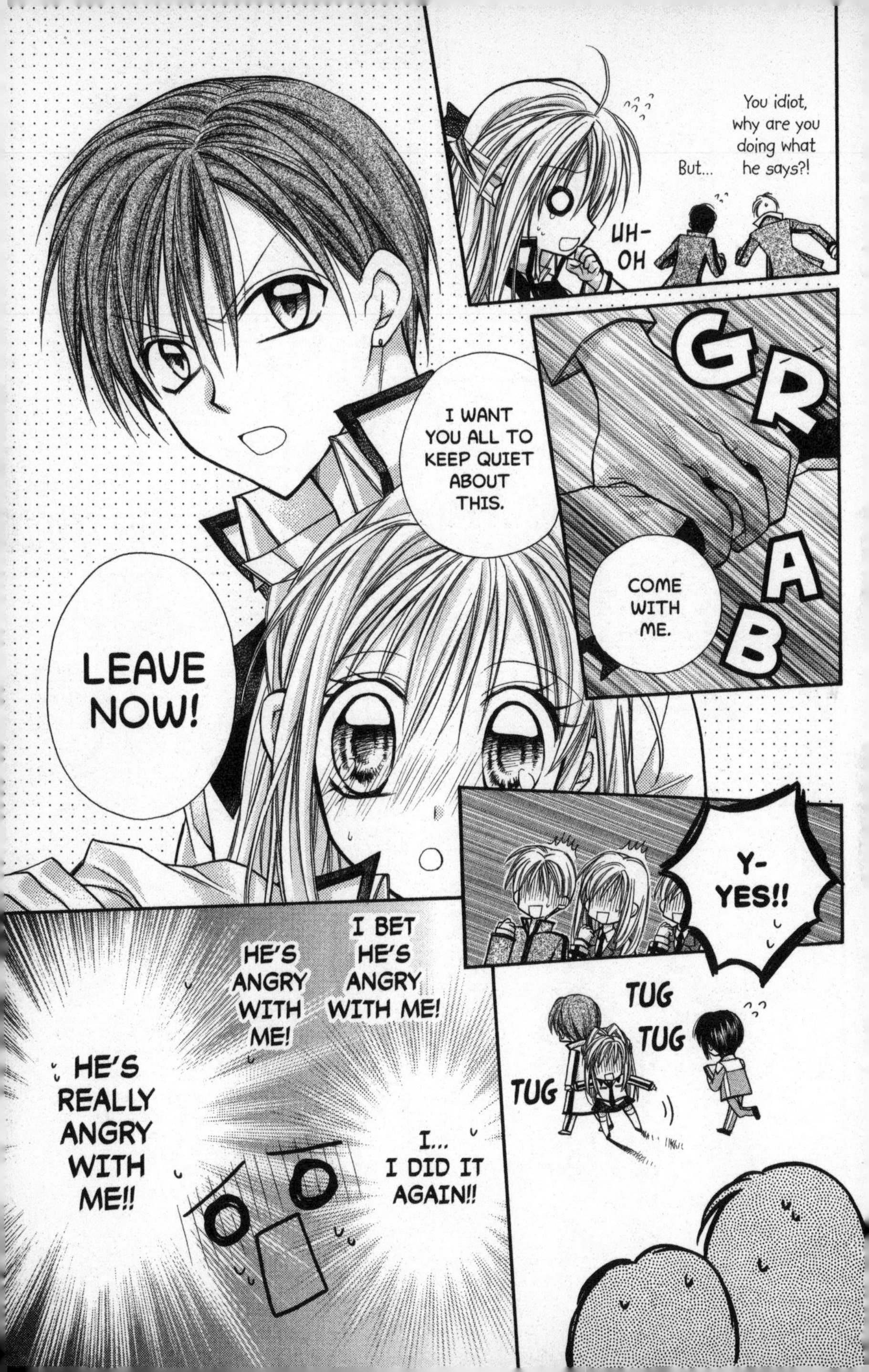
You idiot, why are you doing what he says?!
But...
UH-OH
GRAB
COME WITH ME.
Y-YES!!
I WANT YOU ALL TO KEEP QUIET ABOUT THIS.
LEAVE NOW!
TUG
TUG
TUG
I BET HE'S ANGRY WITH ME!
HE'S ANGRY WITH ME!
I... I DID IT AGAIN!!
HE'S REALLY ANGRY WITH ME!!

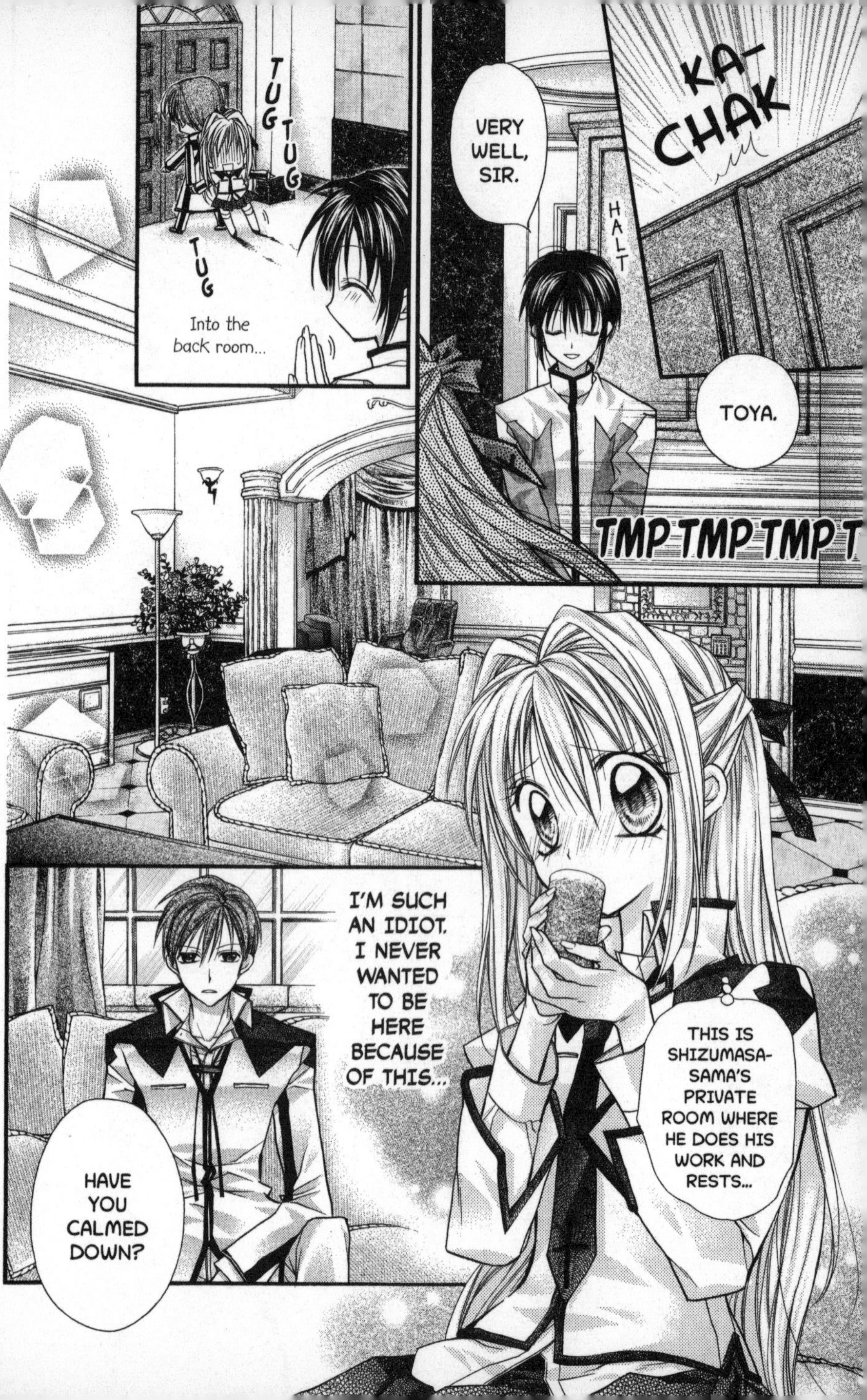
KA-CHAK
TOYA.
TMP TMP TMP T
VERY WELL, SIR.
HALT
TUG TUG
TUG TUG
Into the back room...
THIS IS SHIZUMASA-SAMA'S PRIVATE ROOM WHERE HE DOES HIS WORK AND RESTS...
I'M SUCH AN IDIOT. I NEVER WANTED TO BE HERE BECAUSE OF THIS...
HAVE YOU CALMED DOWN?

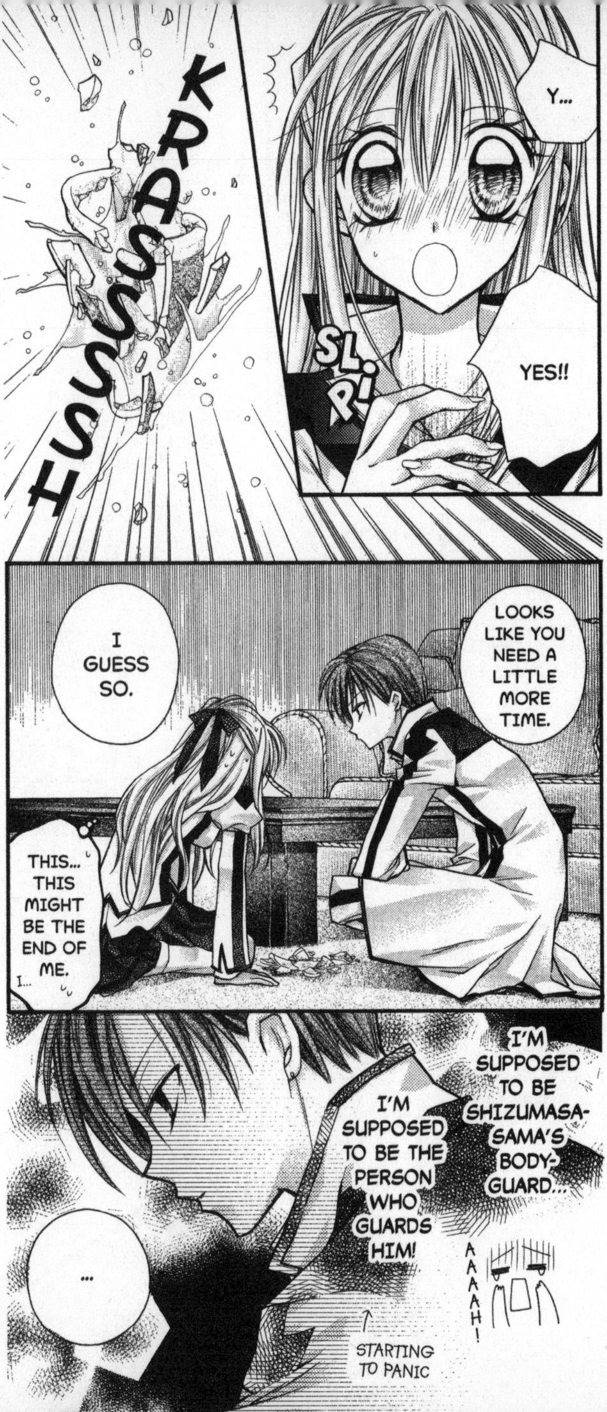
Y...
YES!!
SLIP
KRASSSSH
LOOKS LIKE YOU NEED A LITTLE MORE TIME.
I GUESS SO.
THIS... THIS MIGHT BE THE END OF ME.
I...
I'M SUPPOSED TO BE SHIZUMASA-SAMA'S BODY-GUARD...
I'M SUPPOSED TO BE THE PERSON WHO GUARDS HIM!
AAAAAH!
STARTING TO PANIC
...

Maora

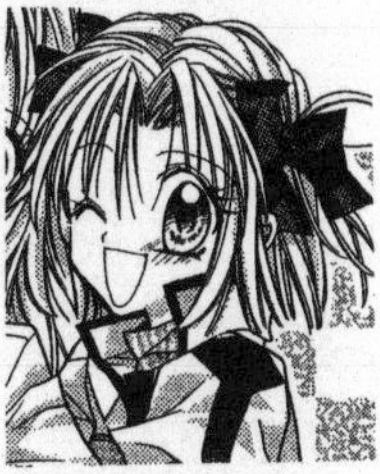

Birthday: August 8
Blood Type: AB

Maora is a nickname for this eccentric character who is highly intelligent and likes to play tricks on people.

But actually, Maora is very kind-hearted...

Has a pet named Okorimakuri-Kun.

Comments

Eccentricity (strangeness) was the basic theme for this character.

Maora is a very strange person!

Oh, I forgot to write it above, but Maora and Maguri are childhood friends who basically have a cat-and-dog relationship. It's rather complicated.

Maora's popularity rose in chapter 5, which will be in volume 2. So please look forward to it if you haven't read it yet!

Many of my assistants are actually Maora fans.

Aah, eccentricity!

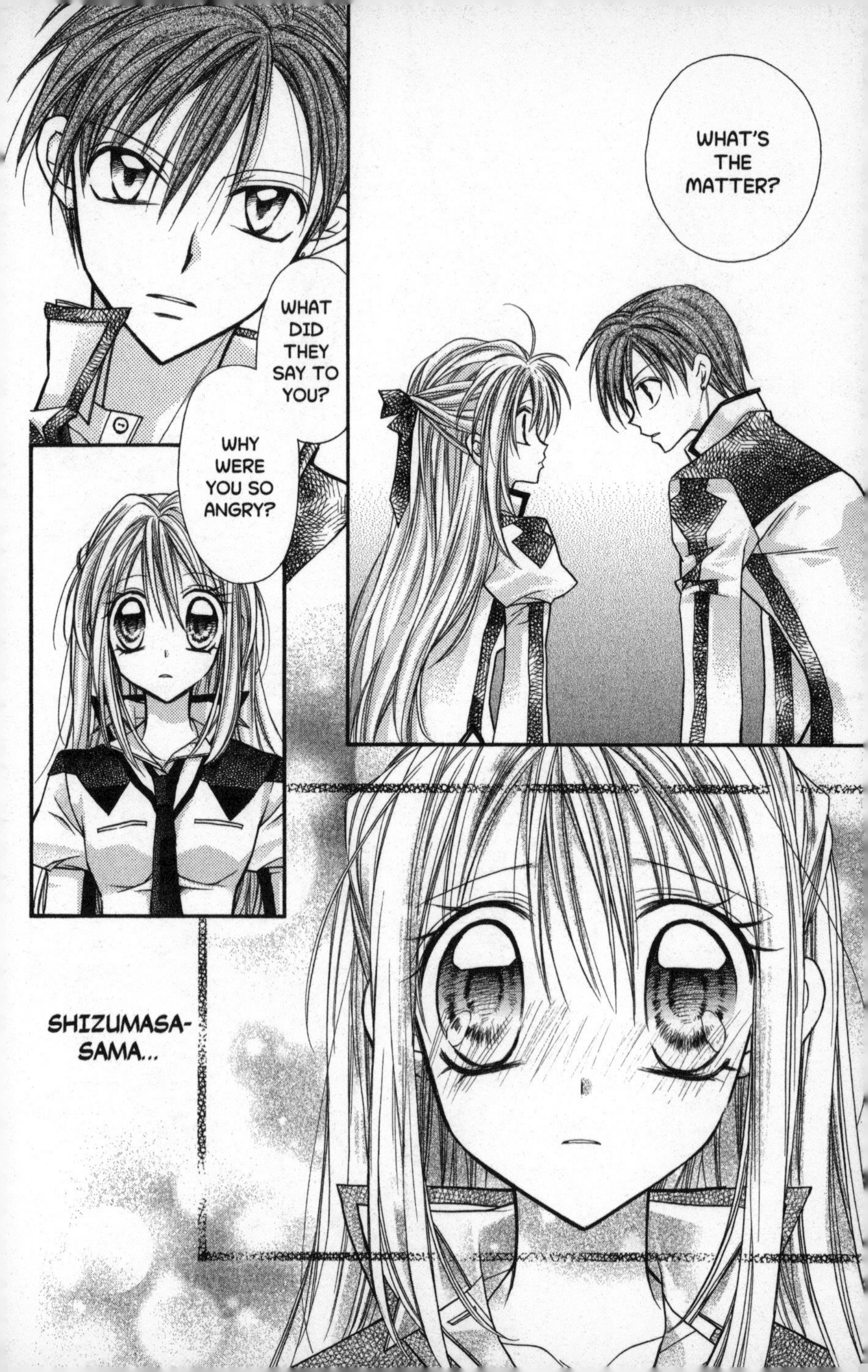
WHAT'S THE MATTER?
WHAT DID THEY SAY TO YOU?
WHY WERE YOU SO ANGRY?
SHIZUMASA-SAMA...

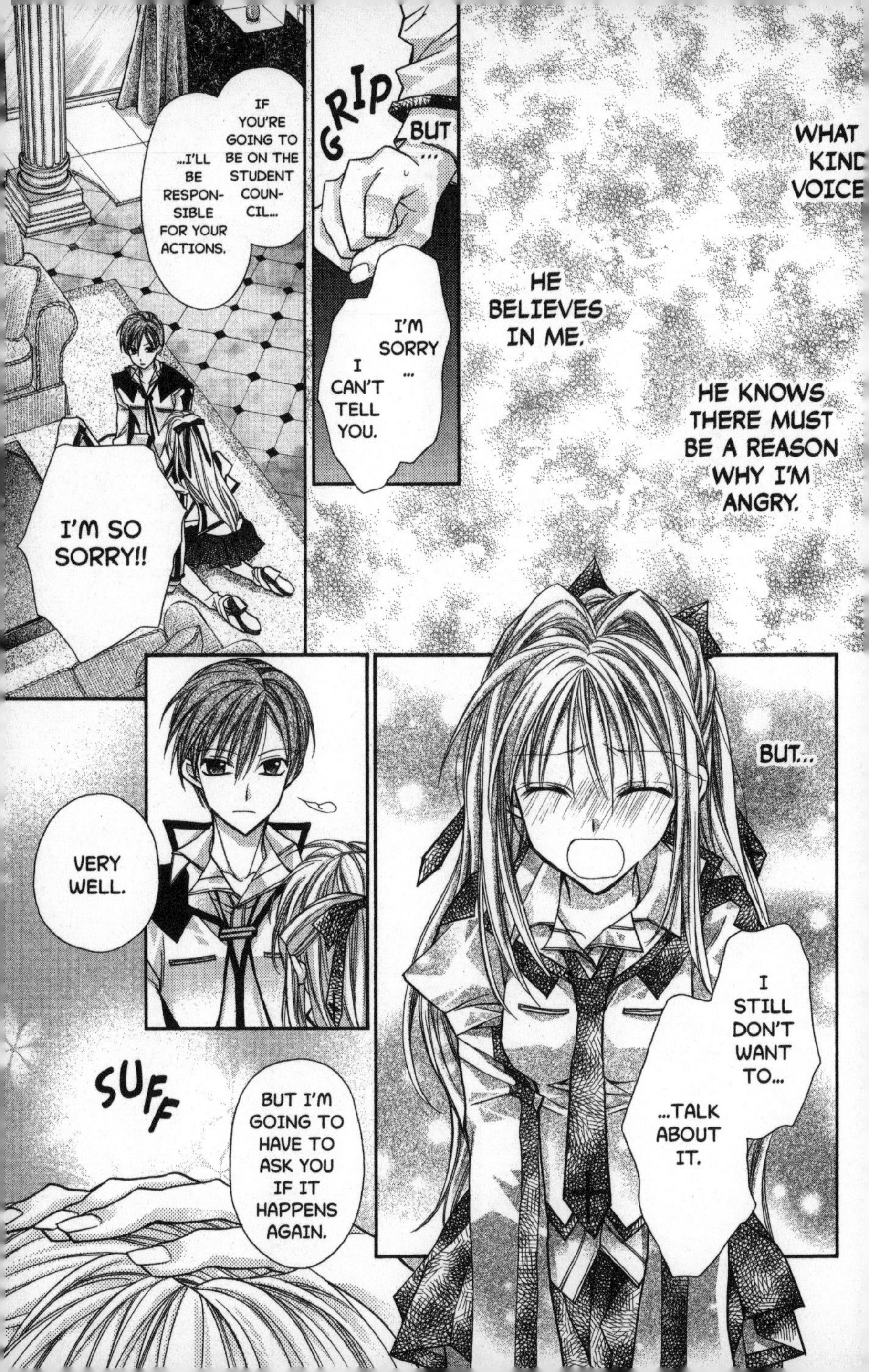
WHAT KIND VOICE
HE BELIEVES IN ME.
HE KNOWS THERE MUST BE A REASON WHY I'M ANGRY.
GRIP
BUT...
I'M SORRY...
I CAN'T TELL YOU.
IF YOU'RE GOING TO BE ON THE STUDENT COUNCIL...
...I'LL BE RESPONSIBLE FOR YOUR ACTIONS.
I'M SO SORRY!!
BUT...
I STILL DON'T WANT TO...
...TALK ABOUT IT.
VERY WELL.
SUFF
BUT I'M GOING TO HAVE TO ASK YOU IF IT HAPPENS AGAIN.

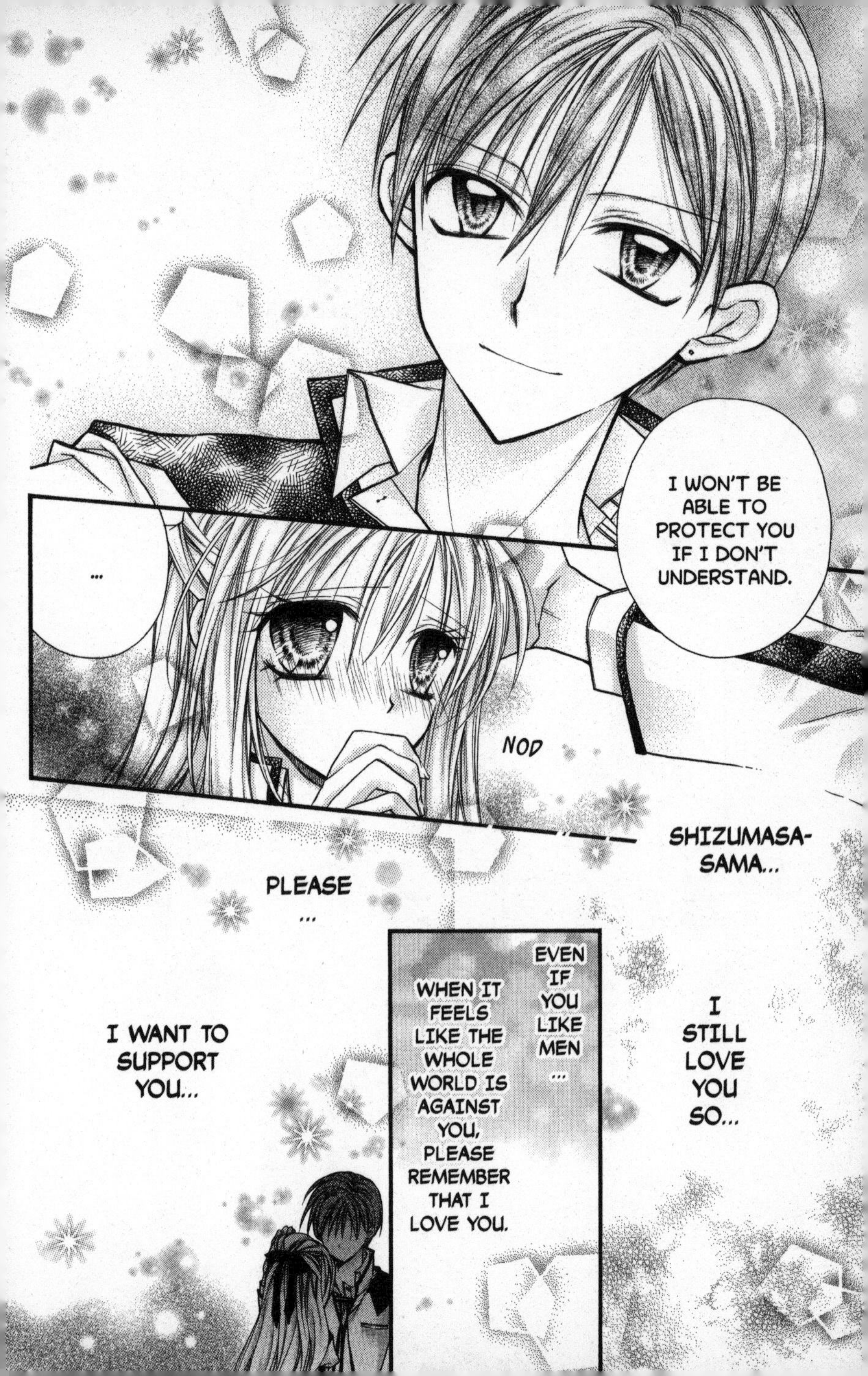
I WON'T BE ABLE TO PROTECT YOU IF I DON'T UNDERSTAND.
...
NOD
SHIZUMASA-SAMA...
PLEASE ...
I STILL LOVE YOU SO...
EVEN IF YOU LIKE MEN ...
WHEN IT FEELS LIKE THE WHOLE WORLD IS AGAINST YOU, PLEASE REMEMBER THAT I LOVE YOU.
I WANT TO SUPPORT YOU...

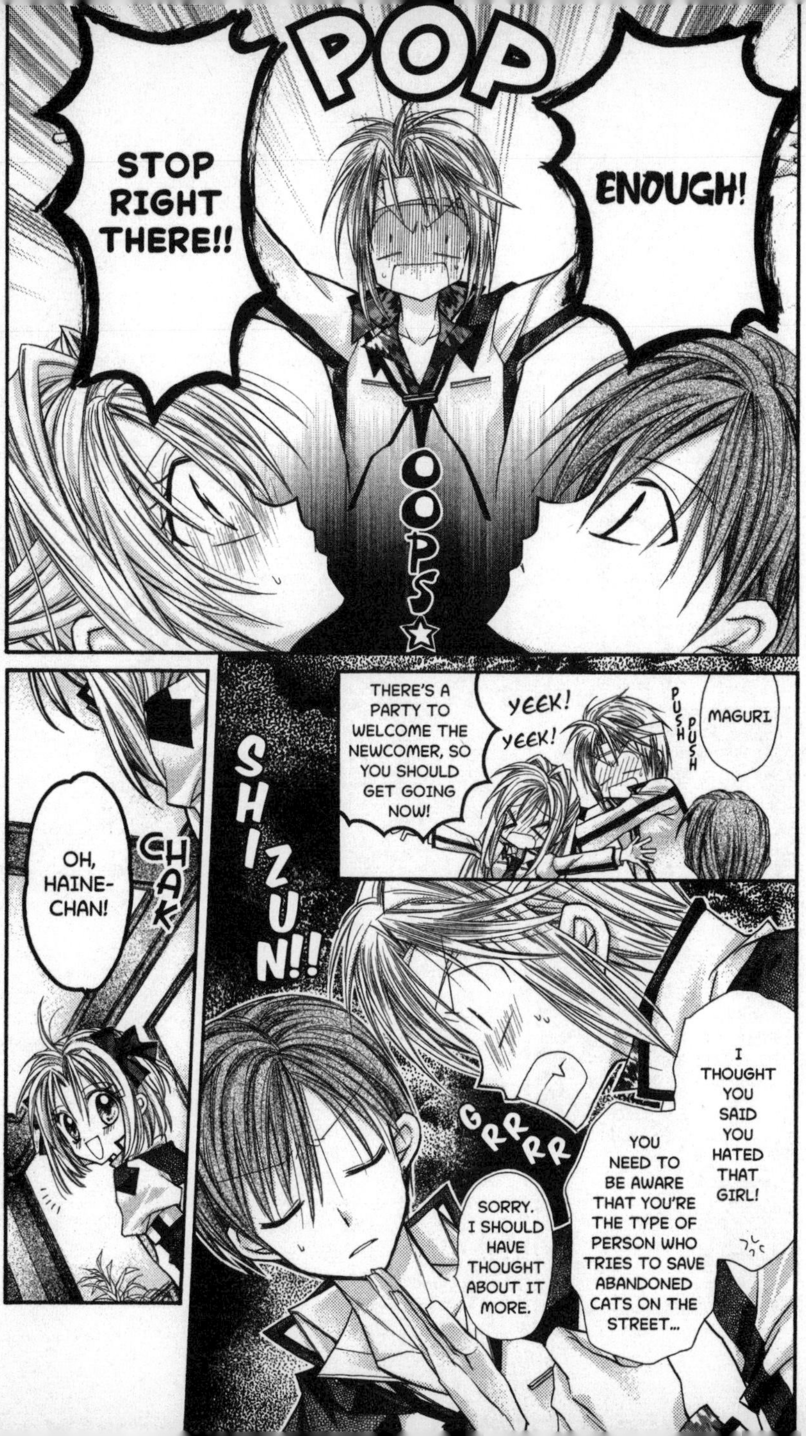
POP
ENOUGH!
STOP RIGHT THERE!!
OOPS☆
MAGURI
PUSH PUSH
YEEK!
YEEK!
THERE'S A PARTY TO WELCOME THE NEWCOMER, SO YOU SHOULD GET GOING NOW!
SHIZUN!!
I THOUGHT YOU SAID YOU HATED THAT GIRL!
YOU NEED TO BE AWARE THAT YOU'RE THE TYPE OF PERSON WHO TRIES TO SAVE ABANDONED CATS ON THE STREET...
GRRRR
SORRY. I SHOULD HAVE THOUGHT ABOUT IT MORE.
CHAK
OH, HAINE-CHAN!

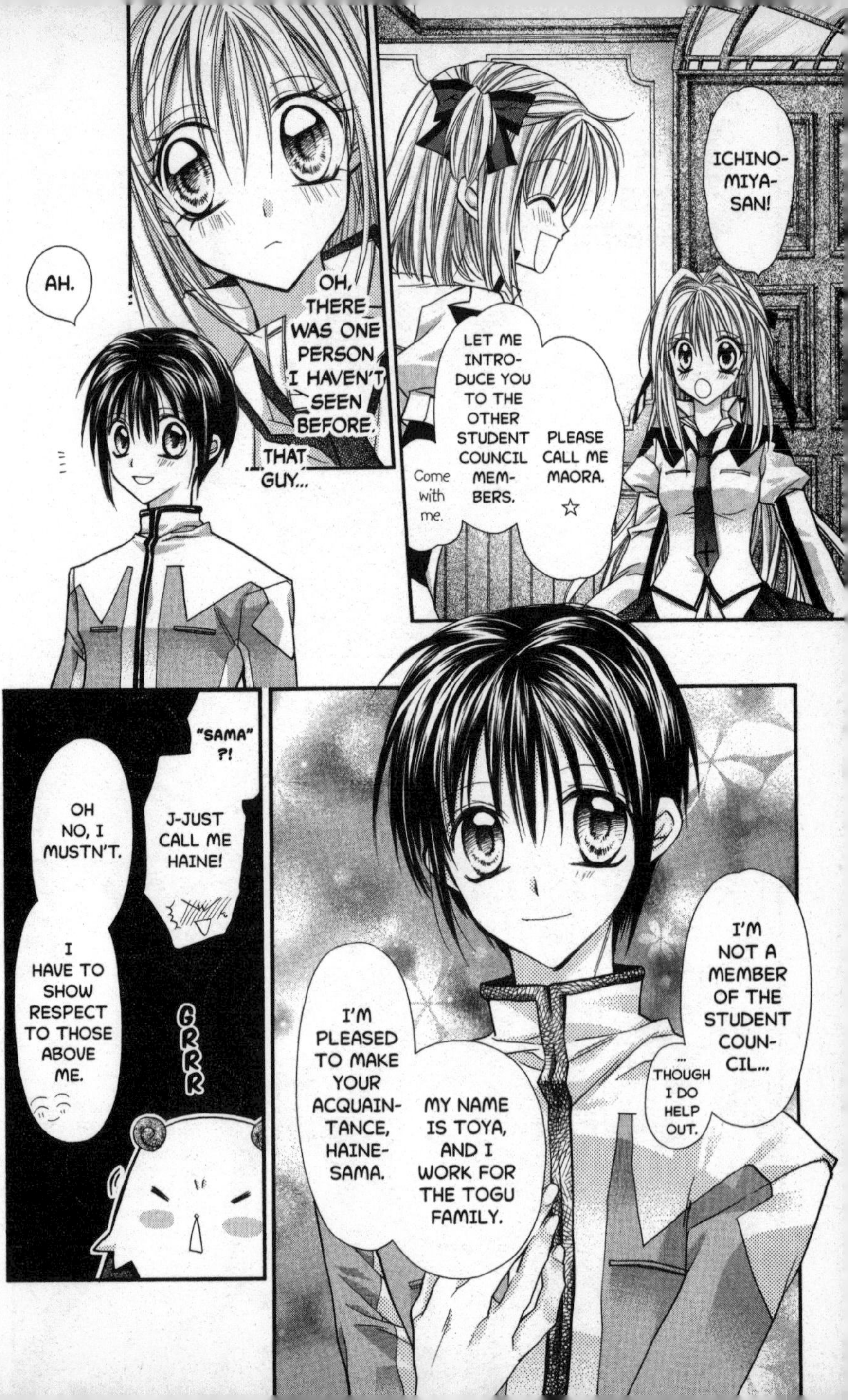
ICHINO-MIYA-SAN!
PLEASE CALL ME MAORA. ☆
LET ME INTRO-DUCE YOU TO THE OTHER STUDENT COUNCIL MEM-BERS.
Come with me.
OH, THERE WAS ONE PERSON I HAVEN'T SEEN BEFORE.
...THAT GUY...
AH.
I'M NOT A MEMBER OF THE STUDENT COUN-CIL...
...THOUGH I DO HELP OUT.
MY NAME IS TOYA, AND I WORK FOR THE TOGU FAMILY.
I'M PLEASED TO MAKE YOUR ACQUAIN-TANCE, HAINE-SAMA.
"SAMA" ?!
J-JUST CALL ME HAINE!
OH NO, I MUSTN'T.
I HAVE TO SHOW RESPECT TO THOSE ABOVE ME.
GRRR

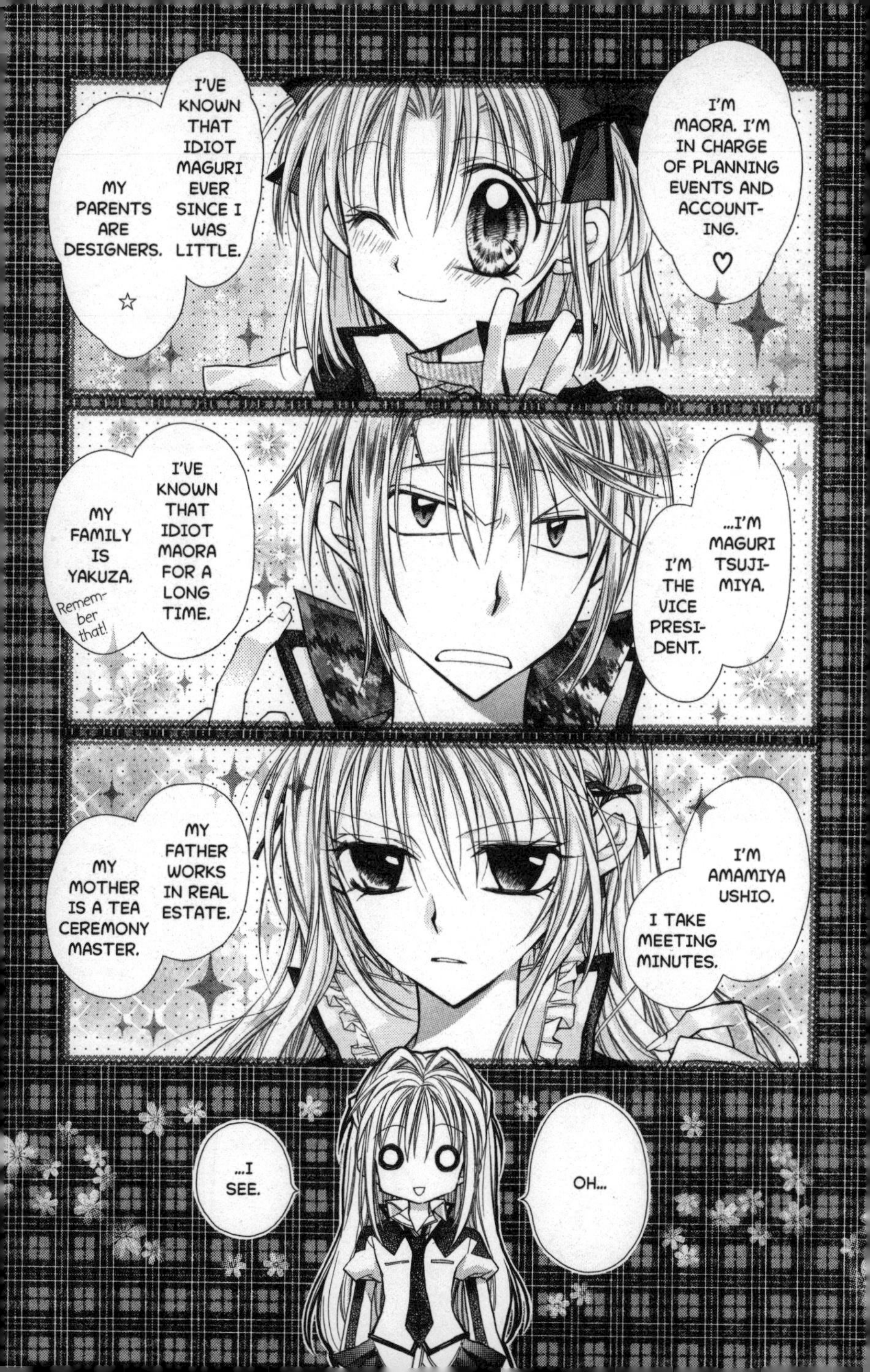
I'M MAORA. I'M IN CHARGE OF PLANNING EVENTS AND ACCOUNTING. ♡
I'VE KNOWN THAT IDIOT MAGURI EVER SINCE I WAS LITTLE.
MY PARENTS ARE DESIGNERS. ☆
...I'M MAGURI TSUJIMIYA.
I'M THE VICE PRESIDENT.
I'VE KNOWN THAT IDIOT MAORA FOR A LONG TIME.
MY FAMILY IS YAKUZA.
Remember that!
I'M AMAMIYA USHIO.
I TAKE MEETING MINUTES.
MY FATHER WORKS IN REAL ESTATE.
MY MOTHER IS A TEA CEREMONY MASTER.
OH...
...I SEE.

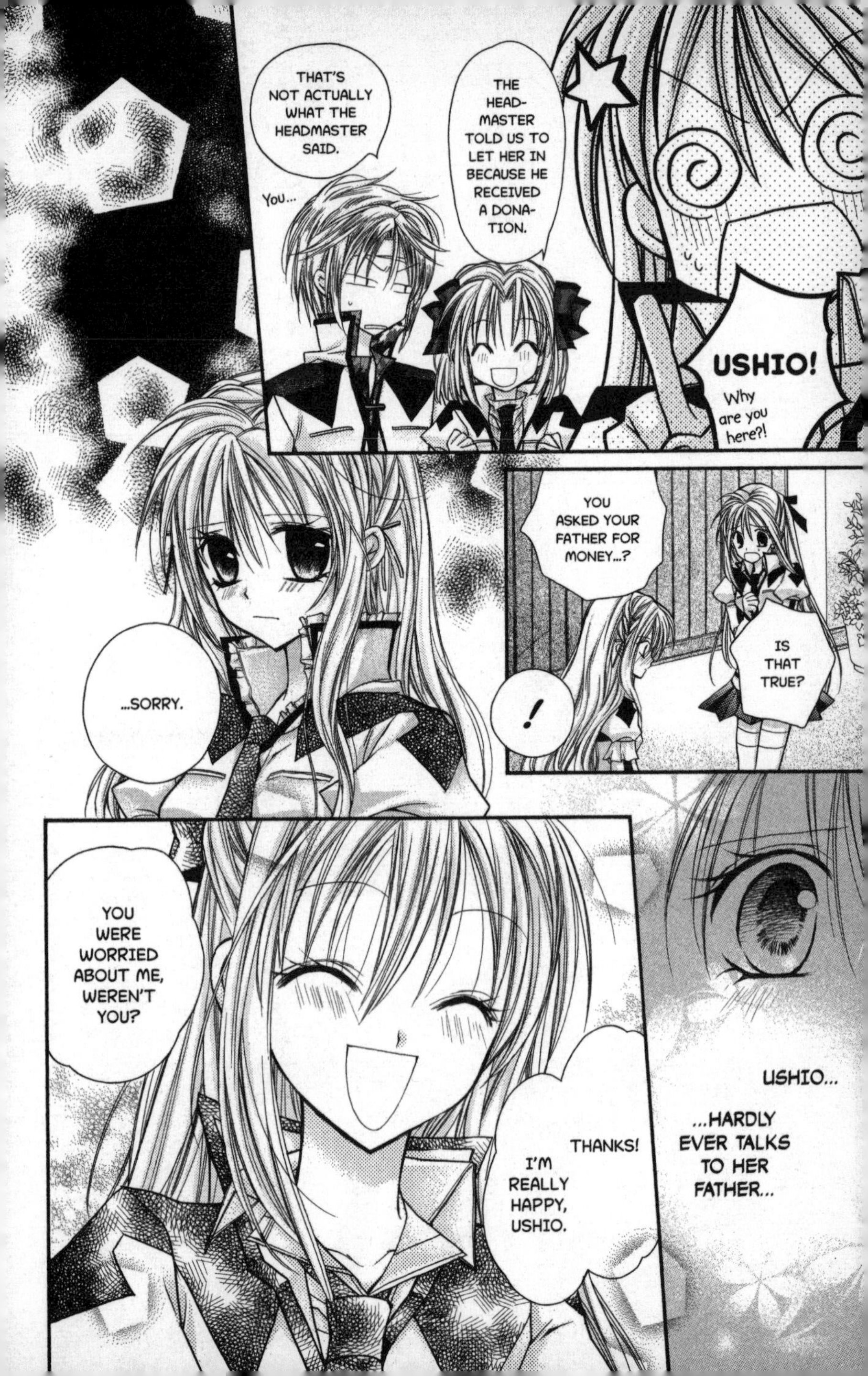
USHIO!
Why are you here?!
THE HEAD-MASTER TOLD US TO LET HER IN BECAUSE HE RECEIVED A DONA-TION.
THAT'S NOT ACTUALLY WHAT THE HEADMASTER SAID.
You...
YOU ASKED YOUR FATHER FOR MONEY...?
IS THAT TRUE?
!
...SORRY.
USHIO...
...HARDLY EVER TALKS TO HER FATHER...
YOU WERE WORRIED ABOUT ME, WEREN'T YOU?
THANKS!
I'M REALLY HAPPY, USHIO.

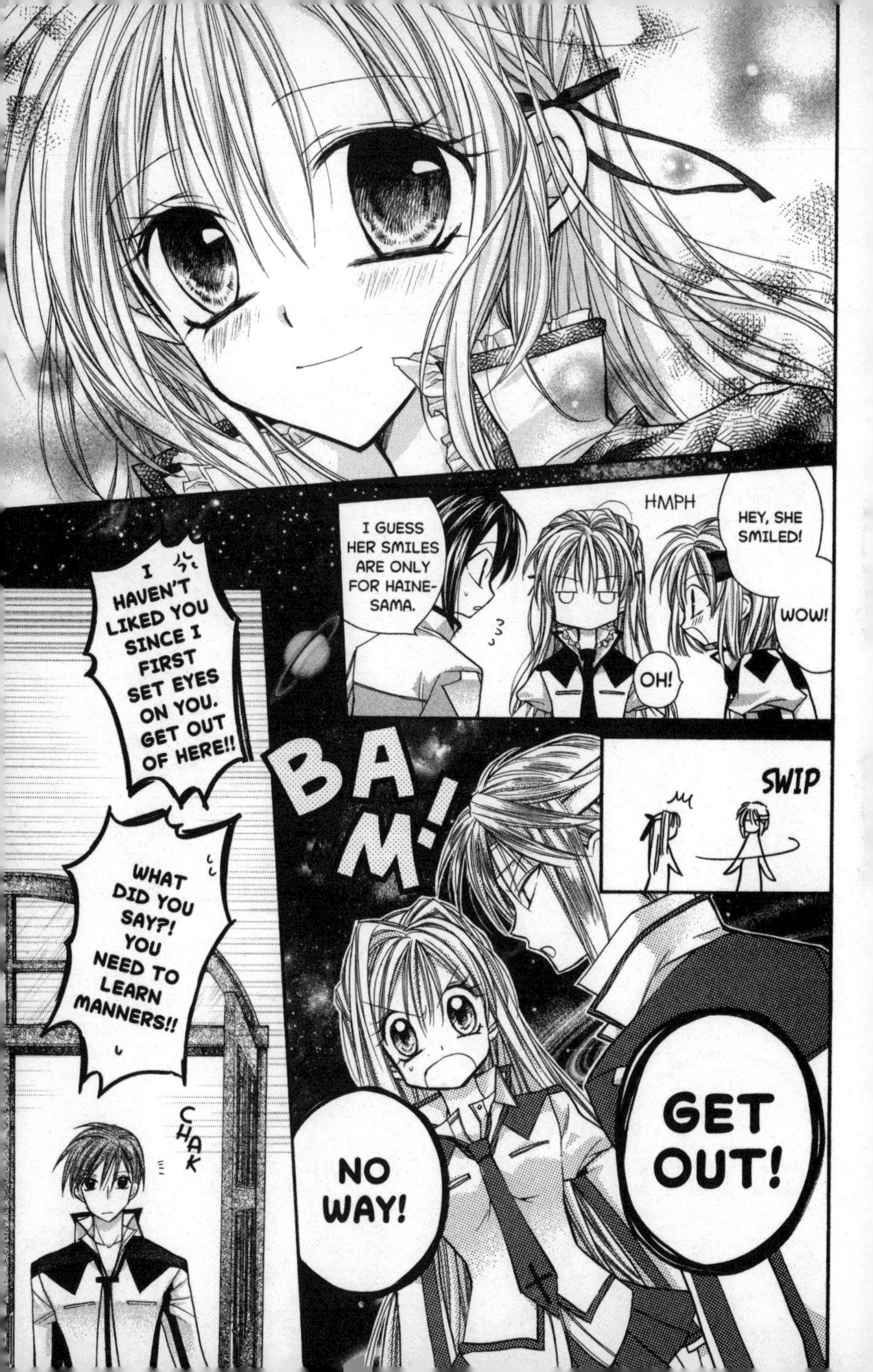
HEY, SHE SMILED!
HMPH
WOW!
OH!
I GUESS HER SMILES ARE ONLY FOR HAINE-SAMA.
SWIP
BAM!
GET OUT!
NO WAY!
I HAVEN'T LIKED YOU SINCE I FIRST SET EYES ON YOU. GET OUT OF HERE!!
WHAT DID YOU SAY?! YOU NEED TO LEARN MANNERS!!
CHAK

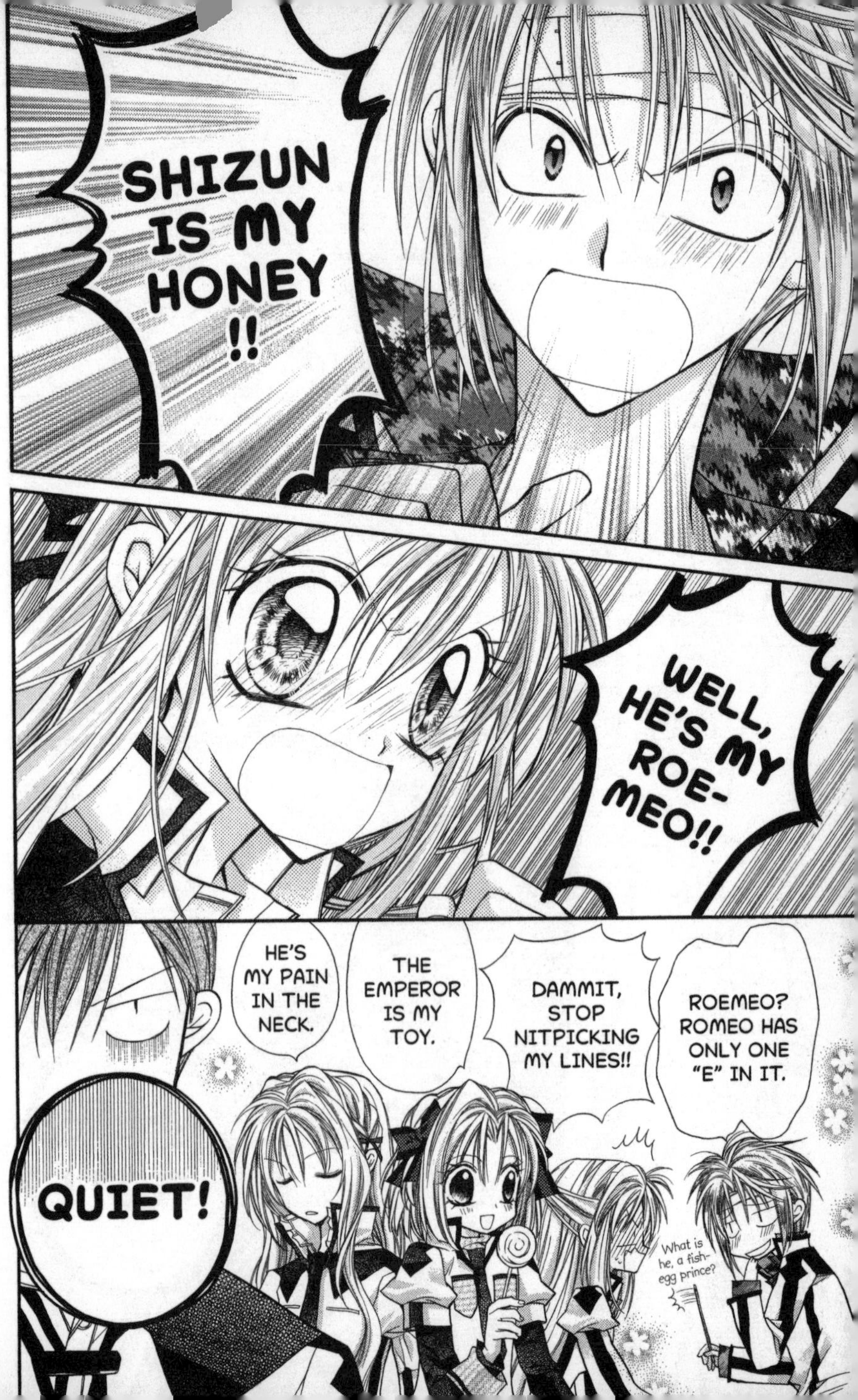
SHIZUN IS MY HONEY!!
WELL, HE'S MY ROE-MEO!!
ROEMEO? ROMEO HAS ONLY ONE "E" IN IT.
DAMMIT, STOP NITPICKING MY LINES!!
THE EMPEROR IS MY TOY.
HE'S MY PAIN IN THE NECK.
What is he, a fish-egg prince?
QUIET!

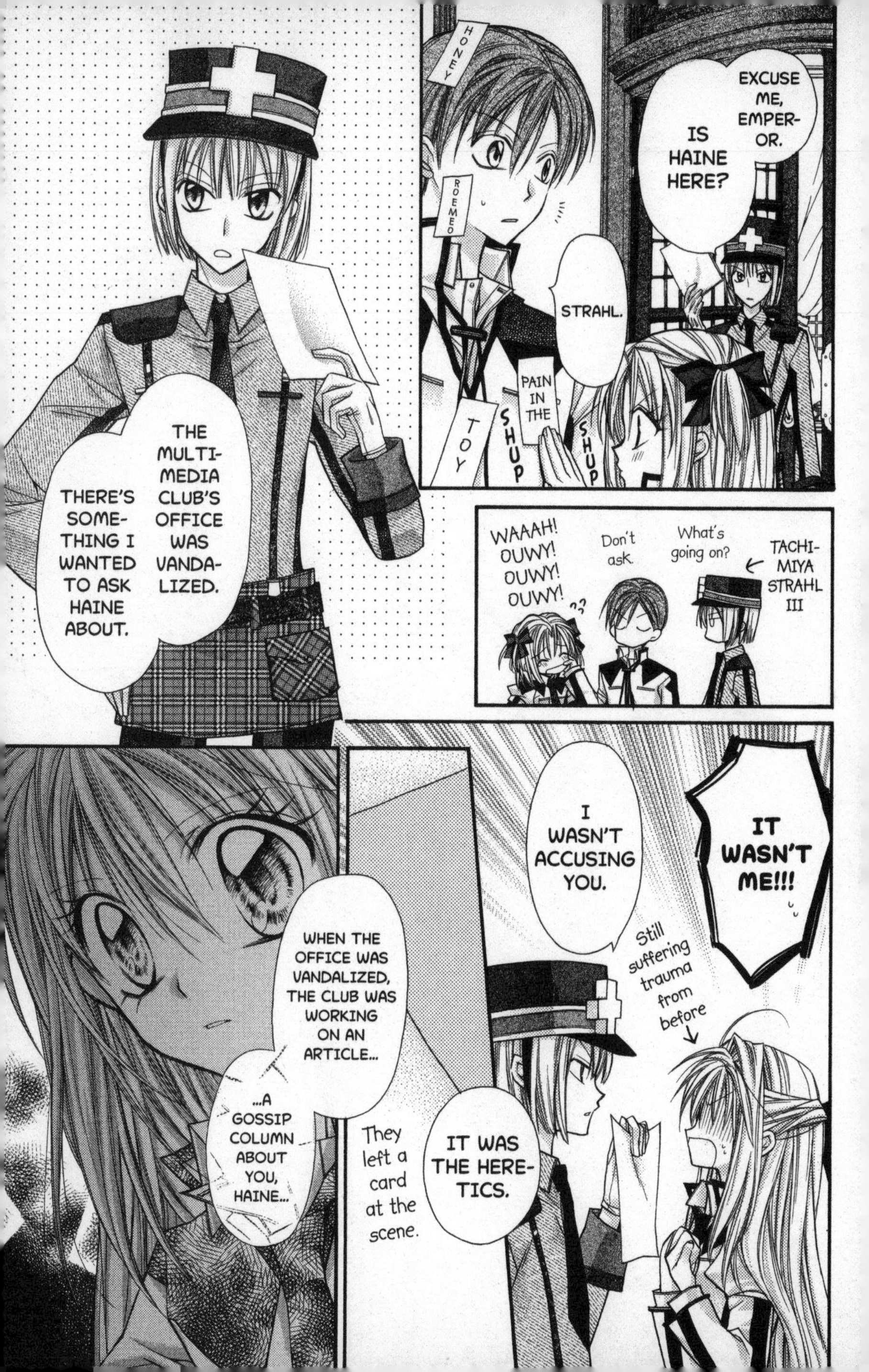
EXCUSE ME, EMPEROR.
IS HAINE HERE?
HONEY
ROEMED
STRAHL.
PAIN IN THE
TOY
SHUP
SHUP
TACHIMIYA STRAHL III
What's going on?
Don't ask.
WAAAH! OUWY! OUWY! OUWY!
THE MULTIMEDIA CLUB'S OFFICE WAS VANDALIZED.
THERE'S SOMETHING I WANTED TO ASK HAINE ABOUT.
IT WASN'T ME!!!
I WASN'T ACCUSING YOU.
Still suffering trauma from before
IT WAS THE HERETICS.
They left a card at the scene.
WHEN THE OFFICE WAS VANDALIZED, THE CLUB WAS WORKING ON AN ARTICLE...
...A GOSSIP COLUMN ABOUT YOU, HAINE...

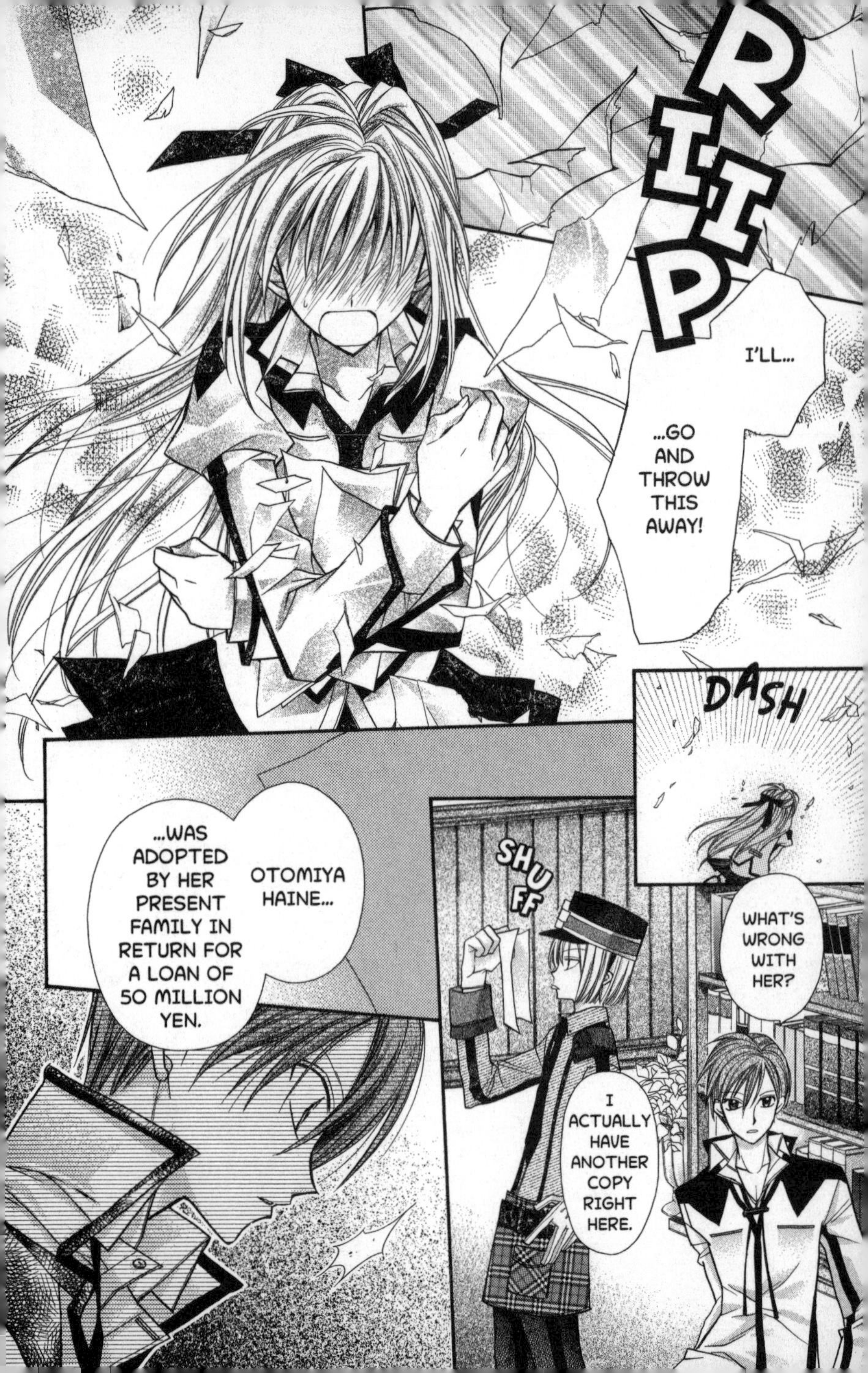
RIIP
I'LL...
...GO AND THROW THIS AWAY!
DASH
WHAT'S WRONG WITH HER?
SHUFF
I ACTUALLY HAVE ANOTHER COPY RIGHT HERE.
OTOMIYA HAINE...
...WAS ADOPTED BY HER PRESENT FAMILY IN RETURN FOR A LOAN OF 50 MILLION YEN.

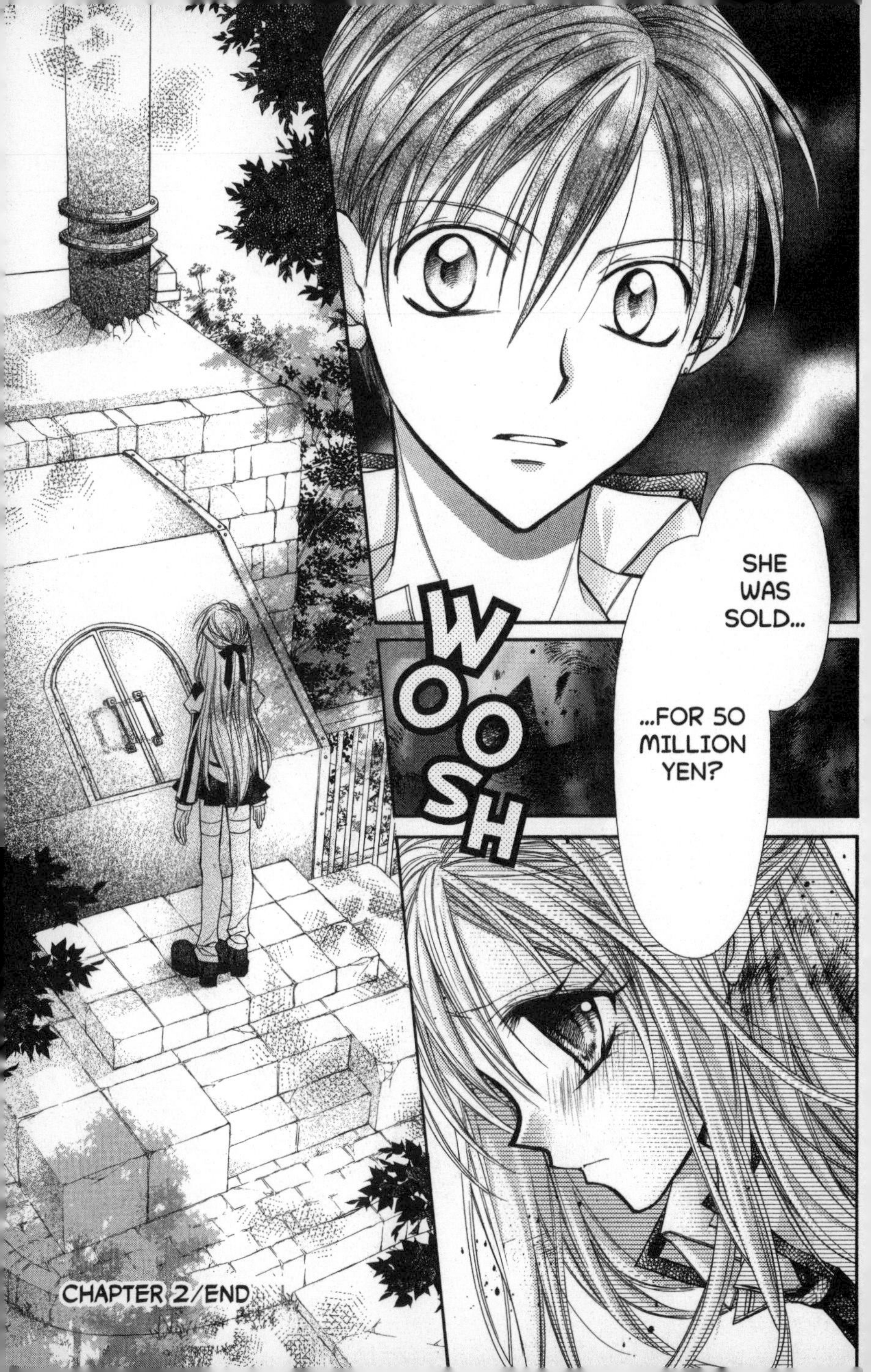
SHE WAS SOLD...
WOOSH
...FOR 50 MILLION YEN?
CHAPTER 2/END

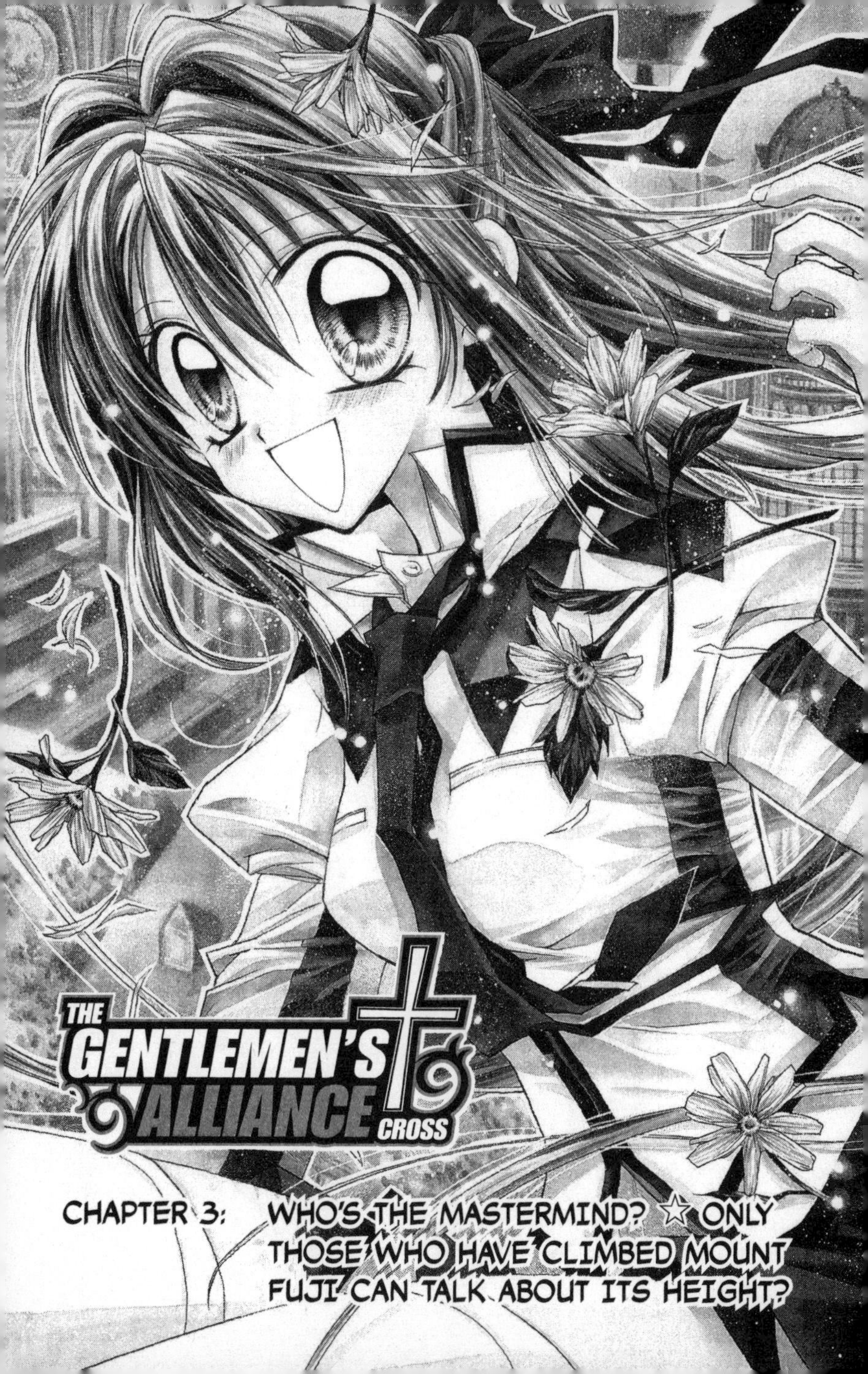
THE GENTLEMEN'S ALLIANCE CROSS
CHAPTER 3: WHO'S THE MASTERMIND? ☆ ONLY THOSE WHO HAVE CLIMBED MOUNT FUJI CAN TALK ABOUT ITS HEIGHT?

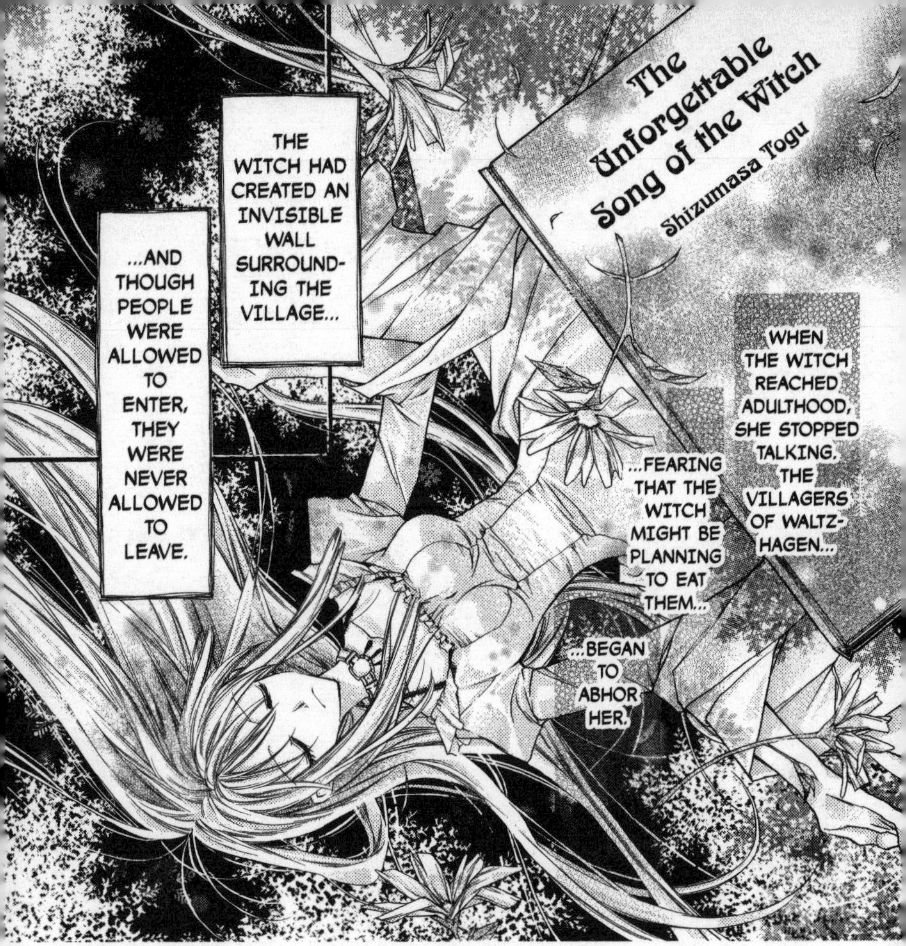
The Unforgettable Song of the Witch
Shizumasa Togu
WHEN THE WITCH REACHED ADULTHOOD, SHE STOPPED TALKING. THE VILLAGERS OF WALTZ-HAGEN...
...FEARING THAT THE WITCH MIGHT BE PLANNING TO EAT THEM...
...BEGAN TO ABHOR HER.
THE WITCH HAD CREATED AN INVISIBLE WALL SURROUNDING THE VILLAGE...
...AND THOUGH PEOPLE WERE ALLOWED TO ENTER, THEY WERE NEVER ALLOWED TO LEAVE.

Chapter 3: Who's the Mastermind? ☆ Only Those Who Have Climbed Mount Fuji Can Talk About Its Height?

"The Unforgettable Song of the Witch" at the start of this chapter is only a rough outline (I couldn't fit the whole story on three pages... Sorry.)
↑ And it would be too much of a hassle to read if it were too long.

Lead-in

To be stronger, all I have to do is think about Shizumasa-sama!

Oh, and there's one more thing. This is actually a story about Yami from *Time Stranger Kyoko*. I created this story back then, but didn't have the chance to include it in *Time Stranger Kyoko* so I decided to include it here. This story is going to provide the base for the Emperor.

Kusame and Haine make a great pair. It's very refreshing for me since I don't create many siblings in my stories. I don't draw these kinds of relationships much, but I really like them.

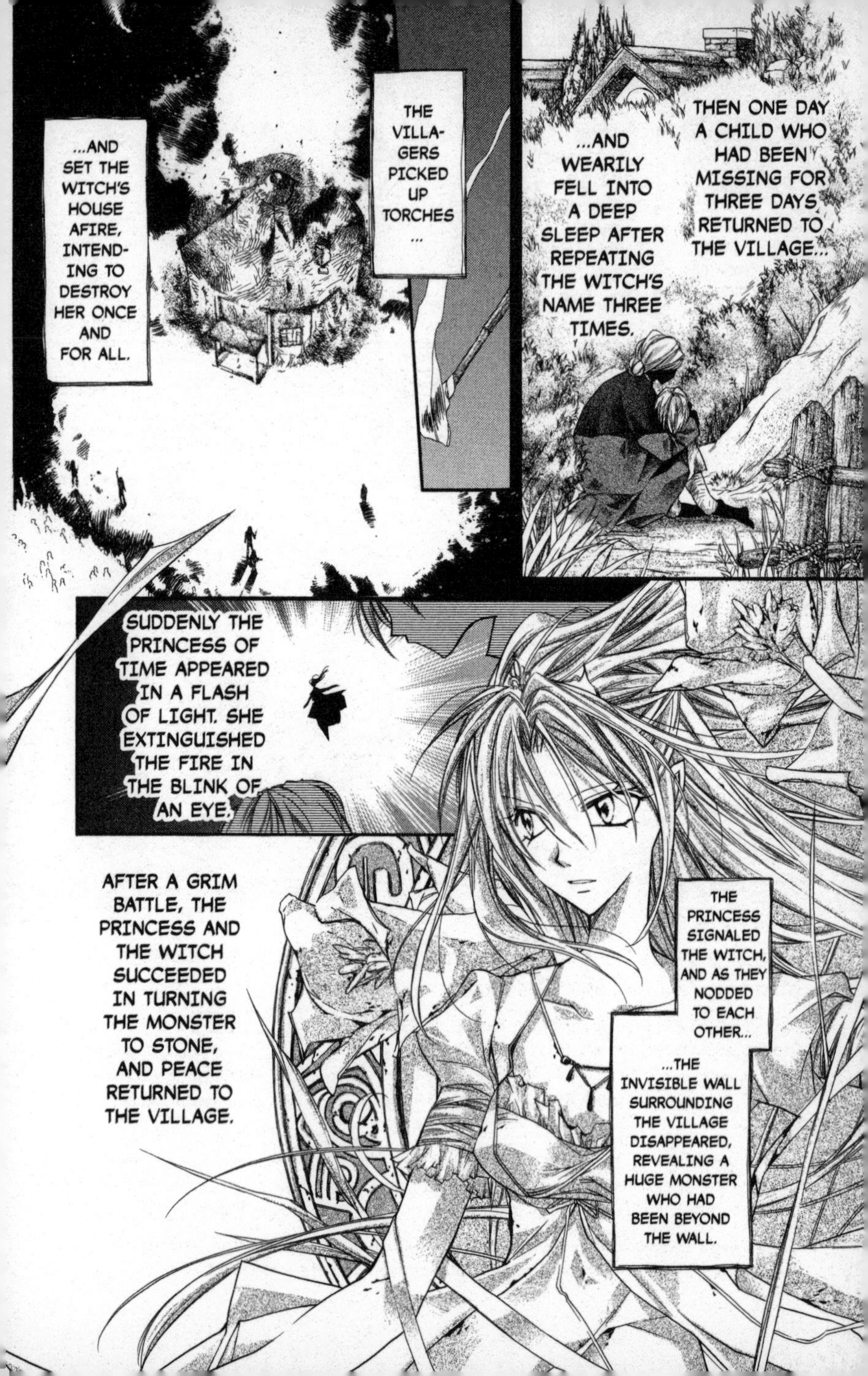
THEN ONE DAY A CHILD WHO HAD BEEN MISSING FOR THREE DAYS RETURNED TO THE VILLAGE...
...AND WEARILY FELL INTO A DEEP SLEEP AFTER REPEATING THE WITCH'S NAME THREE TIMES.
THE VILLAGERS PICKED UP TORCHES...
...AND SET THE WITCH'S HOUSE AFIRE, INTENDING TO DESTROY HER ONCE AND FOR ALL.
SUDDENLY THE PRINCESS OF TIME APPEARED IN A FLASH OF LIGHT. SHE EXTINGUISHED THE FIRE IN THE BLINK OF AN EYE.
THE PRINCESS SIGNALED THE WITCH, AND AS THEY NODDED TO EACH OTHER...
...THE INVISIBLE WALL SURROUNDING THE VILLAGE DISAPPEARED, REVEALING A HUGE MONSTER WHO HAD BEEN BEYOND THE WALL.
AFTER A GRIM BATTLE, THE PRINCESS AND THE WITCH SUCCEEDED IN TURNING THE MONSTER TO STONE, AND PEACE RETURNED TO THE VILLAGE.

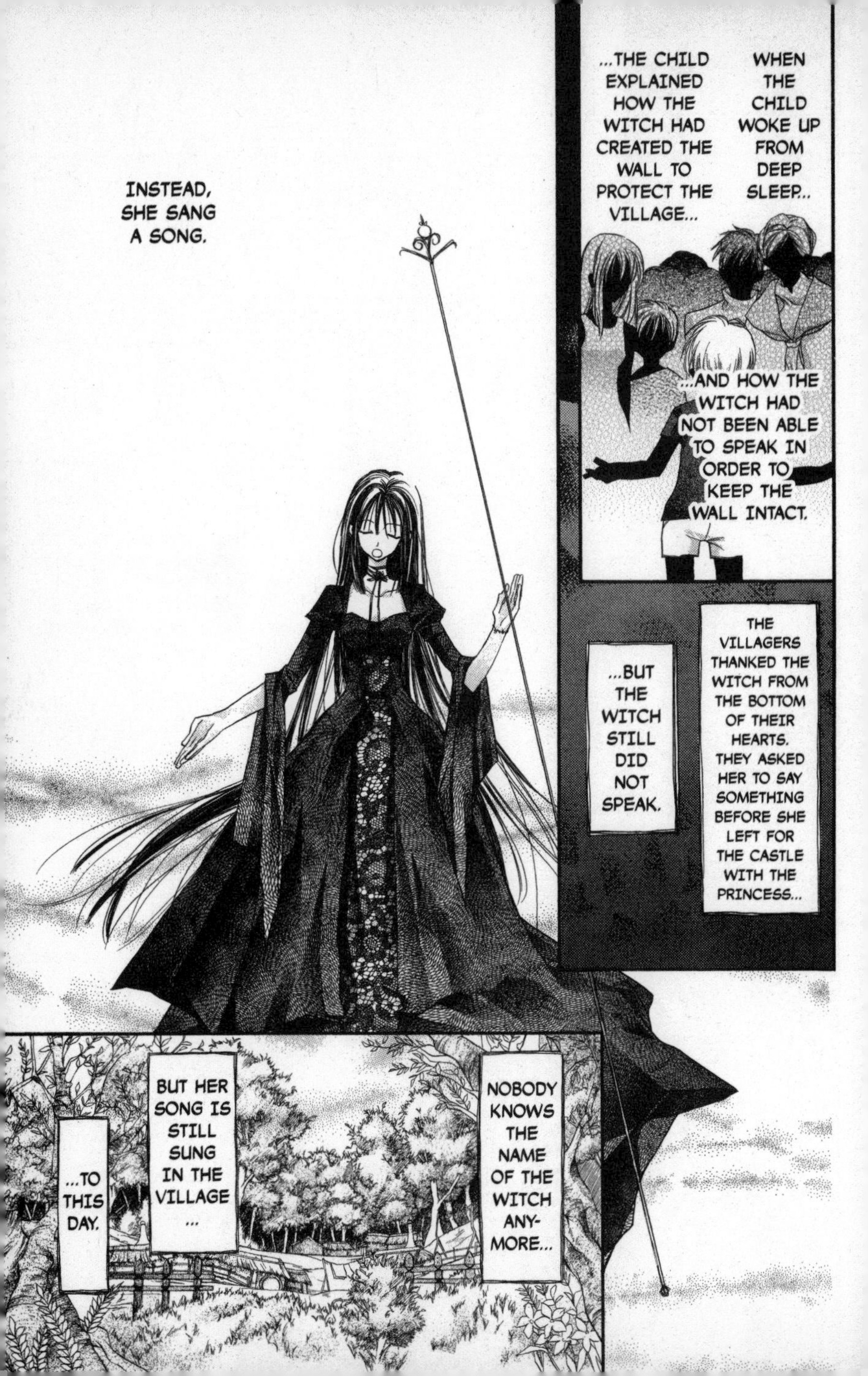
WHEN THE CHILD WOKE UP FROM DEEP SLEEP...
...THE CHILD EXPLAINED HOW THE WITCH HAD CREATED THE WALL TO PROTECT THE VILLAGE...
...AND HOW THE WITCH HAD NOT BEEN ABLE TO SPEAK IN ORDER TO KEEP THE WALL INTACT.
THE VILLAGERS THANKED THE WITCH FROM THE BOTTOM OF THEIR HEARTS. THEY ASKED HER TO SAY SOMETHING BEFORE SHE LEFT FOR THE CASTLE WITH THE PRINCESS...
...BUT THE WITCH STILL DID NOT SPEAK.
INSTEAD, SHE SANG A SONG.
NOBODY KNOWS THE NAME OF THE WITCH ANY-MORE...
BUT HER SONG IS STILL SUNG IN THE VILLAGE ...
...TO THIS DAY.

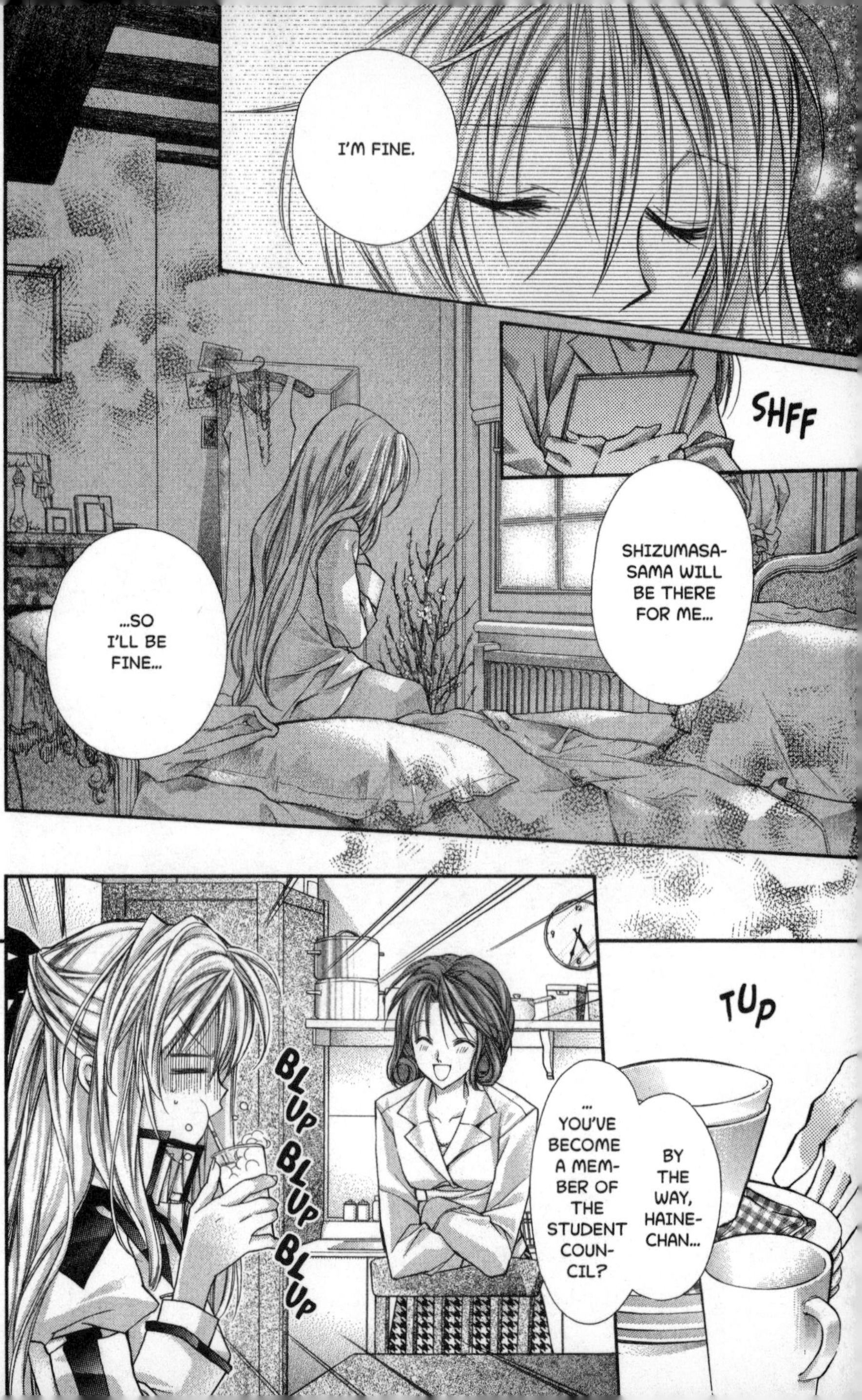
I'M FINE.
SHFF
SHIZUMASA-SAMA WILL BE THERE FOR ME...
...SO I'LL BE FINE...
TUP
BY THE WAY, HAINE-CHAN...
... YOU'VE BECOME A MEMBER OF THE STUDENT COUNCIL?
BLUP BLUP BLUP BLUP

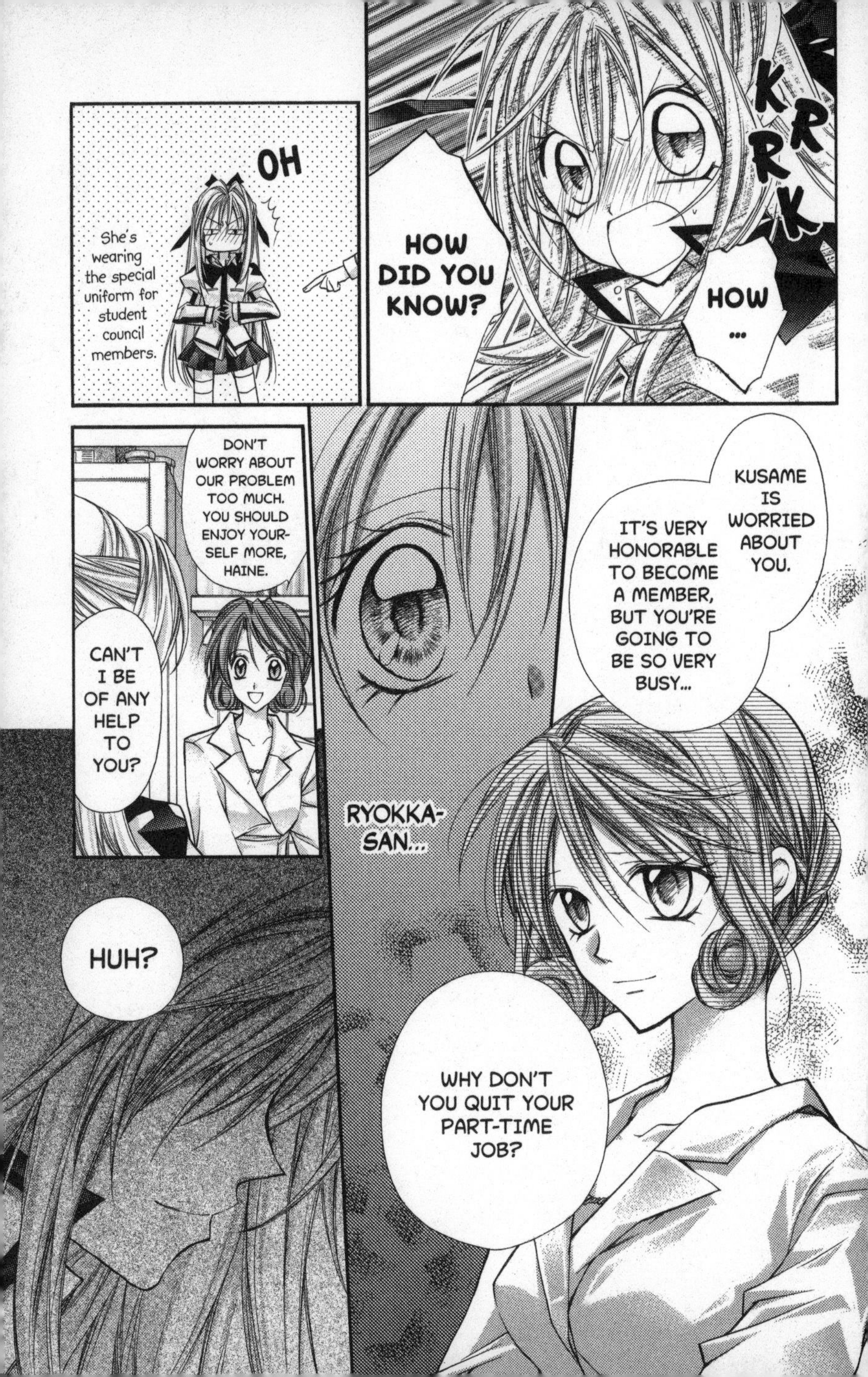
KRRK
HOW...
HOW DID YOU KNOW?
OH
She's wearing the special uniform for student council members.
KUSAME IS WORRIED ABOUT YOU.
IT'S VERY HONORABLE TO BECOME A MEMBER, BUT YOU'RE GOING TO BE SO VERY BUSY...
WHY DON'T YOU QUIT YOUR PART-TIME JOB?
RYOKKA-SAN...
DON'T WORRY ABOUT OUR PROBLEM TOO MUCH. YOU SHOULD ENJOY YOURSELF MORE, HAINE.
CAN'T I BE OF ANY HELP TO YOU?
HUH?

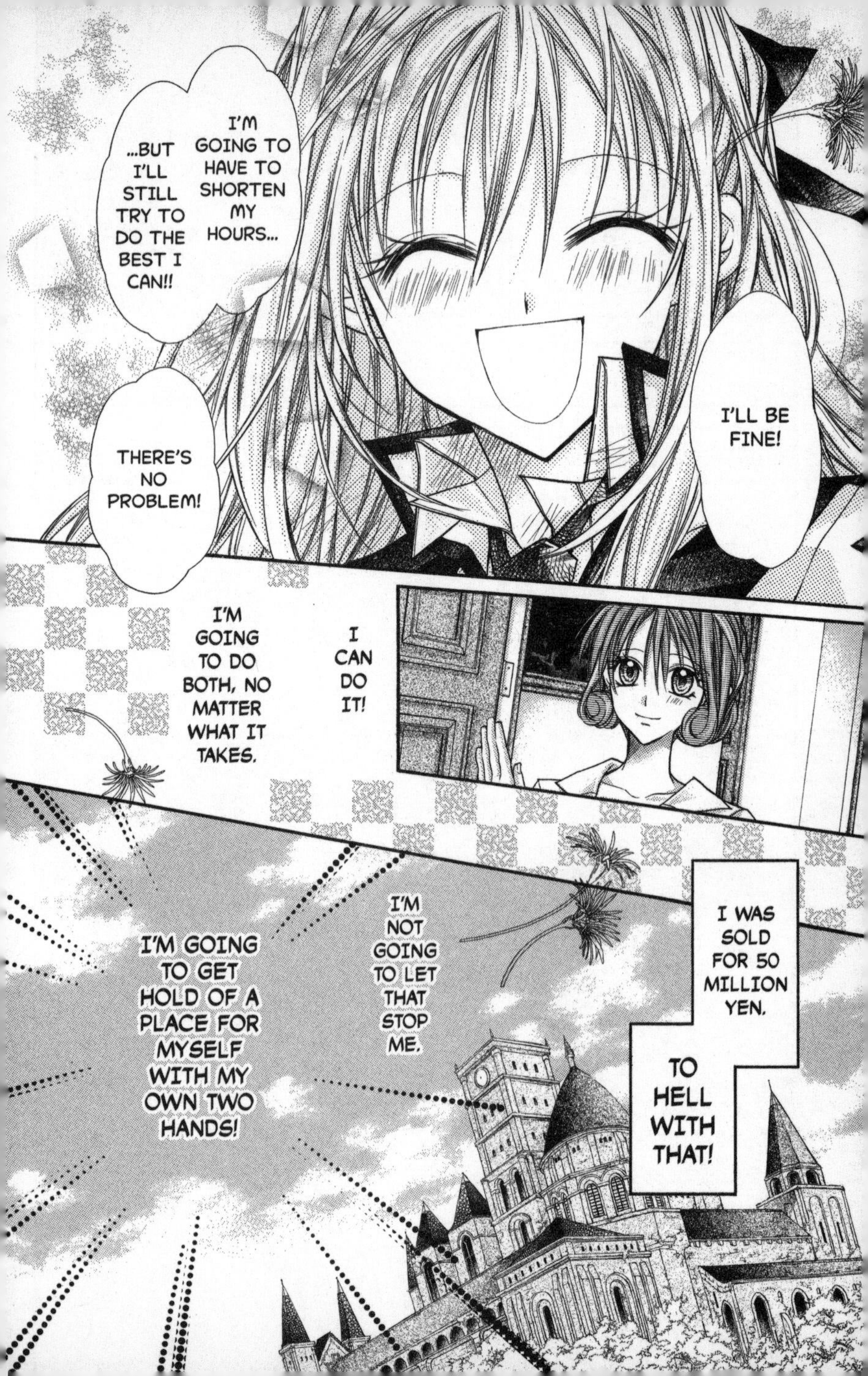
I'LL BE FINE!
I'M GOING TO HAVE TO SHORTEN MY HOURS...
...BUT I'LL STILL TRY TO DO THE BEST I CAN!!
THERE'S NO PROBLEM!
I CAN DO IT!
I'M GOING TO DO BOTH, NO MATTER WHAT IT TAKES.
I WAS SOLD FOR 50 MILLION YEN.
TO HELL WITH THAT!
I'M NOT GOING TO LET THAT STOP ME.
I'M GOING TO GET HOLD OF A PLACE FOR MYSELF WITH MY OWN TWO HANDS!

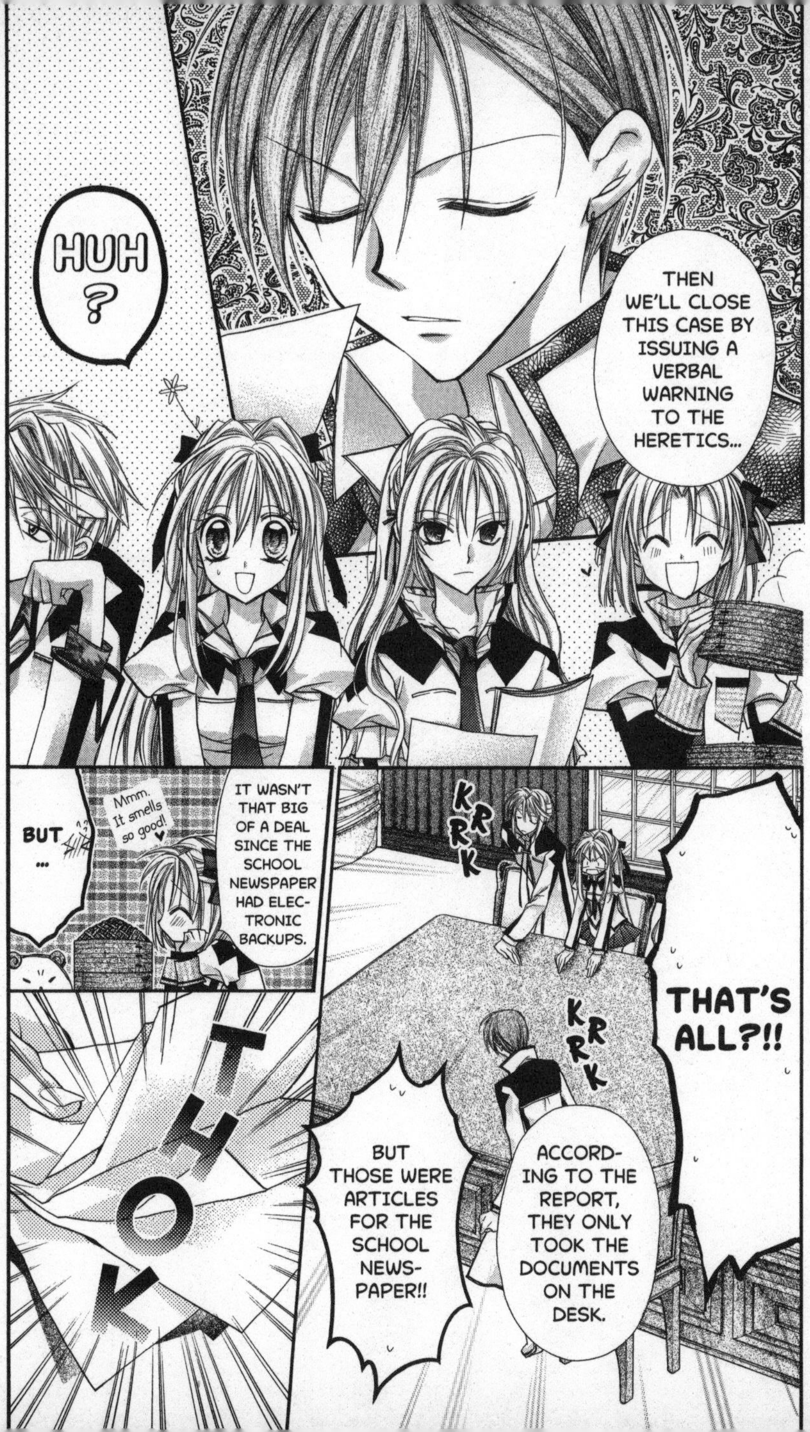
THEN WE'LL CLOSE THIS CASE BY ISSUING A VERBAL WARNING TO THE HERETICS...
HUH ?
KRRK
THAT'S ALL?!!
KRRK
ACCORD-ING TO THE REPORT, THEY ONLY TOOK THE DOCUMENTS ON THE DESK.
BUT THOSE WERE ARTICLES FOR THE SCHOOL NEWS-PAPER!!
IT WASN'T THAT BIG OF A DEAL SINCE THE SCHOOL NEWSPAPER HAD ELEC-TRONIC BACKUPS.
Mmm. It smells so good! ♥
BUT ...
THOK

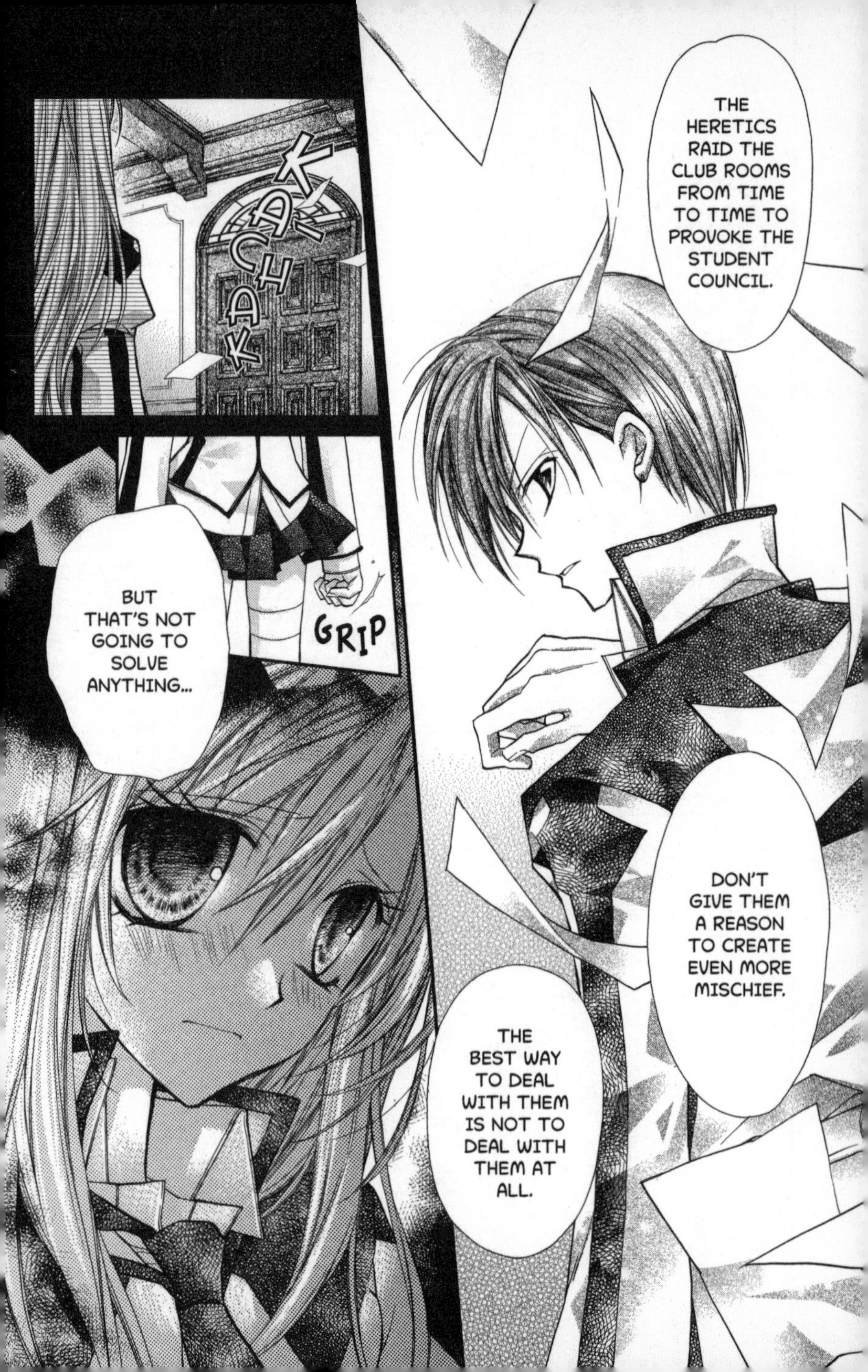
THE HERETICS RAID THE CLUB ROOMS FROM TIME TO TIME TO PROVOKE THE STUDENT COUNCIL.
DON'T GIVE THEM A REASON TO CREATE EVEN MORE MISCHIEF.
THE BEST WAY TO DEAL WITH THEM IS NOT TO DEAL WITH THEM AT ALL.
KACHAK
GRIP
BUT THAT'S NOT GOING TO SOLVE ANYTHING...

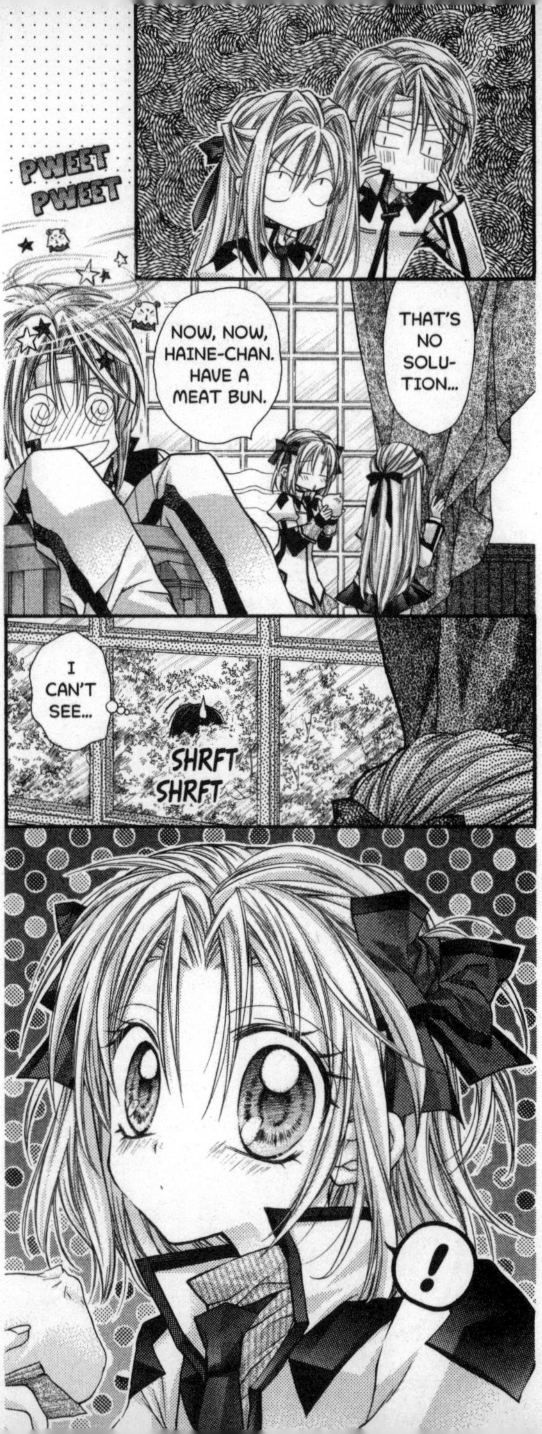
PWEET
PWEET
THAT'S NO SOLU-TION...
NOW, NOW, HAINE-CHAN. HAVE A MEAT BUN.
I CAN'T SEE...
SHRFT
SHRFT
!

Maguri Tsujimiya

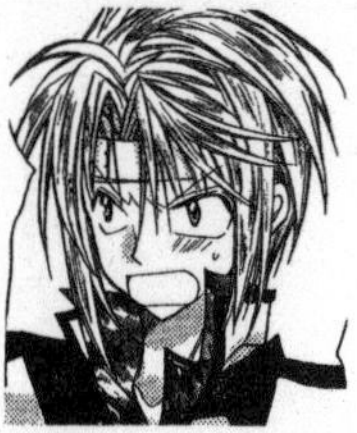

Birthday: November 3
Blood Type: A

Maguri is gay.
He's deeply in love with Shizun (Shizumasa), and he's also the happy-go-lucky vice president.
His family is in the yakuza.
Did you notice he's got a bandage around his head because he's wounded all the time? (This is only meant as a gag, so I might use it in the funnies in the back.)

Comments

I never expected to include a gay guy in my manga...!! (By the way, I'm not interested in those kinds of manga, but I did draw a private version of one because my friend asked me to.)
So I'm really surprised to have him in this!! But that doesn't mean I hate him or anything.
I just wanted to try out many kinds of characters.
Also, since I'm not really interested in that kind of manga, I probably am able to present him in a much lighter context.
Well, I am a professional, so I try not to fill the stories with only my favorite things.
But it's a lot of fun. He's something completely outside of my usual realm of knowledge.
It's very invigorating for me.

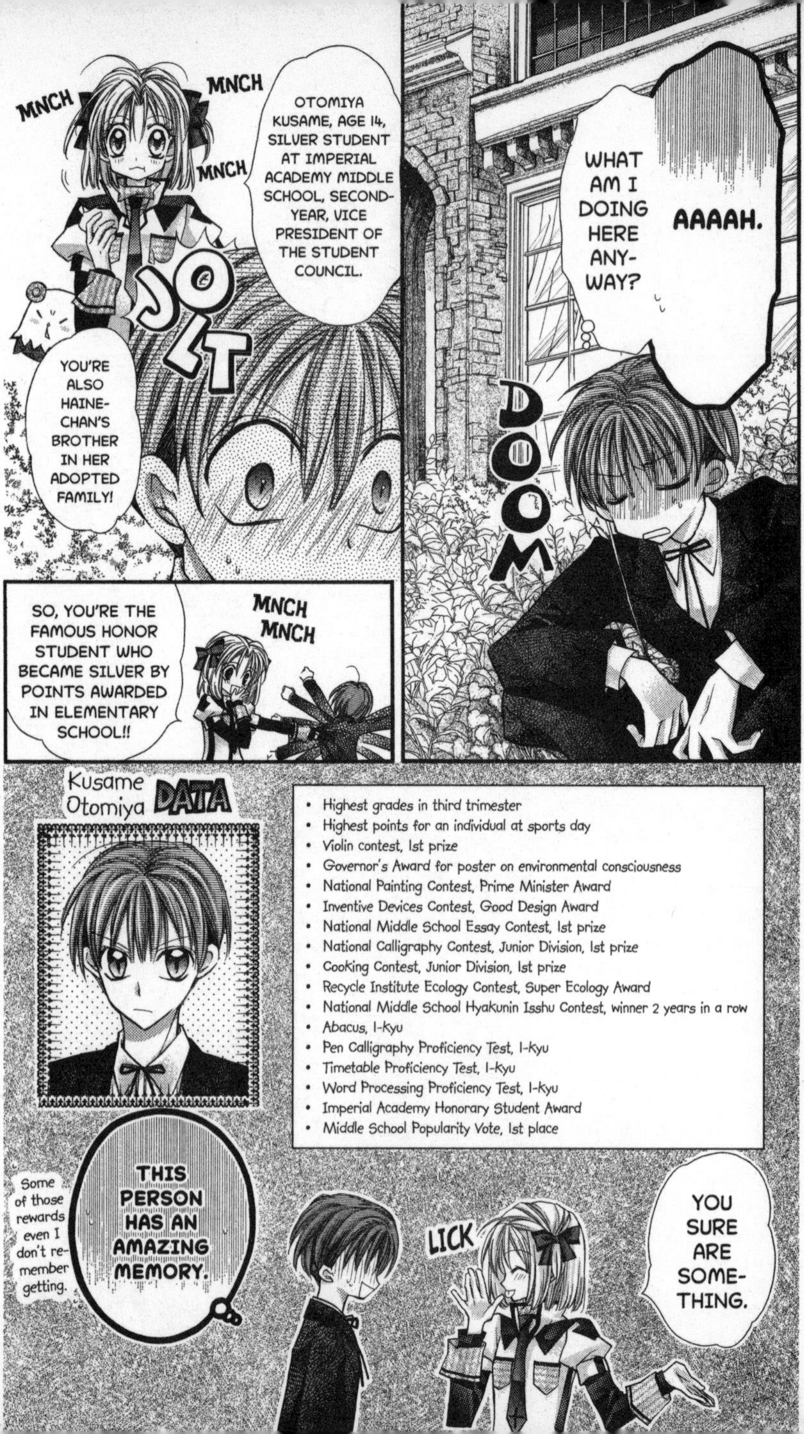
WHAT AM I DOING HERE ANY-WAY?
AAAAH.
DOOOM
MNCH
OTOMIYA KUSAME, AGE 14, SILVER STUDENT AT IMPERIAL ACADEMY MIDDLE SCHOOL, SECOND-YEAR, VICE PRESIDENT OF THE STUDENT COUNCIL.
MNCH
MNCH
JOLT
YOU'RE ALSO HAINE-CHAN'S BROTHER IN HER ADOPTED FAMILY!
MNCH MNCH
SO, YOU'RE THE FAMOUS HONOR STUDENT WHO BECAME SILVER BY POINTS AWARDED IN ELEMENTARY SCHOOL!!
Kusame Otomiya DATA
• Highest grades in third trimester
• Highest points for an individual at sports day
• Violin contest, 1st prize
• Governor's Award for poster on environmental consciousness
• National Painting Contest, Prime Minister Award
• Inventive Devices Contest, Good Design Award
• National Middle School Essay Contest, 1st prize
• National Calligraphy Contest, Junior Division, 1st prize
• Cooking Contest, Junior Division, 1st prize
• Recycle Institute Ecology Contest, Super Ecology Award
• National Middle School Hyakunin Isshu Contest, winner 2 years in a row
• Abacus, 1-Kyu
• Pen Calligraphy Proficiency Test, 1-Kyu
• Timetable Proficiency Test, 1-Kyu
• Word Processing Proficiency Test, 1-Kyu
• Imperial Academy Honorary Student Award
• Middle School Popularity Vote, 1st place
YOU SURE ARE SOME-THING.
LICK
THIS PERSON HAS AN AMAZING MEMORY.
Some of those rewards even I don't re-member getting.

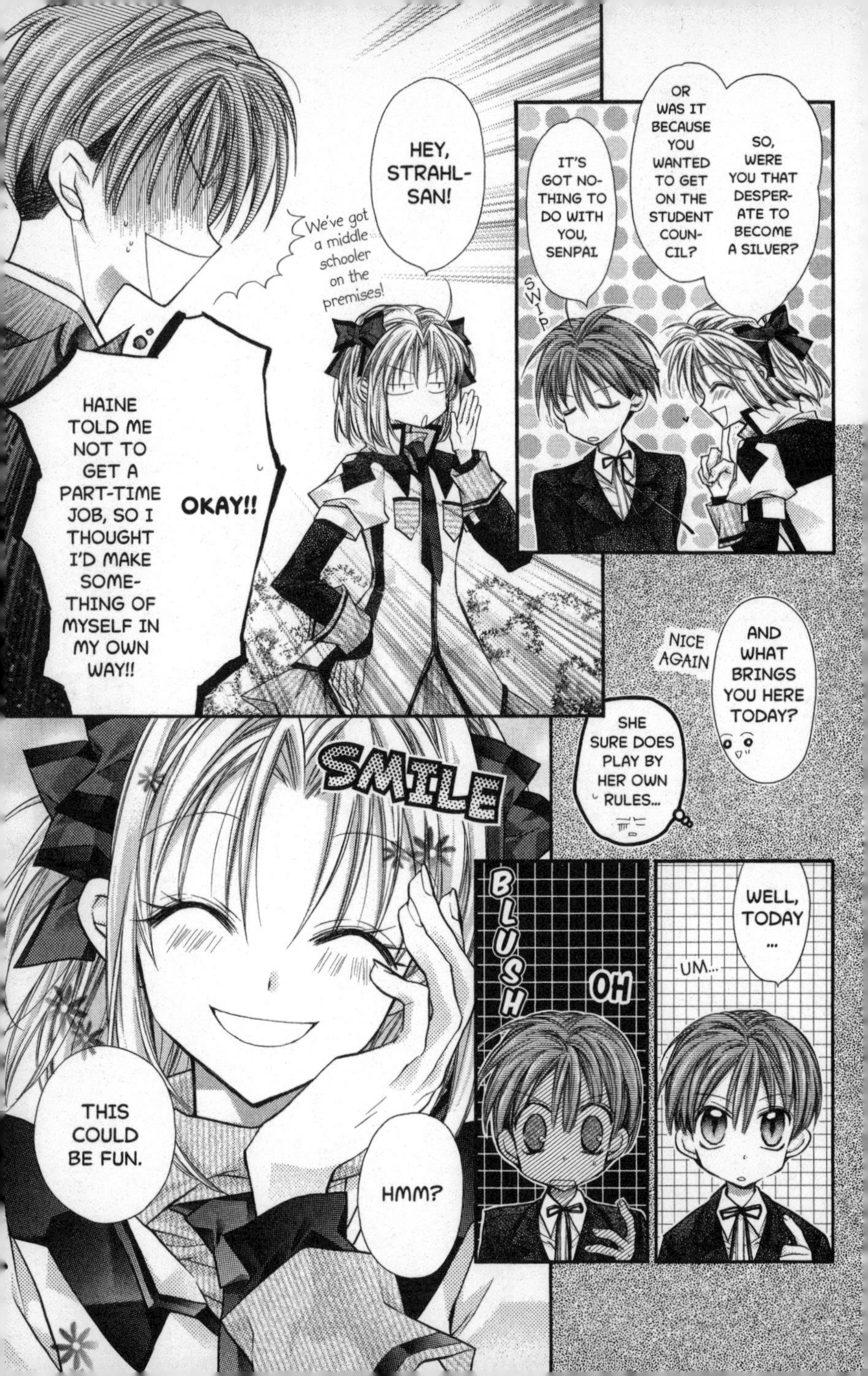
SO, WERE YOU THAT DESPERATE TO BECOME A SILVER?
OR WAS IT BECAUSE YOU WANTED TO GET ON THE STUDENT COUNCIL?
IT'S GOT NOTHING TO DO WITH YOU, SENPAI
SWIP
AND WHAT BRINGS YOU HERE TODAY?
NICE AGAIN
SHE SURE DOES PLAY BY HER OWN RULES...
HEY, STRAHL-SAN!
We've got a middle schooler on the premises!
OKAY!!
HAINE TOLD ME NOT TO GET A PART-TIME JOB, SO I THOUGHT I'D MAKE SOMETHING OF MYSELF IN MY OWN WAY!!
WELL, TODAY ...
UM...
OH
BLUSH
SMILE
HMM?
THIS COULD BE FUN.

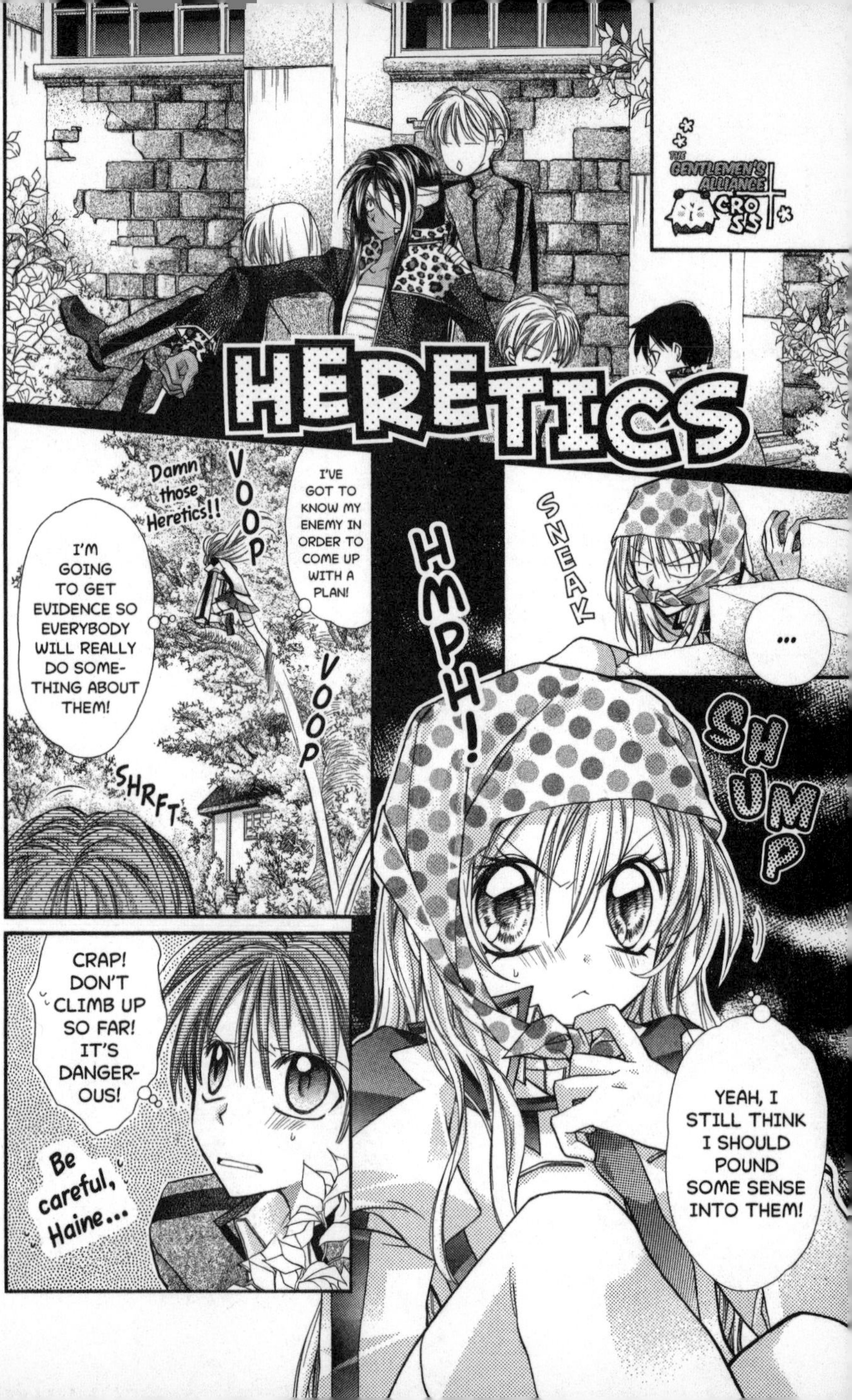

THE GENTLEMEN'S ALLIANCE CROSS
HERETICS
SNEAK
...
HMPH!
SHUMP
YEAH, I STILL THINK I SHOULD POUND SOME SENSE INTO THEM!
I'VE GOT TO KNOW MY ENEMY IN ORDER TO COME UP WITH A PLAN!
Damn those Heretics!!
VOOP
I'M GOING TO GET EVIDENCE SO EVERYBODY WILL REALLY DO SOME-THING ABOUT THEM!
VOOP
SHRFT
CRAP! DON'T CLIMB UP SO FAR! IT'S DANGER-OUS!
Be careful, Haine...

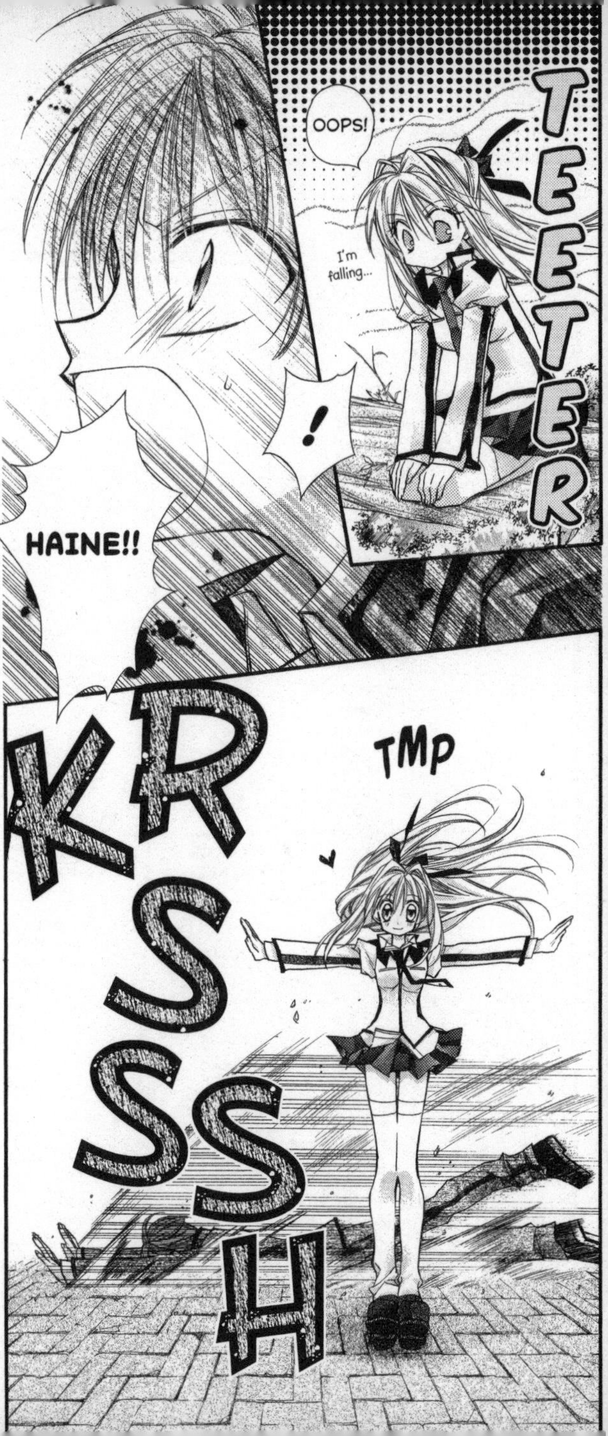
TEETER
OOPS!
I'm falling...
!
HAINE!!
TMp
KRSSSH

Toya

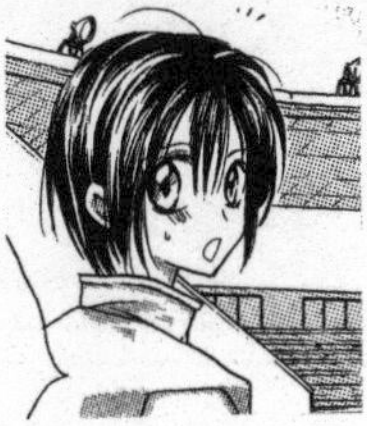

Birthday: May 31
Blood Type: A

He was an abandoned child who was saved by Shizumasa.

He's a boy who lives for Shizumasa-sama and strives to protect him.

He's determined to dedicate his life to serving him. He hopes Haine and Shizumasa-sama will become a true couple one day.

Comments

To tell the truth, this character is actually a rehash of Kagura in *Phantom Thief Jeanne.* (It's only the hairstyle that makes them look alike, but their personalities are basically the same.)

I thought it would be good to create somebody who really understands Shizumasa.

But Toya is like a part of the body to Shizun, so it doesn't mean Shizun opens up to him...

I would like Aya Hisakawa or Noriko Hidaka to do his voice...

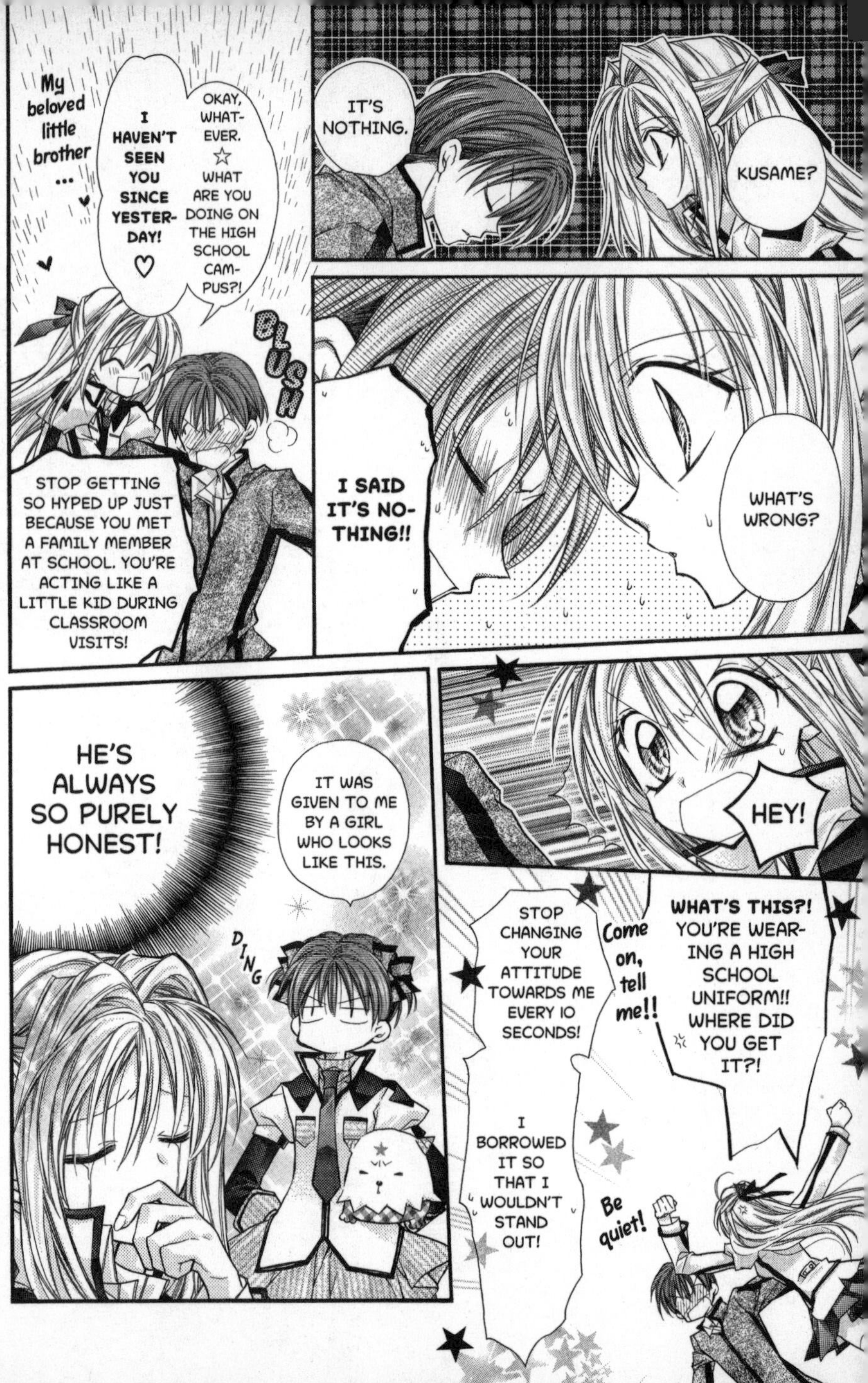
KUSAME?
IT'S NOTHING.
WHAT'S WRONG?
I SAID IT'S NOTHING!!
OKAY, WHATEVER. ☆ WHAT ARE YOU DOING ON THE HIGH SCHOOL CAMPUS?!
I HAVEN'T SEEN YOU SINCE YESTERDAY! ♡
My beloved little brother...
BLUSH
STOP GETTING SO HYPED UP JUST BECAUSE YOU MET A FAMILY MEMBER AT SCHOOL. YOU'RE ACTING LIKE A LITTLE KID DURING CLASSROOM VISITS!
HEY!
WHAT'S THIS?! YOU'RE WEARING A HIGH SCHOOL UNIFORM!! WHERE DID YOU GET IT?!
Come on, tell me!!
STOP CHANGING YOUR ATTITUDE TOWARDS ME EVERY 10 SECONDS!
I BORROWED IT SO THAT I WOULDN'T STAND OUT!
Be quiet!
IT WAS GIVEN TO ME BY A GIRL WHO LOOKS LIKE THIS.
DING
HE'S ALWAYS SO PURELY HONEST!

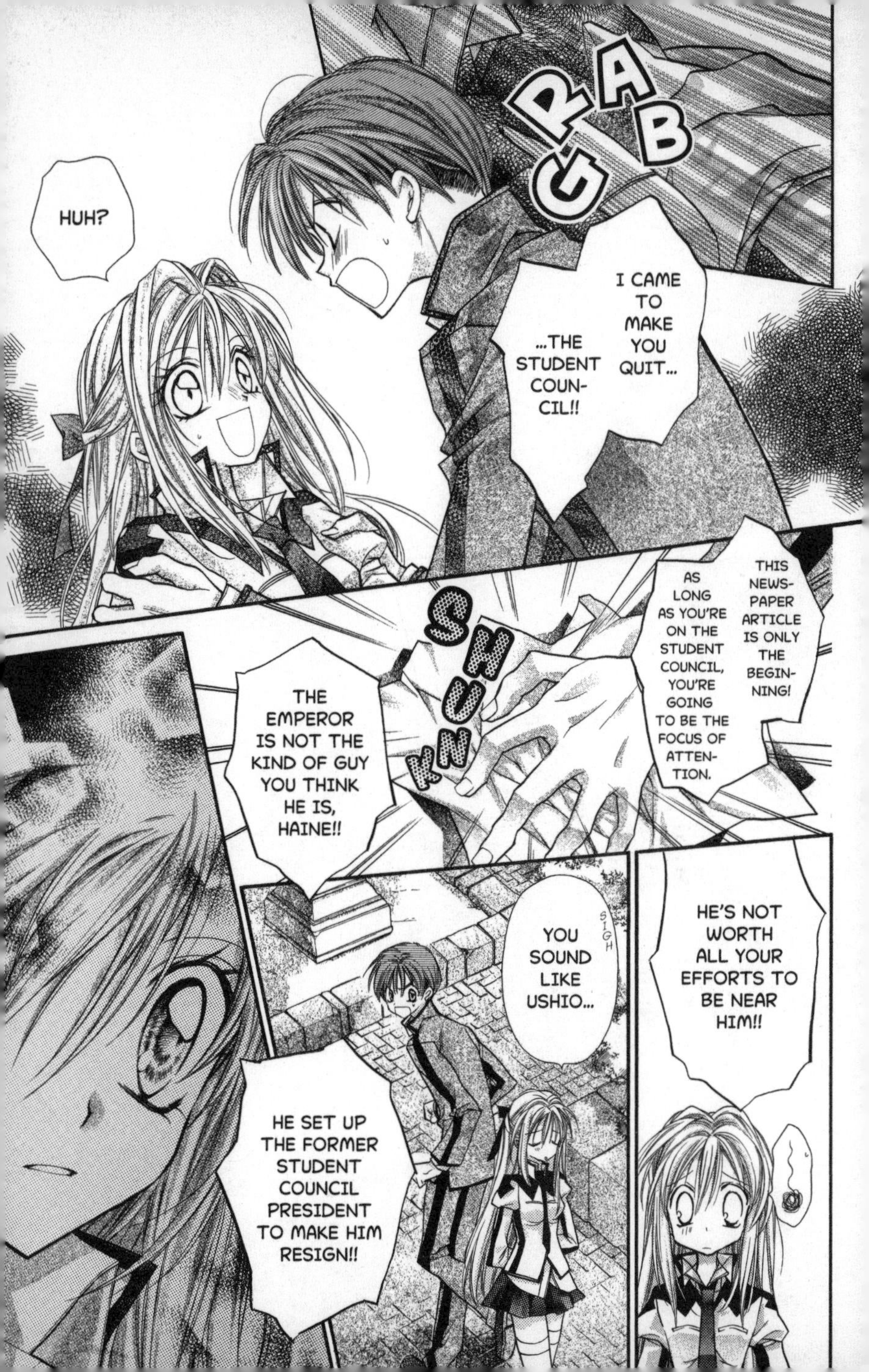
GRAB
I CAME TO MAKE YOU QUIT...
...THE STUDENT COUNCIL!!
HUH?
THIS NEWSPAPER ARTICLE IS ONLY THE BEGINNING!
AS LONG AS YOU'RE ON THE STUDENT COUNCIL, YOU'RE GOING TO BE THE FOCUS OF ATTENTION.
SHUNK
THE EMPEROR IS NOT THE KIND OF GUY YOU THINK HE IS, HAINE!!
HE SET UP THE FORMER STUDENT COUNCIL PRESIDENT TO MAKE HIM RESIGN!!
HE'S NOT WORTH ALL YOUR EFFORTS TO BE NEAR HIM!!
SIGH
YOU SOUND LIKE USHIO...

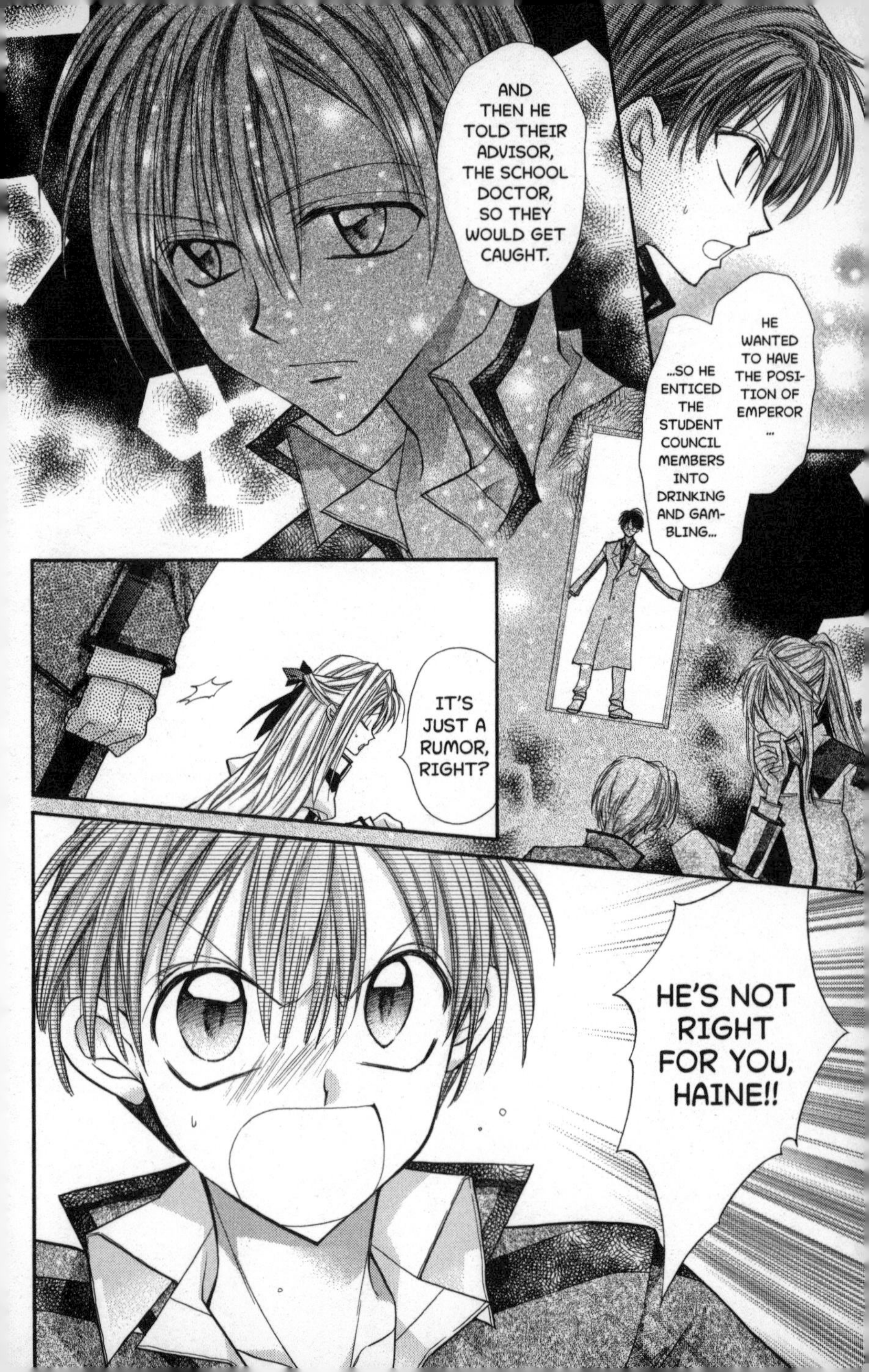
HE WANTED TO HAVE THE POSITION OF EMPEROR ...
...SO HE ENTICED THE STUDENT COUNCIL MEMBERS INTO DRINKING AND GAMBLING...
AND THEN HE TOLD THEIR ADVISOR, THE SCHOOL DOCTOR, SO THEY WOULD GET CAUGHT.
IT'S JUST A RUMOR, RIGHT?
HE'S NOT RIGHT FOR YOU, HAINE!!

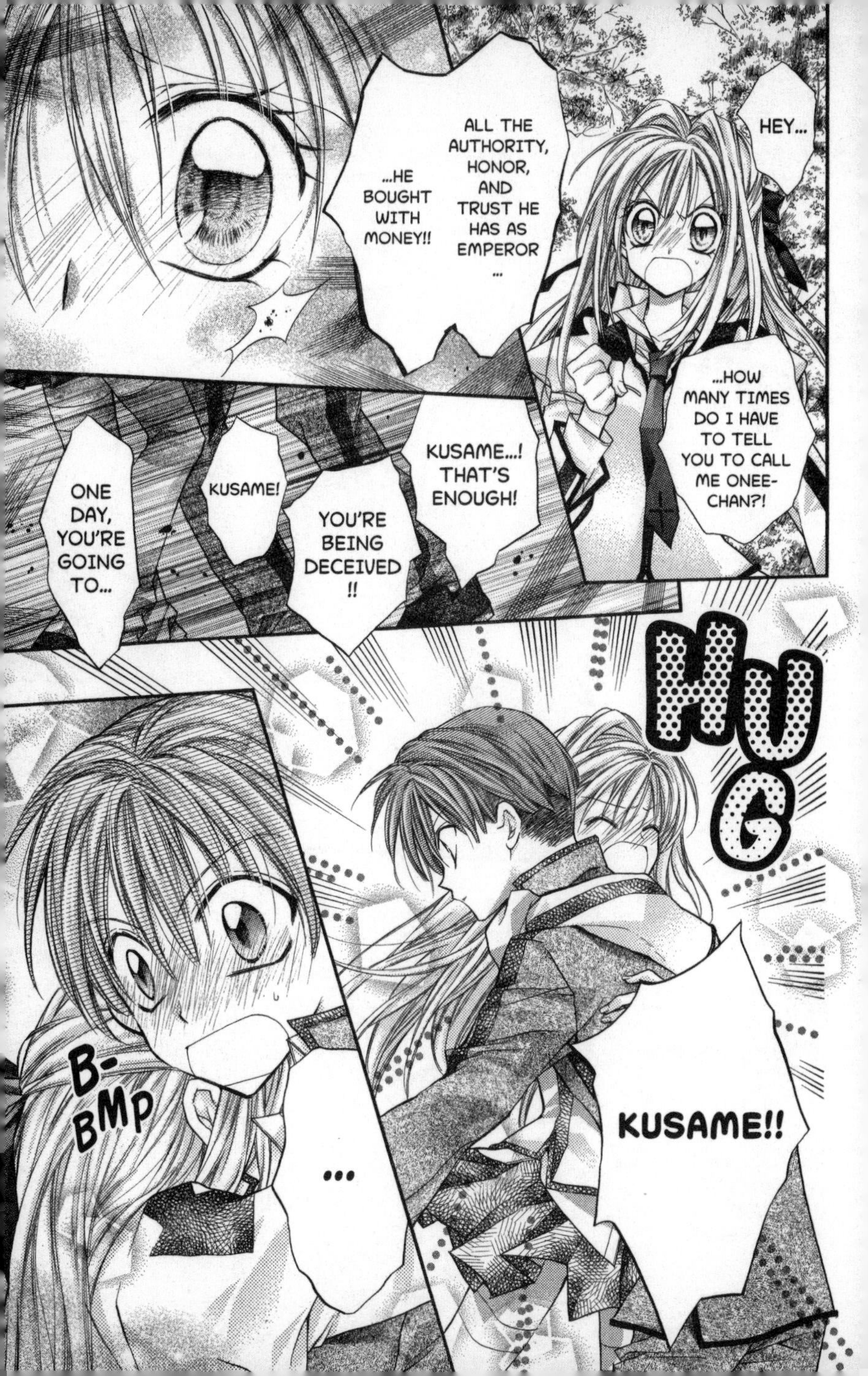
HEY...
...HOW MANY TIMES DO I HAVE TO TELL YOU TO CALL ME ONEE-CHAN?!
ALL THE AUTHORITY, HONOR, AND TRUST HE HAS AS EMPEROR...
...HE BOUGHT WITH MONEY!!
KUSAME...! THAT'S ENOUGH!
YOU'RE BEING DECEIVED!!
KUSAME!
ONE DAY, YOU'RE GOING TO...
HUG
KUSAME!!
...
B-BMP

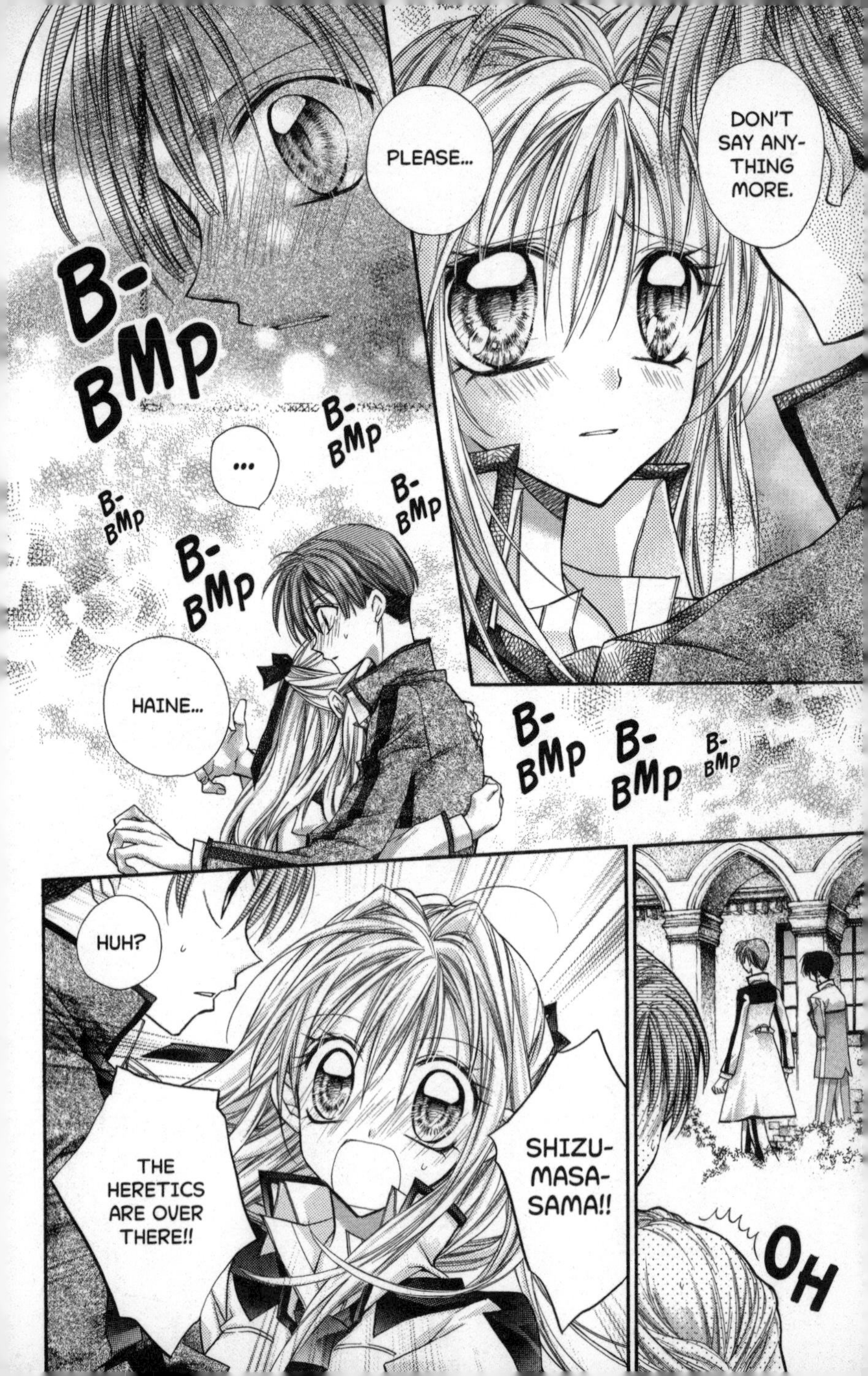
DON'T SAY ANY-THING MORE.
PLEASE...
B-BMP
...
B-BMP
B-BMP
B-BMP
B-BMP
HAINE...
B-BMP
B-BMP
B-BMP
OH
SHIZU-MASA-SAMA!!
HUH?
THE HERETICS ARE OVER THERE!!

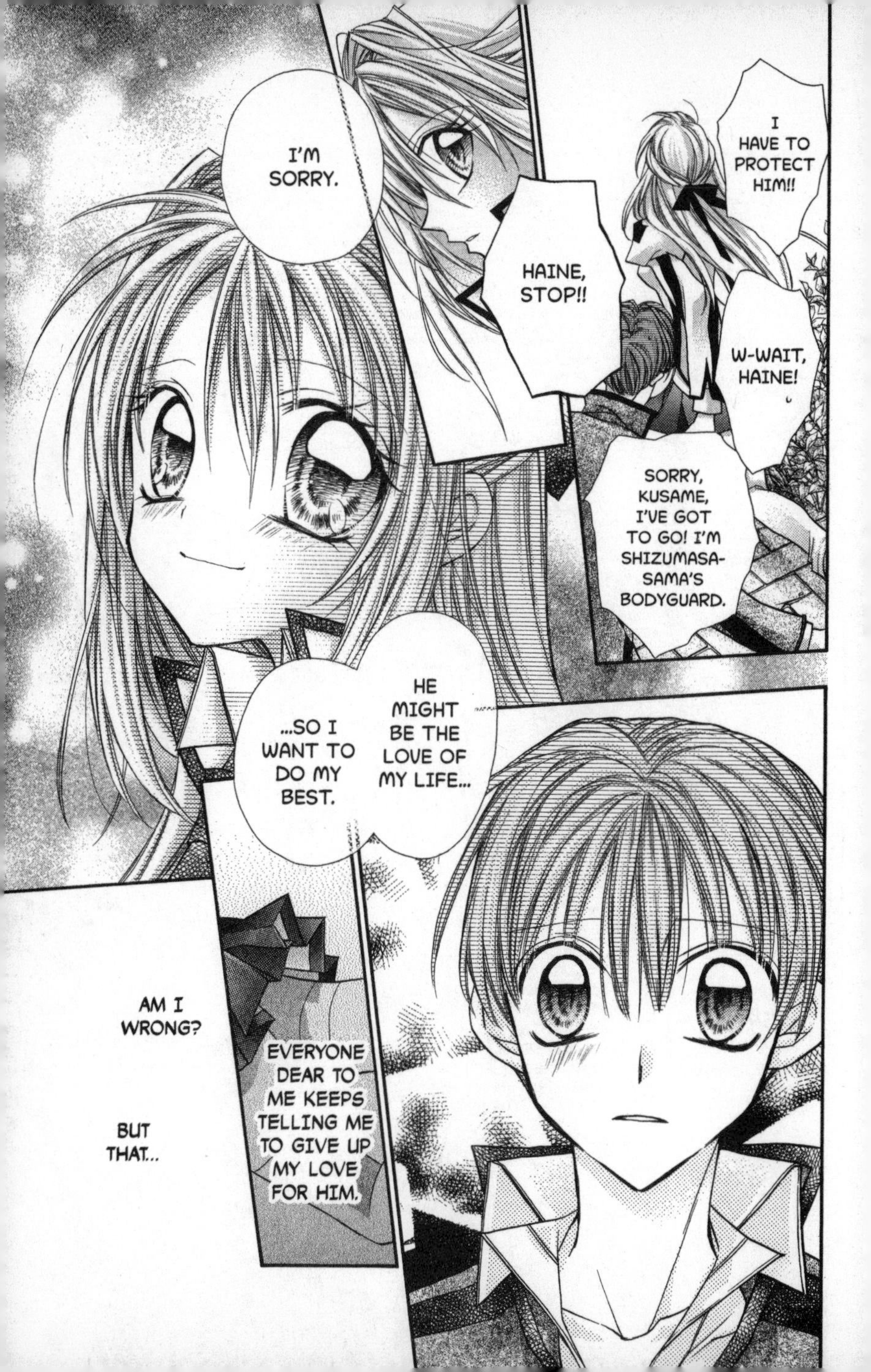
I HAVE TO PROTECT HIM!!
W-WAIT, HAINE!
SORRY, KUSAME, I'VE GOT TO GO! I'M SHIZUMASA-SAMA'S BODYGUARD.
HAINE, STOP!!
I'M SORRY.
HE MIGHT BE THE LOVE OF MY LIFE...
...SO I WANT TO DO MY BEST.
EVERYONE DEAR TO ME KEEPS TELLING ME TO GIVE UP MY LOVE FOR HIM.
AM I WRONG?
BUT THAT...

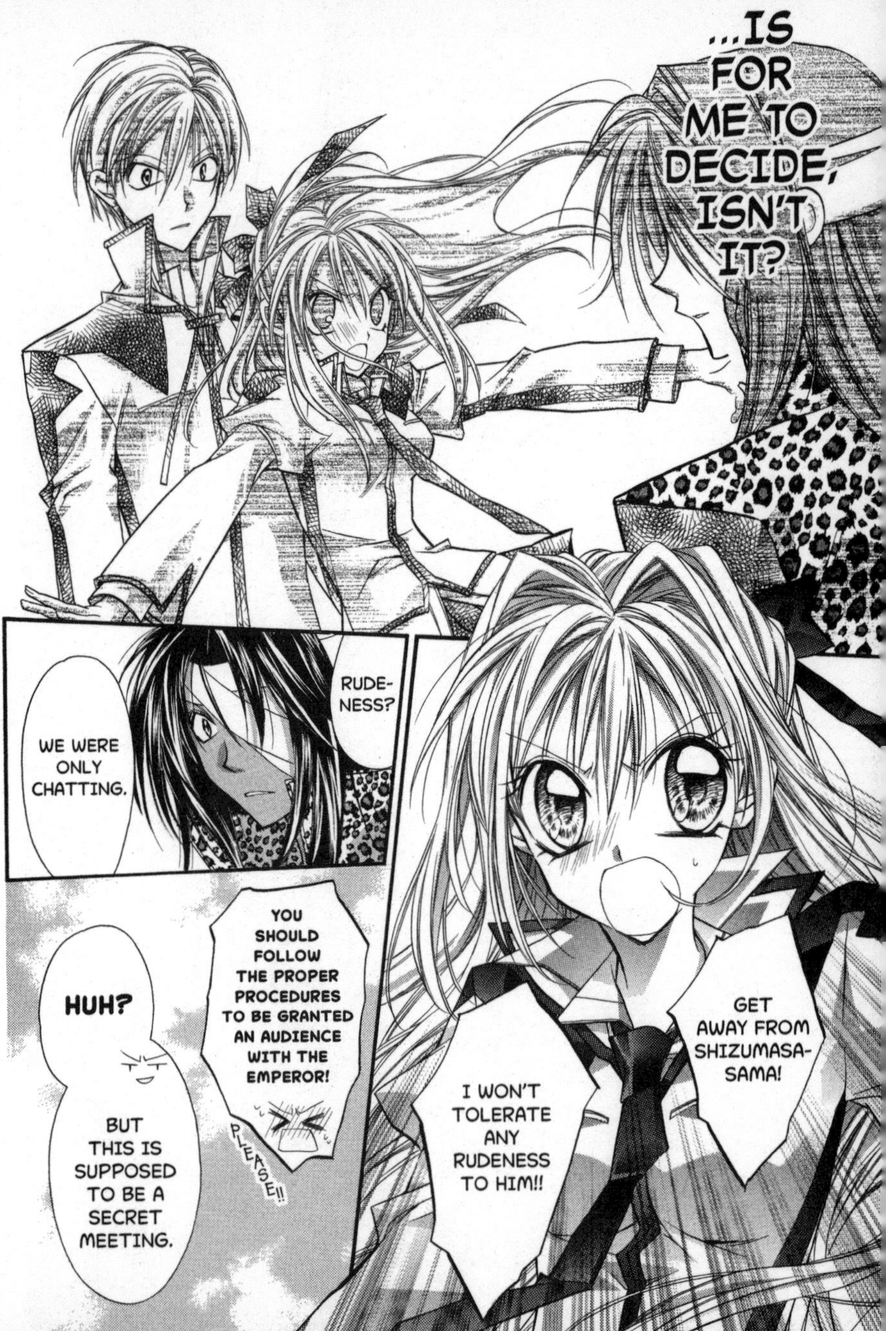
...IS FOR ME TO DECIDE, ISN'T IT?
GET AWAY FROM SHIZUMASA-SAMA!
I WON'T TOLERATE ANY RUDENESS TO HIM!!
RUDENESS?
WE WERE ONLY CHATTING.
YOU SHOULD FOLLOW THE PROPER PROCEDURES TO BE GRANTED AN AUDIENCE WITH THE EMPEROR!
PLEASE!!
HUH?
BUT THIS IS SUPPOSED TO BE A SECRET MEETING.

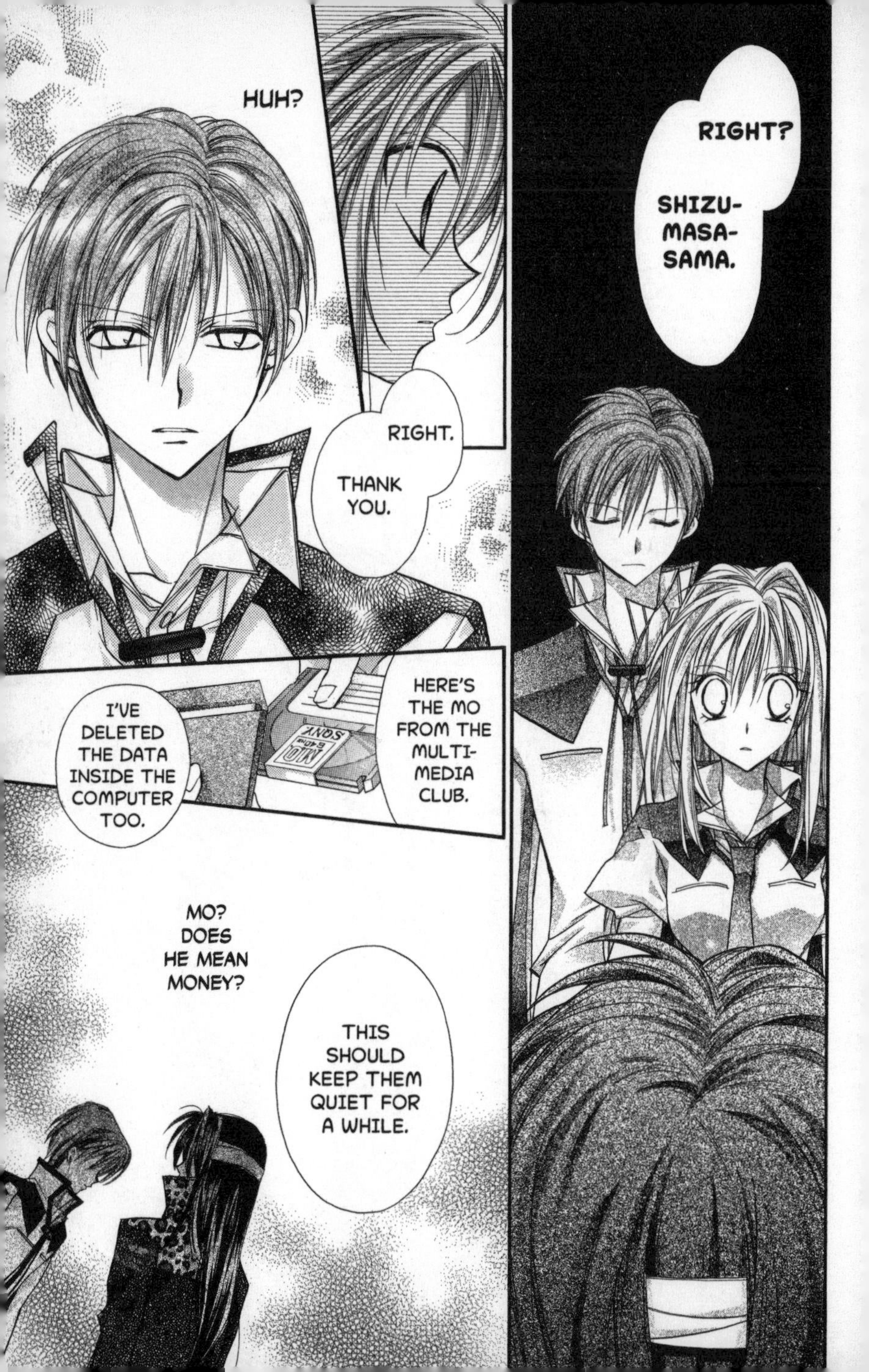
RIGHT?
SHIZU-MASA-SAMA.
RIGHT.
THANK YOU.
HUH?
HERE'S THE MO FROM THE MULTI-MEDIA CLUB.
I'VE DELETED THE DATA INSIDE THE COMPUTER TOO.
THIS SHOULD KEEP THEM QUIET FOR A WHILE.
MO? DOES HE MEAN MONEY?

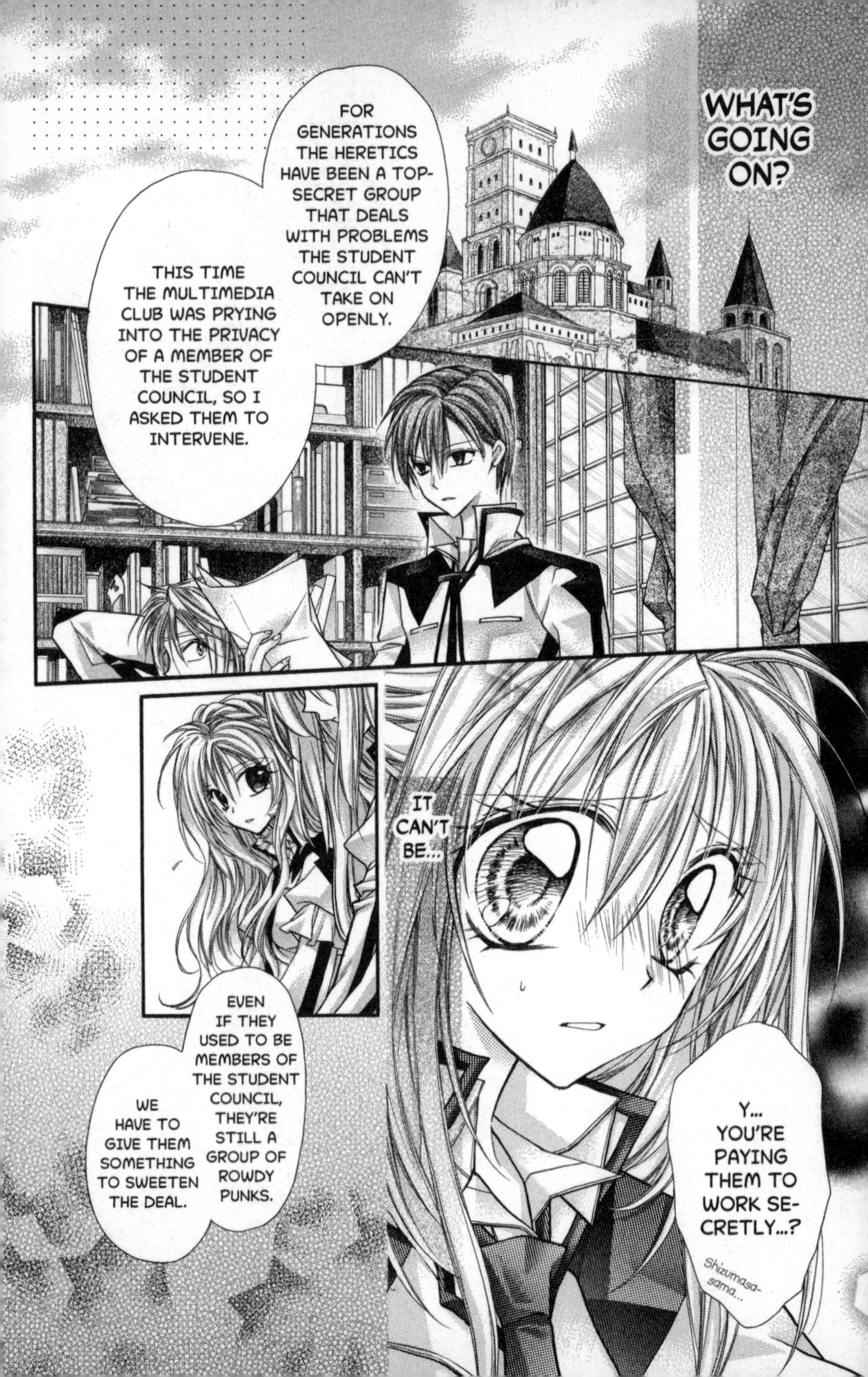
WHAT'S GOING ON?
FOR GENERATIONS THE HERETICS HAVE BEEN A TOP-SECRET GROUP THAT DEALS WITH PROBLEMS THE STUDENT COUNCIL CAN'T TAKE ON OPENLY.
THIS TIME THE MULTIMEDIA CLUB WAS PRYING INTO THE PRIVACY OF A MEMBER OF THE STUDENT COUNCIL, SO I ASKED THEM TO INTERVENE.
IT CAN'T BE...
Y... YOU'RE PAYING THEM TO WORK SE-CRETLY...?
Shizumasa-sama...
EVEN IF THEY USED TO BE MEMBERS OF THE STUDENT COUNCIL, THEY'RE STILL A GROUP OF ROWDY PUNKS.
WE HAVE TO GIVE THEM SOMETHING TO SWEETEN THE DEAL.

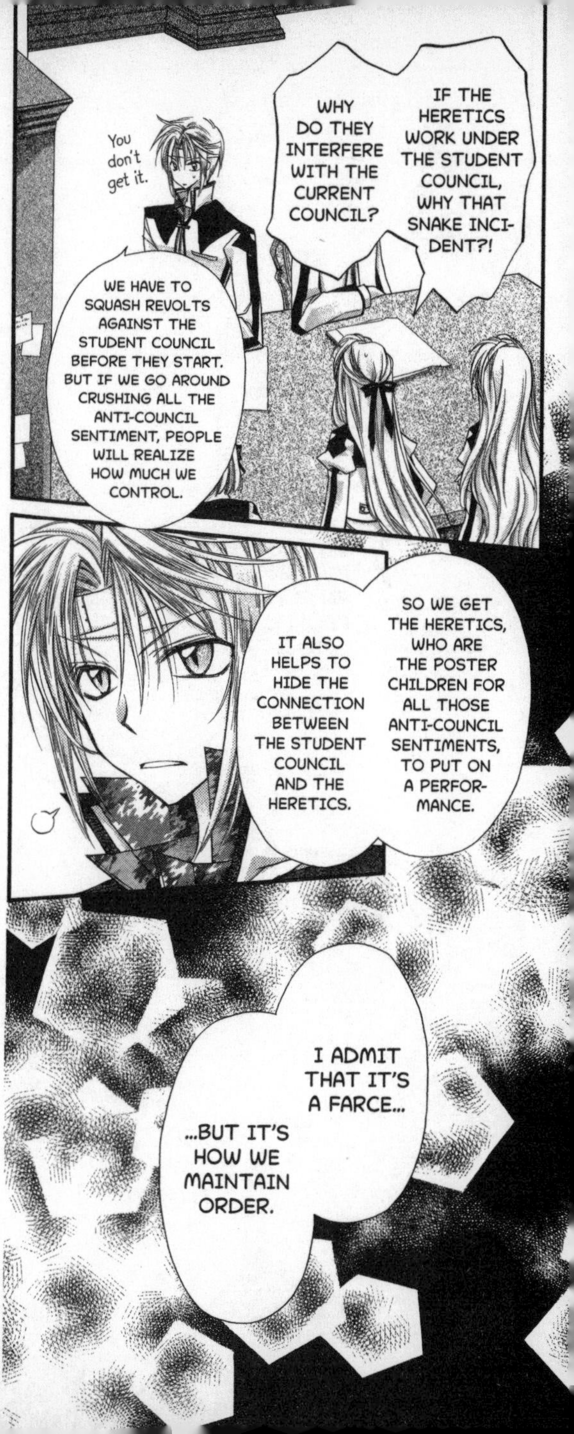

IF THE HERETICS WORK UNDER THE STUDENT COUNCIL, WHY THAT SNAKE INCI-DENT?!
WHY DO THEY INTERFERE WITH THE CURRENT COUNCIL?
You don't get it.
WE HAVE TO SQUASH REVOLTS AGAINST THE STUDENT COUNCIL BEFORE THEY START. BUT IF WE GO AROUND CRUSHING ALL THE ANTI-COUNCIL SENTIMENT, PEOPLE WILL REALIZE HOW MUCH WE CONTROL.
SO WE GET THE HERETICS, WHO ARE THE POSTER CHILDREN FOR ALL THOSE ANTI-COUNCIL SENTIMENTS, TO PUT ON A PERFOR-MANCE.
IT ALSO HELPS TO HIDE THE CONNECTION BETWEEN THE STUDENT COUNCIL AND THE HERETICS.
I ADMIT THAT IT'S A FARCE...
...BUT IT'S HOW WE MAINTAIN ORDER.

Postman

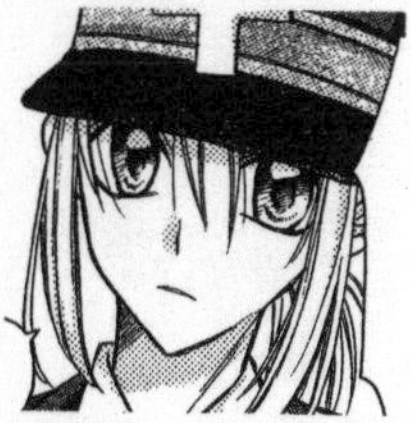

Birthday: Unknown
Blood Type: Unknown

He's the postman of love and hope who carries letters all over the academy.

He's Haine's workmate at her part-time job, and he seems to be interested in her...?

Warden

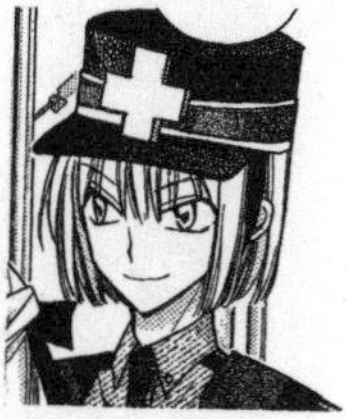

Birthday: Unknown
Blood Type: Unknown

He may be slight, but he's still the warden. (Tachimiya Strahl III)

A German-born Swiss who wears a British-style uniform (it doesn't make sense). He seems to be interested in everything, yet he's also indifferent towards everything. He's a person who is very hard to grasp.

Comments

I like these two as a set.

Come to think of it...there's a lot of people with *bobbed* hair in this series.

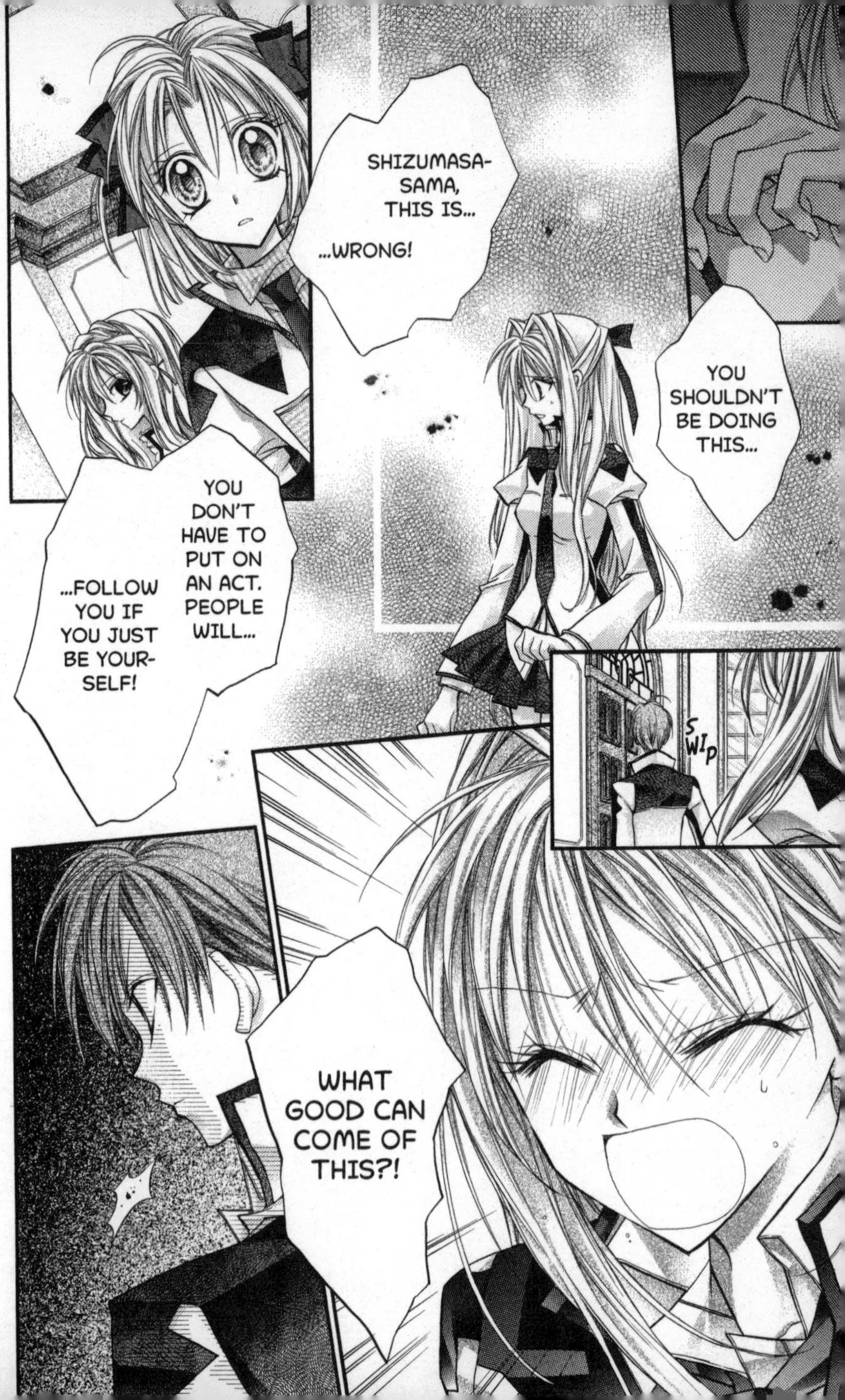
SHIZUMASA-SAMA, THIS IS... ...WRONG!
YOU SHOULDN'T BE DOING THIS...
YOU DON'T HAVE TO PUT ON AN ACT. PEOPLE WILL...
...FOLLOW YOU IF YOU JUST BE YOURSELF!
SWIP
WHAT GOOD CAN COME OF THIS?!

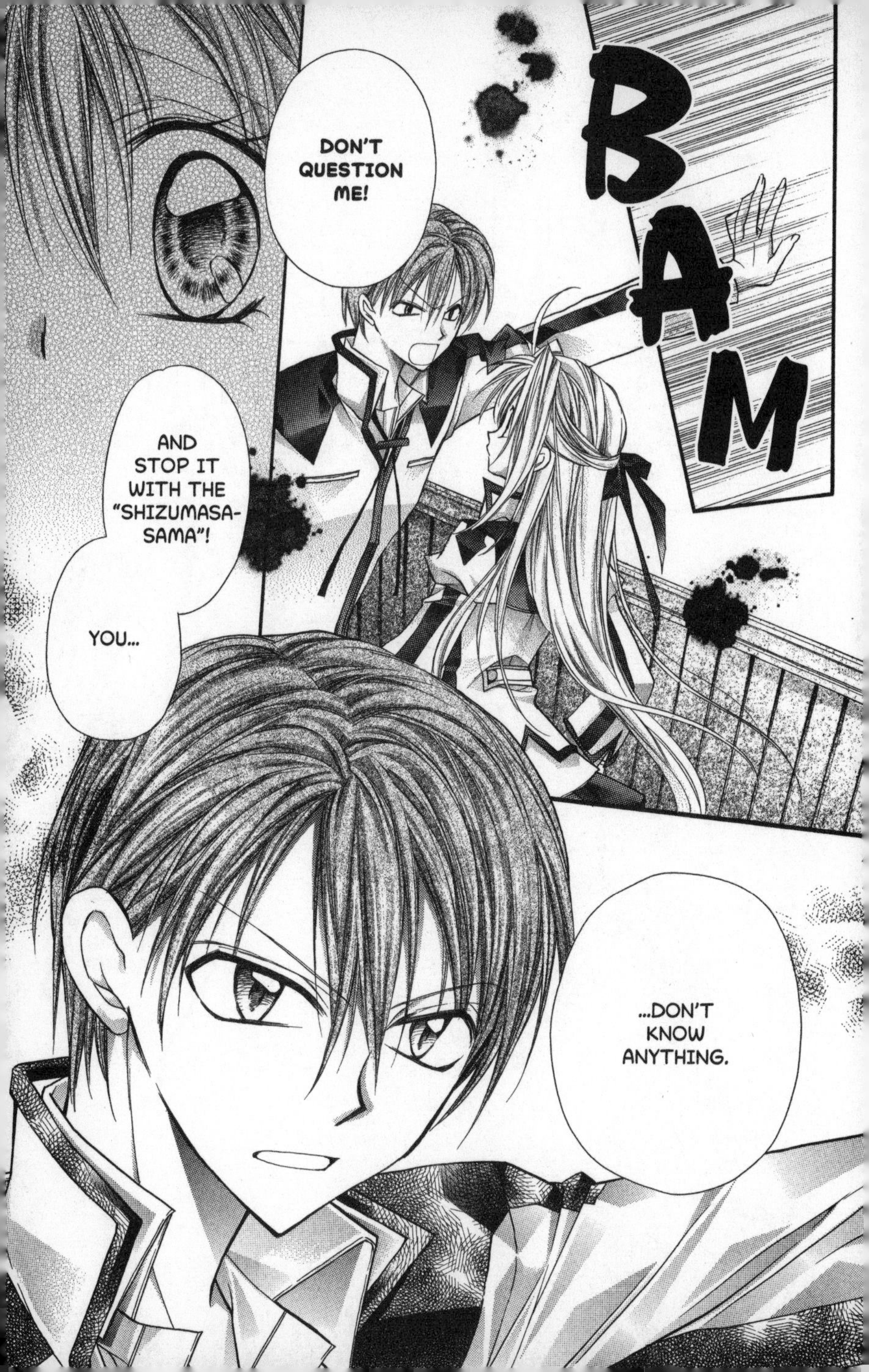
BAM
DON'T QUESTION ME!
AND STOP IT WITH THE "SHIZUMASA-SAMA"!
YOU...
...DON'T KNOW ANYTHING.

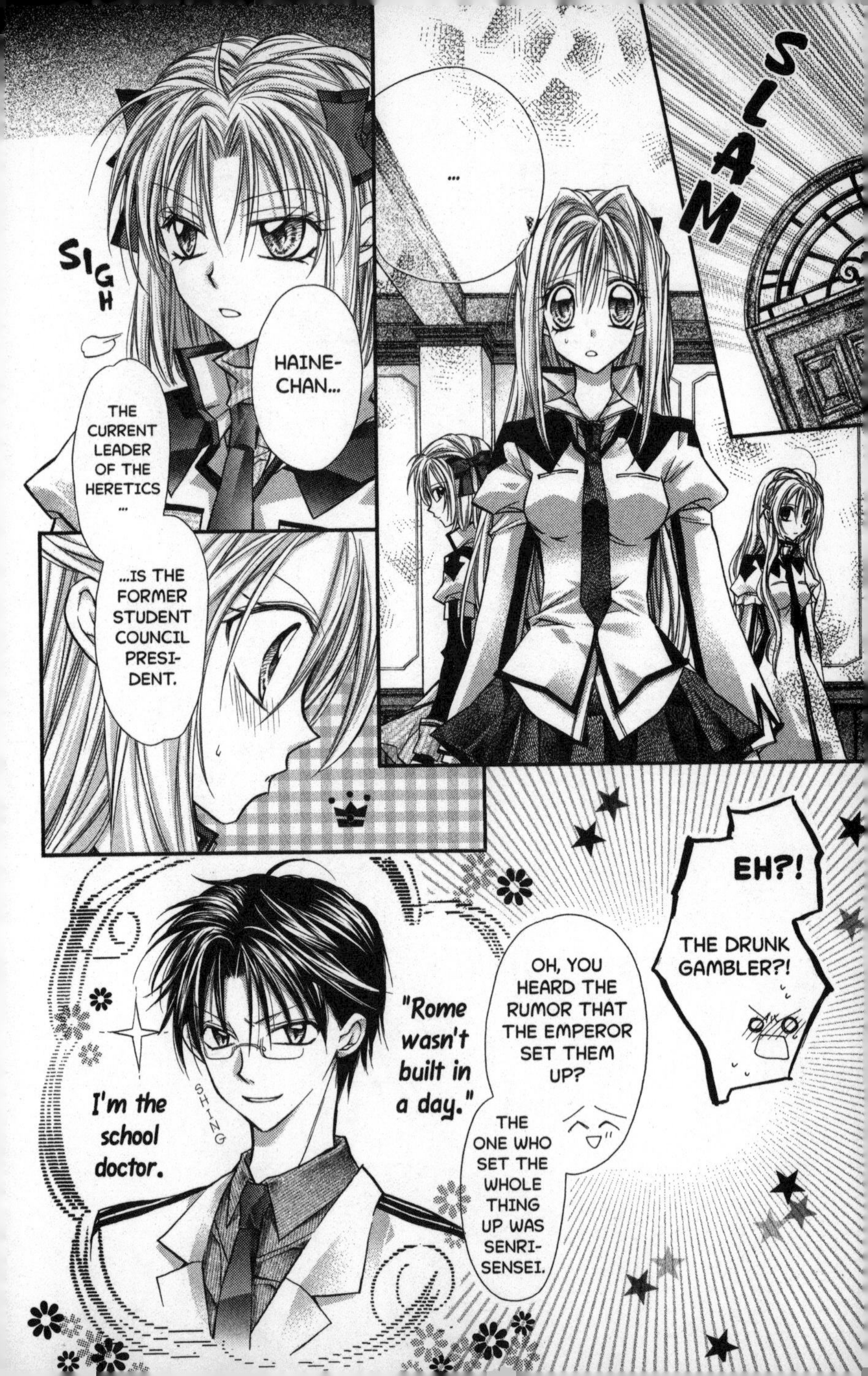

SLAM
...
SIGH
HAINE-CHAN...
THE CURRENT LEADER OF THE HERETICS...
...IS THE FORMER STUDENT COUNCIL PRESIDENT.
EH?!
THE DRUNK GAMBLER?!
OH, YOU HEARD THE RUMOR THAT THE EMPEROR SET THEM UP?
THE ONE WHO SET THE WHOLE THING UP WAS SENRI-SENSEI.
"Rome wasn't built in a day."
SHING
I'm the school doctor.

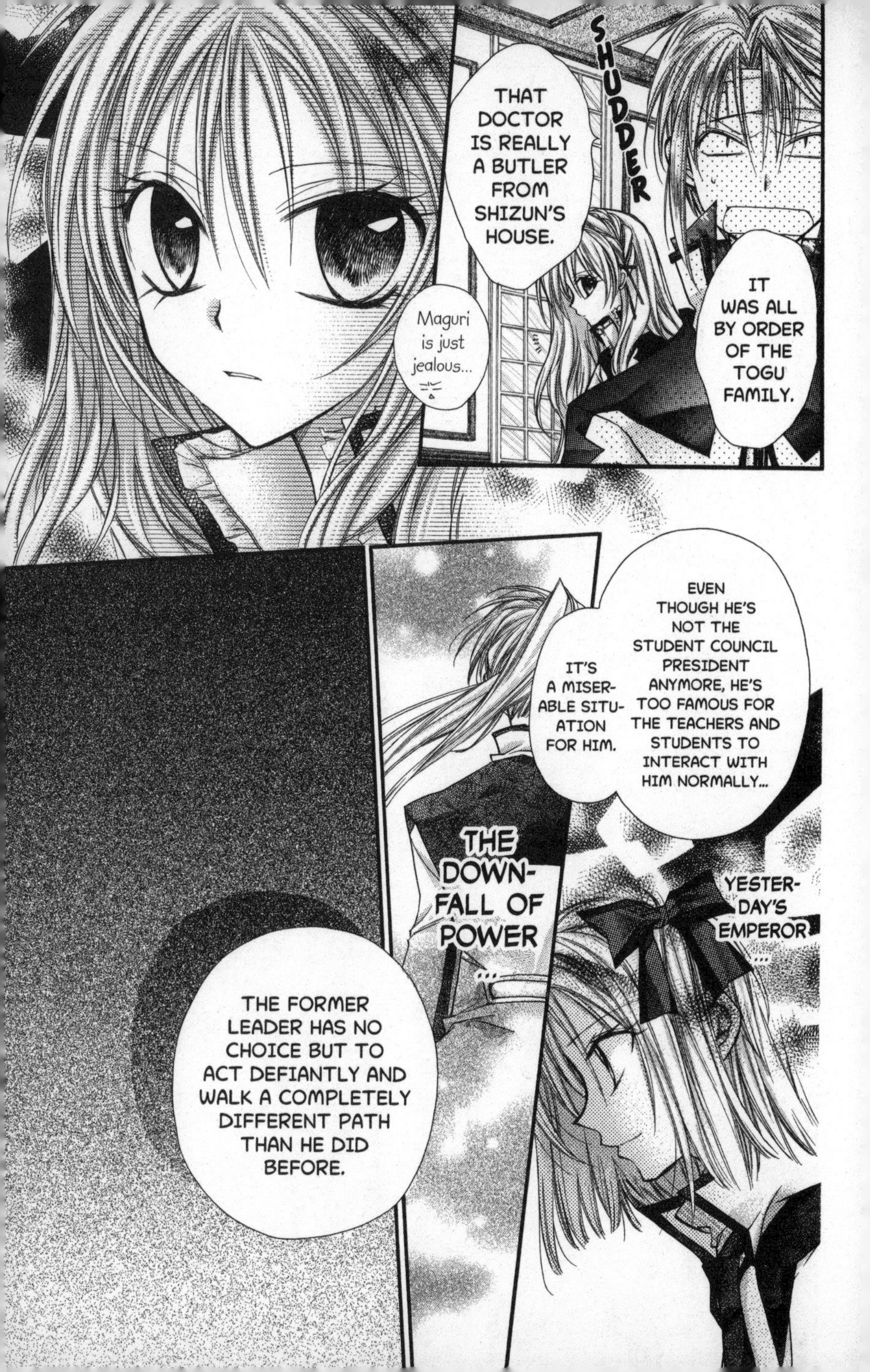
SHUDDER
THAT DOCTOR IS REALLY A BUTLER FROM SHIZUN'S HOUSE.
IT WAS ALL BY ORDER OF THE TOGU FAMILY.
Maguri is just jealous...
EVEN THOUGH HE'S NOT THE STUDENT COUNCIL PRESIDENT ANYMORE, HE'S TOO FAMOUS FOR THE TEACHERS AND STUDENTS TO INTERACT WITH HIM NORMALLY...
IT'S A MISERABLE SITUATION FOR HIM.
YESTERDAY'S EMPEROR...
THE DOWNFALL OF POWER...
THE FORMER LEADER HAS NO CHOICE BUT TO ACT DEFIANTLY AND WALK A COMPLETELY DIFFERENT PATH THAN HE DID BEFORE.

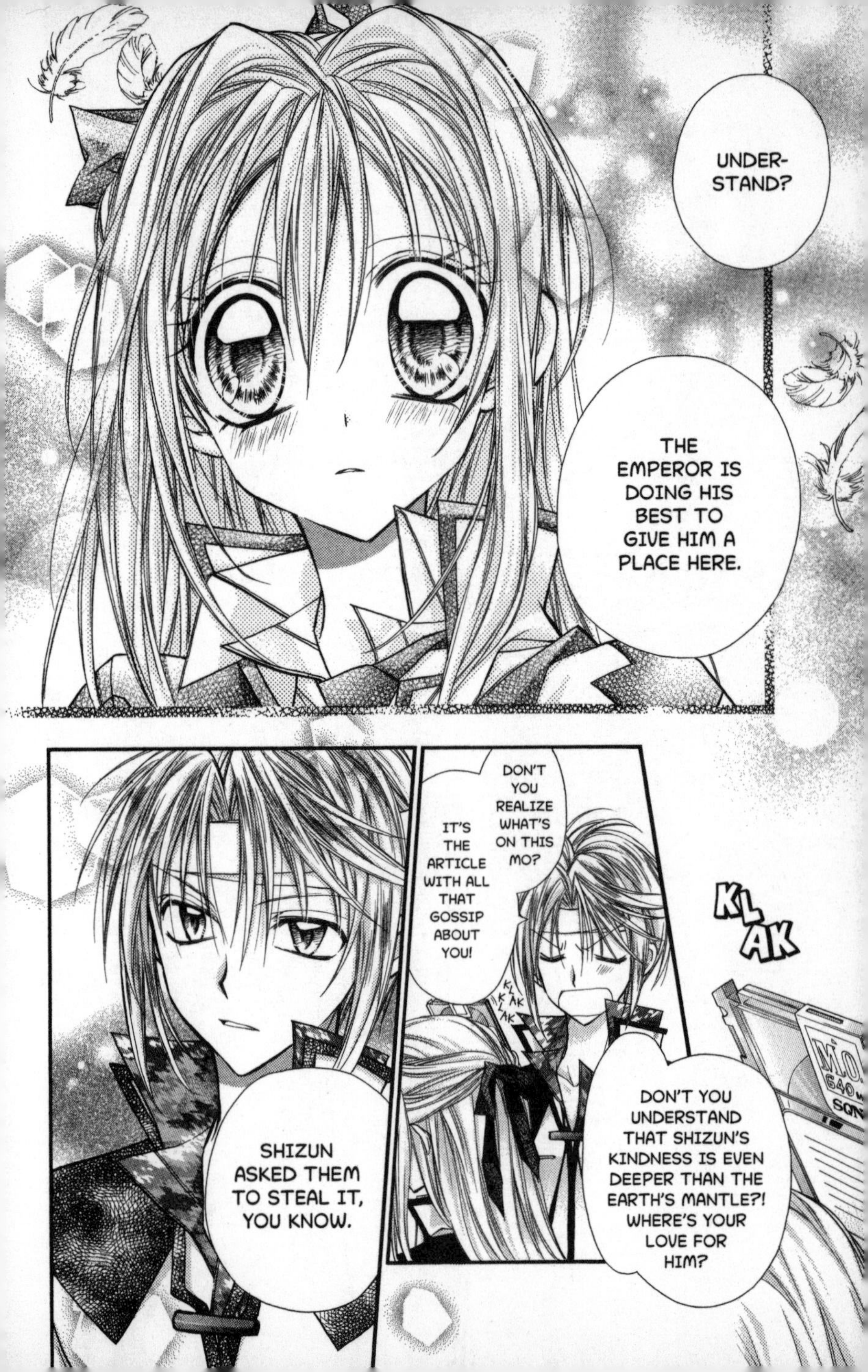

UNDER-STAND?
THE EMPEROR IS DOING HIS BEST TO GIVE HIM A PLACE HERE.
DON'T YOU REALIZE WHAT'S ON THIS MO?
IT'S THE ARTICLE WITH ALL THAT GOSSIP ABOUT YOU!
KLAK
KLAK KLAK KLAK
M.O. 640
DON'T YOU UNDERSTAND THAT SHIZUN'S KINDNESS IS EVEN DEEPER THAN THE EARTH'S MANTLE?! WHERE'S YOUR LOVE FOR HIM?
SHIZUN ASKED THEM TO STEAL IT, YOU KNOW.

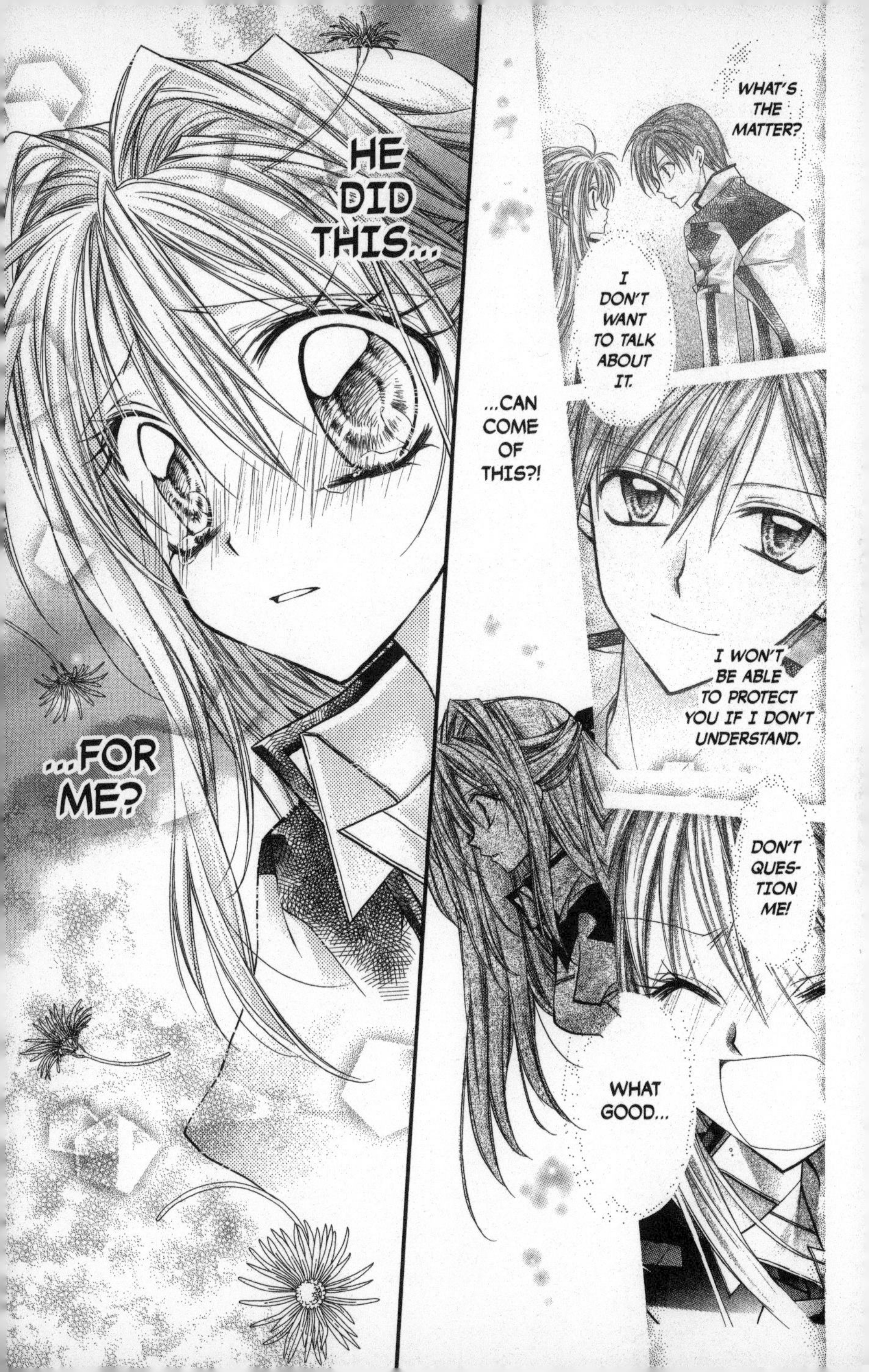
WHAT'S THE MATTER?
I DON'T WANT TO TALK ABOUT IT.
I WON'T BE ABLE TO PROTECT YOU IF I DON'T UNDERSTAND.
DON'T QUES-TION ME!
WHAT GOOD...
...CAN COME OF THIS?!
HE DID THIS...
...FOR ME?

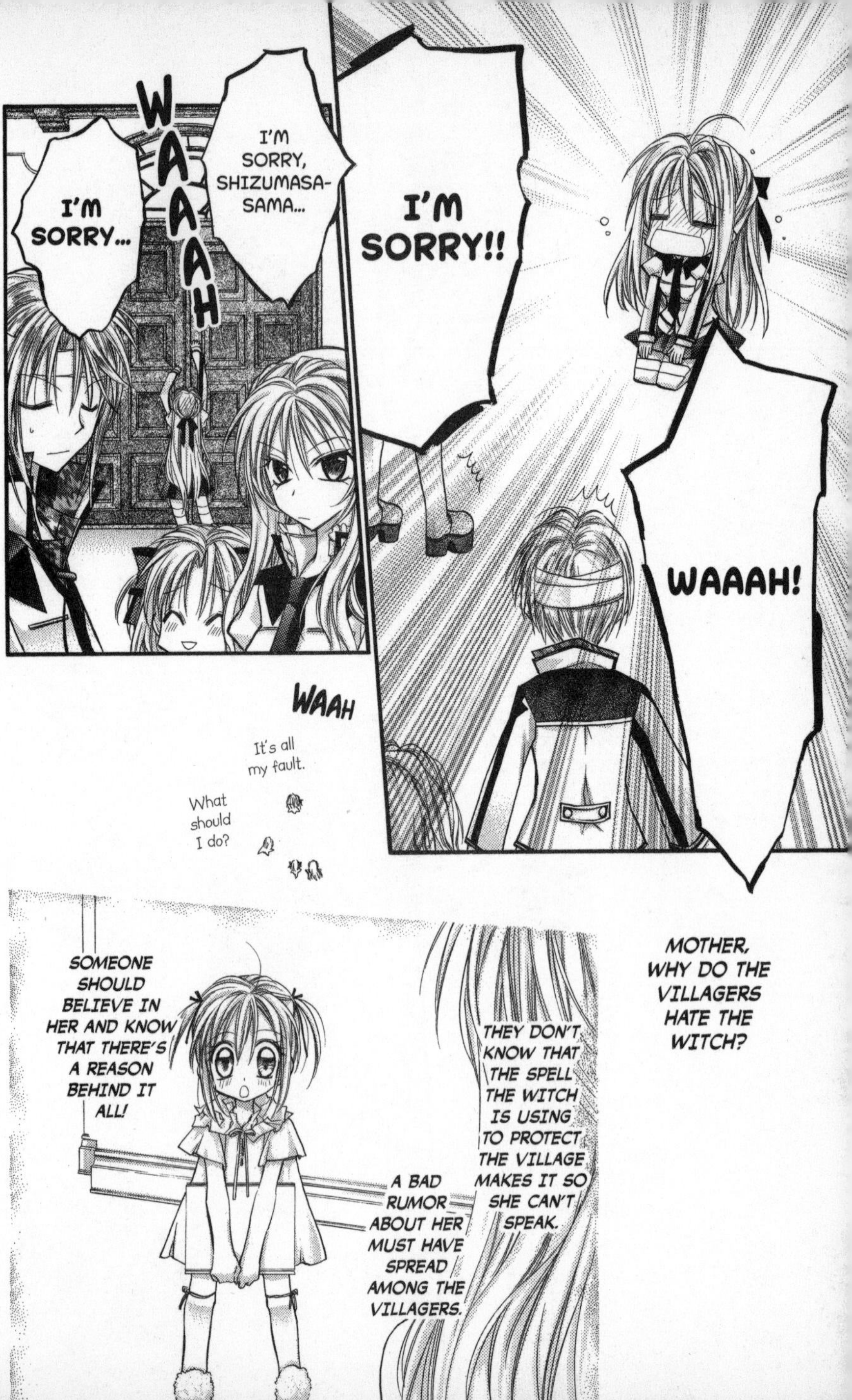
I'M SORRY!!
WAAAH!
I'M SORRY, SHIZUMASA-SAMA...
WAAAAH
I'M SORRY...
WAAH
It's all my fault.
What should I do?
MOTHER, WHY DO THE VILLAGERS HATE THE WITCH?
THEY DON'T KNOW THAT THE SPELL THE WITCH IS USING TO PROTECT THE VILLAGE MAKES IT SO SHE CAN'T SPEAK.
A BAD RUMOR ABOUT HER MUST HAVE SPREAD AMONG THE VILLAGERS.
SOMEONE SHOULD BELIEVE IN HER AND KNOW THAT THERE'S A REASON BEHIND IT ALL!

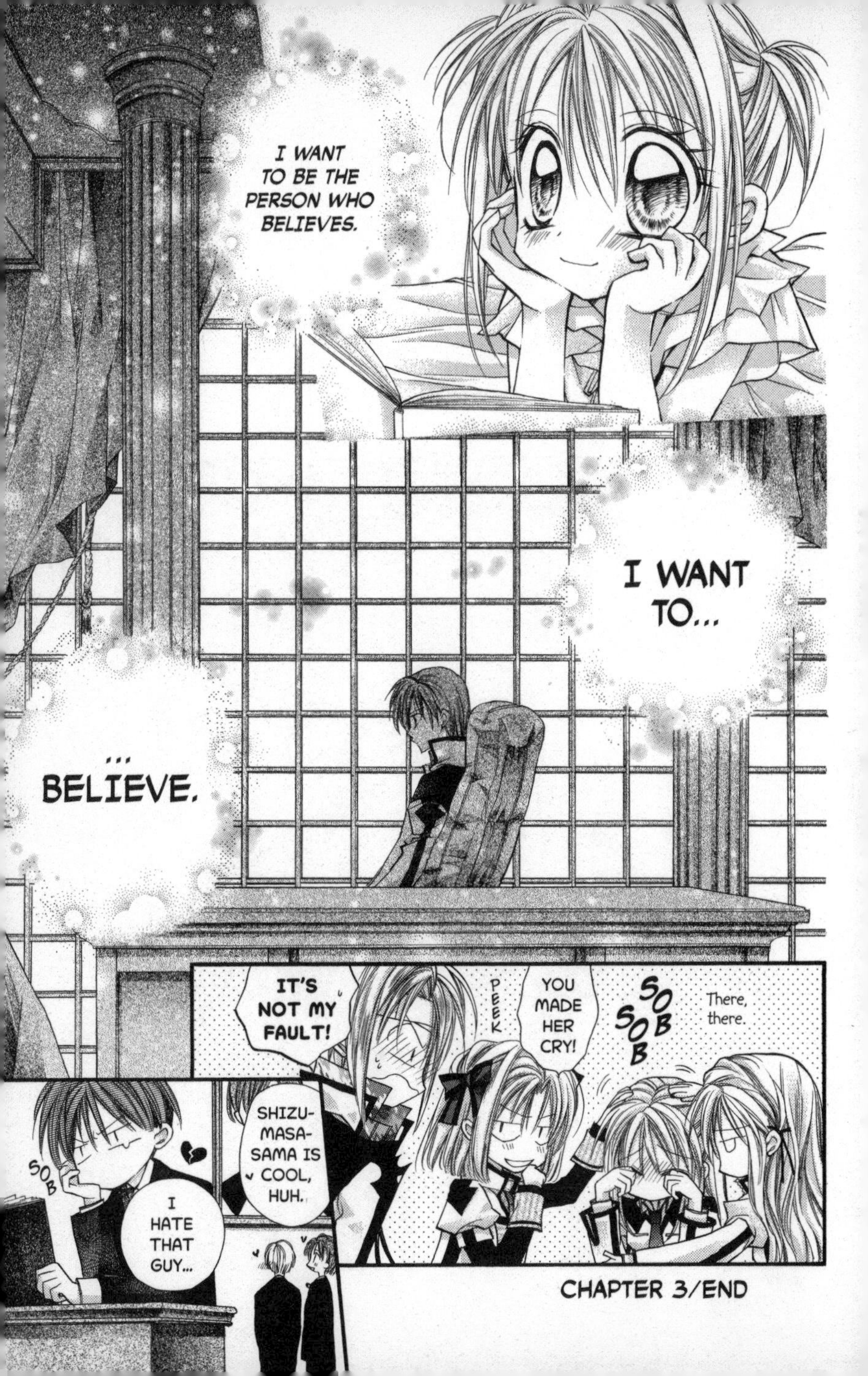
I WANT TO BE THE PERSON WHO BELIEVES.
I WANT TO...
...BELIEVE.
There, there.
SOB SOB
YOU MADE HER CRY!
PEEK
IT'S NOT MY FAULT!
SHIZU-MASA-SAMA IS COOL, HUH.
SOB
I HATE THAT GUY...
CHAPTER 3/END

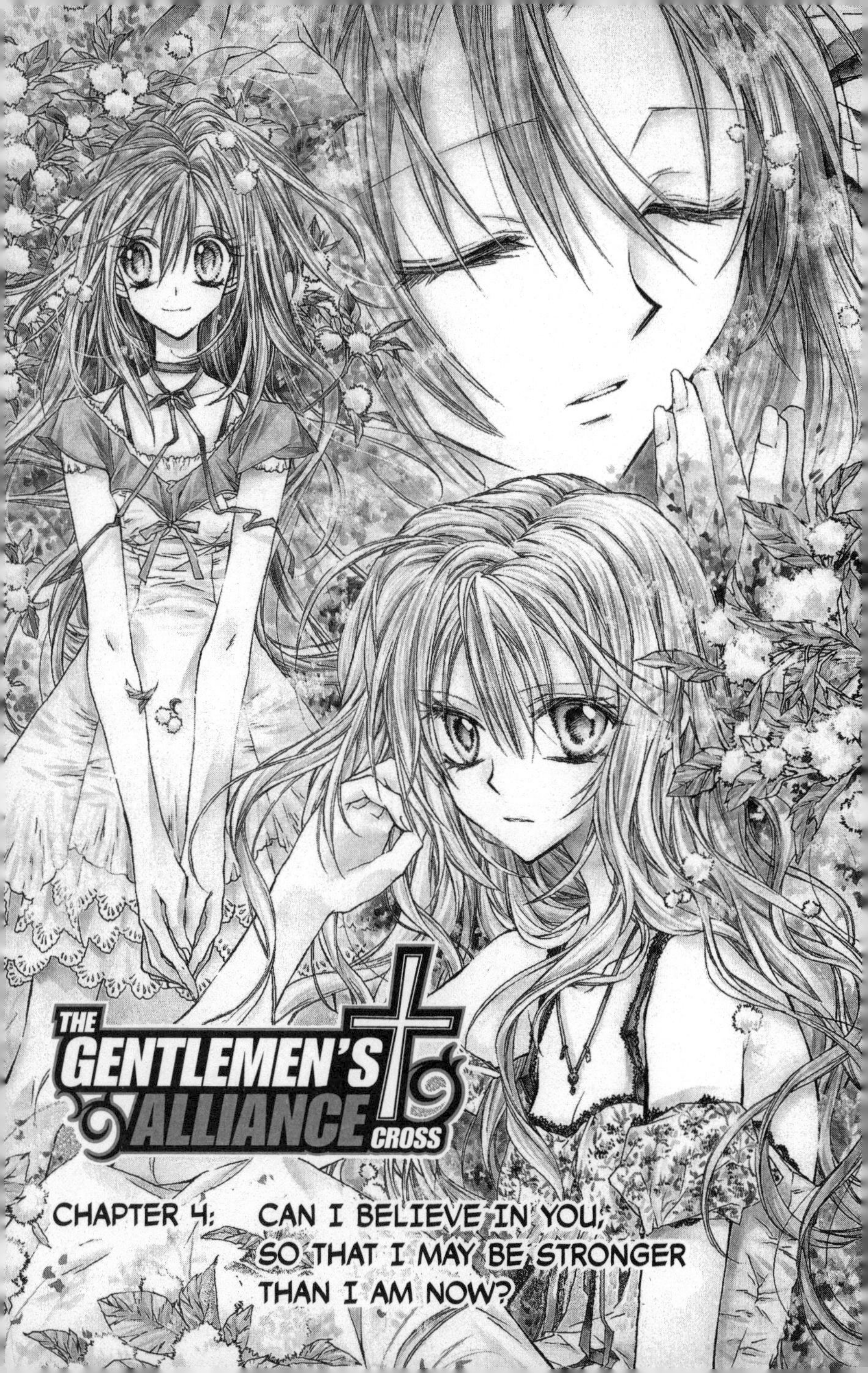
THE GENTLEMEN'S ALLIANCE CROSS
CHAPTER 4: CAN I BELIEVE IN YOU, SO THAT I MAY BE STRONGER THAN I AM NOW?

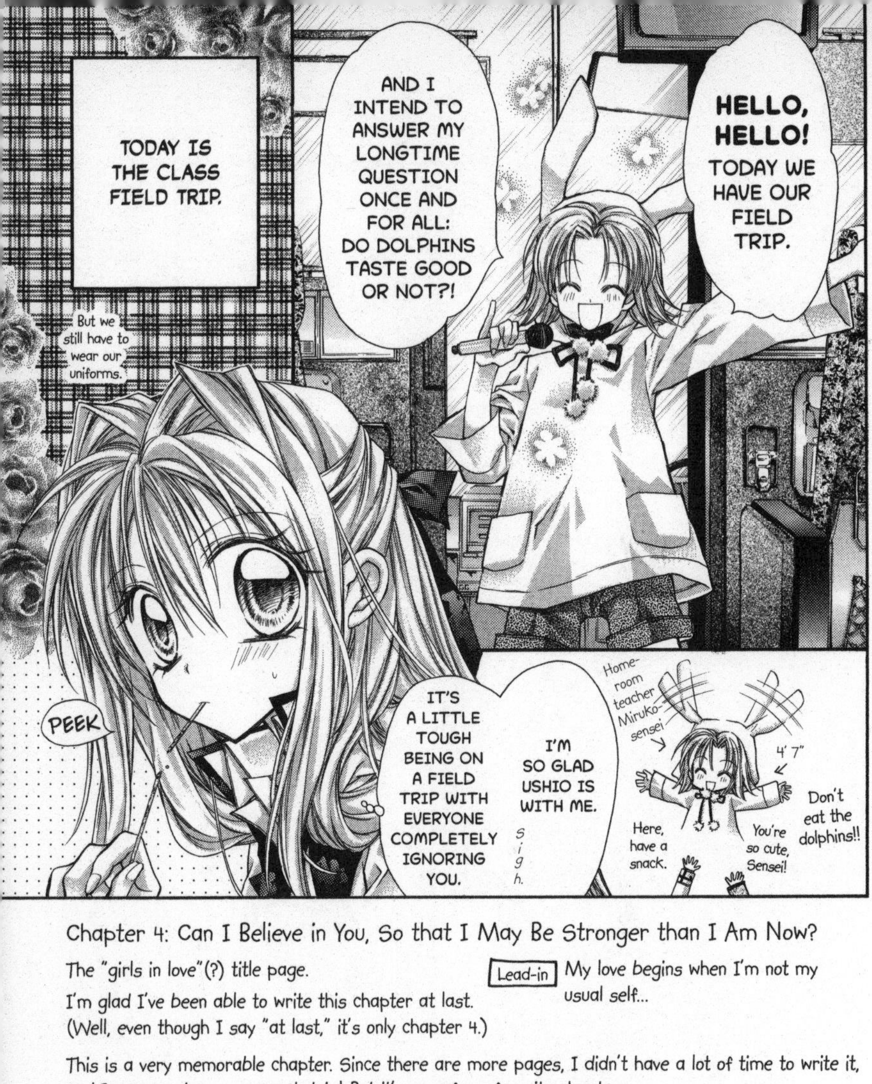
HELLO, HELLO! TODAY WE HAVE OUR FIELD TRIP.
AND I INTEND TO ANSWER MY LONGTIME QUESTION ONCE AND FOR ALL: DO DOLPHINS TASTE GOOD OR NOT?!
TODAY IS THE CLASS FIELD TRIP.
But we still have to wear our uniforms.
Homeroom teacher Miruko-sensei
4' 7"
Don't eat the dolphins!!
You're so cute, Sensei!
Here, have a snack.
I'M SO GLAD USHIO IS WITH ME.
Sigh.
IT'S A LITTLE TOUGH BEING ON A FIELD TRIP WITH EVERYONE COMPLETELY IGNORING YOU.
PEEK

Chapter 4: Can I Believe in You, So that I May Be Stronger than I Am Now?

The "girls in love"(?) title page.

I'm glad I've been able to write this chapter at last.
(Well, even though I say "at last," it's only chapter 4.)

Lead-in: My love begins when I'm not my usual self...

This is a very memorable chapter. Since there are more pages, I didn't have a lot of time to write it, and I even went on a research trip! But it's one of my favorite chapters.

The Emperor really is a strange guy, isn't he? I haven't written about his private life yet, so I really can't talk much about him... But I'll write about him gradually.

He's actually a nice guy at heart. I wonder if I'm ever going to be able to draw him and Haine as a loving couple... I don't have a lot of confidence in it...

Another person I'm keeping an eye on is Toya. I never expected him to appear in the story this much, but it's always a nice scene when he's in it. It's a big help for me to have him around, so I'm really glad to have created him.

I'm really sorry that I haven't written much.
But this series has just began, so...

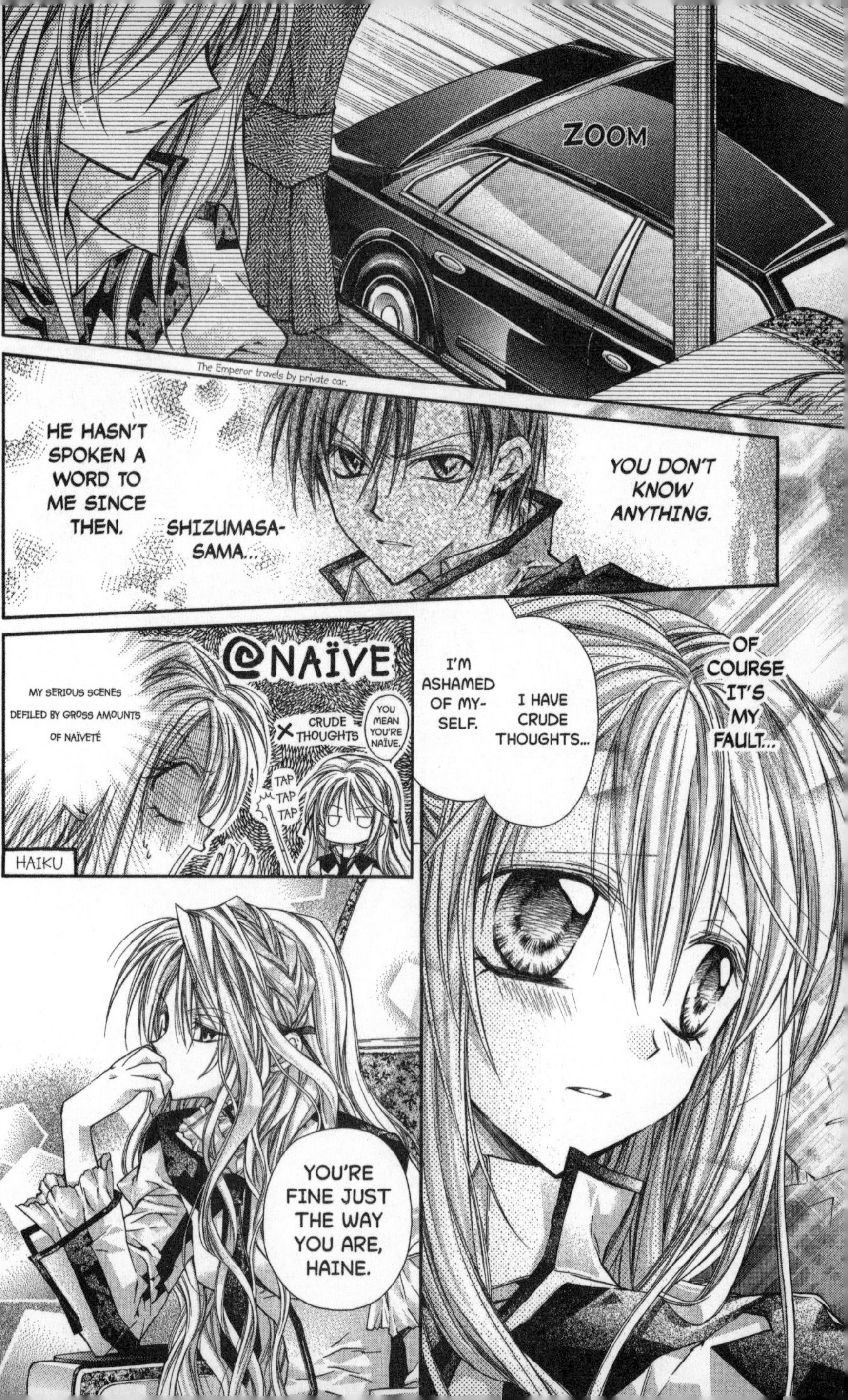
ZOOM
The Emperor travels by private car.
YOU DON'T KNOW ANYTHING.
SHIZUMASA-SAMA...
HE HASN'T SPOKEN A WORD TO ME SINCE THEN.
OF COURSE IT'S MY FAULT...
I HAVE CRUDE THOUGHTS...
I'M ASHAMED OF MY-SELF.
@NAÏVE
MY SERIOUS SCENES DEFILED BY GROSS AMOUNTS OF NAÏVETÉ
× CRUDE THOUGHTS
YOU MEAN YOU'RE NAÏVE.
TAP TAP TAP
HAIKU
YOU'RE FINE JUST THE WAY YOU ARE, HAINE.

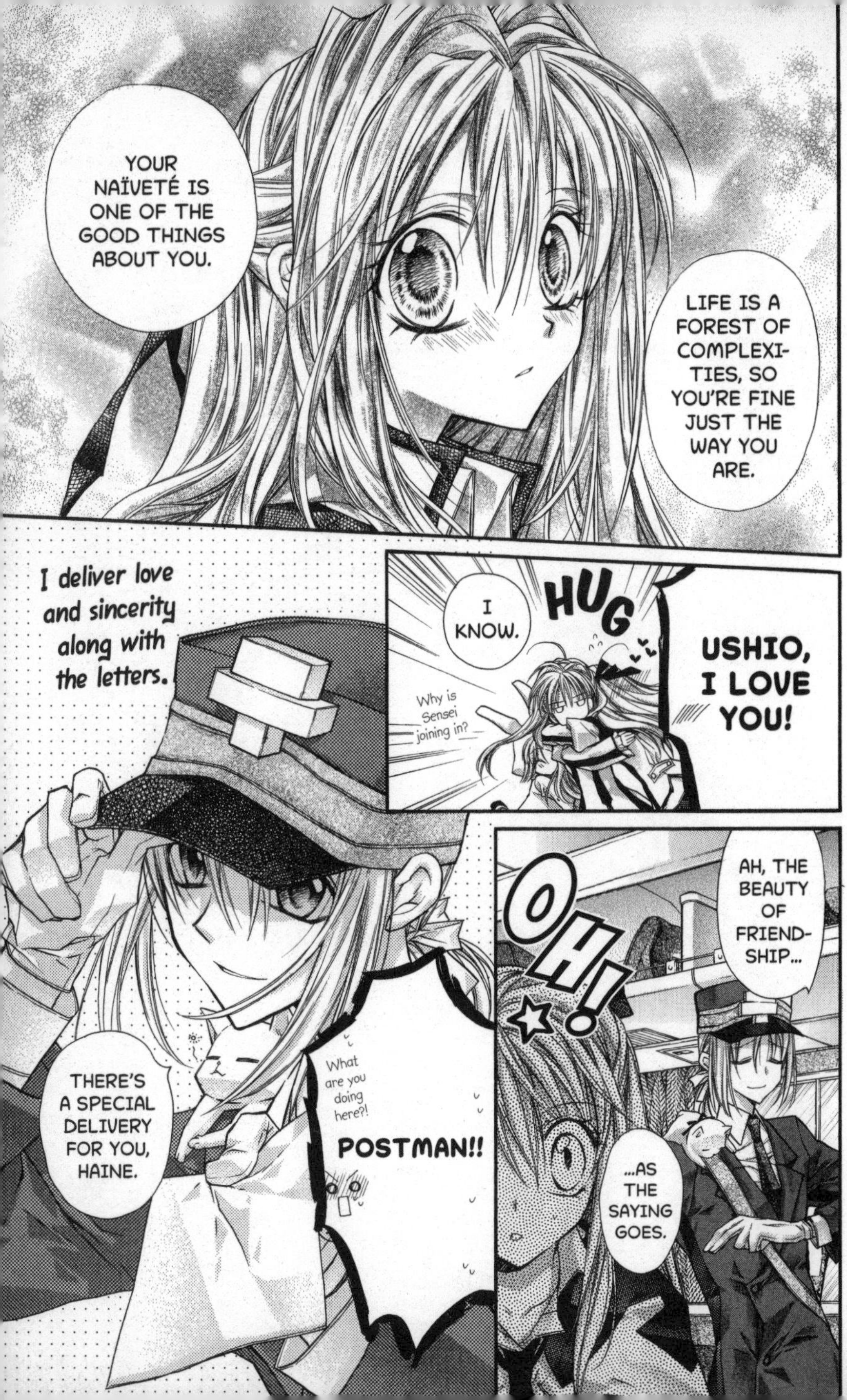
YOUR NAÏVETÉ IS ONE OF THE GOOD THINGS ABOUT YOU.
LIFE IS A FOREST OF COMPLEXI-TIES, SO YOU'RE FINE JUST THE WAY YOU ARE.
USHIO, I LOVE YOU!
HUG
I KNOW.
Why is Sensei joining in?
AH, THE BEAUTY OF FRIEND-SHIP...
OH!
...AS THE SAYING GOES.
I deliver love and sincerity along with the letters.
POSTMAN!!
What are you doing here?!
THERE'S A SPECIAL DELIVERY FOR YOU, HAINE.

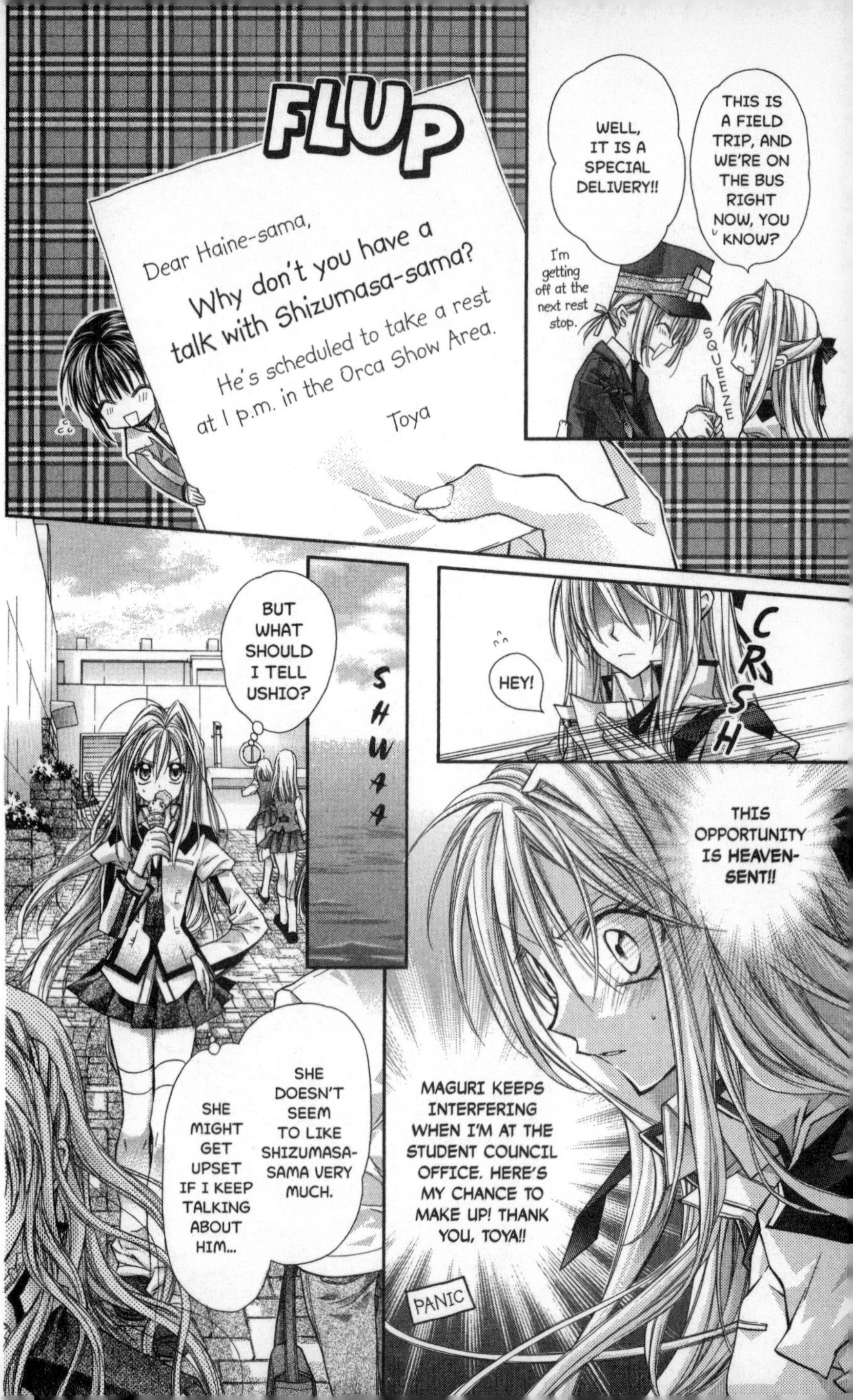
THIS IS A FIELD TRIP, AND WE'RE ON THE BUS RIGHT NOW, YOU KNOW?
WELL, IT IS A SPECIAL DELIVERY!!
I'm getting off at the next rest stop.
SQUEEZE
FLUP
Dear Haine-sama,
Why don't you have a talk with Shizumasa-sama?
He's scheduled to take a rest at 1 p.m. in the Orca Show Area.
Toya
CRSH
HEY!
BUT WHAT SHOULD I TELL USHIO?
SHWAA
THIS OPPORTUNITY IS HEAVEN-SENT!!
MAGURI KEEPS INTERFERING WHEN I'M AT THE STUDENT COUNCIL OFFICE. HERE'S MY CHANCE TO MAKE UP! THANK YOU, TOYA!!
PANIC
SHE DOESN'T SEEM TO LIKE SHIZUMASA-SAMA VERY MUCH.
SHE MIGHT GET UPSET IF I KEEP TALKING ABOUT HIM...

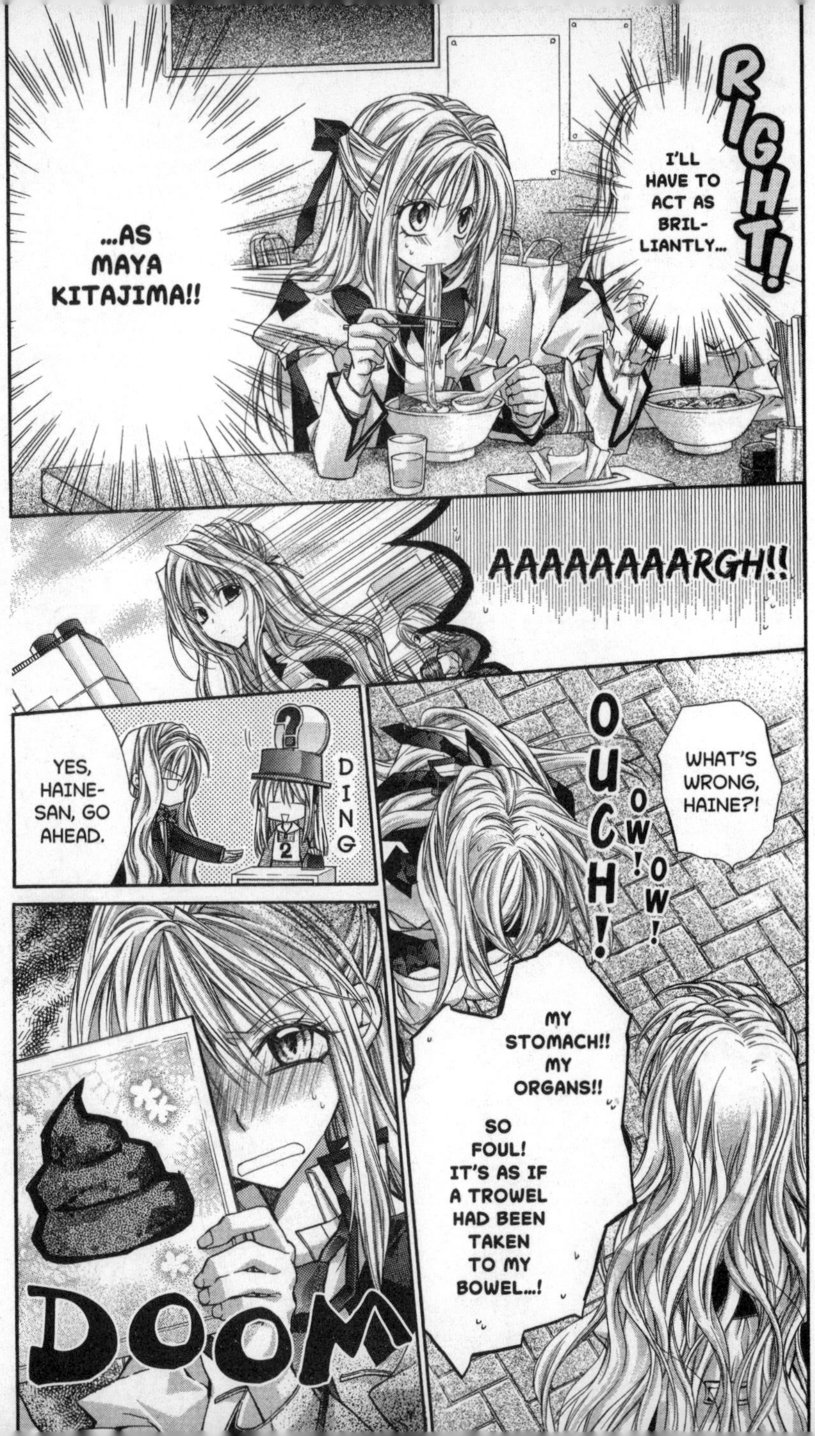
RIGHT!
I'LL HAVE TO ACT AS BRIL-LIANTLY...
...AS MAYA KITAJIMA!!
AAAAAAAARGH!!
WHAT'S WRONG, HAINE?!
OW! OW!
OUCH!
DING
YES, HAINE-SAN, GO AHEAD.
MY STOMACH!! MY ORGANS!!
SO FOUL! IT'S AS IF A TROWEL HAD BEEN TAKEN TO MY BOWEL...!
DOOM

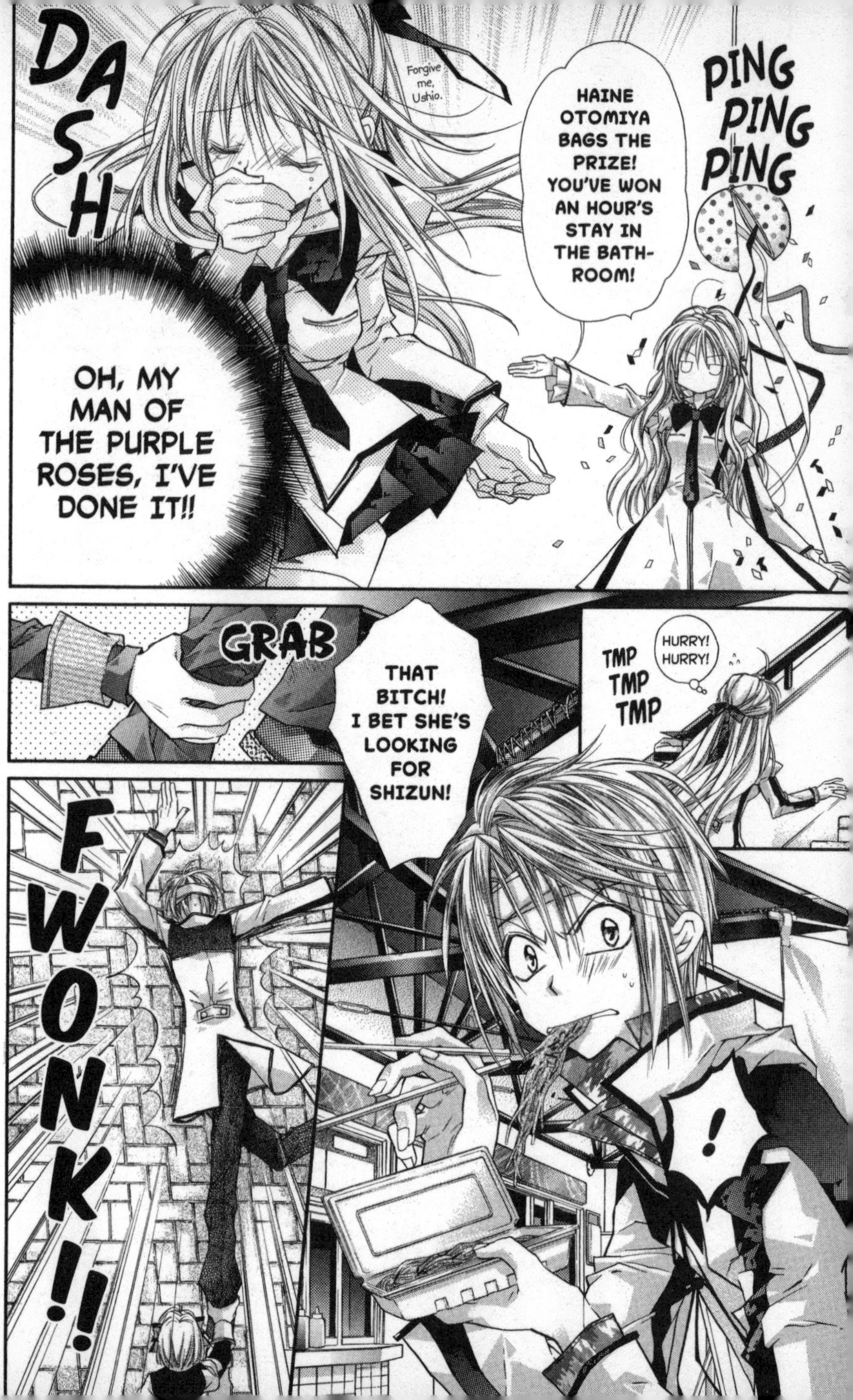
PING PING PING
HAINE OTOMIYA BAGS THE PRIZE! YOU'VE WON AN HOUR'S STAY IN THE BATH-ROOM!
Forgive me, Ushio.
DASH
OH, MY MAN OF THE PURPLE ROSES, I'VE DONE IT!!
HURRY! HURRY!
TMP TMP TMP
GRAB
THAT BITCH! I BET SHE'S LOOKING FOR SHIZUN!
!
FWONK!!

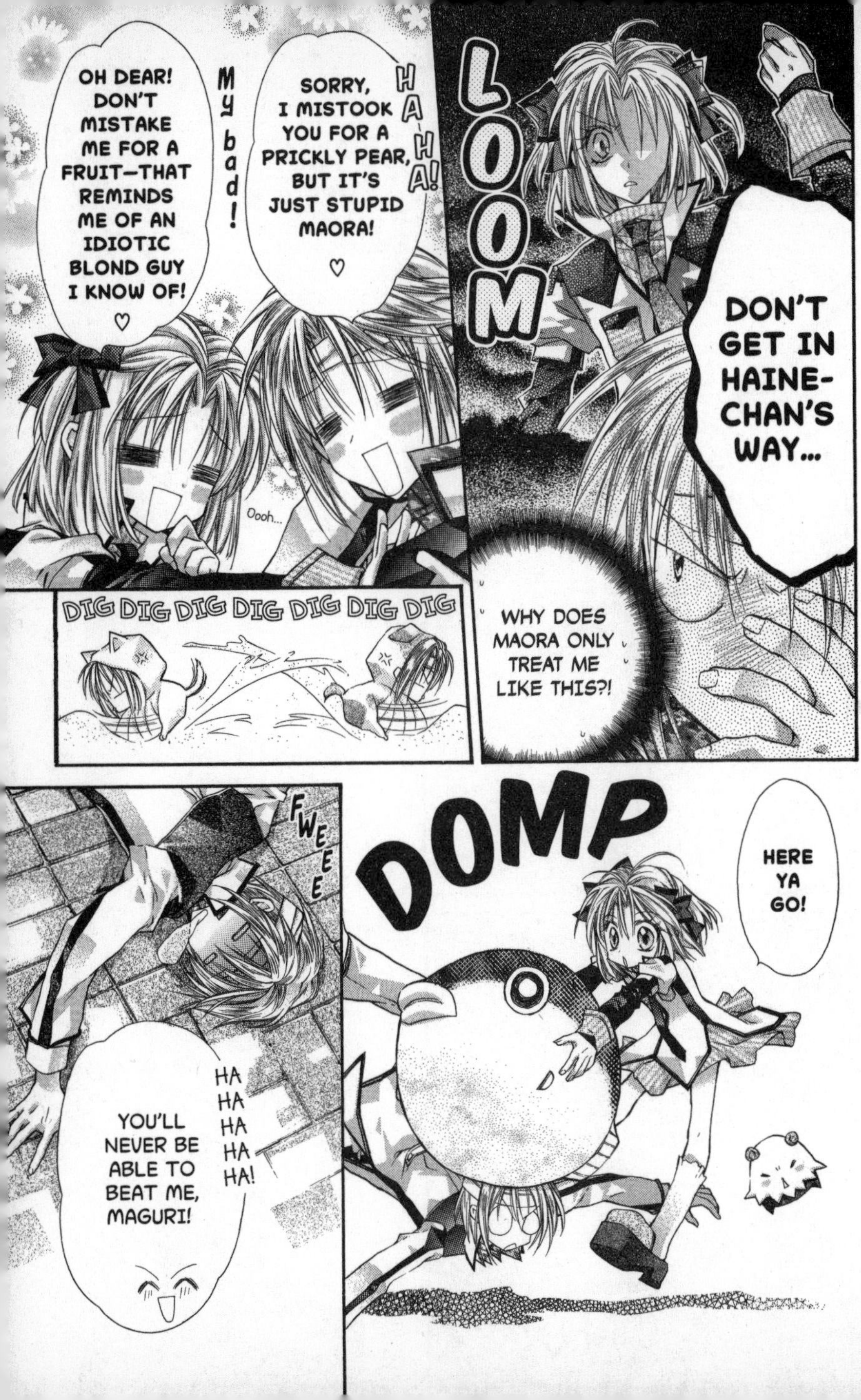
LOOM
DON'T GET IN HAINE-CHAN'S WAY...
WHY DOES MAORA ONLY TREAT ME LIKE THIS?!
SORRY, I MISTOOK YOU FOR A PRICKLY PEAR, BUT IT'S JUST STUPID MAORA! ♡
HAHAHA!
My bad!
OH DEAR! DON'T MISTAKE ME FOR A FRUIT—THAT REMINDS ME OF AN IDIOTIC BLOND GUY I KNOW OF! ♡
Oooh...
DIG DIG DIG DIG DIG DIG DIG
DOMP
HERE YA GO!
FWEEE
HA HA HA HA HA!
YOU'LL NEVER BE ABLE TO BEAT ME, MAGURI!

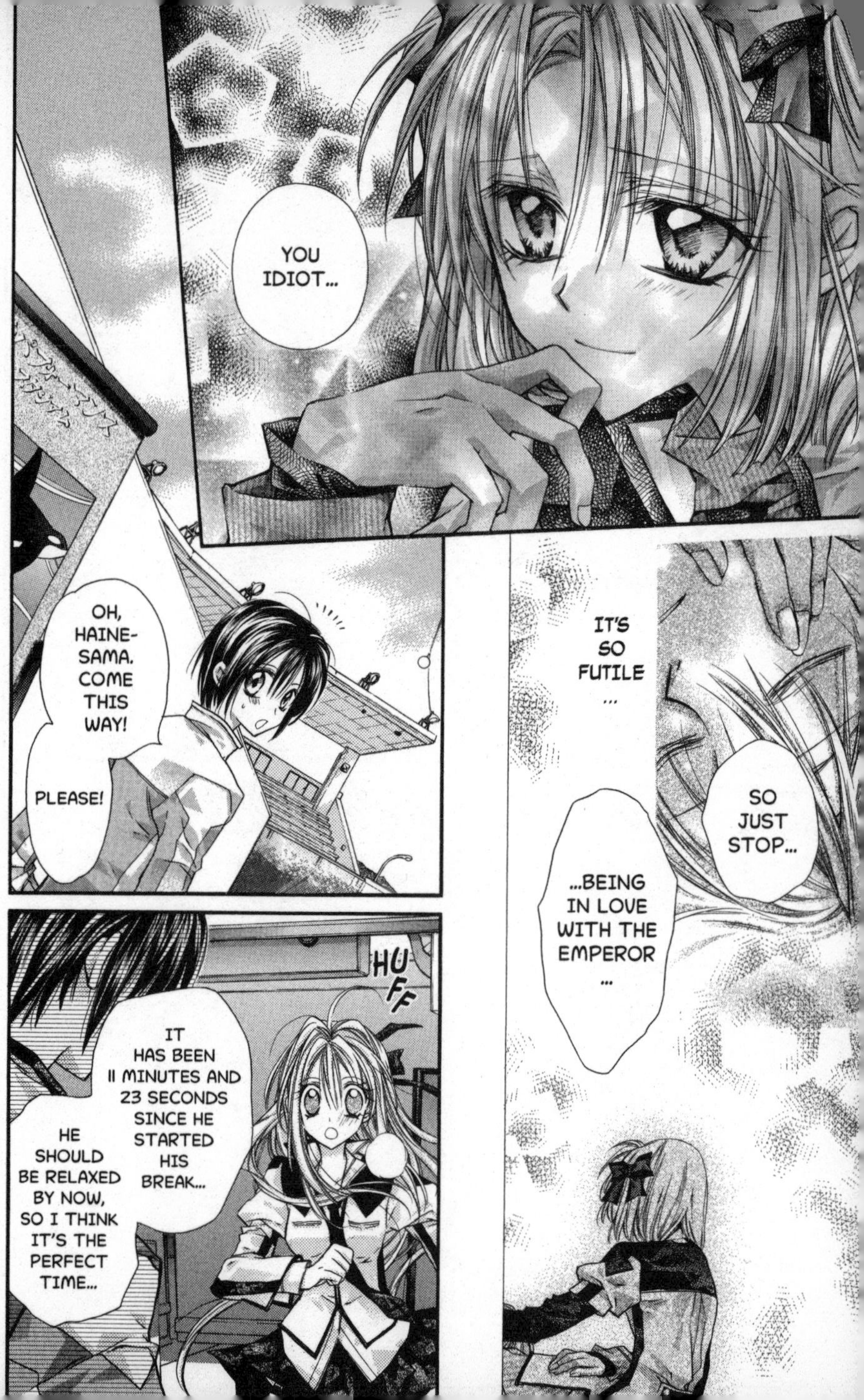
YOU IDIOT...
IT'S SO FUTILE ...
SO JUST STOP...
...BEING IN LOVE WITH THE EMPEROR ...
OH, HAINE-SAMA. COME THIS WAY!
PLEASE!
HUFF
IT HAS BEEN 11 MINUTES AND 23 SECONDS SINCE HE STARTED HIS BREAK...
HE SHOULD BE RELAXED BY NOW, SO I THINK IT'S THE PERFECT TIME...

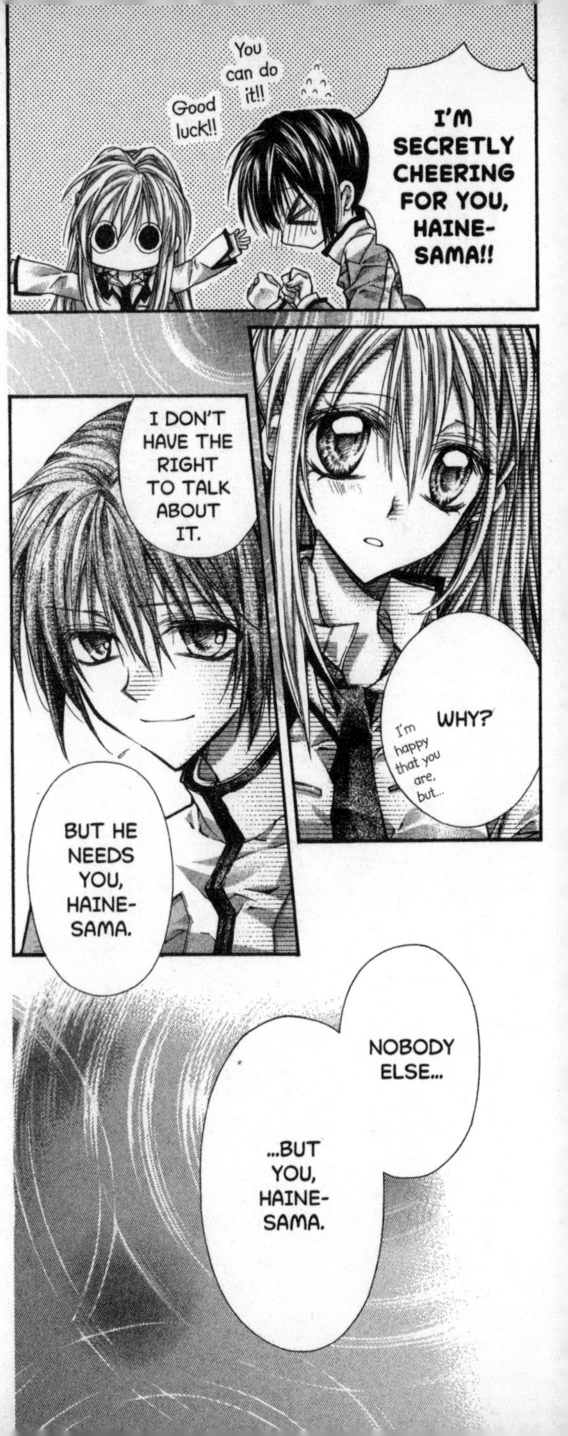
I'M SECRETLY CHEERING FOR YOU, HAINE-SAMA!!
You can do it!!
Good luck!!
WHY?
I'm happy that you are, but...
I DON'T HAVE THE RIGHT TO TALK ABOUT IT.
BUT HE NEEDS YOU, HAINE-SAMA.
NOBODY ELSE...
...BUT YOU, HAINE-SAMA.

Senri Narumiya

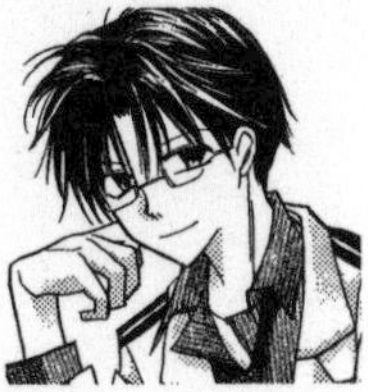

Birthday: September 27
Blood Type: A

He's the perverted school doctor at the academy, but he's actually the butler of the Togu family.

He seems to be interested in Ushio...or not?

Comments

For me, he's actually a serious person, but since he's so flirtatious on the outside, nobody takes him seriously. ᵕ

I'm looking forward to writing about his life in the Togu family.

Kusame Otomiya

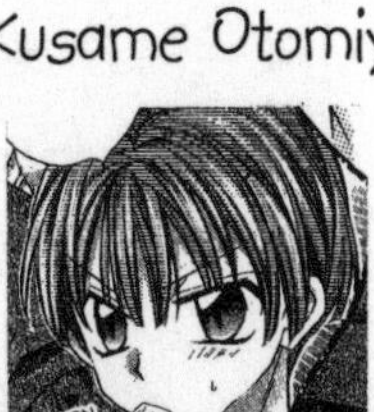
DAIKON RADISH

Birthday: May 1
Blood Type: AB

He's Haine's brother after she was adopted by the Otomiya's. There is a reason why he does not call Haine "Onee-chan."

He's a model student, and he's the vice-president of the student council at Imperial Academy Middle School.

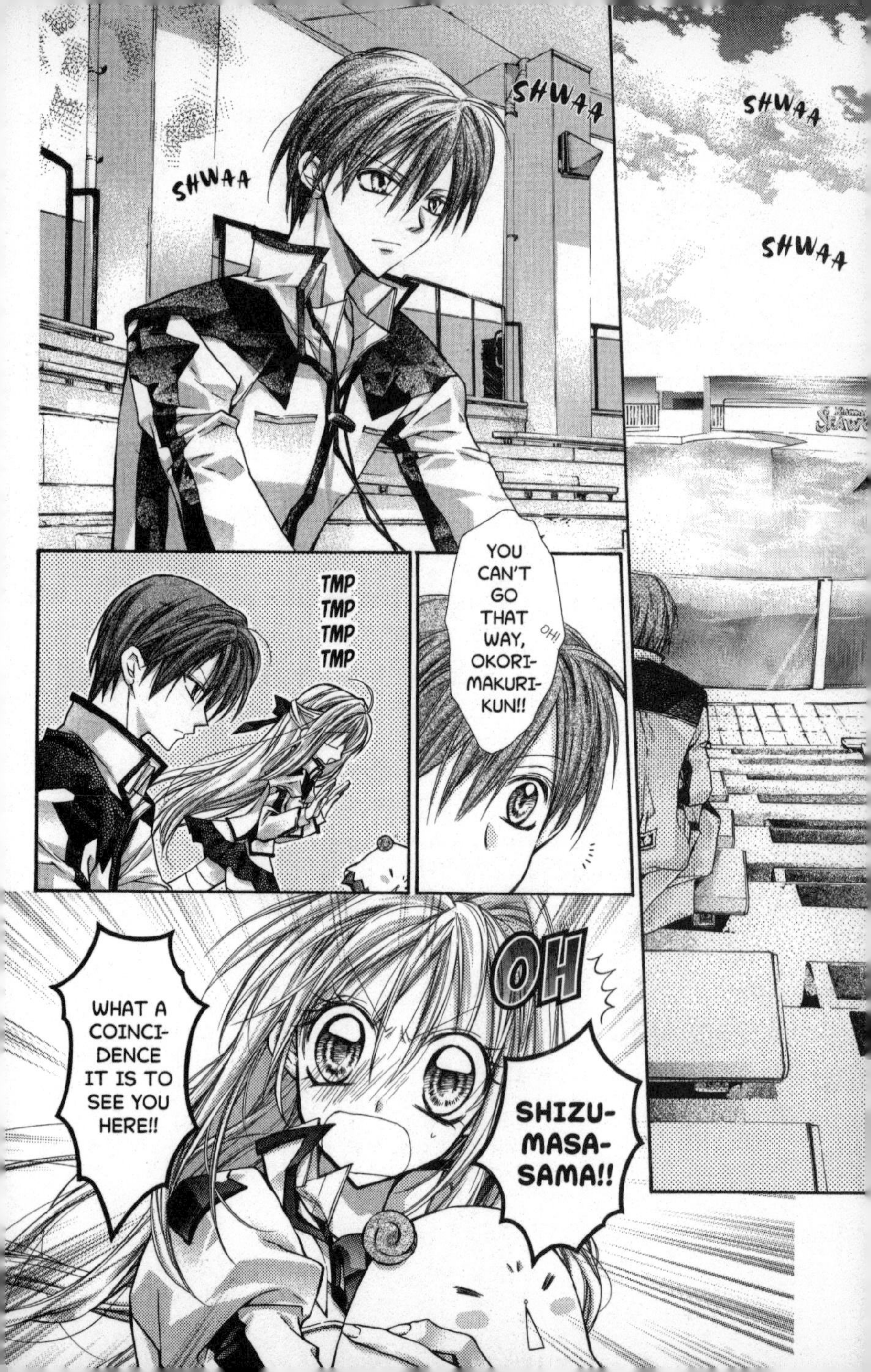
SHWAA
SHWAA
SHWAA
SHWAA
YOU CAN'T GO THAT WAY, OKORI-MAKURI-KUN!!
OH!
TMP TMP TMP TMP
OH
SHIZU-MASA-SAMA!!
WHAT A COINCI-DENCE IT IS TO SEE YOU HERE!!

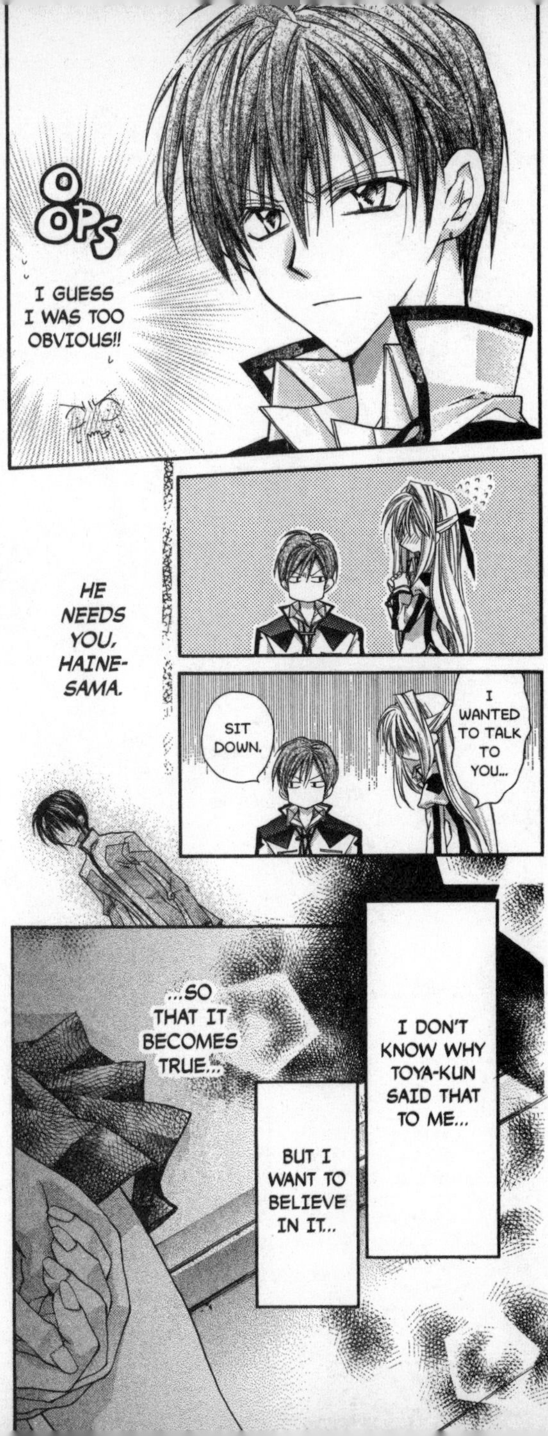
OOPS
I GUESS I WAS TOO OBVIOUS!!
I WANTED TO TALK TO YOU...
SIT DOWN.
HE NEEDS YOU, HAINE-SAMA.
I DON'T KNOW WHY TOYA-KUN SAID THAT TO ME...
BUT I WANT TO BELIEVE IN IT...
...SO THAT IT BECOMES TRUE...

Final Words

- Well, I'll see you in volume 2.
- The cover for the next volume will feature Shizun.
- It's a pain to have so many characters.
- But that means all the more love for them!
- I especially like Ushio.
- She's even better when she's together with Hainekko.
- I want to push Shizun to the ground and hug him.
- Maora is an eccentric.
- But it's the eccentricity that makes Maora cute.
- Maguri is stupid.
- But it's the stupidity that makes him cute.
- Maguri has a Hiroshima accent, but that does not mean he speaks in Hiroshima dialect.
- The school doctor is perverted.
- The school doctor is very unpopular among the elementary school readers, but I don't care.
- "Shinshi Domei Cross" can be shortened to "Shinkuro."
- I want to keep writing this series for a long looooong time.
- See you in volume 2!!!

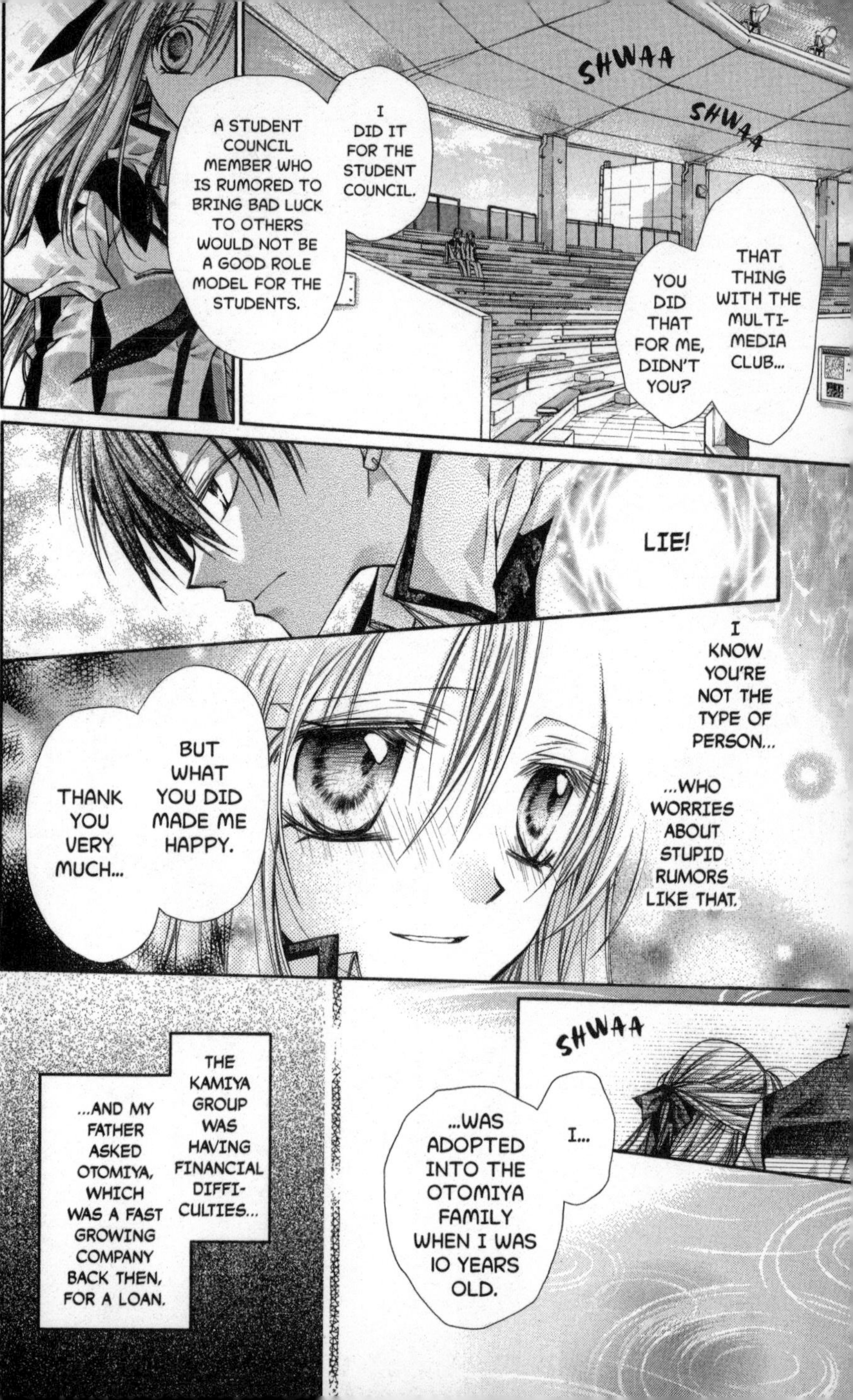
SHWAA
SHWAA
THAT THING WITH THE MULTI-MEDIA CLUB...
YOU DID THAT FOR ME, DIDN'T YOU?
I DID IT FOR THE STUDENT COUNCIL.
A STUDENT COUNCIL MEMBER WHO IS RUMORED TO BRING BAD LUCK TO OTHERS WOULD NOT BE A GOOD ROLE MODEL FOR THE STUDENTS.
LIE!
I KNOW YOU'RE NOT THE TYPE OF PERSON...
...WHO WORRIES ABOUT STUPID RUMORS LIKE THAT.
BUT WHAT YOU DID MADE ME HAPPY.
THANK YOU VERY MUCH...
SHWAA
I...
...WAS ADOPTED INTO THE OTOMIYA FAMILY WHEN I WAS 10 YEARS OLD.
THE KAMIYA GROUP WAS HAVING FINANCIAL DIFFICULTIES...
...AND MY FATHER ASKED OTOMIYA, WHICH WAS A FAST GROWING COMPANY BACK THEN, FOR A LOAN.

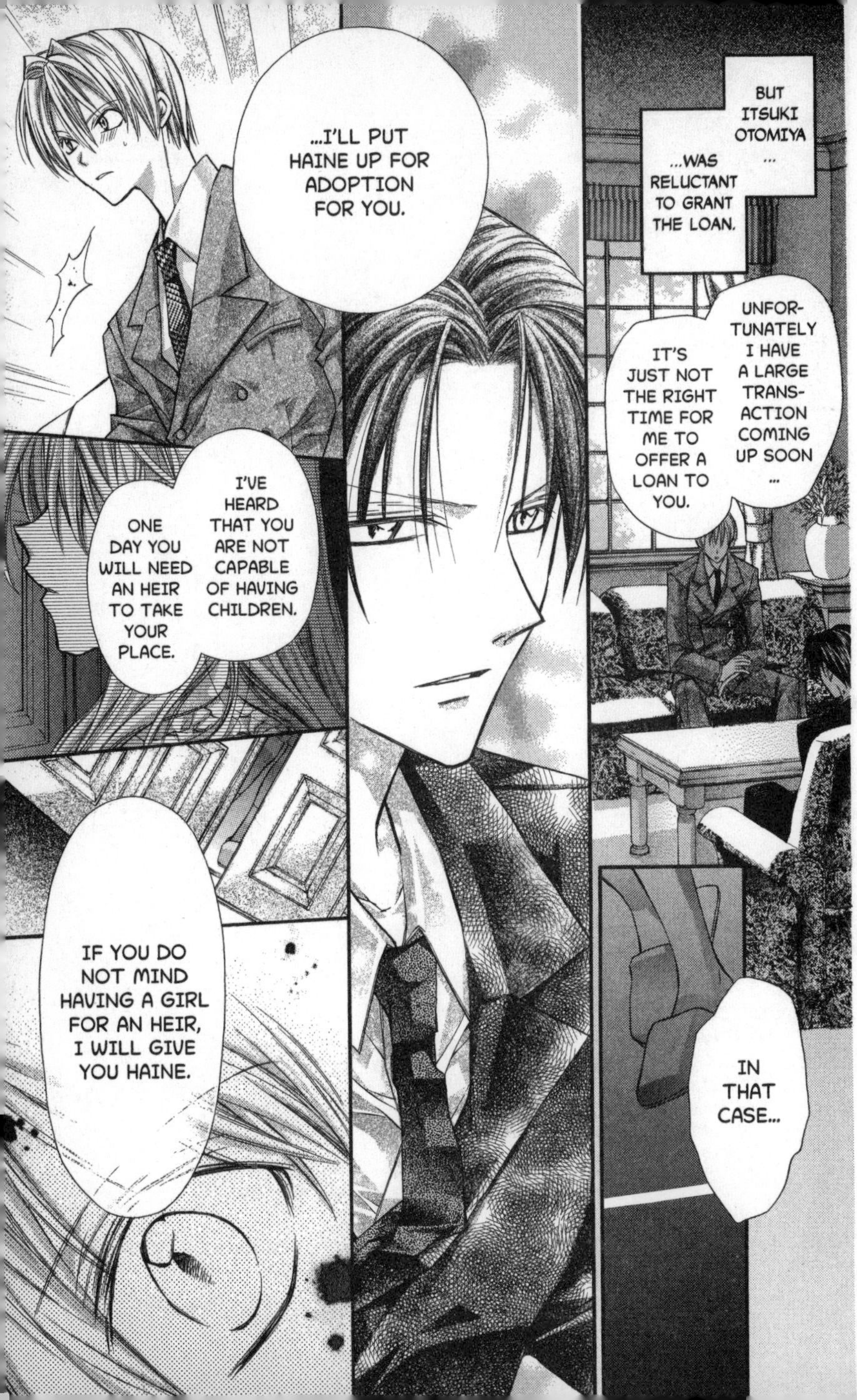
BUT ITSUKI OTOMIYA ...
...WAS RELUCTANT TO GRANT THE LOAN.
UNFORTUNATELY I HAVE A LARGE TRANSACTION COMING UP SOON ...
IT'S JUST NOT THE RIGHT TIME FOR ME TO OFFER A LOAN TO YOU.
IN THAT CASE...
...I'LL PUT HAINE UP FOR ADOPTION FOR YOU.
I'VE HEARD THAT YOU ARE NOT CAPABLE OF HAVING CHILDREN.
ONE DAY YOU WILL NEED AN HEIR TO TAKE YOUR PLACE.
IF YOU DO NOT MIND HAVING A GIRL FOR AN HEIR, I WILL GIVE YOU HAINE.

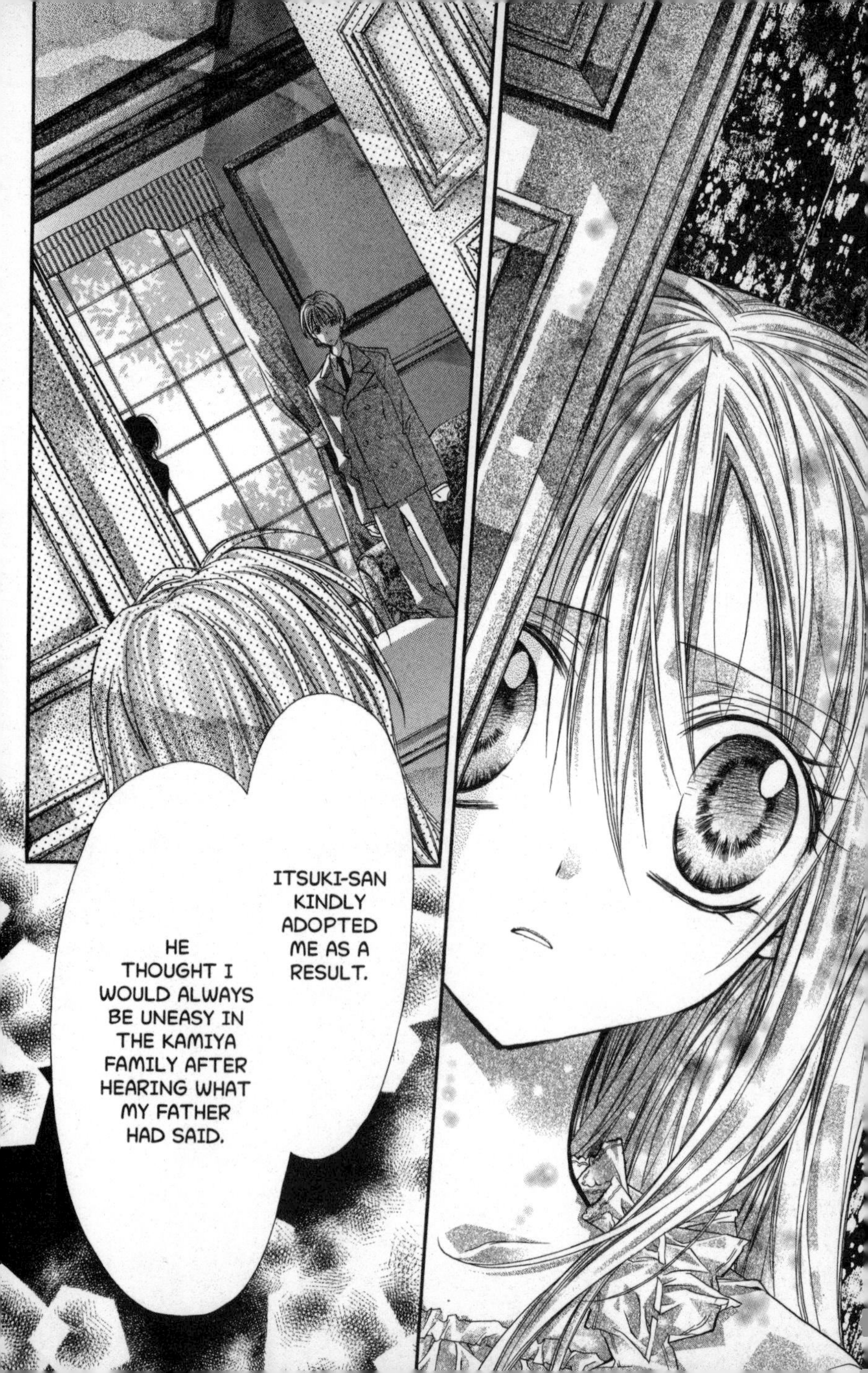
ITSUKI-SAN KINDLY ADOPTED ME AS A RESULT.
HE THOUGHT I WOULD ALWAYS BE UNEASY IN THE KAMIYA FAMILY AFTER HEARING WHAT MY FATHER HAD SAID.

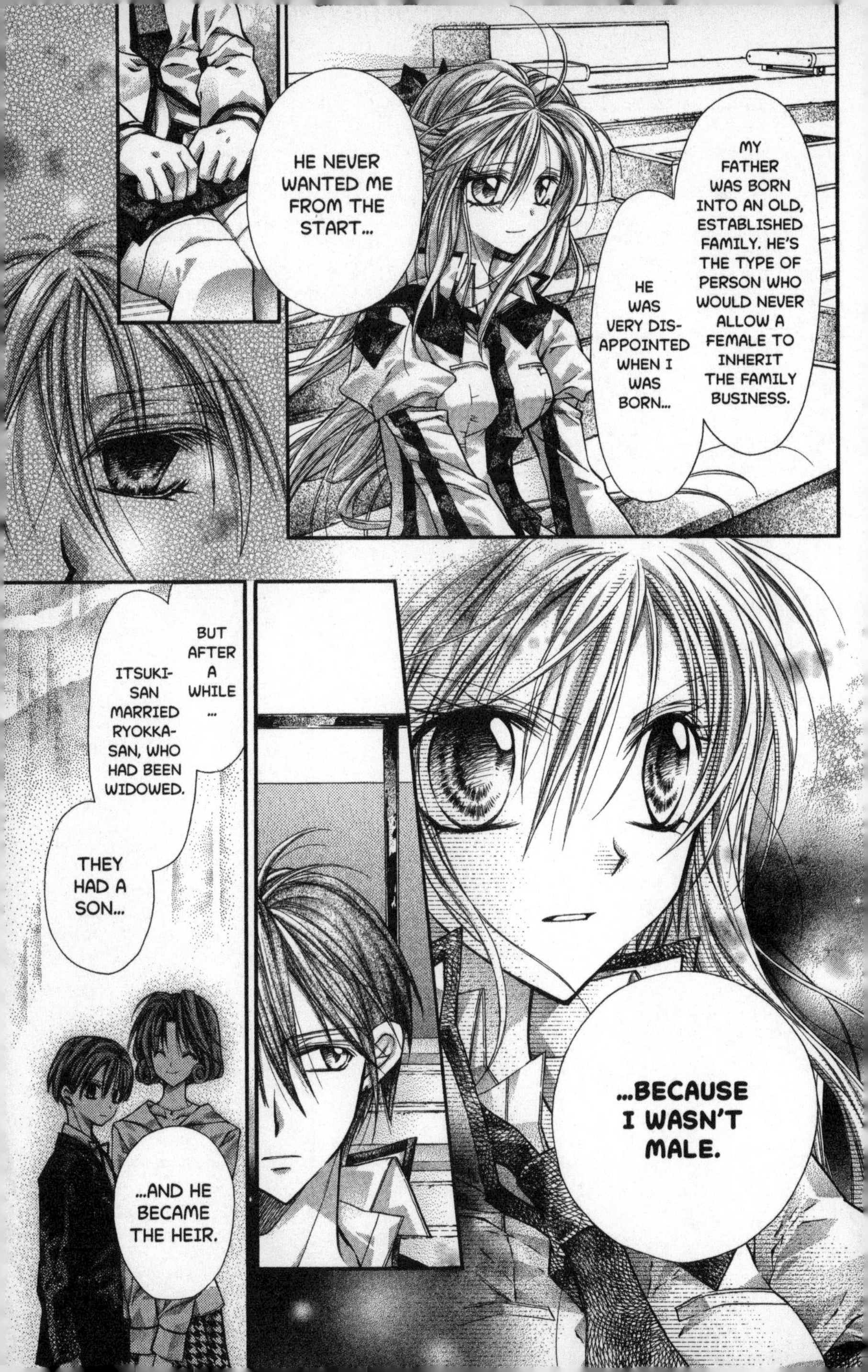
MY FATHER WAS BORN INTO AN OLD, ESTABLISHED FAMILY. HE'S THE TYPE OF PERSON WHO WOULD NEVER ALLOW A FEMALE TO INHERIT THE FAMILY BUSINESS.
HE WAS VERY DIS-APPOINTED WHEN I WAS BORN...
HE NEVER WANTED ME FROM THE START...
...BECAUSE I WASN'T MALE.
BUT AFTER A WHILE...
ITSUKI-SAN MARRIED RYOKKA-SAN, WHO HAD BEEN WIDOWED.
THEY HAD A SON...
...AND HE BECAME THE HEIR.

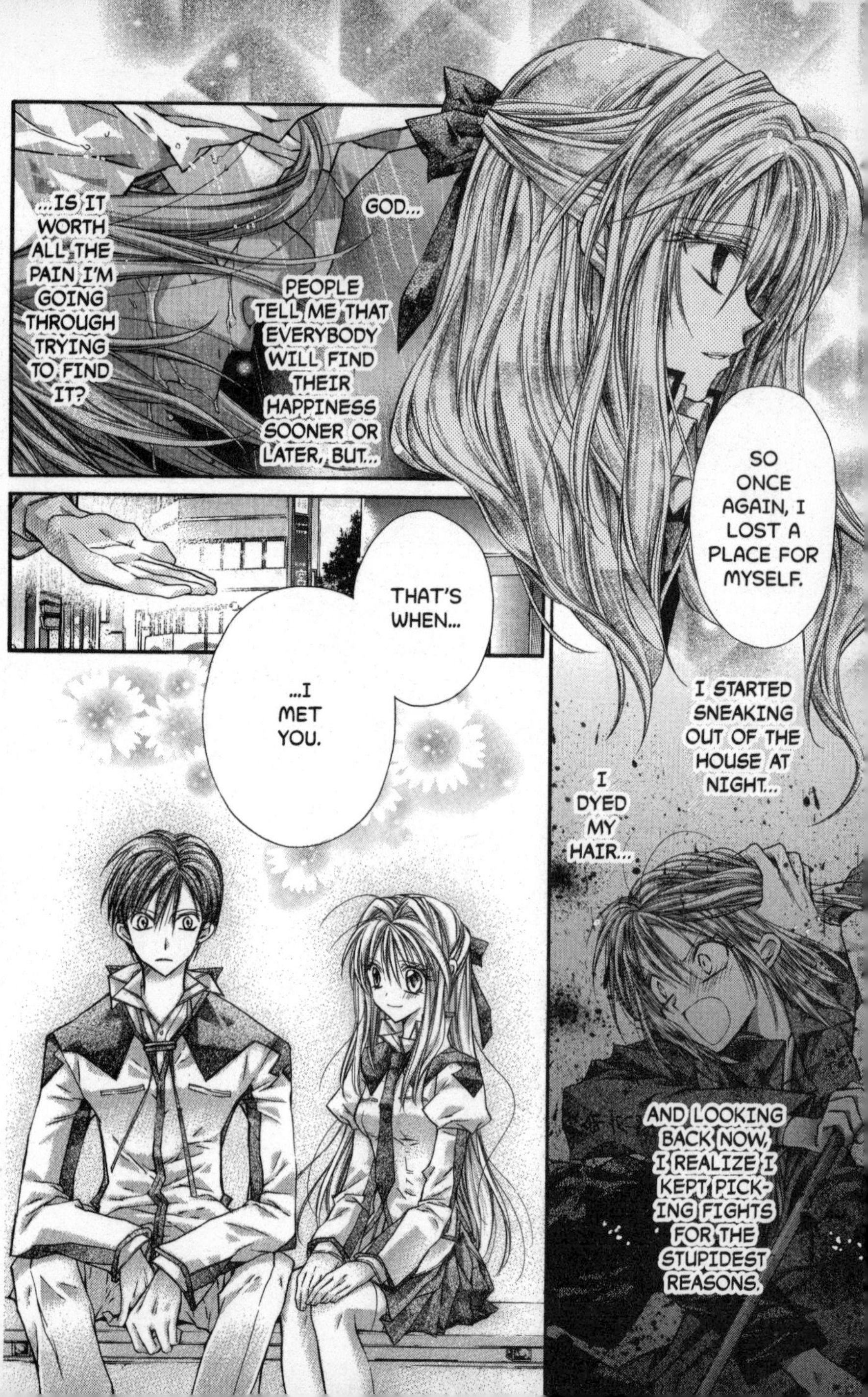
GOD...
PEOPLE TELL ME THAT EVERYBODY WILL FIND THEIR HAPPINESS SOONER OR LATER, BUT...
...IS IT WORTH ALL THE PAIN I'M GOING THROUGH TRYING TO FIND IT?
SO ONCE AGAIN, I LOST A PLACE FOR MYSELF.
I STARTED SNEAKING OUT OF THE HOUSE AT NIGHT...
I DYED MY HAIR...
AND LOOKING BACK NOW, I REALIZE I KEPT PICK-ING FIGHTS FOR THE STUPIDEST REASONS.
THAT'S WHEN...
...I MET YOU.

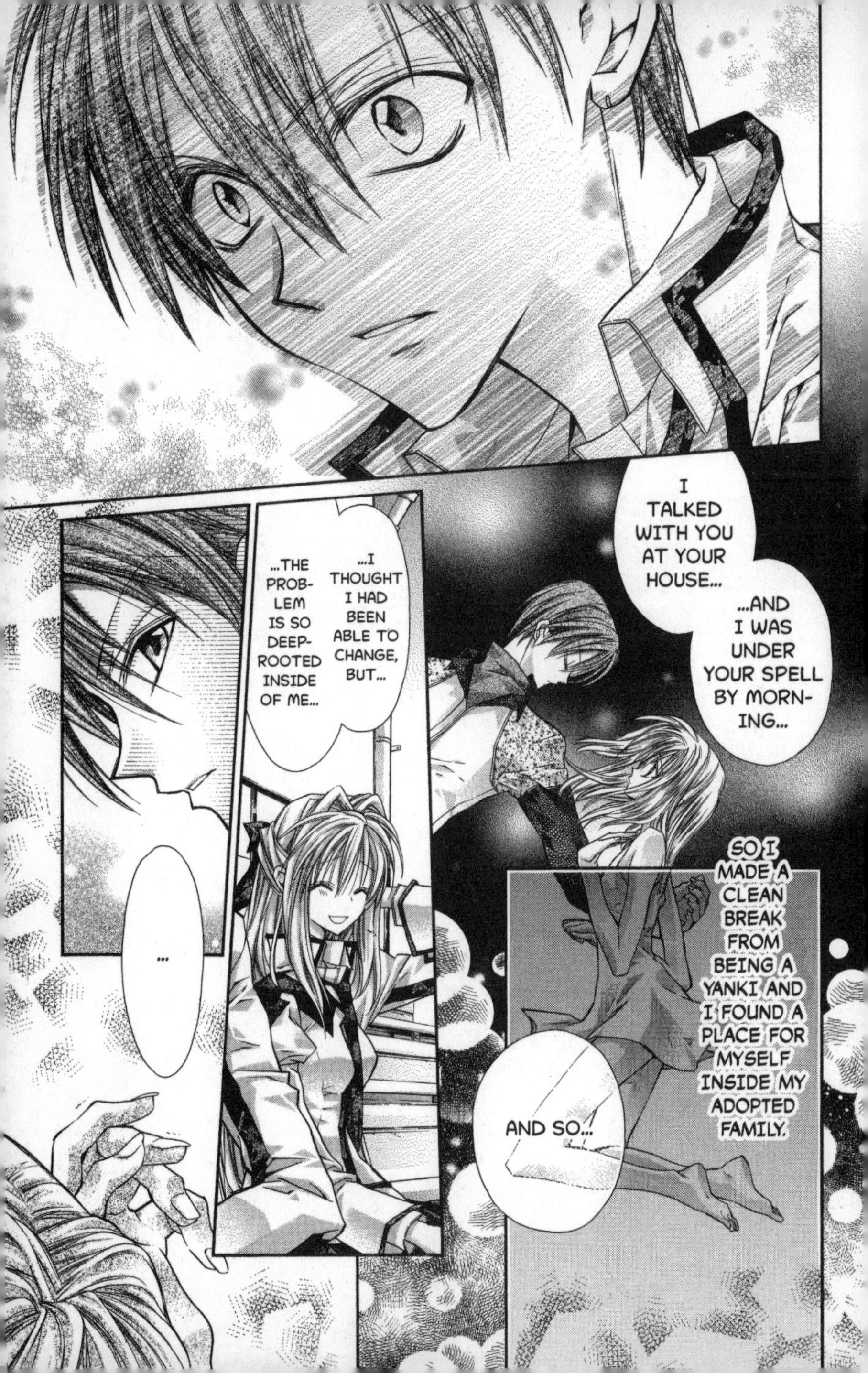
I TALKED WITH YOU AT YOUR HOUSE...
...AND I WAS UNDER YOUR SPELL BY MORNING...
SO I MADE A CLEAN BREAK FROM BEING A YANKI AND I FOUND A PLACE FOR MYSELF INSIDE MY ADOPTED FAMILY.
AND SO...
...I THOUGHT I HAD BEEN ABLE TO CHANGE, BUT...
...THE PROBLEM IS SO DEEP-ROOTED INSIDE OF ME...
...

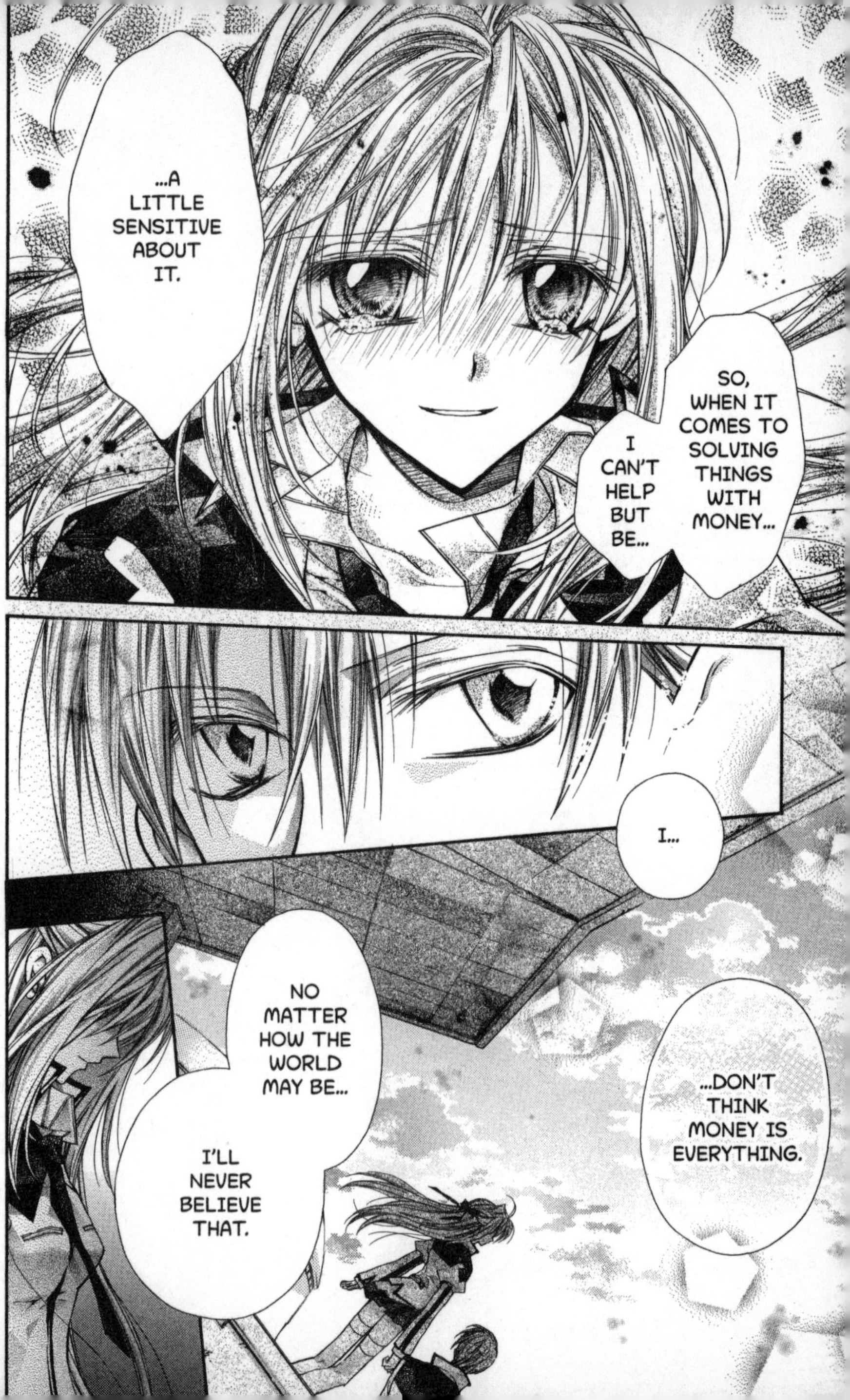
SO, WHEN IT COMES TO SOLVING THINGS WITH MONEY...
I CAN'T HELP BUT BE...
...A LITTLE SENSITIVE ABOUT IT.
I...
...DON'T THINK MONEY IS EVERYTHING.
NO MATTER HOW THE WORLD MAY BE...
I'LL NEVER BELIEVE THAT.

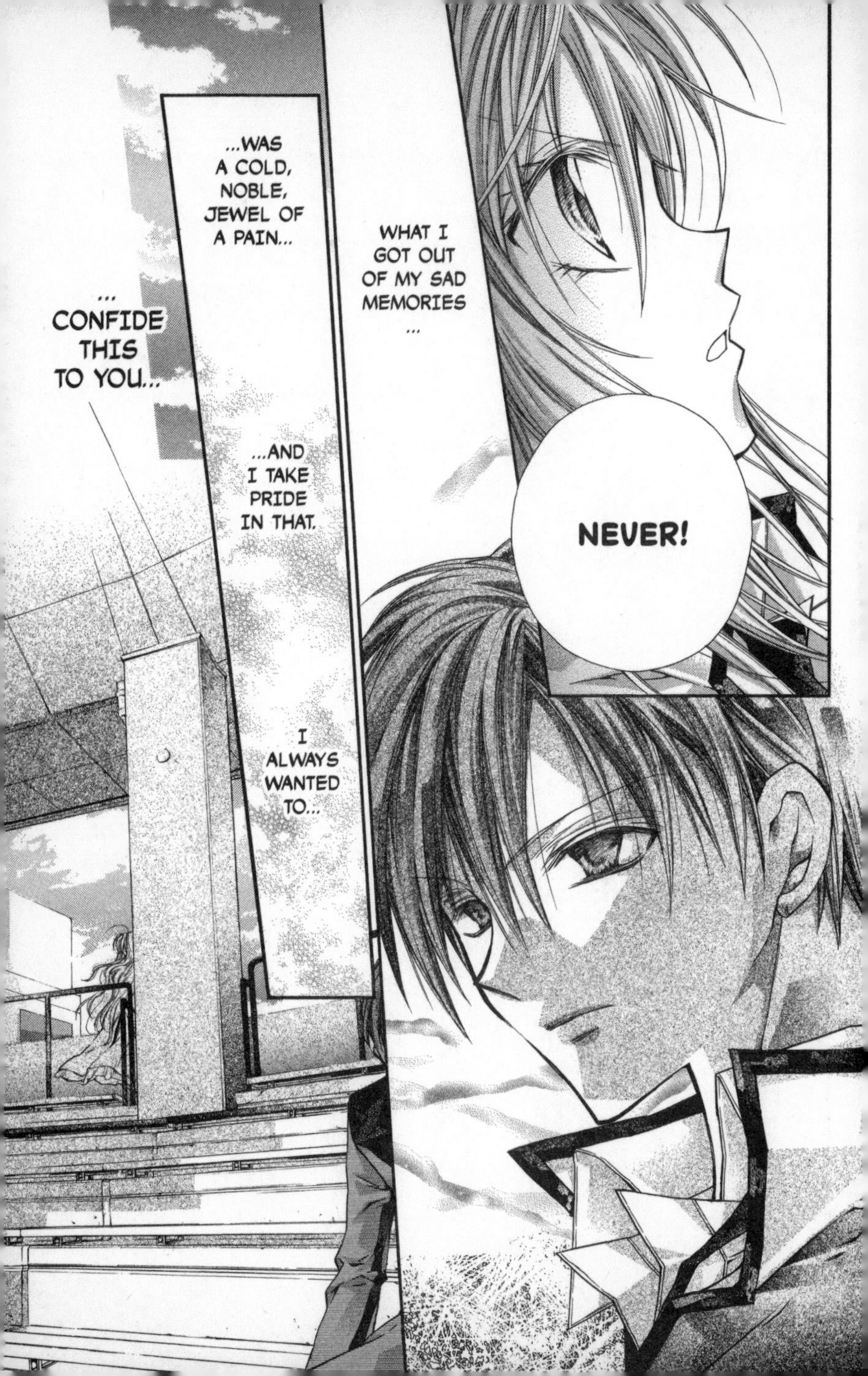
NEVER!
WHAT I GOT OUT OF MY SAD MEMORIES ...
...WAS A COLD, NOBLE, JEWEL OF A PAIN...
...AND I TAKE PRIDE IN THAT.
I ALWAYS WANTED TO...
... CONFIDE THIS TO YOU...

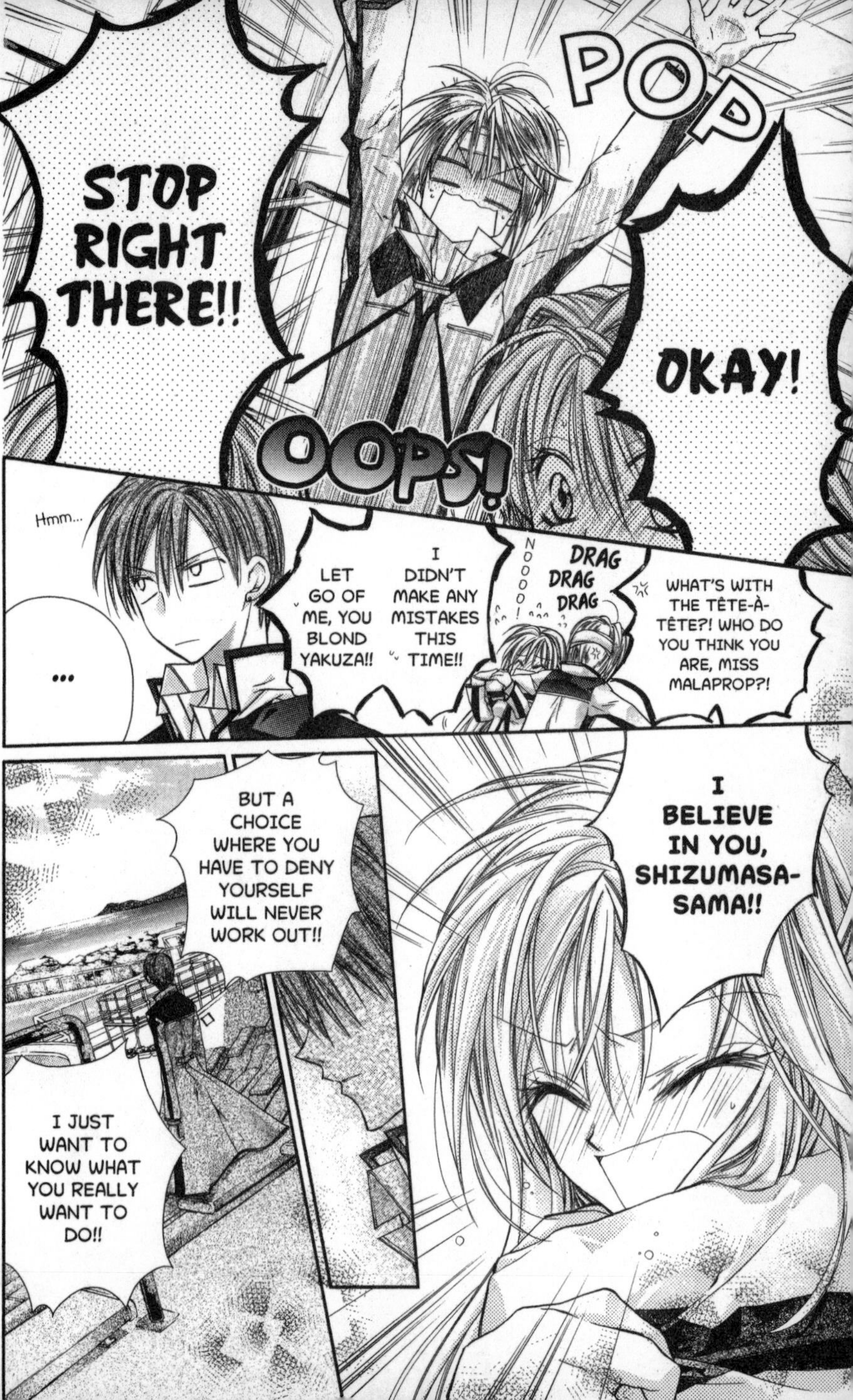
POP
STOP RIGHT THERE!!
OKAY!
OOPS!
WHAT'S WITH THE TÊTE-À-TÊTE?! WHO DO YOU THINK YOU ARE, MISS MALAPROP?!
DRAG DRAG DRAG
NOOOOO!
I DIDN'T MAKE ANY MISTAKES THIS TIME!!
LET GO OF ME, YOU BLOND YAKUZA!!
Hmm...
...
I BELIEVE IN YOU, SHIZUMASA-SAMA!!
BUT A CHOICE WHERE YOU HAVE TO DENY YOURSELF WILL NEVER WORK OUT!!
I JUST WANT TO KNOW WHAT YOU REALLY WANT TO DO!!

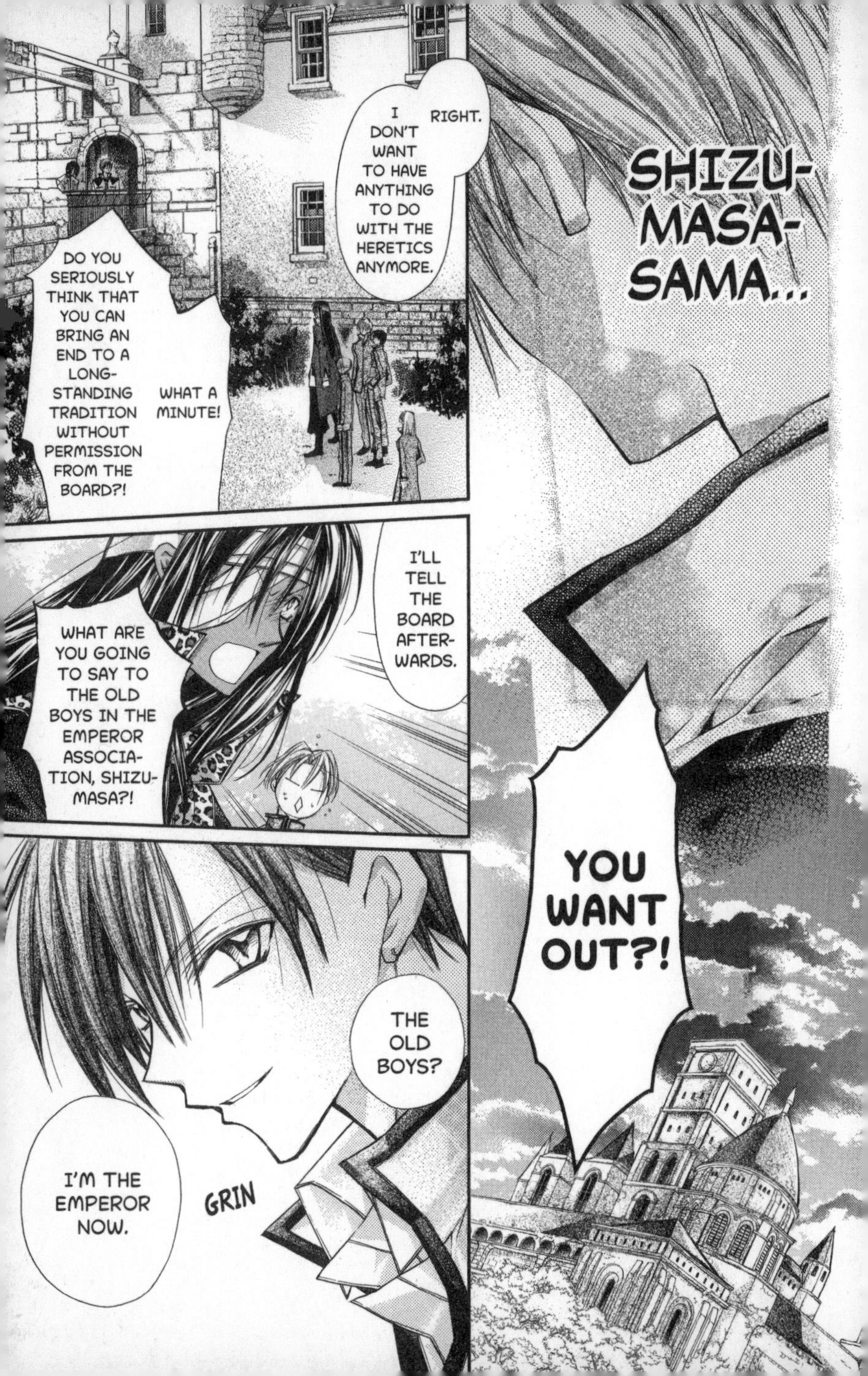
SHIZU-MASA-SAMA...
YOU WANT OUT?!
RIGHT. I DON'T WANT TO HAVE ANYTHING TO DO WITH THE HERETICS ANYMORE.
WHAT A MINUTE!
DO YOU SERIOUSLY THINK THAT YOU CAN BRING AN END TO A LONG-STANDING TRADITION WITHOUT PERMISSION FROM THE BOARD?!
I'LL TELL THE BOARD AFTER-WARDS.
WHAT ARE YOU GOING TO SAY TO THE OLD BOYS IN THE EMPEROR ASSOCIA-TION, SHIZU-MASA?!
THE OLD BOYS?
I'M THE EMPEROR NOW.
GRIN

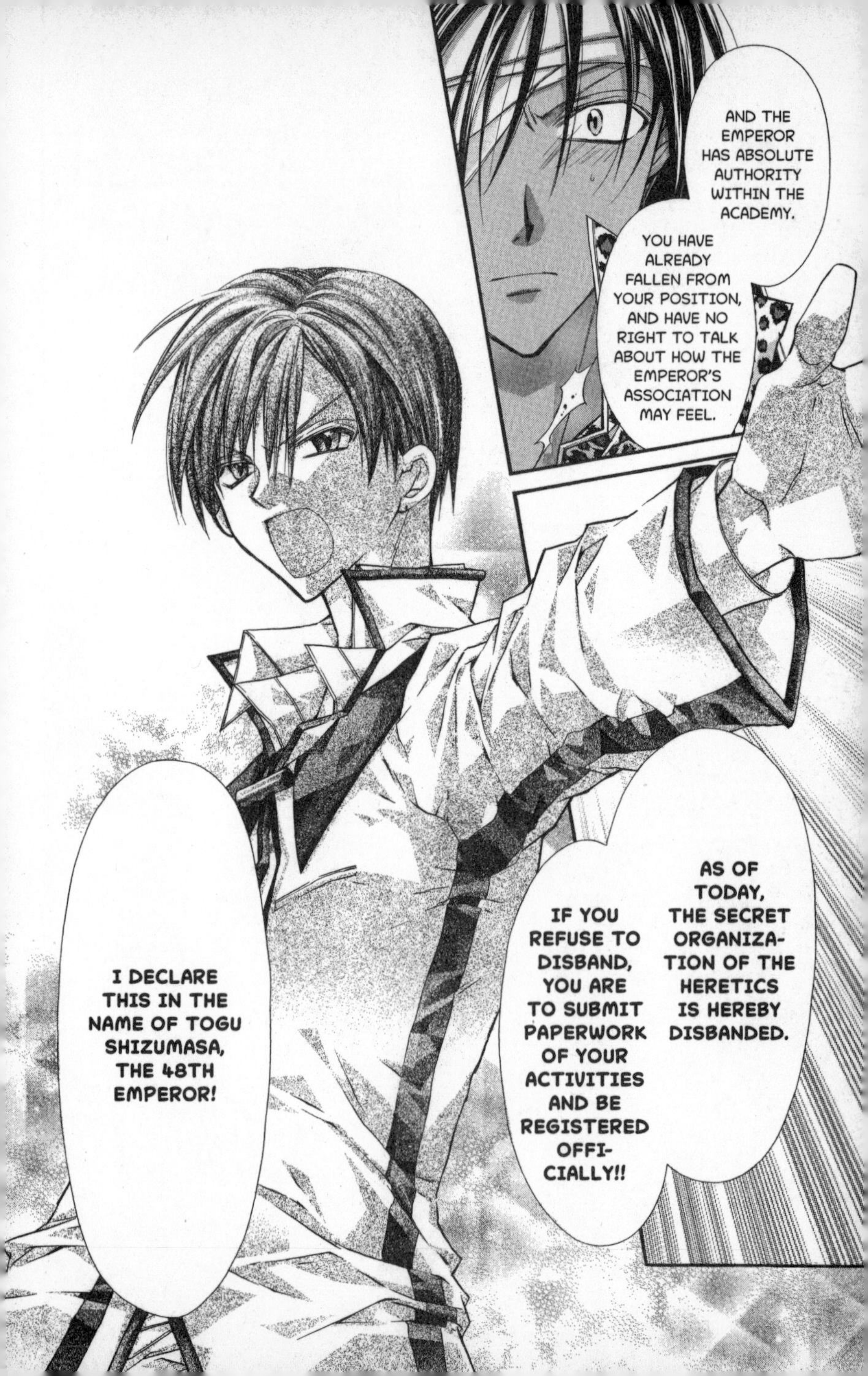
AND THE EMPEROR HAS ABSOLUTE AUTHORITY WITHIN THE ACADEMY.
YOU HAVE ALREADY FALLEN FROM YOUR POSITION, AND HAVE NO RIGHT TO TALK ABOUT HOW THE EMPEROR'S ASSOCIATION MAY FEEL.
AS OF TODAY, THE SECRET ORGANIZA-TION OF THE HERETICS IS HEREBY DISBANDED.
IF YOU REFUSE TO DISBAND, YOU ARE TO SUBMIT PAPERWORK OF YOUR ACTIVITIES AND BE REGISTERED OFFI-CIALLY!!
I DECLARE THIS IN THE NAME OF TOGU SHIZUMASA, THE 48TH EMPEROR!

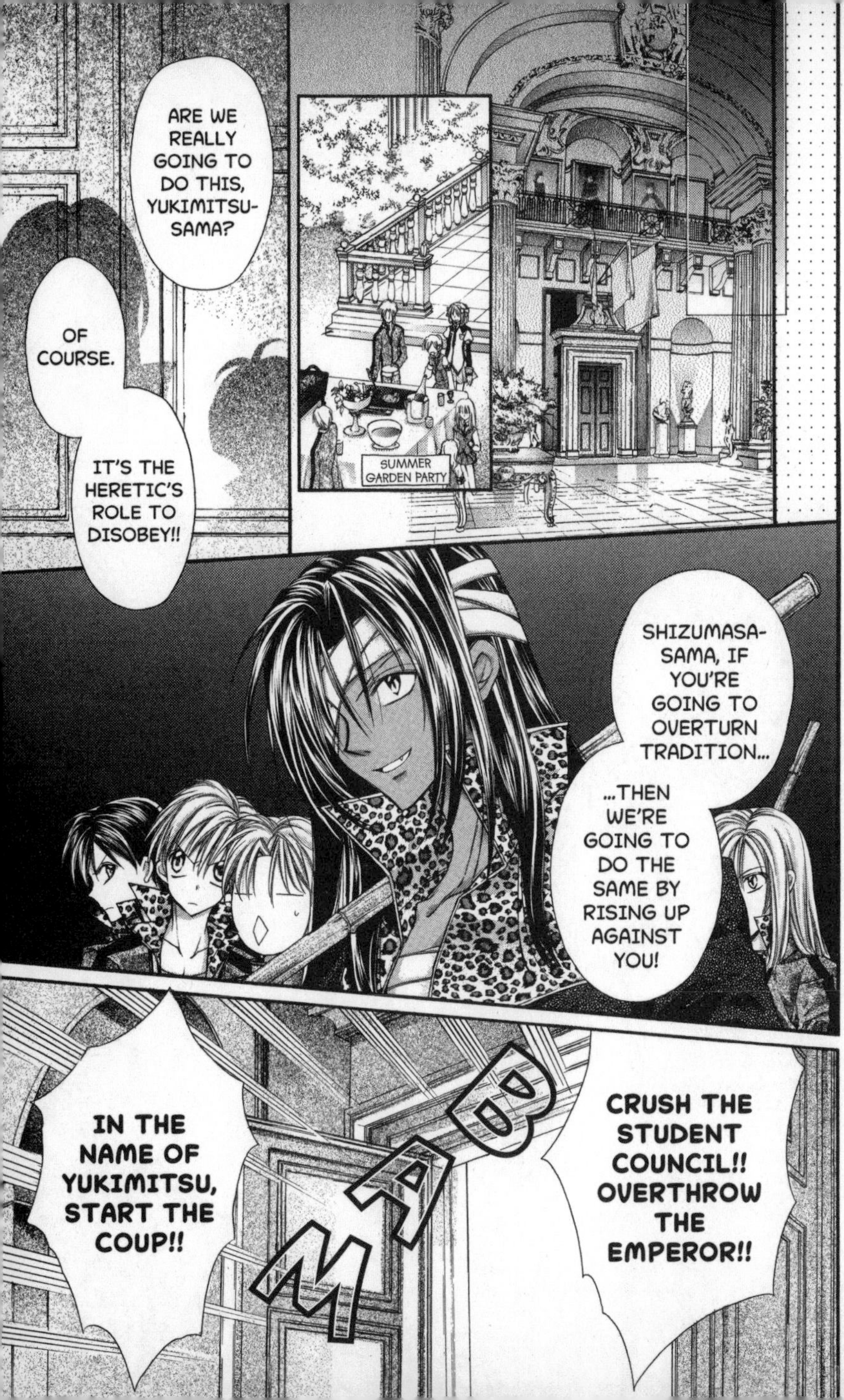
SUMMER GARDEN PARTY
ARE WE REALLY GOING TO DO THIS, YUKIMITSU-SAMA?
OF COURSE.
IT'S THE HERETIC'S ROLE TO DISOBEY!!
SHIZUMASA-SAMA, IF YOU'RE GOING TO OVERTURN TRADITION...
...THEN WE'RE GOING TO DO THE SAME BY RISING UP AGAINST YOU!
CRUSH THE STUDENT COUNCIL!! OVERTHROW THE EMPEROR!!
BAM
IN THE NAME OF YUKIMITSU, START THE COUP!!

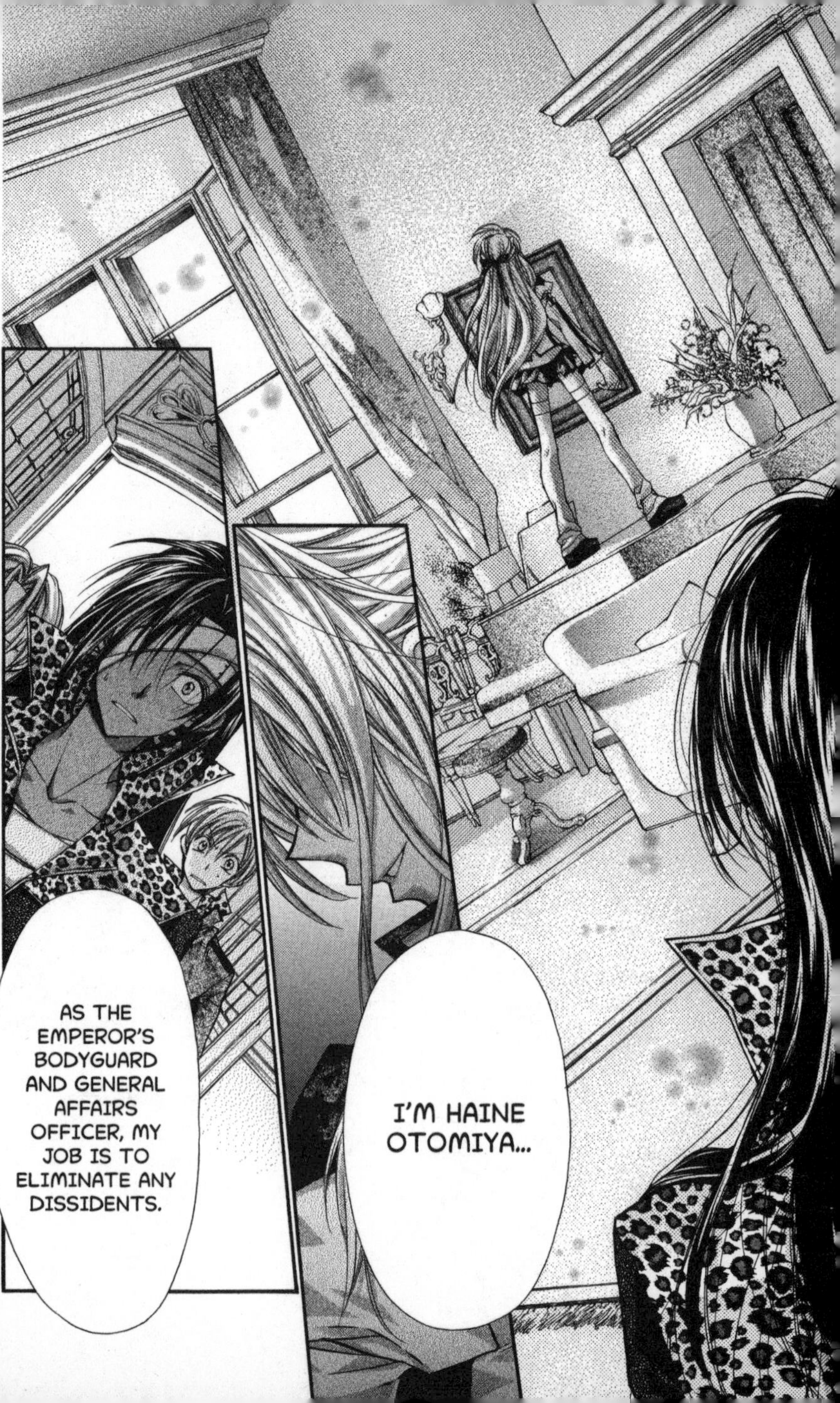
I'M HAINE OTOMIYA...
AS THE EMPEROR'S BODYGUARD AND GENERAL AFFAIRS OFFICER, MY JOB IS TO ELIMINATE ANY DISSIDENTS.

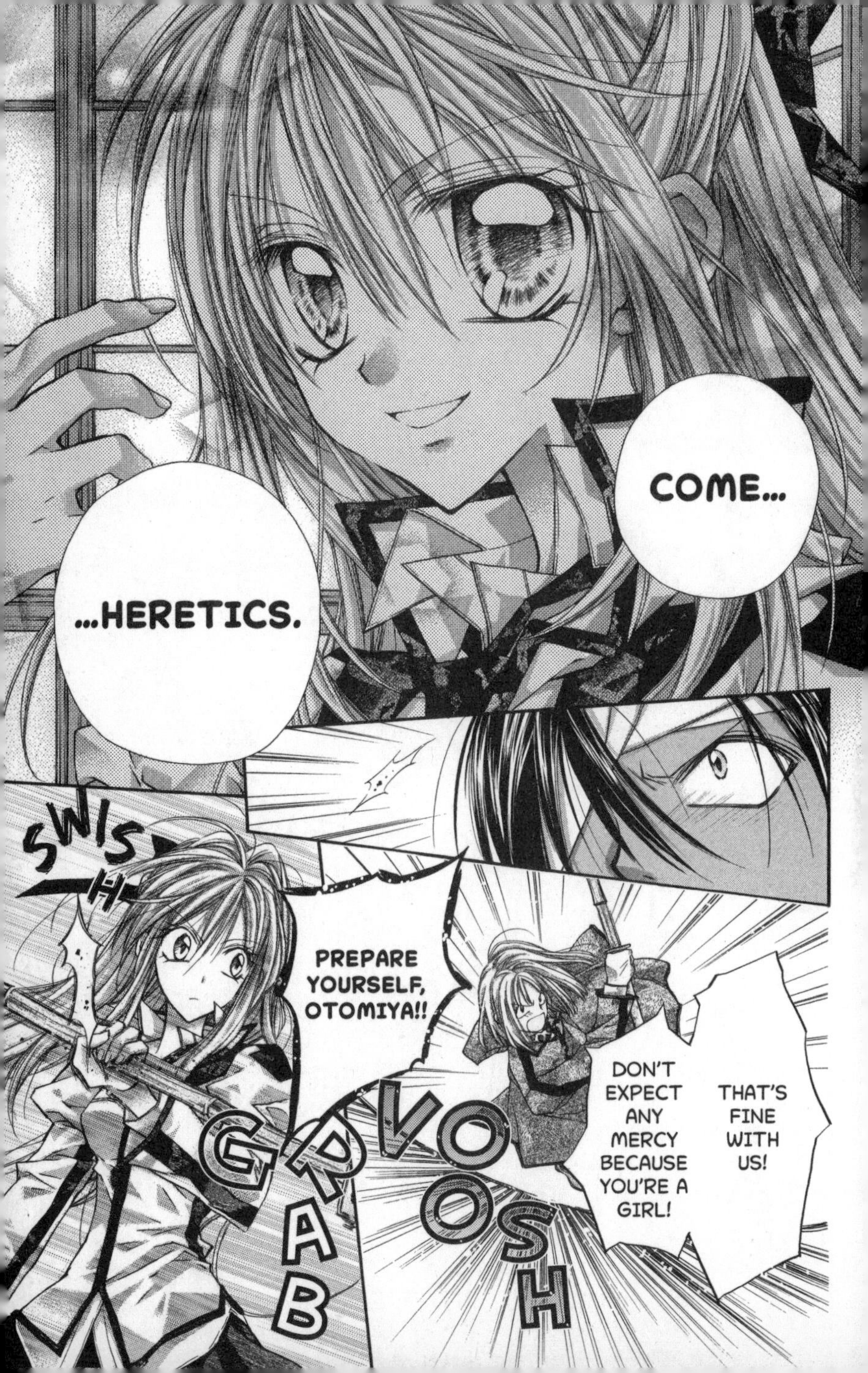
COME...
...HERETICS.
THAT'S FINE WITH US!
DON'T EXPECT ANY MERCY BECAUSE YOU'RE A GIRL!
PREPARE YOURSELF, OTOMIYA!!
VOOSH
GRAB
SWISH

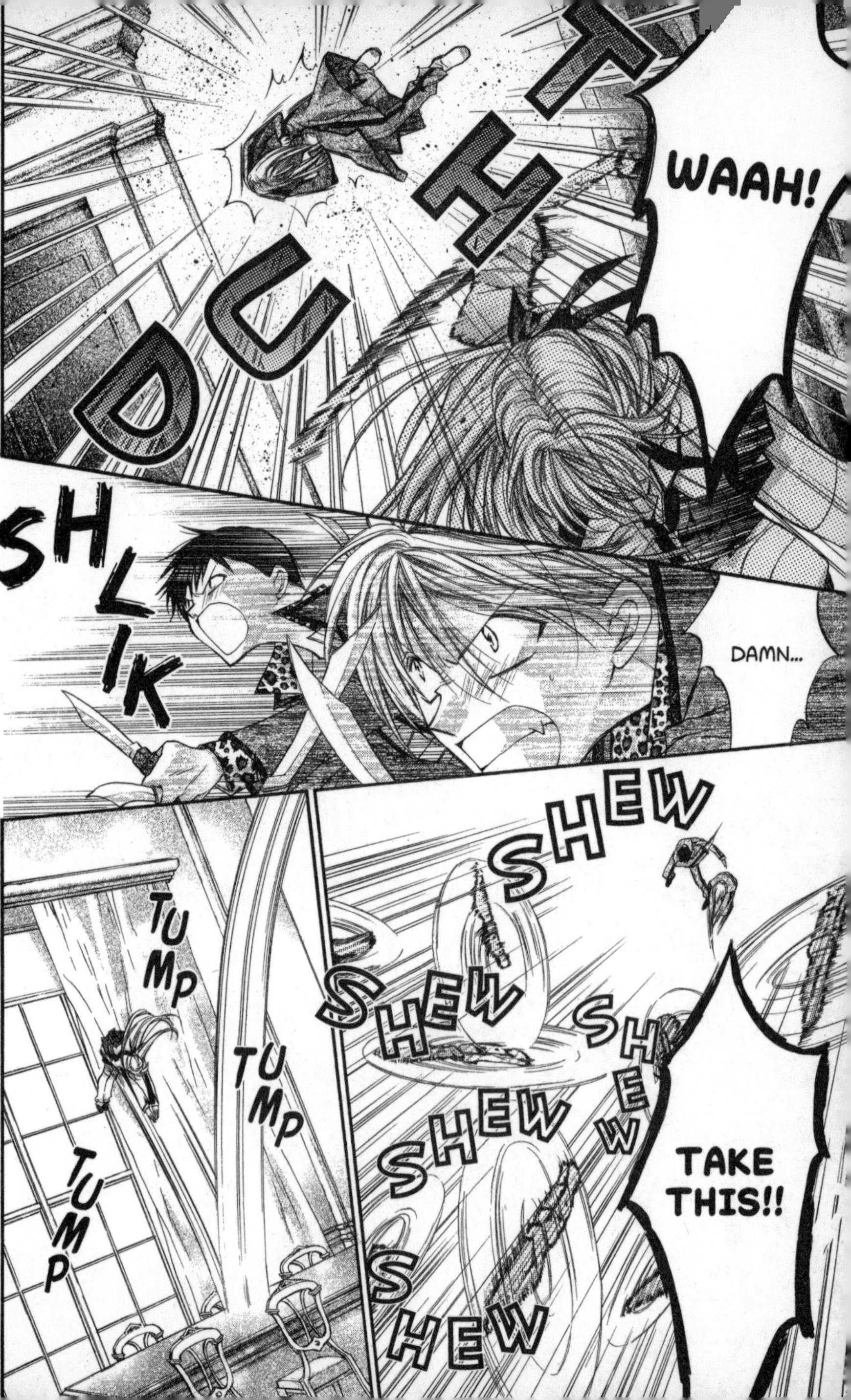
THUD
WAAH!
DAMN...
SHLIK
TAKE THIS!!
SHEW
SHEW
SHEW
SHEW
SHEW
SHEW
TUMP
TUMP
TUMP

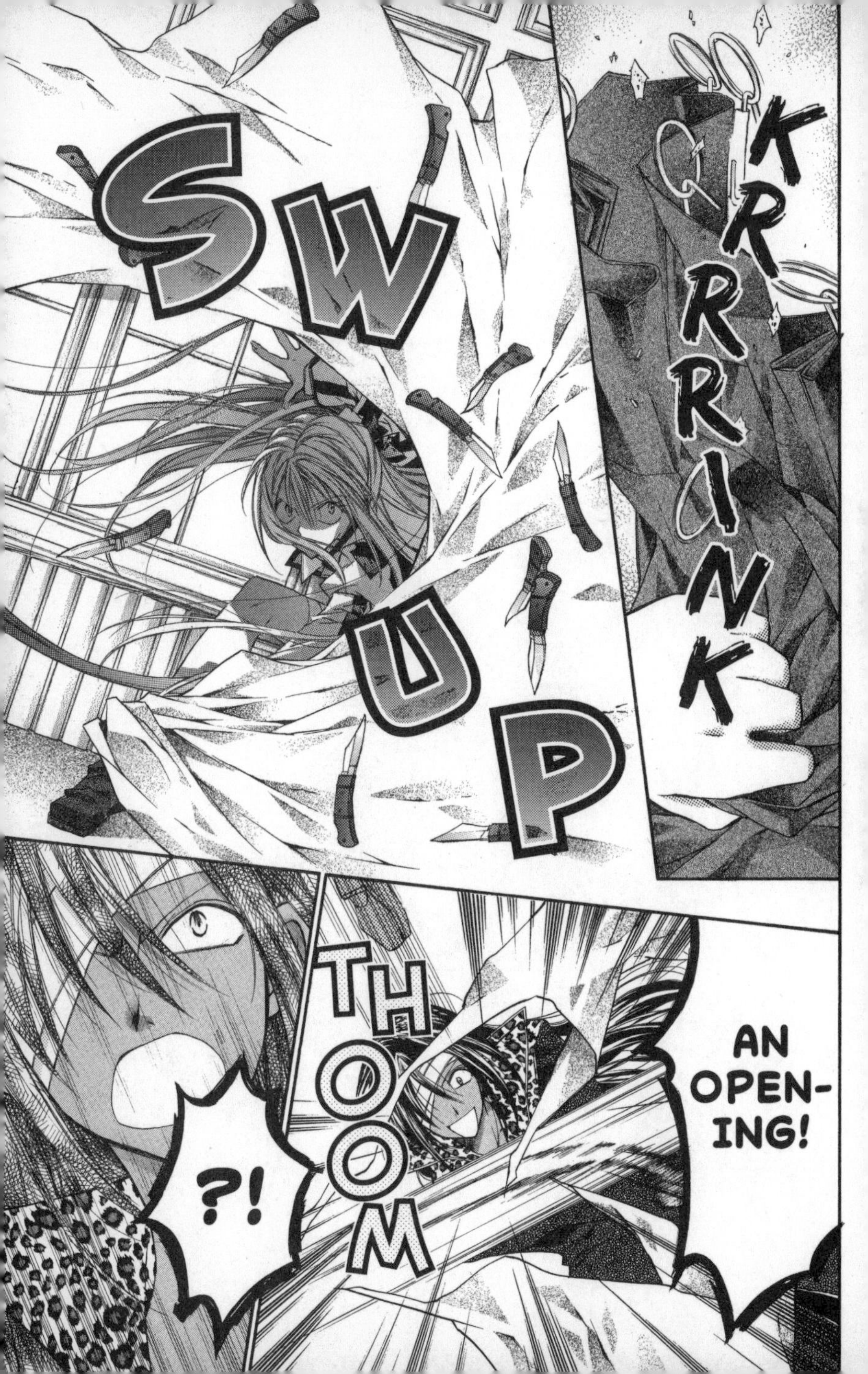
KRRRINK
SWUP
AN OPEN-
ING!
THOOOM
?!

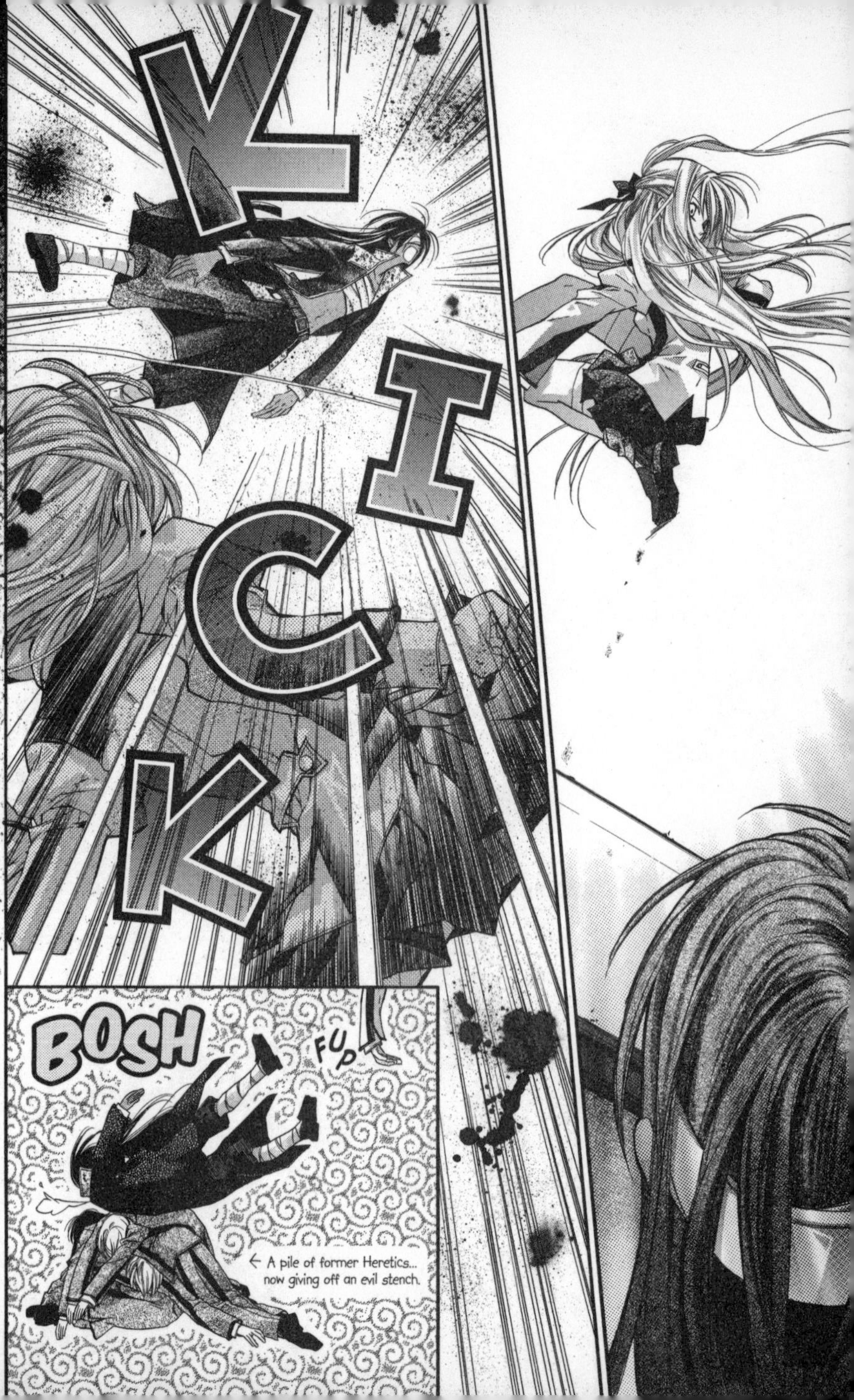
KICK
BOSH
FUP
← A pile of former Heretics... now giving off an evil stench.

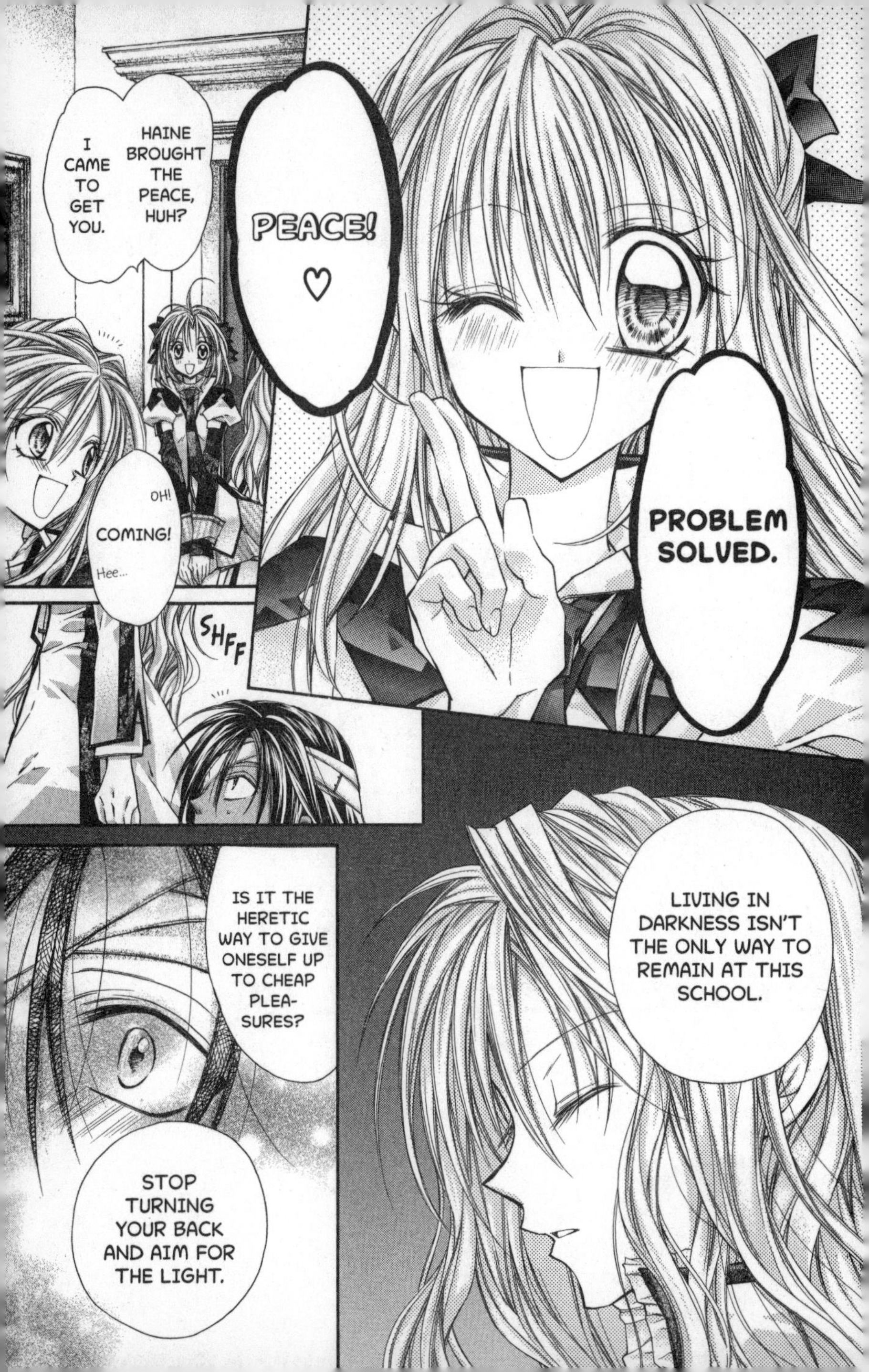
PEACE!
♥
PROBLEM SOLVED.
HAINE BROUGHT THE PEACE, HUH?
I CAME TO GET YOU.
OH!
COMING!
Hee...
SHFF
LIVING IN DARKNESS ISN'T THE ONLY WAY TO REMAIN AT THIS SCHOOL.
IS IT THE HERETIC WAY TO GIVE ONESELF UP TO CHEAP PLEA-SURES?
STOP TURNING YOUR BACK AND AIM FOR THE LIGHT.

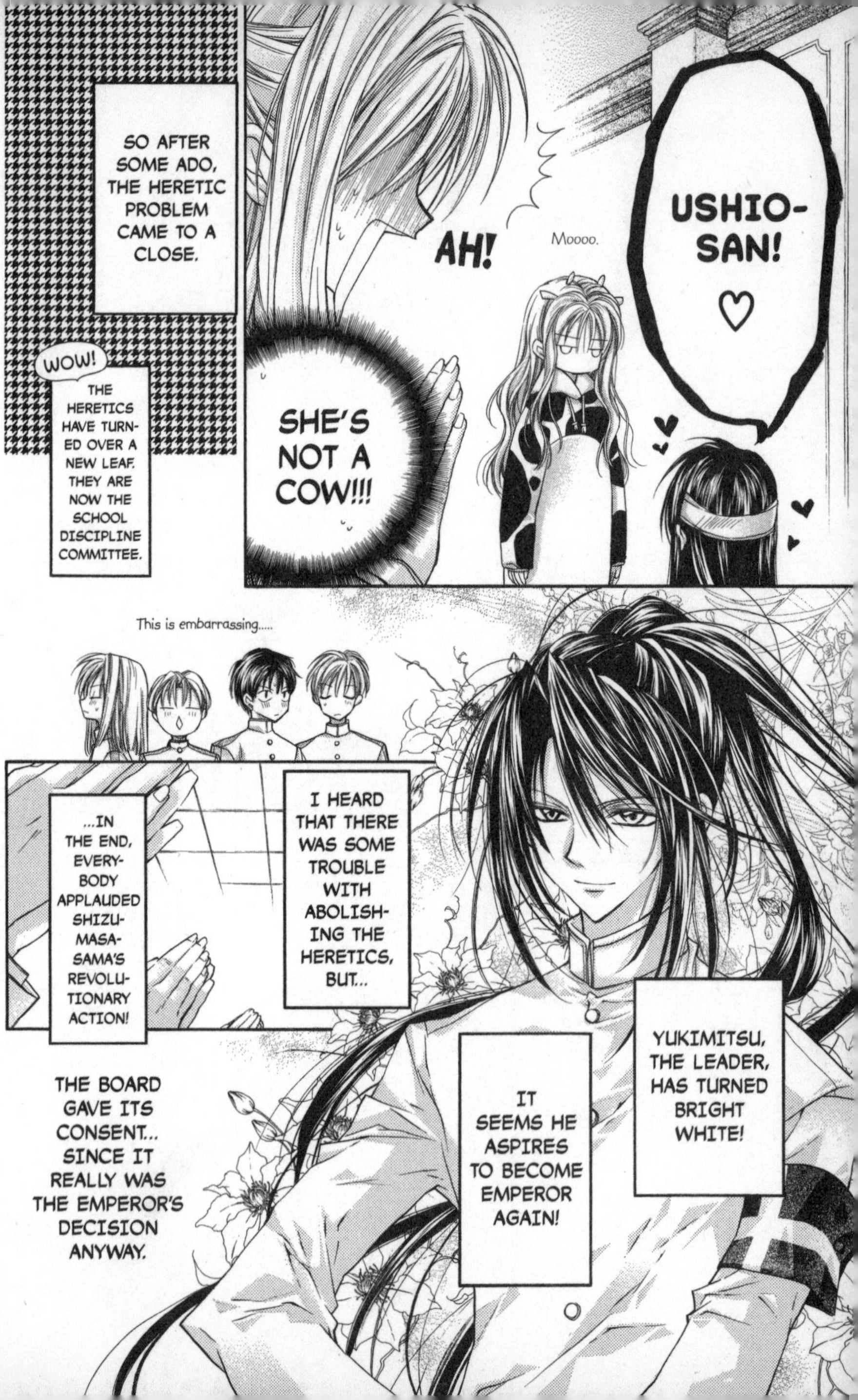
USHIO-SAN! ♡
AH!
Moooo.
SHE'S NOT A COW!!!
SO AFTER SOME ADO, THE HERETIC PROBLEM CAME TO A CLOSE.
WOW!
THE HERETICS HAVE TURNED OVER A NEW LEAF. THEY ARE NOW THE SCHOOL DISCIPLINE COMMITTEE.
YUKIMITSU, THE LEADER, HAS TURNED BRIGHT WHITE!
IT SEEMS HE ASPIRES TO BECOME EMPEROR AGAIN!
This is embarrassing.....
I HEARD THAT THERE WAS SOME TROUBLE WITH ABOLISHING THE HERETICS, BUT...
...IN THE END, EVERYBODY APPLAUDED SHIZUMASA-SAMA'S REVOLUTIONARY ACTION!
THE BOARD GAVE ITS CONSENT... SINCE IT REALLY WAS THE EMPEROR'S DECISION ANYWAY.

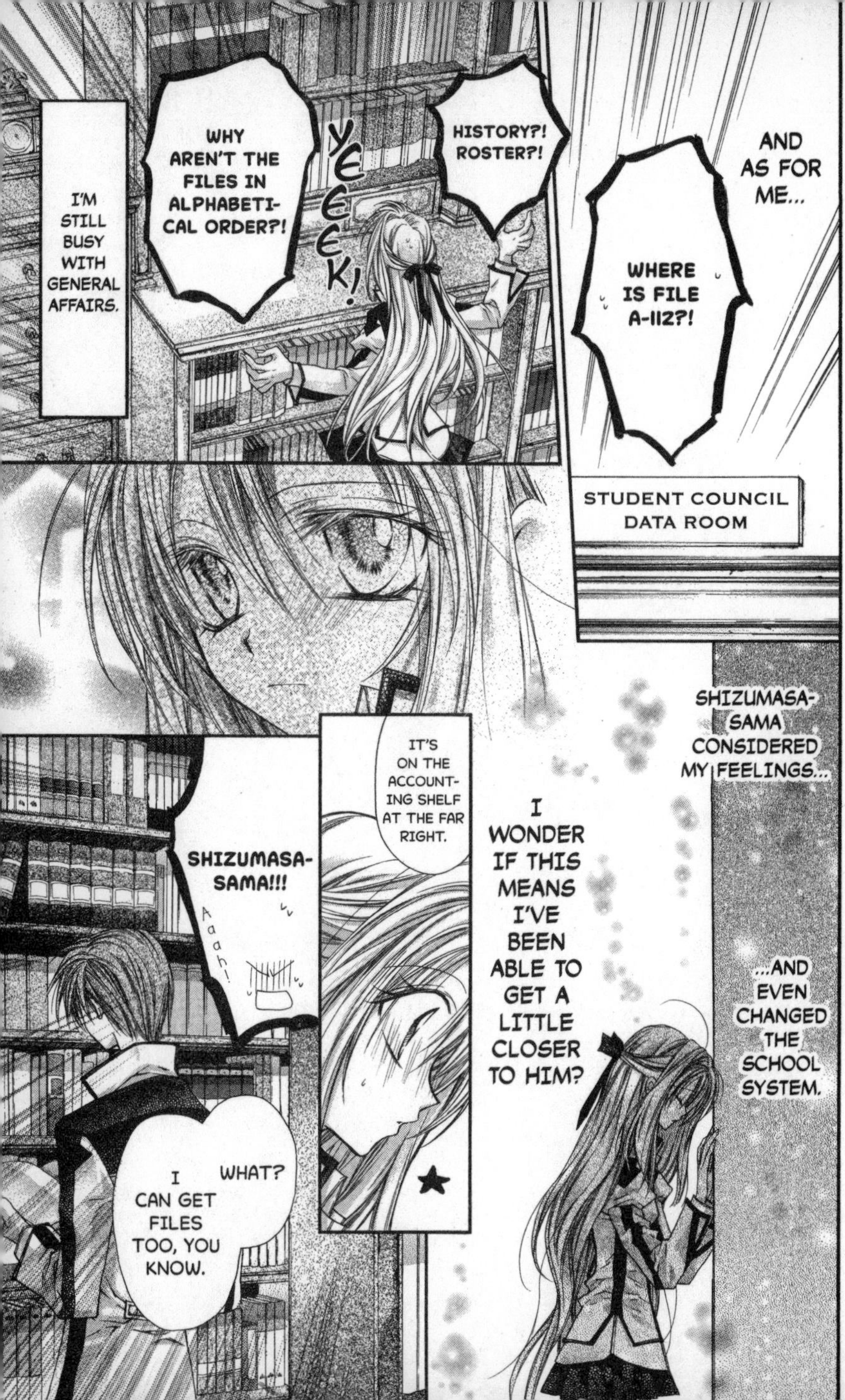
AND AS FOR ME...
WHERE IS FILE A-112?!
STUDENT COUNCIL DATA ROOM
HISTORY?! ROSTER?!
YEEEK!
WHY AREN'T THE FILES IN ALPHABETICAL ORDER?!
I'M STILL BUSY WITH GENERAL AFFAIRS.
SHIZUMASA-SAMA CONSIDERED MY FEELINGS...
...AND EVEN CHANGED THE SCHOOL SYSTEM.
I WONDER IF THIS MEANS I'VE BEEN ABLE TO GET A LITTLE CLOSER TO HIM?
IT'S ON THE ACCOUNTING SHELF AT THE FAR RIGHT.
SHIZUMASA-SAMA!!!
Aaah!
WHAT?
I CAN GET FILES TOO, YOU KNOW.

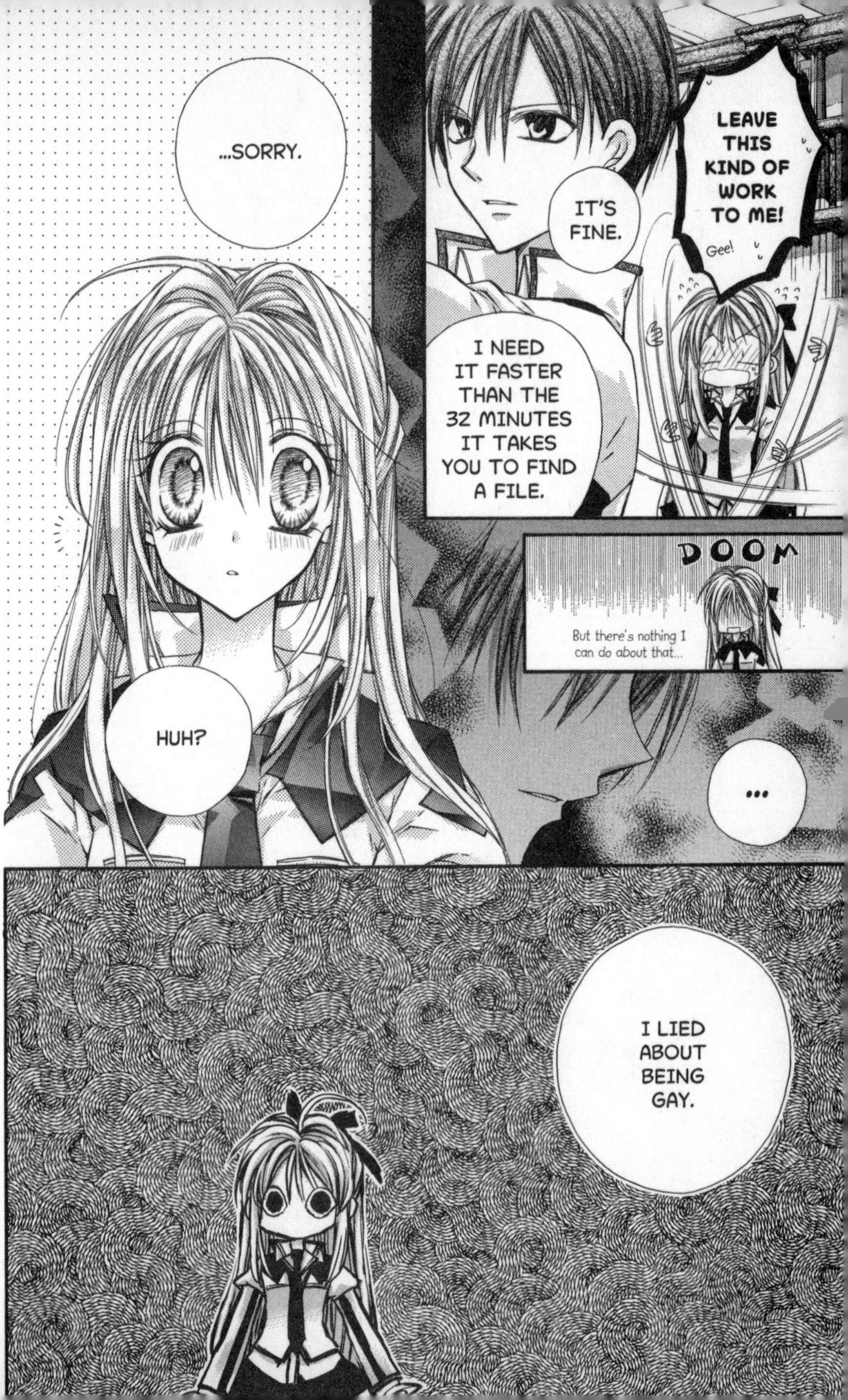
LEAVE THIS KIND OF WORK TO ME!
Gee!
IT'S FINE.
I NEED IT FASTER THAN THE 32 MINUTES IT TAKES YOU TO FIND A FILE.
DOOM
But there's nothing I can do about that...
...
...SORRY.
HUH?
I LIED ABOUT BEING GAY.

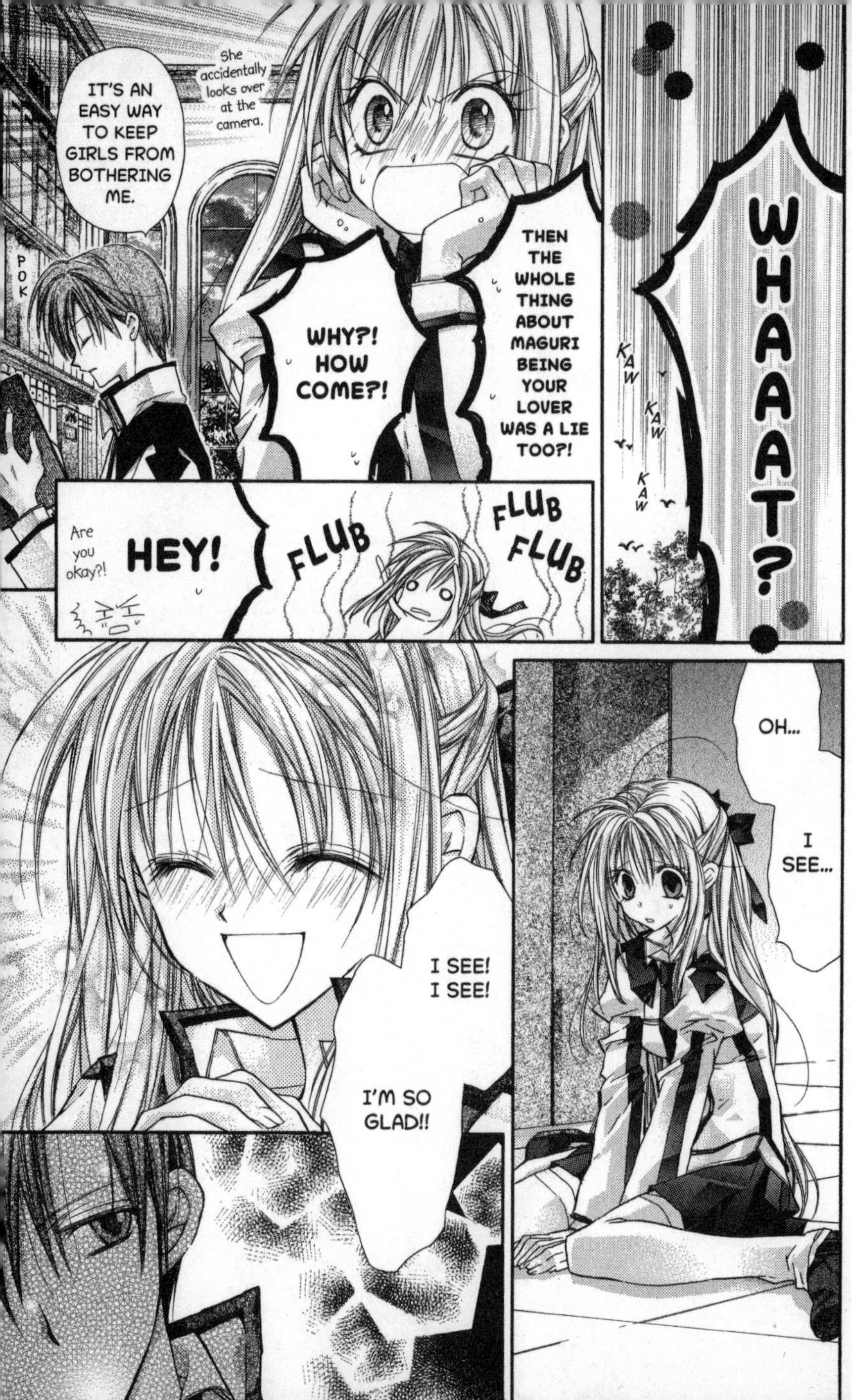
WHAAAT?
KAW
KAW
KAW
THEN THE WHOLE THING ABOUT MAGURI BEING YOUR LOVER WAS A LIE TOO?!
WHY?! HOW COME?!
She accidentally looks over at the camera.
IT'S AN EASY WAY TO KEEP GIRLS FROM BOTHERING ME.
POK
FLUB
FLUB
FLUB
HEY!
Are you okay?!
OH...
I SEE...
I SEE! I SEE!
I'M SO GLAD!!

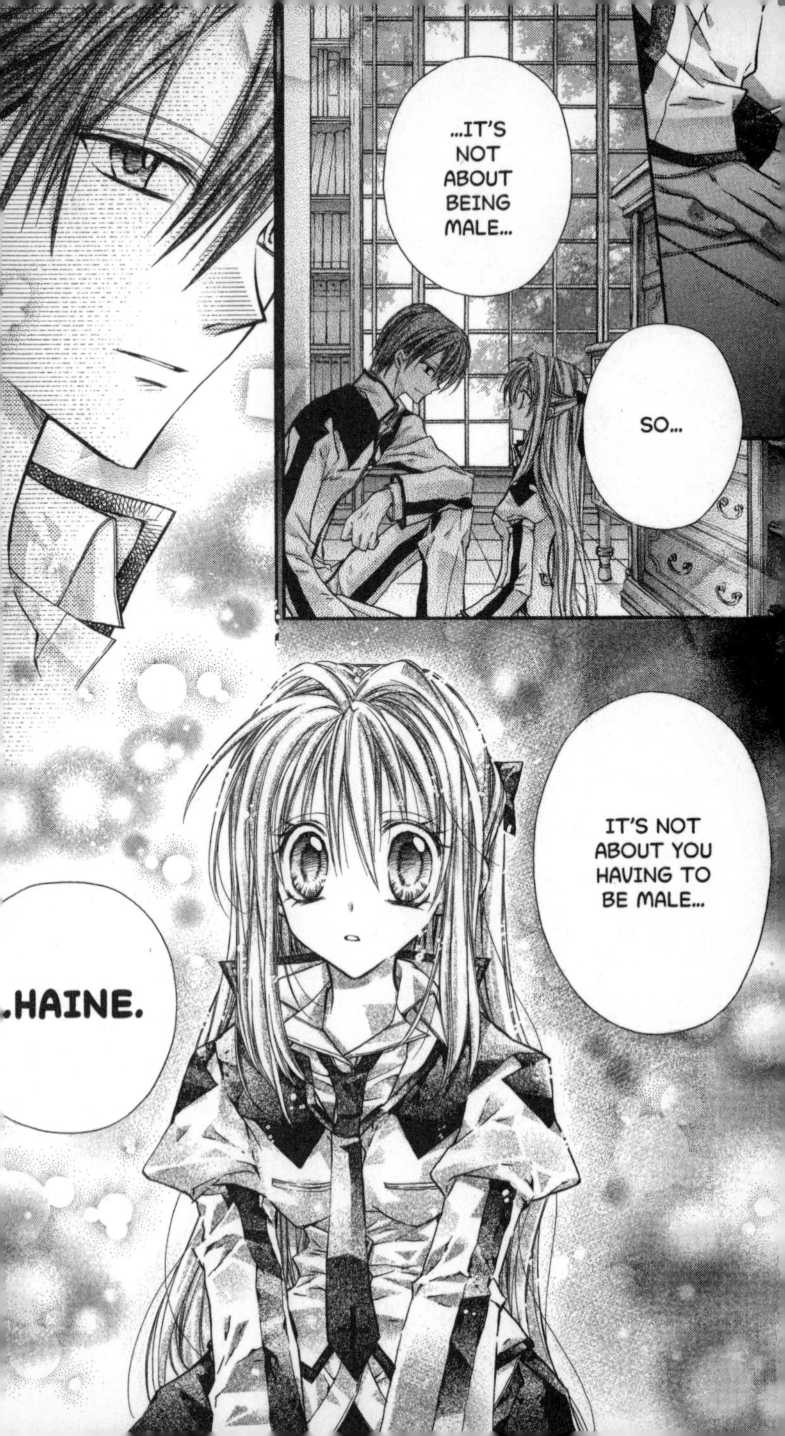
...IT'S NOT ABOUT BEING MALE...
SO...
IT'S NOT ABOUT YOU HAVING TO BE MALE...
.HAINE.

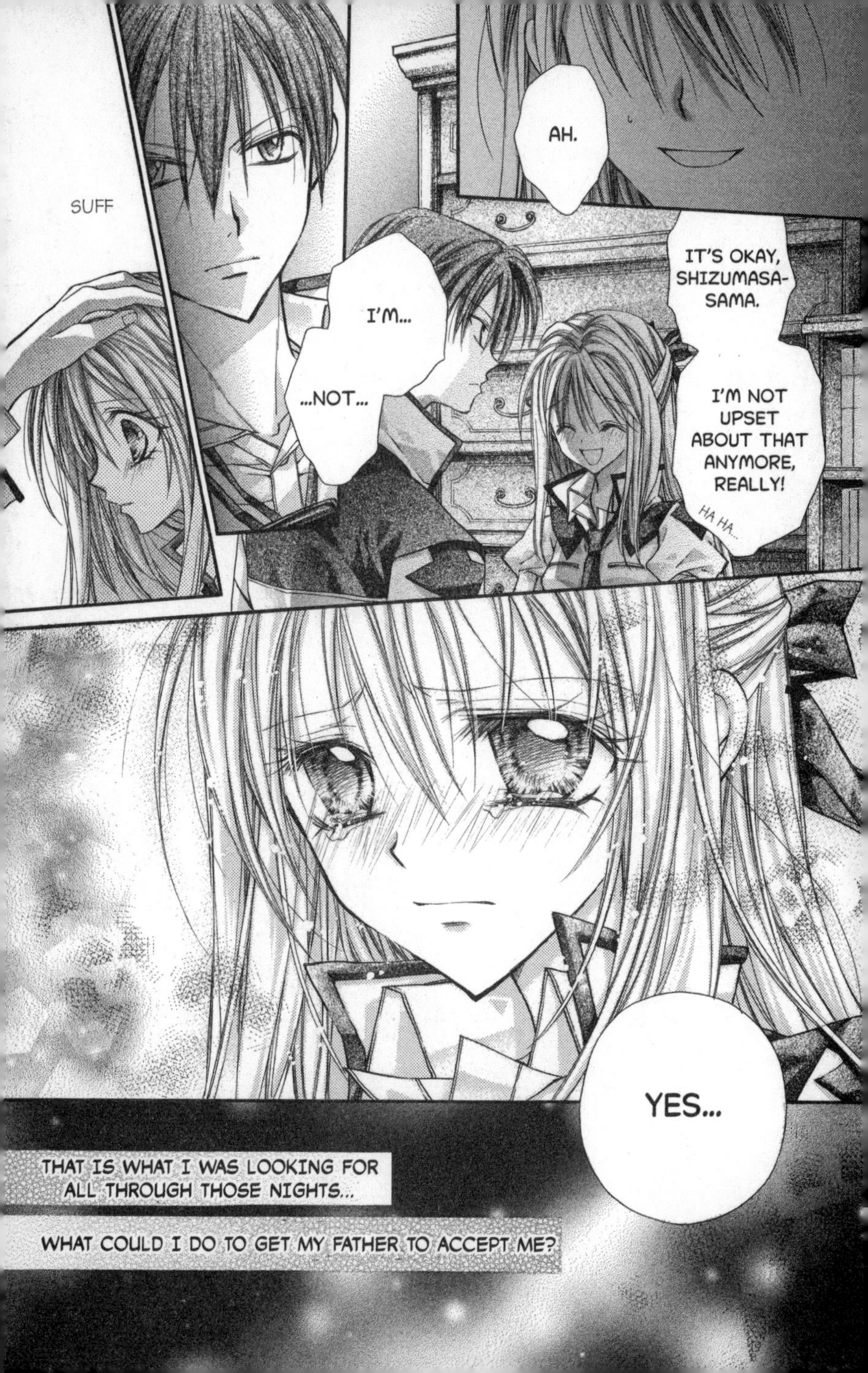
AH.
IT'S OKAY, SHIZUMASA-SAMA.
I'M NOT UPSET ABOUT THAT ANYMORE, REALLY!
HA HA...
I'M...
...NOT...
SUFF
YES...
THAT IS WHAT I WAS LOOKING FOR ALL THROUGH THOSE NIGHTS...
WHAT COULD I DO TO GET MY FATHER TO ACCEPT ME?

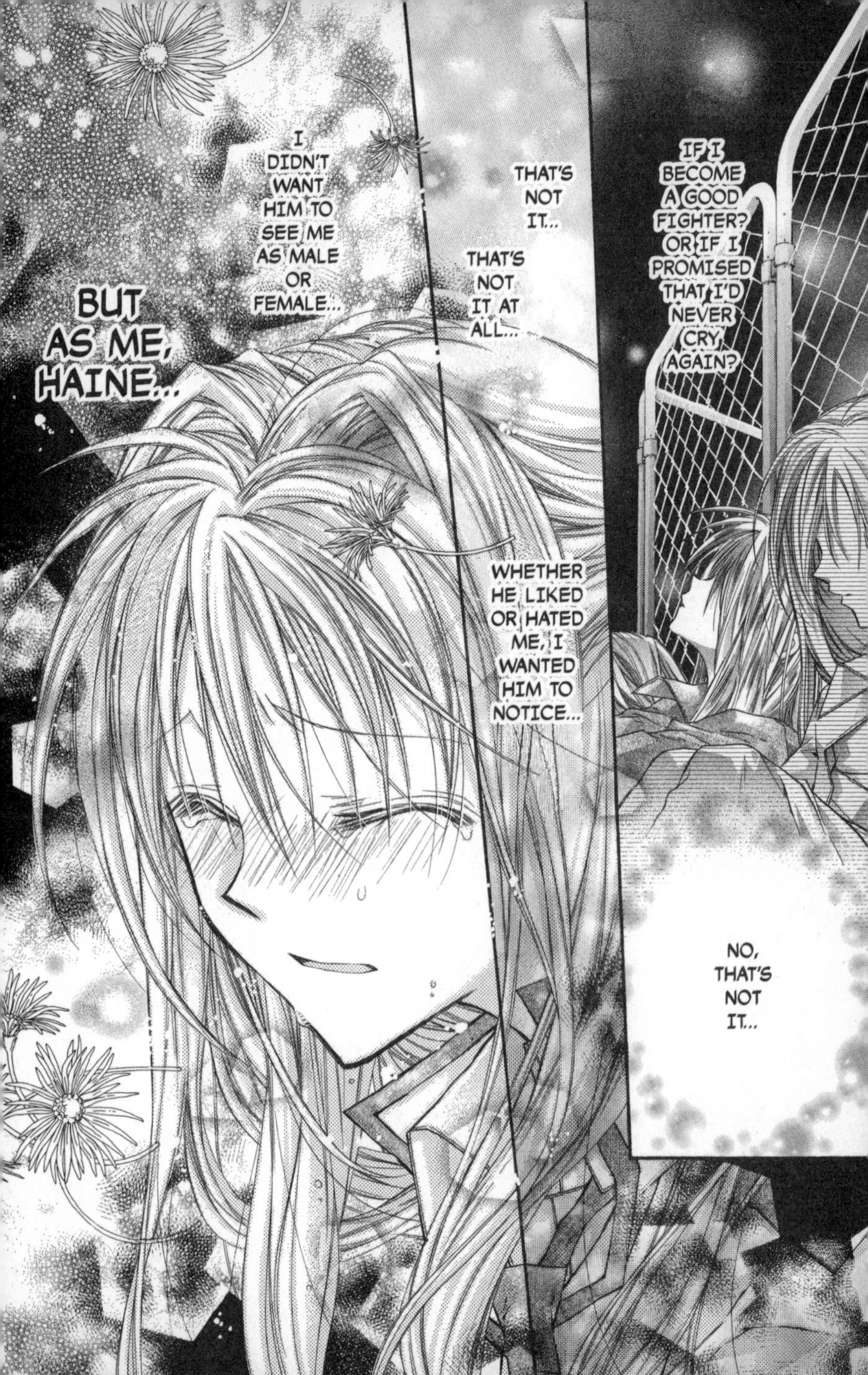
IF I BECOME A GOOD FIGHTER? OR IF I PROMISED THAT I'D NEVER CRY AGAIN?
NO, THAT'S NOT IT...
THAT'S NOT IT...
THAT'S NOT IT AT ALL...
WHETHER HE LIKED OR HATED ME, I WANTED HIM TO NOTICE...
I DIDN'T WANT HIM TO SEE ME AS MALE OR FEMALE...
BUT AS ME, HAINE...

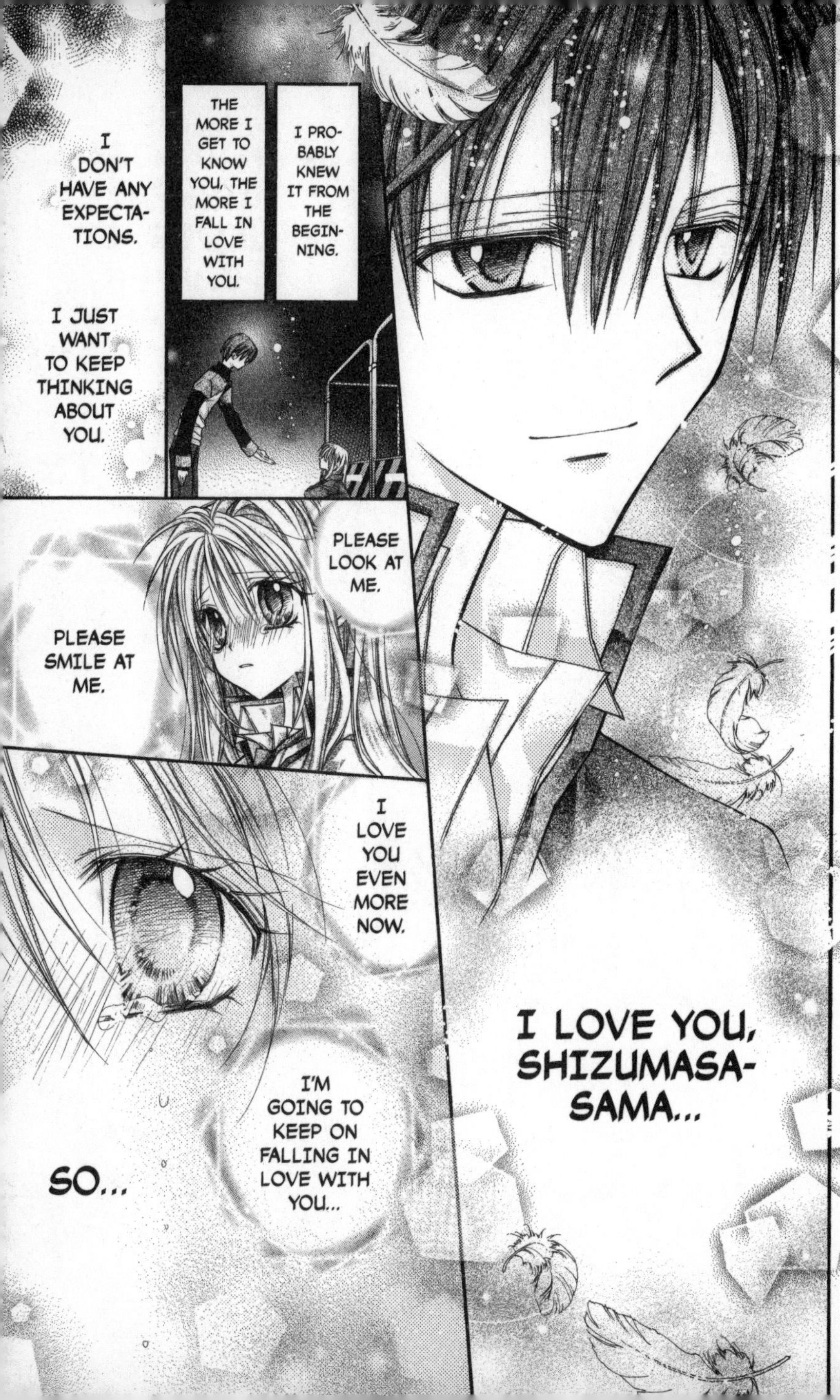

I PROBABLY KNEW IT FROM THE BEGINNING.
THE MORE I GET TO KNOW YOU, THE MORE I FALL IN LOVE WITH YOU.
I DON'T HAVE ANY EXPECTATIONS.
I JUST WANT TO KEEP THINKING ABOUT YOU.
PLEASE LOOK AT ME.
PLEASE SMILE AT ME.
I LOVE YOU EVEN MORE NOW.
I'M GOING TO KEEP ON FALLING IN LOVE WITH YOU...
SO...
I LOVE YOU, SHIZUMASA-SAMA...

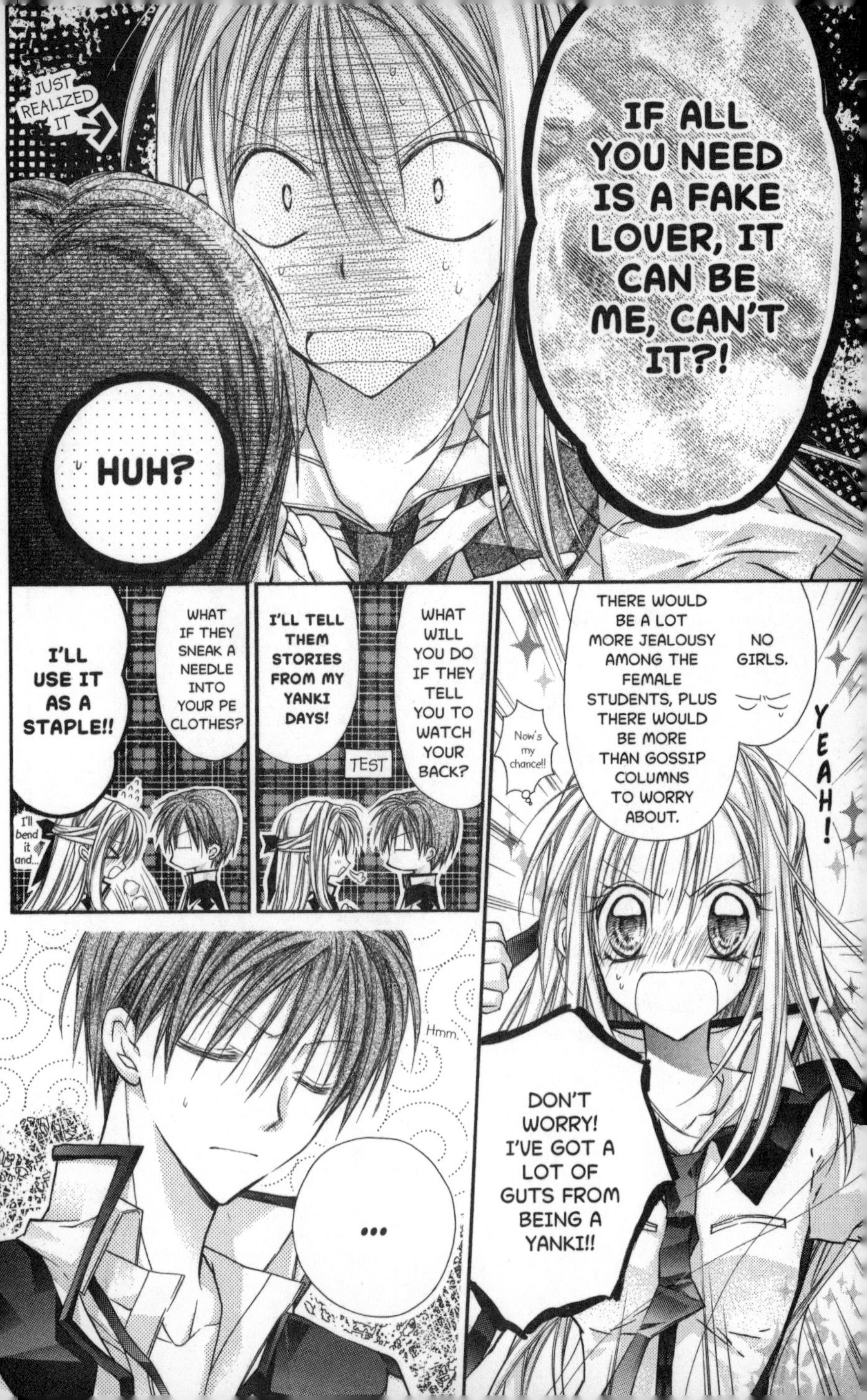
IF ALL YOU NEED IS A FAKE LOVER, IT CAN BE ME, CAN'T IT?!
JUST REALIZED IT
HUH?
NO GIRLS.
THERE WOULD BE A LOT MORE JEALOUSY AMONG THE FEMALE STUDENTS, PLUS THERE WOULD BE MORE THAN GOSSIP COLUMNS TO WORRY ABOUT.
YEAH!
Now's my chance!!
DON'T WORRY! I'VE GOT A LOT OF GUTS FROM BEING A YANKI!!
WHAT WILL YOU DO IF THEY TELL YOU TO WATCH YOUR BACK?
I'LL TELL THEM STORIES FROM MY YANKI DAYS!
TEST
WHAT IF THEY SNEAK A NEEDLE INTO YOUR PE CLOTHES?
I'LL USE IT AS A STAPLE!!
I'll bend it and...
Hmm.
...

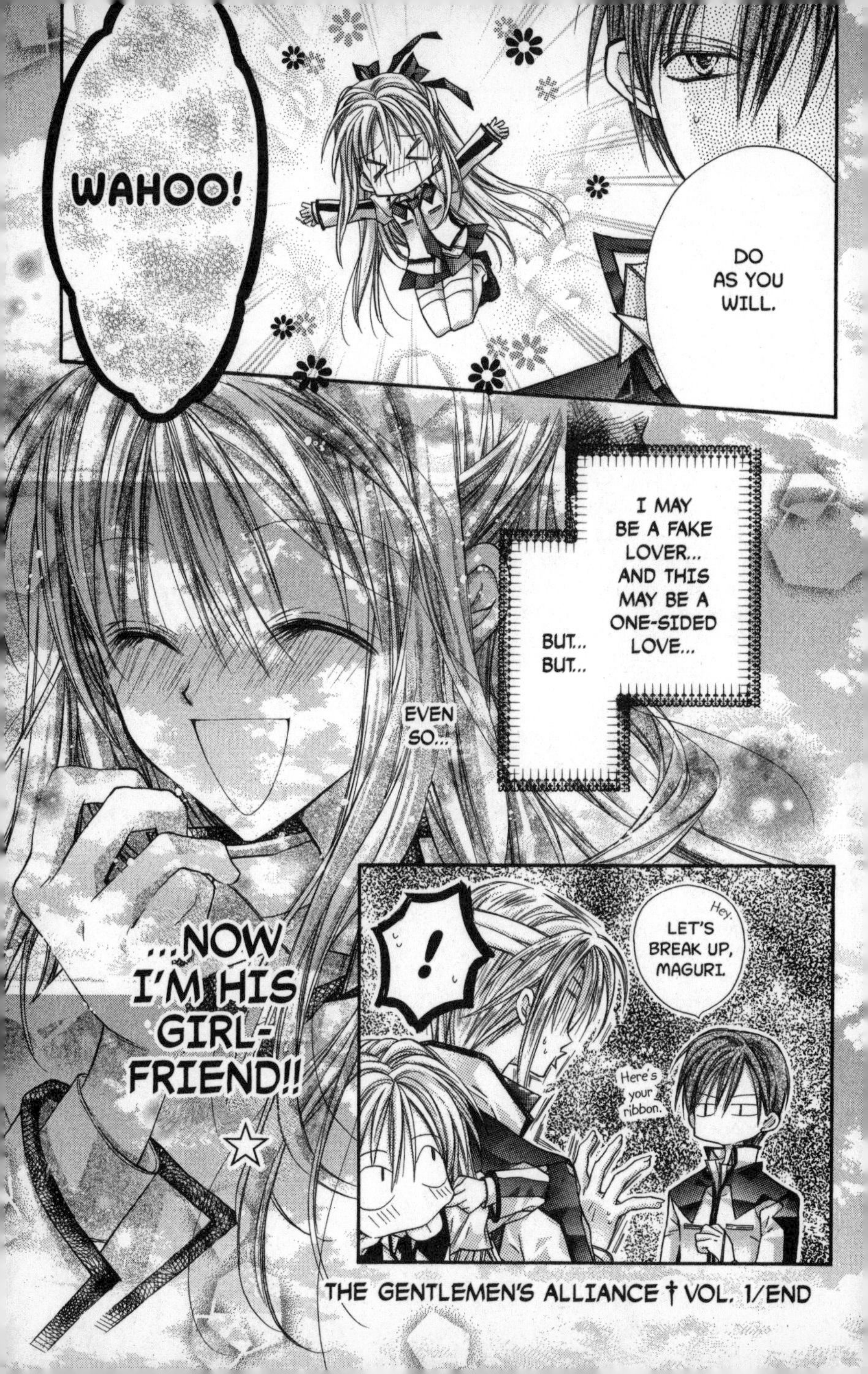
DO AS YOU WILL.
WAHOO!
I MAY BE A FAKE LOVER... AND THIS MAY BE A ONE-SIDED LOVE...
BUT... BUT...
EVEN SO...
...NOW I'M HIS GIRL-FRIEND!! ☆
Hey.
LET'S BREAK UP, MAGURI.
Here's your ribbon.
!

THE GENTLEMEN'S ALLIANCE † VOL. 1/END

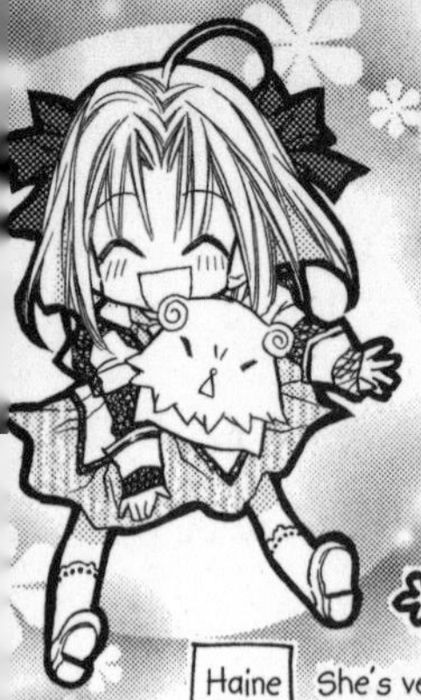

THE GENTLEMEN'S ALLIANCE CROSS

INTRODUCTION

Character Creation

Haine She's very cheerful! I gave her long hair to emphasize the girlish aspect even though she's a former yanki.

Apart from that, I've created her with everything I like and idealize. She's strong at fighting, but she's still the daughter of a prestigious family (though she's going through hard times), so she needed to have a touch of elegance... I guess that's about it? I call her "Hainekko," by the way.

She was shown wearing the student council uniform in the magazine before the manga started, which was a slight spoiler (laugh). But I also like the regular student uniform too because it's easy to draw (easy to make a sketch of).

She seems to have liked tying her hair with the necktie in chapter one, so she still does it.

She's single-minded, and she's determined to do her very best. The slightly tough, silly aspect of her is cute too. She really is easy to draw! I've got perfect chemistry with her.

The Emperor Shizumasa I created this character long before anything else:

One-length hairstyle, sandy screentoned eyes, unsociable, and he's a misanthrope (laugh). Shizumasa does confide more in Maguri, so I guess Maguri is special. Shizumasa is filled with mysteries. For this series, I was aiming to create a main character with no mysteries. So he's taken on all the two-faced, mysterious aspects.

Ushio She was created pretty much before everything too.

She seems to like clothes with laces and frills. I really like her name and the way she talks, since they're both a little mannish!!

She kind of resembles the Emperor since she too is a misanthrope...

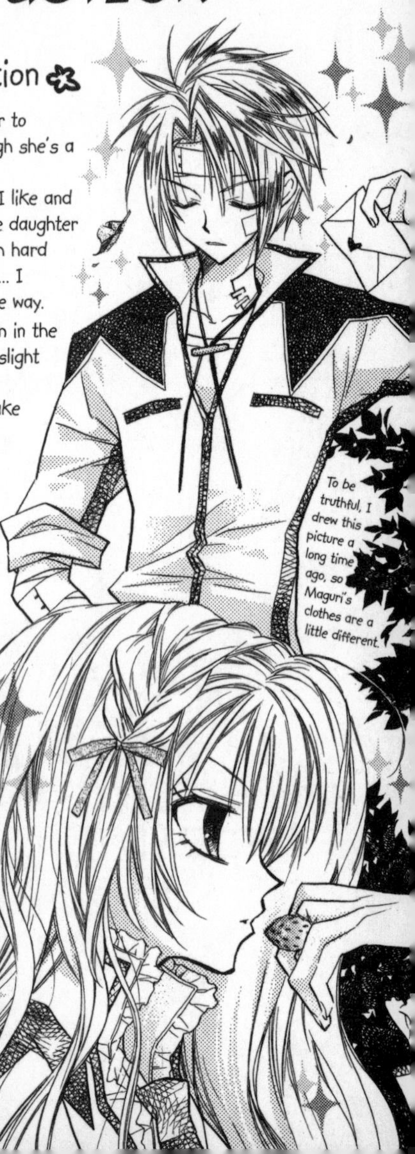
To be truthful, I drew this picture a long time ago, so Maguri's clothes are a little different.

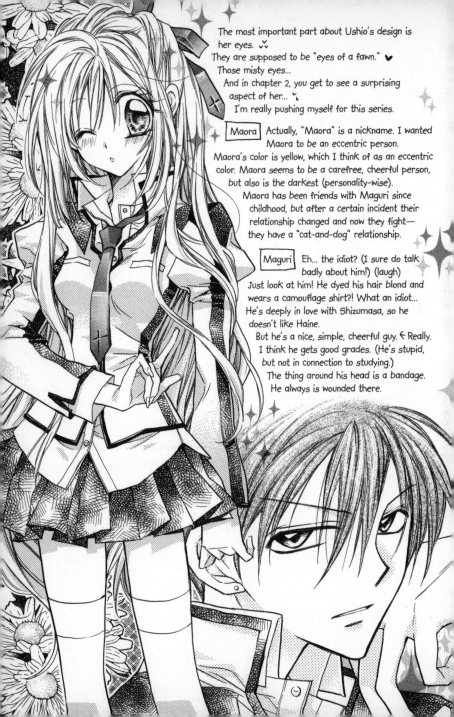

The most important part about Ushio's design is her eyes. ♥
They are supposed to be "eyes of a fawn." ♥
Those misty eyes...
    And in chapter 2, you get to see a surprising aspect of her... ♥
    I'm really pushing myself for this series.

Maora | Actually, "Maora" is a nickname. I wanted Maora to be an eccentric person.
Maora's color is yellow, which I think of as an eccentric color. Maora seems to be a carefree, cheerful person, but also is the darkest (personality-wise).
    Maora has been friends with Maguri since childhood, but after a certain incident their relationship changed and now they fight— they have a "cat-and-dog" relationship.

Maguri | Eh... the idiot? (I sure do talk badly about him!) (laugh)
Just look at him! He dyed his hair blond and wears a camouflage shirt?! What an idiot...
He's deeply in love with Shizumasa, so he doesn't like Haine.
    But he's a nice, simple, cheerful guy. ↤ Really.
    I think he gets good grades. (He's stupid, but not in connection to studying.)
    The thing around his head is a bandage. He always is wounded there.

Research

I went over to Aoyama High School to do some research. (But at first glance, I don't think the manga really shows how it helped...) But the school was a great source of inspiration!! There really was a guardsman (warden) there too. Going there was an enlightening experience for me!! Thank you very much to all the teachers and the student council members.

Imperial Academy

I came up with the idea for the postman when I was at Shueisha. There was a person who distributed all the letters and packages to the people in each department (I'm sure that other companies have this too). I was fascinated by it, so I wanted to incorporate that idea into my manga.

Also, since it's a rich school, there's got to be a guardsman, right? So that's why I created the warden.

I hope you will all read this manga as if you were actually a student at Imperial Academy.

Storyline

The story is going to get to a break after chapter 4 or so, I think. I'm thinking about really pushing the love aspect of the story at the beginning.

So, I don't intend to write about why the Emperor does not like Haine for some time. I'm thinking about unfolding the whole story through various fun and silly incidents, so please look forward to it!

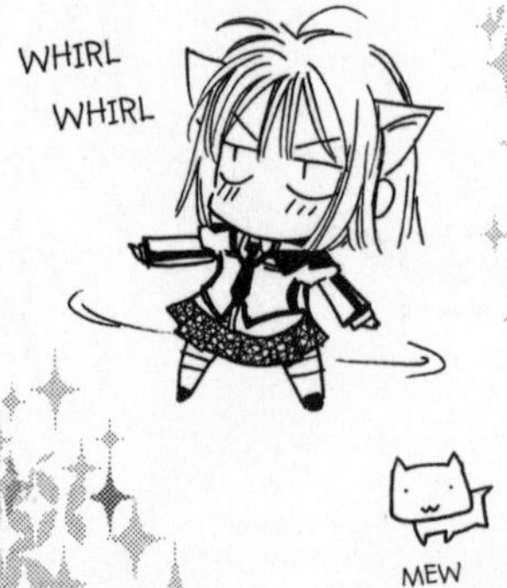
WHIRL
WHIRL
MEW

A word or two from the supervisor, Matsuda:

The stories are going to pick up speed with various turns of events...

Dear readers, please look forward to reading it!

松

Matsu

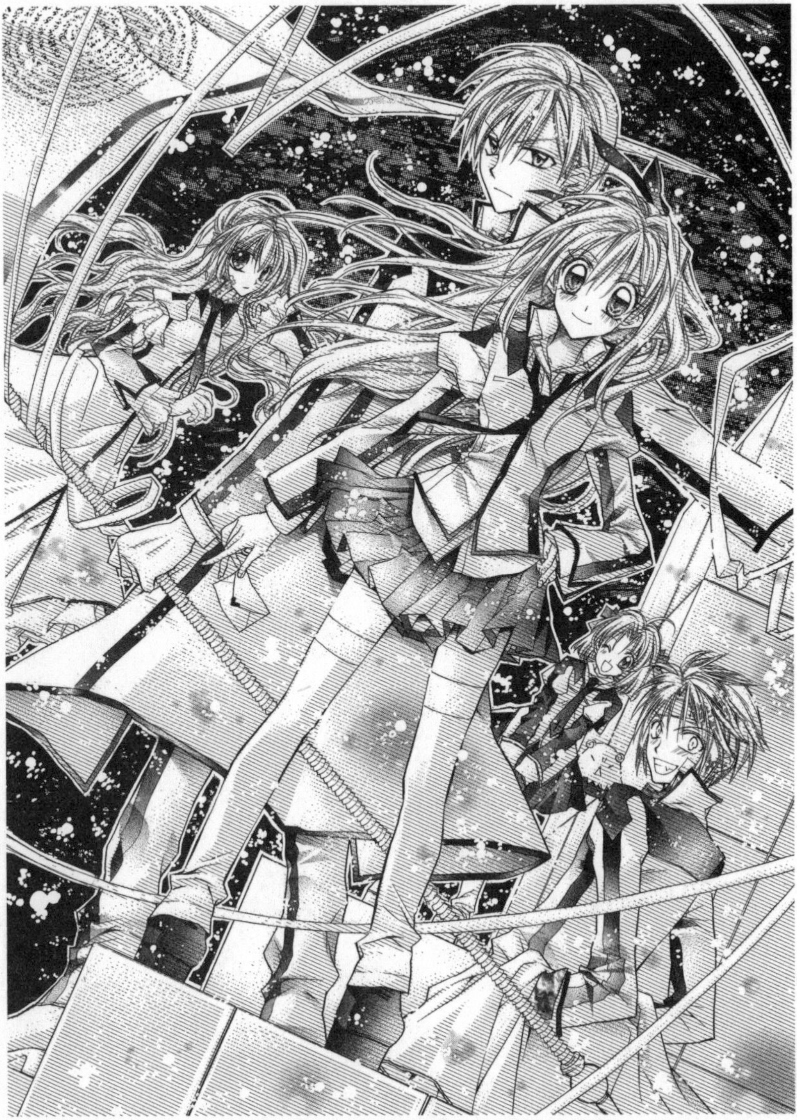

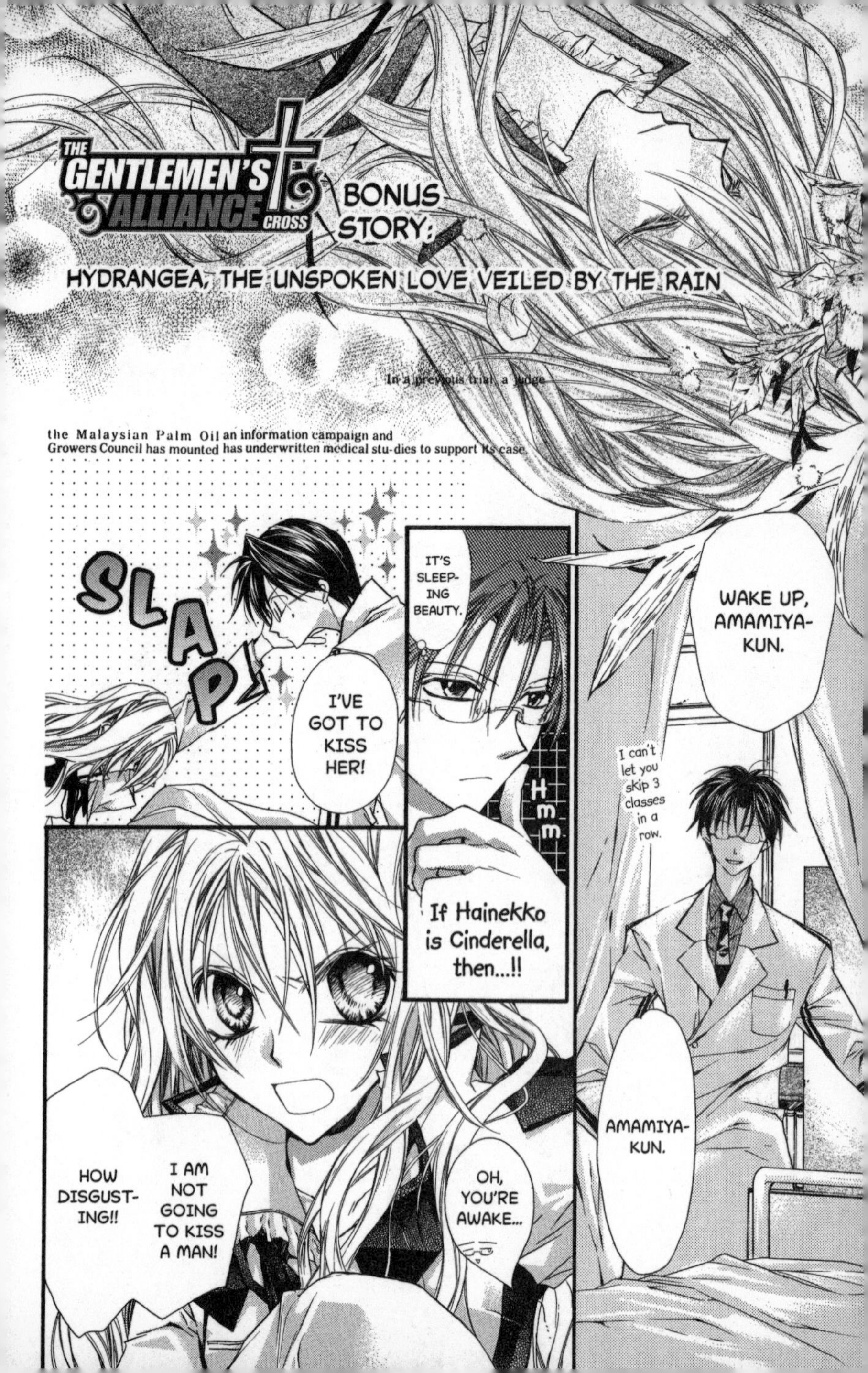
THE GENTLEMEN'S ALLIANCE CROSS
BONUS STORY:
HYDRANGEA, THE UNSPOKEN LOVE VEILED BY THE RAIN
WAKE UP, AMAMIYA-KUN.
I can't let you skip 3 classes in a row.
AMAMIYA-KUN.
IT'S SLEEPING BEAUTY.
I'VE GOT TO KISS HER!
If Hainekko is Cinderella, then...!!
Hmm
SLAP
OH, YOU'RE AWAKE...
I AM NOT GOING TO KISS A MAN!
HOW DISGUSTING!!

In a previous trial, a judge

the Malaysian Palm Oil an information campaign and Growers Council has mounted has underwritten medical stu-dies to support its case.

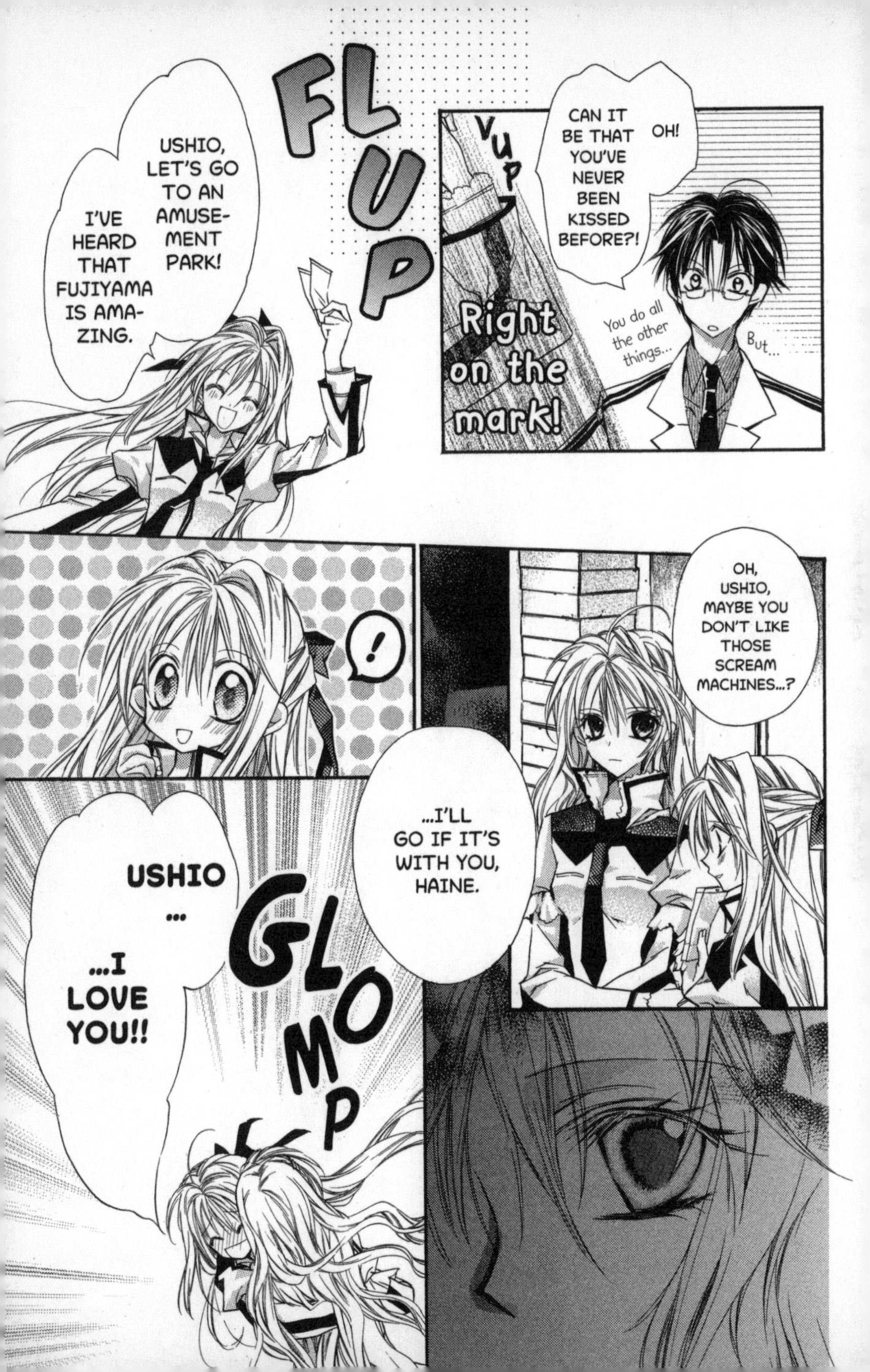
OH!
CAN IT BE THAT YOU'VE NEVER BEEN KISSED BEFORE?!
VUP
But...
You do all the other things...
Right on the mark!
FLUP
USHIO, LET'S GO TO AN AMUSEMENT PARK!
I'VE HEARD THAT FUJIYAMA IS AMAZING.
OH, USHIO, MAYBE YOU DON'T LIKE THOSE SCREAM MACHINES...?
...I'LL GO IF IT'S WITH YOU, HAINE.
!
USHIO ...
...I LOVE YOU!!
GLOMP

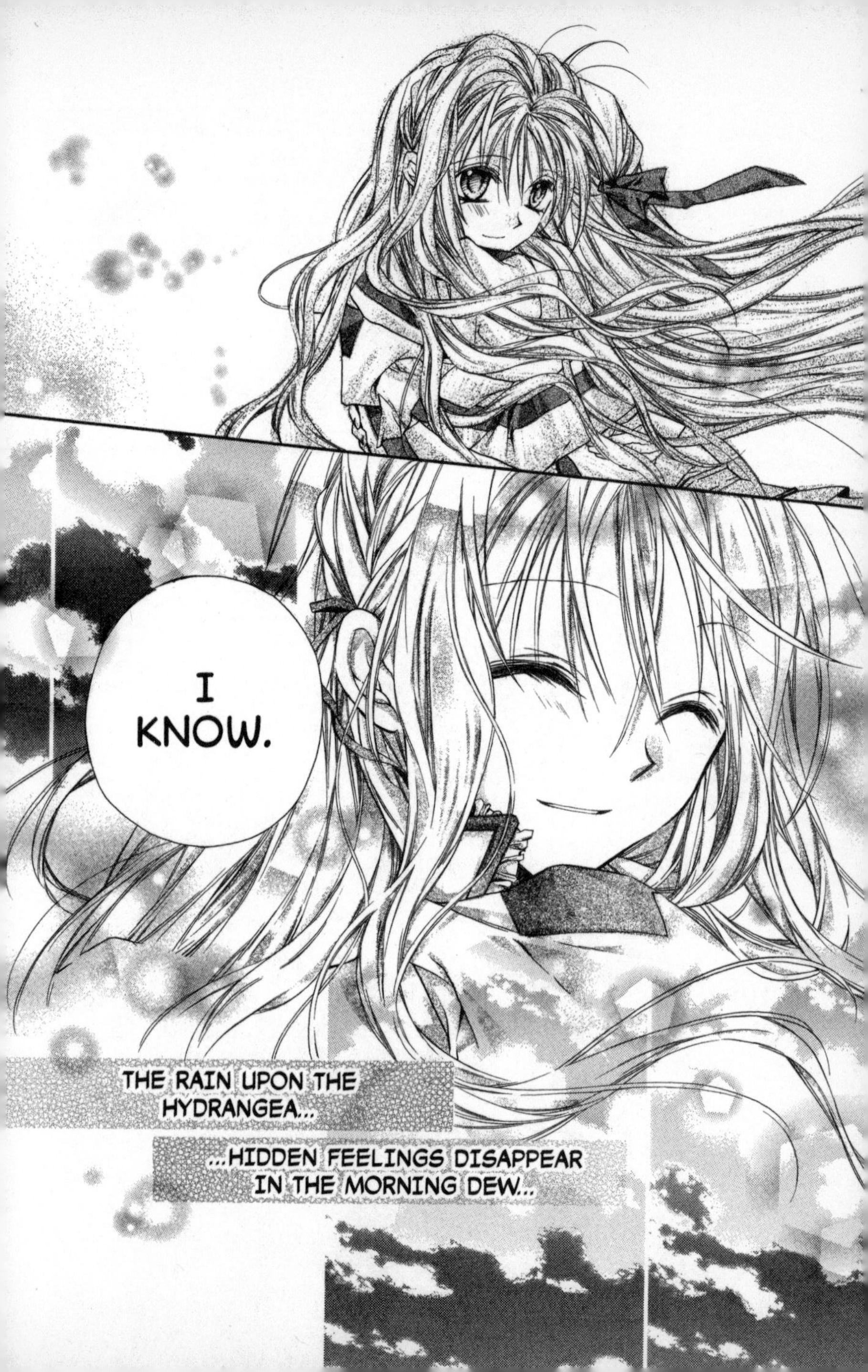
I KNOW.
THE RAIN UPON THE HYDRANGEA...
...HIDDEN FEELINGS DISAPPEAR IN THE MORNING DEW...

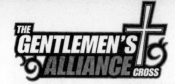

THE GENTLEMEN'S ALLIANCE CROSS BONUS FUNNIES

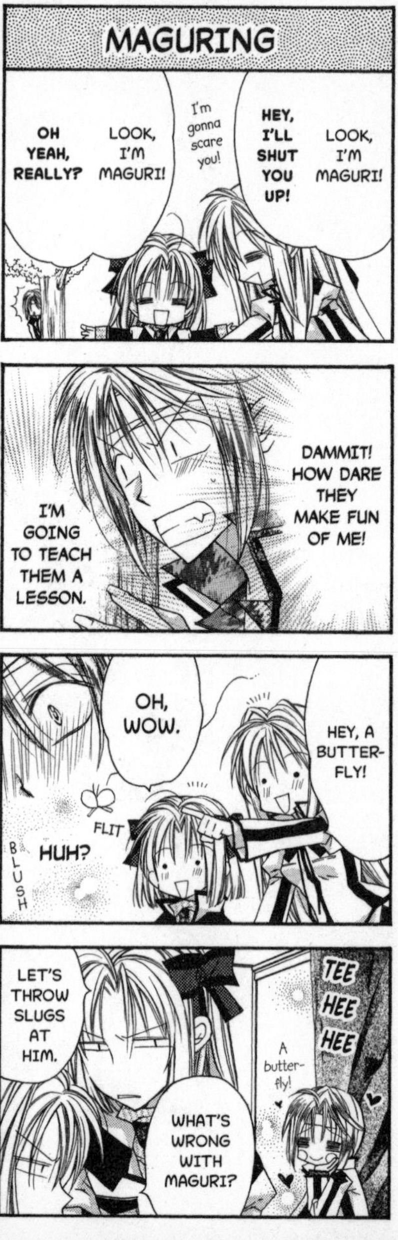
MAGURING
LOOK, I'M MAGURI!
HEY, I'LL SHUT YOU UP!
I'm gonna scare you!
LOOK, I'M MAGURI!
OH YEAH, REALLY?
DAMMIT! HOW DARE THEY MAKE FUN OF ME!
I'M GOING TO TEACH THEM A LESSON.
HEY, A BUTTER-FLY!
OH, WOW.
FLIT
HUH?
BLUSH
TEE HEE HEE
A butter-fly!
WHAT'S WRONG WITH MAGURI?
LET'S THROW SLUGS AT HIM.

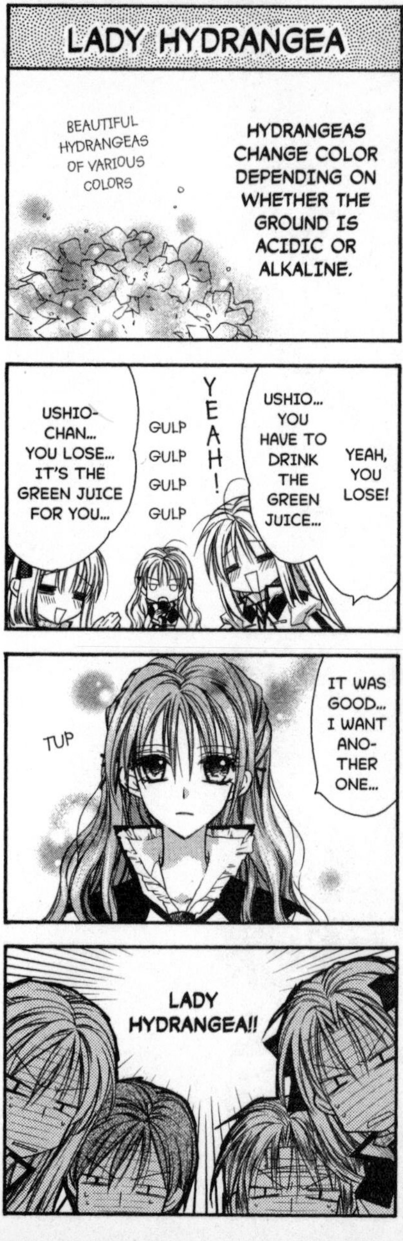
LADY HYDRANGEA
HYDRANGEAS CHANGE COLOR DEPENDING ON WHETHER THE GROUND IS ACIDIC OR ALKALINE.
BEAUTIFUL HYDRANGEAS OF VARIOUS COLORS
YEAH, YOU LOSE!
USHIO... YOU HAVE TO DRINK THE GREEN JUICE...
YEAH!
GULP
GULP
GULP
GULP
USHIO-CHAN... YOU LOSE... IT'S THE GREEN JUICE FOR YOU...
IT WAS GOOD... I WANT ANO-THER ONE...
TUP
LADY HYDRANGEA!!

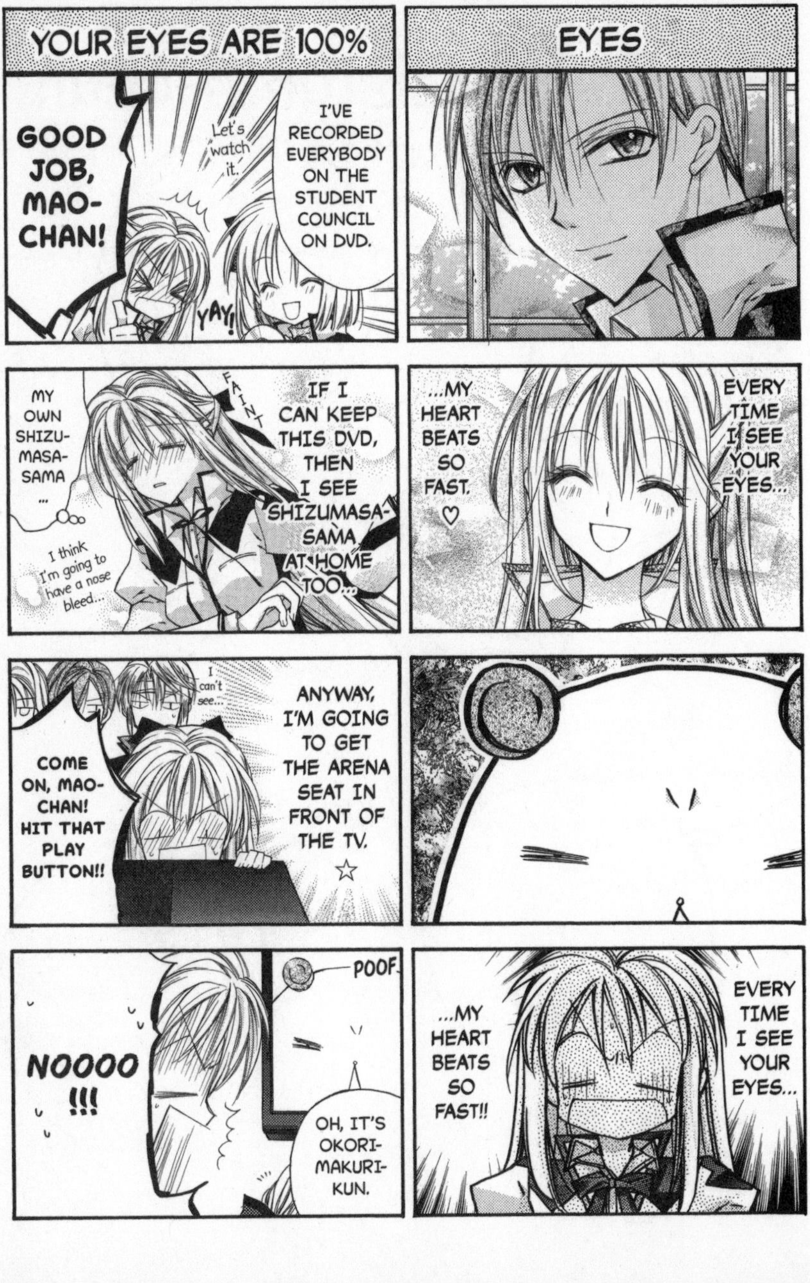
EYES
EVERY TIME I SEE YOUR EYES...
...MY HEART BEATS SO FAST. ♡
EVERY TIME I SEE YOUR EYES...
...MY HEART BEATS SO FAST!!
YOUR EYES ARE 100%
I'VE RECORDED EVERYBODY ON THE STUDENT COUNCIL ON DVD.
Let's watch it.
GOOD JOB, MAO-CHAN!
YAY!
IF I CAN KEEP THIS DVD, THEN I SEE SHIZUMASA-SAMA AT HOME TOO...
FAINT
MY OWN SHIZUMASA-SAMA ...
I think I'm going to have a nose bleed...
ANYWAY, I'M GOING TO GET THE ARENA SEAT IN FRONT OF THE TV. ☆
I can't see...
COME ON, MAO-CHAN! HIT THAT PLAY BUTTON!!
POOF
OH, IT'S OKORI-MAKURI-KUN.
NOOOO !!!

Saint ☆ Assistants-chan

From Sensei Being the nice person I am, I gave everybody pocket money for New Year's. Make sure you don't spend it wastefully.

I'm in charge of the backgrounds. ☆

I also do the laundry and the dishes every now and then.

Nakame

I promise to use the pocket money wisely. ♥

I'm in charge of drawing the backgrounds. I love drawing.

I love Mao-chan!!

I wish I could eat snacks with her. (laugh)

Thanks for the money.

Thorn
Asano Kyakya

★ I ink as well as do screentones for the background.
I just **love** Mao-chan!! Especially when paired up with Maguri. I really want to know what happened to them in the past!
Thank you very much for the pocket money, Tanemura-sensei!

星聖二季
2005. XXX
Seisou Niki

Special Thanks!

Noriko
Takki
Rukacchi
Ribon Editorial Department
Ammonite

I draw backgrounds.
I'm really looking forward for the Emperor and Haine to be a real couple. I love Maguri and the postman. I also love the way Tanemura-sensei draws herself!!

Tanemura-sensei, let's go to karaoke. Concerts too...

AIRI
Teito
Airi

Pocket money!

✚ I do screentones, draw the panels, and do all the copying.
I love Ushio-chan. ♥

Thank you, Sensei.

Pocket money!!

Hinano Saori

❋ I paste the screentones.
It's such a great feeling to be able to apply screentones to my favorite characters. ♪
I especially like the school doctor and Ushio-chan.

Thank you very much for the pocket money.

2005 XXX
Minase Ai

◎ I paste the screentones.
I enjoy trimming them. ♥
Recently I've begun lettering.

I love Mao-chan. And I'm not going to lose against Niki-sama. (laugh) I **love** it when Mao-chan is paired up with Haine.

I'm going to hide the pocket money in my room in case I need it. (laugh)

Asano Kaori

MEW

MEW

MEW

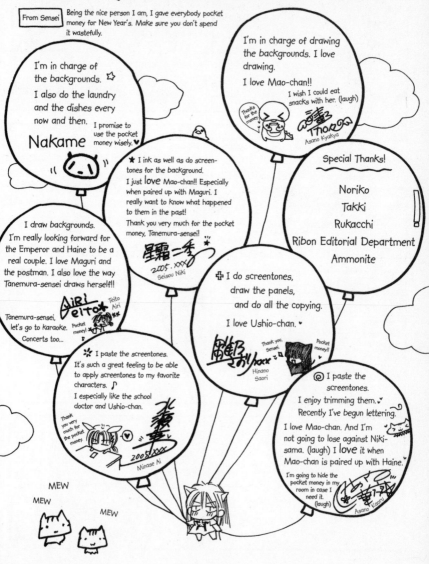

NOTES ON THE TEXT

PAGE 4:

I'm Not Afraid of the Emperor! ☆
The word *jyoto* is used in the Japanese chapter title.
It is yanki slang for "I'm not afraid of."

PAGE 9:

Riko-chan
The suffix *-chan* is usually added to female names to show
familiarity or friendship.

PAGE 10:

**"I have no need for people who just suck up to those
above them."**
Ushio is actually using a common saying here: "You may as well
be bound by a long twine," basically stating that she hates
people who kiss up to those above them.

PAGE 11:

Hanging Garden
The Hanging Garden is a garden that is built high up.

Riku and Kai
Riku means "land," and *Kai* means "sea."

PAGE 13:

Shizumasa-sama
The suffix *-sama* is added to show respect to someone who is
higher up in the social hierarchy. Fan girls also use this suffix
when they are addressing the object of their adoration.

The correct uniform
In Imperial Academy, boys wear the ribbon and the girls wear
the necktie. It should be the other way around, but in this
school it is purposely done so that you only wear the "correct"
uniform after you have found a girlfriend/boyfriend and swap
the ribbon and necktie. Having the correct uniform marks the
students' coming of age.

PAGE 14:

Cherry blossoms

There is a famous myth in Japan that dead bodies make cherry blossoms more beautiful. If a dead body is buried underneath a cherry blossom tree, the blood will dye the flowers, making them more beautiful.

Mount Fuji

There actually is a lot of trash on Mount Fuji. This is the main reason why UNESCO will not approve Mount Fuji as a World Heritage site.

Grade D

Haine's grade in *Genkoku*—the equivalent of an English class where one reads books, writes essays, and makes speeches— is a 3, which is not a very good grade.

PAGE 18:

Heretic

The Japanese term for "heretic" is *gedo*. It is a Buddhist term that means "those who have strayed from the true path."

PAGE 19:

Yanki

A *yanki* is a juvenile delinquent or young gangster. They're young people who smoke, start fights, etc. Some create gangs, and some just wander the streets alone.

PAGE 20:

Haine-san

The suffix -*san* is added to a person's name to show respect.

"Here's my special move…"

The term here is *hissatsu*, which literally means "special move" or "the killing blow." It's often used in shonen manga when one of the characters uses a special move to defeat the enemy.

PAGE 21:

"I've gained a reputation in Sakuragi-cho as the Hama Cinderella, you know!!"
Sakuragi-cho is an area in Yokohama. *Hama* is a shortened version of *Yokohama*.

"Ora ora!!!"
Ora ora is like a stereotypical yanki shout often used in manga and movies. The word itself doesn't really have a meaning–it's like a "Huh!!" or "Yeargh!!"

PAGE 22:

Wooden sword
Another stereotype about yankis is that they use wooden swords in fights. The wooden sword is called a *bokuto*, and it's used like a bat.

"Normal words"
Yankis write using different kanji for words that sound the same in Japanese.

PAGE 26:

Okorimakuri-kun
Maora's pet is named *Okorimakuri*, which means "always angry." The suffix *-kun* is usually added to boy's names to show familiarity or friendship.

PAGE 28:

"Like robbing his wallet…"
When yankis bully people to get their money it's called *katsuage*. There is also an initiation-like ritual called *konjyo-yaki* where yankis will press a lit cigarette on their skin to show how tough they are. *Konjyo-yaki* is also used to bully others.

PAGE 37:

Lunch money
In Japanese public schools, the students will hand in their lunch money, or *kyushokuhi*, on a monthly basis to the teacher. Every now and then a bad student will steal this money.

PAGE 53:

50 million yen
50 million yen is roughly $450,694 at a rate of 110.9 yen to the dollar.

PAGE 56:

"I was well aware from the beginning I was starting from the bottom!!"
The literal translation is "I knew from the beginning that I had a bunker start!!" "Bunker" is a golf term for the sand pit on the course. Haine is basically saying that she knew very well she was going to have a long way to climb before getting to Shizumasa.

"To hell with it!"
Tanan jyoto means "I'm not afraid of those difficulties!" or "To hell with those difficulties!"

Working assiduously
In the Japanese version, Haine mixes up the kanji for "working diligently" with "anger."

Infirmary
In Japanese schools this is basically the nurse's office, where the school nurse or doctor resides and takes care of students who are sick or injured.

PAGE 57:

Miya/Gu (宮)
There are two ways to read the character 宮. One is "Miya" and the other is "Gu." For instance, 東宮 is "Togu" and 乙宮 is "Otomiya."

PAGE 59:

Lady Hydrangea
Ushio's nickname is *Ajisai no hime*, or "Lady Hydrangea." The title *no hime* is given to women of noble birth. It is slightly different from the Western concept of a princess since the princess is usually the daughter of the ruler.

PAGE 75:

Shizun!!
Shizun is Maguri's pet name for Shizumasa. The literal translation would be "season."

PAGE 76:

"I have to show respect to those above me."
In Japanese culture it is important be aware of one's level in society.

PAGE 77:

Yakuza
Yakuza is the Japanese mafia.

PAGE 80:

Roemeo
In the Japanese version, Haine mixes up the kanji for "prince" with "egg."

PAGE 95:

Meat Bun
Niku-man, or "meat bun," is basically a Chinese *baozi* (a bun stuffed with flavored meat.) It's a popular snack in Japan, especially during winter.

PAGE 96:

Hyakunin Isshu
Hyakunin Isshu ("a hundred poems by a hundred poets") is a traditional Japanese card game. Usually the first half of the poem is read out loud, and the aim is to pick up the card with the second half of the poem on it. People will often memorize all 100 poems so they can pick the card up while the first half of the poem is still being read out loud.

1-kyu
Kyu is a term used to rank an amateur's level of proficiency in various sports and games. "1-kyu" is the best possible rank before becoming a professional.

PAGE 96:
Timetable Proficiency Test
This is an actual proficiency test based on the Japanese Rail timetables. It includes detailed questions on all modes of public transportation in Japan.

PAGE 97:
Senpai
Senpai literally means "senior." Students in a lower grade, or *kouhai*, will use this term when referring to students who are in a higher grade.

PAGE 99:
Phantom Thief Jeanne
Kamikaze Kaito Jeanne, or "Phantom Thief Jeanne," is one of Arina Tanemura's manga series.

"I would like Aya Hisakawa or Noriko Hidaka to do his voice…"
Aya Hisakawa is a famous voice actress who played Kerberos in the anime for *Card Captor Sakura*. Noriko Hidaka is another famous voice actress. She played Minami in the *Touch* anime.

Classroom visits
"Classroom visits" are certain days in nursery and elementary school when parents visit to see how their children are doing in class.

PAGE 103:
Onee-chan
Onee-chan means "big sister."

PAGE 122:
Crude thoughts
In the Japanese version, Haine misspells *tanjun*, or "naïve," using kanji that means "faulty purity."

Haiku
Here Haine says her lines in the form of haiku.

PAGE 125:

Maya Kitajima

Maya Kitajima is the main character of the famous classic manga *Garasu no Kamen* (The Glass Mask). It's the story of a girl with brilliant acting skills who rises to stardom in the theater world.

My organs!

Gozo roppu literally means "the five solid organs and six hollow organs": *gozo* (liver, heart, spleen, lung, kidney) and *roppu* (gallbladder, ventricles, bladder, large intestine, small intestine, and *shansho*). *Shansho* does not exist in the human body, but the ancient Chinese believed it controlled "Qi" within the body.

PAGE 126:

Oh, my man of the purple roses, I've done it!!

This is also a gag using the *Garasu no Kamen* manga. In the manga, Maya has an anonymous fan who sends her purple roses in support of her career.

PAGE 127:

"I mistook you for a prickly pear, but it's just stupid Maora! ♡ "

In the Japanese version, the wordplay is on chestnuts and Maguri's last name, which contains the kanji for *guri*, or "chestnut."

PAGE 131:

Hainekko

Hainekko is the way Tanemura often refers to Haine. It doesn't have a specific meaning, but the literal translation is "Haine-girl" or "Haine-kid." The ending is added as an endearment.

Shinkuro

This is an abbrevation of the Japanese title, *Shinshi Domei Kurosu*, or "The Gentlemen's Alliance Cross."

PAGE 150:

"Ushio-san! ♡"
This is another pun. Yukimitsu misspells the kanji for Ushio's name, calling her "cow man-san."

School discipline committee
Many schools in Japan have a school discipline committee. It is composed of a group of students under the student council who take care of school discipline. They make sure students wear their uniforms properly and are well-mannered, etc.

PAGE 159:

"...now I'm his girlfriend!! ☆"
In the Japanese version, this is a play on the movie title *A Star is Born*.

PAGE 164:

Wake up, Amamiya-kun.
The suffix *-kun* often connected to boys, but it can be used for girls as well when calling them by their family name to show respect. In this case, it's roughly the same as "Miss" in English.

PAGE 165:

Fujiyama
Fujiyama is a rollercoaster in the Fuji-Q Highland amusement park.

PAGE 168:

Maguring
Haine and Maora are imitating Maguri's Hiroshima accent.

Green juice
Green juice is a vegetable juice made of kale and other green vegetables. It's known for tasting terrible. Ushio is referencing a Japanese commercial for green juice when she says it's good and asks for another one.

The Gentlemen's Alliance†
is the first manga series by
me, Arina Tanemura, that
is not magical shojo. But
that doesn't mean there is
something different about
this, and as always, I am
relaxed and enjoy creating
the story. No matter what
kind of scene I am drawing,
I always feel absolutely
happy when I'm creating it!
Right now I just want to keep
working on this series for as
long as possible.

—*Arina Tanemura*

Arina Tanemura was born in Aichi, Japan. She got her start in 1996,
publishing *Nibanme no Koi no Katachi* (The Style of the Second Love) in
Ribon Original magazine. Her early work includes a collection of short stories
called *Kanshaku Dama no Yuutsu* (Short-Tempered Melancholic). Two of her
titles, *Kamikaze Kaito Jeanne* and *Full Moon*, were made into popular TV
series. Tanemura enjoys karaoke and is a huge *Lord of the Rings* fan.

THE GENTLEMEN'S ALLIANCE † vol.1
The Shojo Beat Manga Edition

STORY & ART BY
ARINA TANEMURA

English Translation & Adaptation/Tetsuichiro Miyaki
Touch-up Art & Lettering/Rachel Galliano
Design/Amy Martin
Editor/Nancy Thistlethwaite

Managing Editor/Megan Bates
Editorial Director/Elizabeth Kawasaki
VP & Editor in Chief/Yumi Hoashi
Sr. Director of Acquisitions/Rika Inouye
Sr. VP of Marketing/Liza Coppola
Exec. VP of Sales & Marketing/John Easum
Publisher/Hyoe Narita

THE GENTLEMEN ALLIANCE -CROSS- © 2004 by Arina Tanemura. All rights reserved.
First published in Japan in 2004 by SHUEISHA Inc., Tokyo. English translation rights
in the United States of America and Canada arranged by SHUEISHA Inc. The stories,
characters, and incidents mentioned in this publication are entirely fictional.

Printed in Canada

Published by VIZ Media, LLC
P.O. Box 77010
San Francisco, CA 94107

Shojo Beat Manga Edition
10 9 8 7 6 5 4 3 2 1
First printing, March 2007

store.viz.com

PARENTAL ADVISORY
THE GENTLEMEN'S ALLIANCE † is rated T+ for Older Teen and is recom-
mended for ages 16 and up. This volume contains suggestive themes.

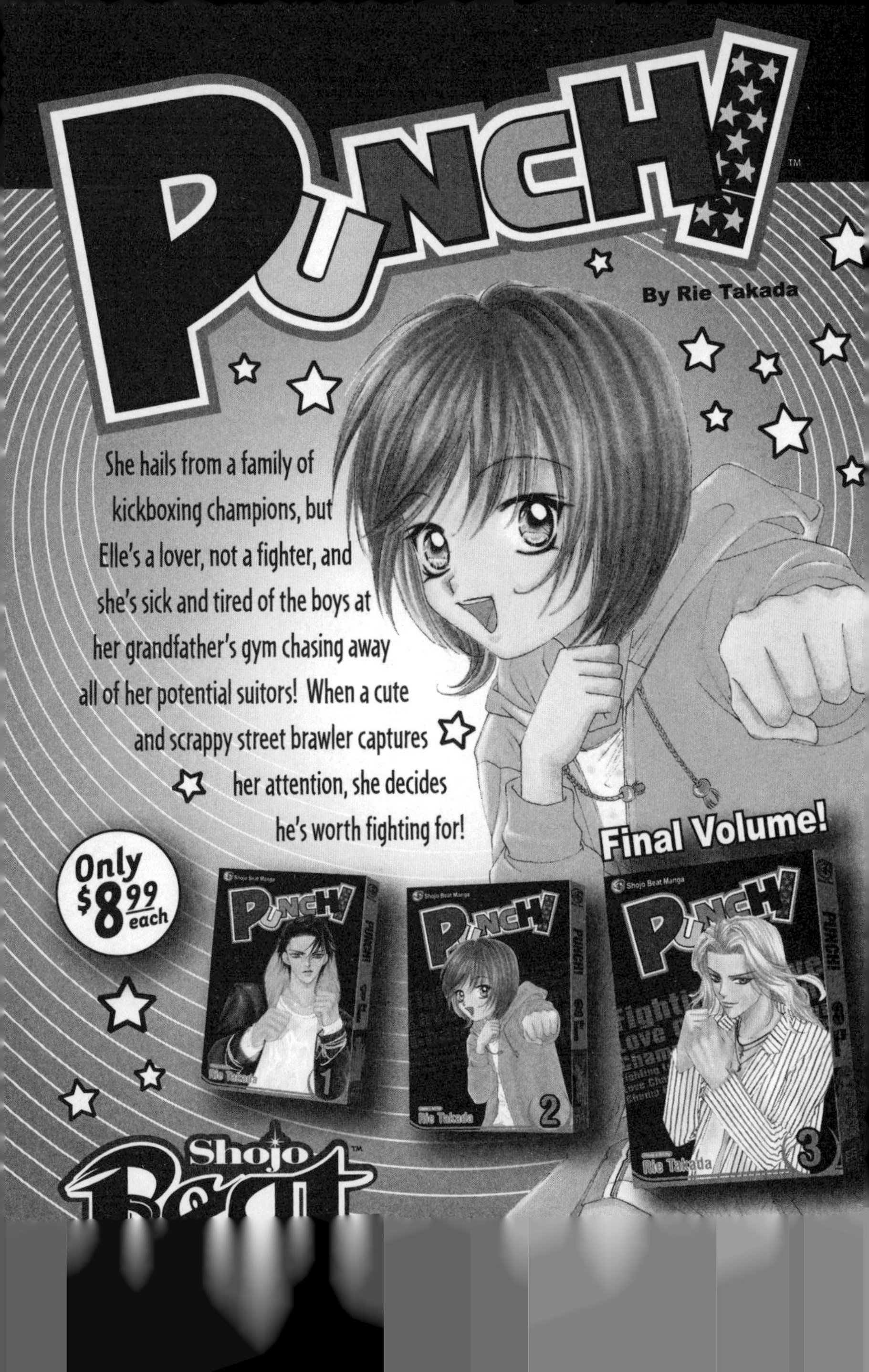

PUNCH!™
By Rie Takada
She hails from a family of kickboxing champions, but Elle's a lover, not a fighter, and she's sick and tired of the boys at her grandfather's gym chasing away all of her potential suitors! When a cute and scrappy street brawler captures her attention, she decides he's worth fighting for!
Only $8.99 each
Final Volume!
Shojo Beat Manga
PUNCH!
Rie Takada
1
Shojo Beat Manga
PUNCH!
Rie Takada
2
Shojo Beat Manga
PUNCH!
Rie Takada
3
Shojo Beat™